HOLDEN'S STATEN ISLAND:

THE HISTORY OF RICHMOND COUNTY

Edited & Compiled By RICHARD DICKENSON

MAP OF

STATEN ISLAND

RICHMOND COUNTY

STATE OF NEW YORK.

PREPARED BY G.W.& C.B.COLTON & CO 182 WILLIAM STREET NEW YORK.

HOLDEN'S STATEN ISLAND:
THE HISTORY OF RICHMOND COUNTY

REVISED RESOURCE MANUAL SKETCHES
FOR THE YEAR TWO THOUSAND TWO

Edited & Compiled By
RICHARD DICKENSON
Staten Island Public/Borough Historian

Reprinted from *Staten Island:
A Resource Manual for Schools and Community* by permission of the
Board of Education of the City of New York.

Funded by:
The Ann H. and Norbert H. Leeseberg Trust
Hon. John Marchi, State Senator
Staten Island Rotary Foundation
Staten Island Savings Bank Community Foundation
Cultural Coalition (a.k.a. Council on the Arts and Humanities of Staten
Island)

CENTER FOR MIGRATION STUDIES
2002

HOLDEN'S STATEN ISLAND:

THE HISTORY OF RICHMOND COUNTY

REVISED RESOURCE MANUAL SKETCHES FOR THE YEAR TWO THOUSAND TWO

Edited & Compiled By

RICHARD DICKENSON

CMS

2002
Center for Migration Studies
New York

HOLDEN'S
STATEN ISLAND:
THE HISTORY OF RICHMOND COUNTY
REVISED RESOURCE MANUAL SKETCHES
FOR THE YEAR TWO THOUSAND TWO

First Edition
Copyright © 2002 by
The Center for Migration Studies of New York, Inc.

Center for Migration Studies
209 Flagg Place
Staten Island, New York 10304–1199

Library of Congress Cataloging-in-Publication Data

Dickenson, Richard B.
    Holden's Staten Island: the history of Richmond: revised resource manual sketches for the year two thousand two/edited & compiled by Richard Dickenson.   1st ed.   p.cm.
    Rev. ed. of: Staten Island: a resource manual for school and community. 1964.
    Previously catalogued under the heading: New York (City). Board of Education, Bureau of Curriculum Research. Manual written by Edna Holden.
    Includes bibliographical references (p.) and index.
ISBN 1-57703-025-7 (PBK) (alk. paper)
ISBN 1-57703-028-1 (HC) (alk. paper)
    1. Staten Island (New York, N.Y.) – History. 2. Richmond County (N.Y.) – History. I. Title: Staten Island. II. Holden, Edna. III. Center for Migration Studies (U.S.) IV. New York (N.Y.). Bureau of Curriculum Research. Staten Island: a resource manual for school and community. V. Title.

F127.S7D53 2003
974.7'26–dc21   2002041514

CONTENTS

Dedicated to Edward Aspinall
A man of consummate knowledge
And the thread on which the exemption documents hung

FOREWORD

New York City schools place high value on giving children an understanding of, and a feeling of pride in the heritage of the community, the state and the nation.

The concern of the Bureau of Curriculum Research in assisting in developing materials for local needs, and the interest of the Assistant Superintendent and his staff in Staten Island were brought together in a project which resulted in this publication.

A Social Studies Committee in Districts 53-54 undertook a study of ways and means of giving teachers materials which would assist them in creating a background in, and an understanding of, the history and developments in Staten Island.

The need for this was highlighted by the construction of the Verrazzano-Narrows Bridge and the concurrent changes which it was bringing in population, housing, and industry.

The research which was carried on in this joint project revealed that the Island was rich in American tradition and in institutions which have contributed to the growth of democratic traditions. It is presented in this publication as an example of scholarly research and of good curriculum material, possible only because of the services of devoted staff members and the cooperation and collaboration of institutions and individuals on Staten Island.

This report serves to highlight the cultural and historical heritage of Staten Island. It is prepared as an aid to the teachers of that borough in their work with children and as a resource document of material not otherwise available for teachers generally.

WILLIAM H. BRISTOW
Assistant Superintendent
Bureau of Curriculum Research

MAURICE WOLLIN
Assistant Superintendent
Districts 53-54

January, 1964

ACKNOWLEDGEMENTS

When the Borough Historian's Advisory Board was functioning, Judy McMillan, the director of education for Historic Richmond Town, made the key recommendation to have *Staten Island: A Resource Manual* reprinted. From there we slowly plodded to this publication.

I'm deeply indebted to Edna Holden, author of the original *Resource Manual* for entrusting to me, prior to her impending permanent departure for New Mexico in 1996, materials she had gathered, mostly in 1974, for updating the *Resource Manual.* Some of the material may be outdated, but some is not, and all was useful. This revision has been named in her honor.

Edward Aspinall, Lorraine McSwegan, Bennet Minko and Fred Cerullo III, all of the Department of Finance, made it possible for me to mine voluminous manuscripts relating to Staten Island (e.g., properties, and incorporations). Between 7:30 and 8:30 A. M., I was enabled through Fred Cerullo, Eddie and Ben to review Works Progress Administration tax photos of Staten Island. Lorraine allowed access to the copying machine and helped with errant tax block and lot numbers. There were also other friendly staff members, of especial note were Richard, John, Leslie and Mary. I am very grateful to everyone in Real Property. Their support was most helpful.

The highly competent David Ment and Manuscript Curator Ms. Bette Weneck most ably assisted in obtaining photographs and texts from the Board of Education Archives at the Special Collections of the Teachers College Library of Columbia University.

Taking Toni Dickenson to the 7:20 — or earlier — ferry, five days a week, set the wheels in motion for me to stop three days a week at the Staten Island Real Property Office of the Department of Finance.

Dr. Lydio Tomasi, the lively and supportive director of the Center for Migration Studies, graciously provided his services not only as a publisher but also as a fiscal conduit for funding sources.

When he was a summer intern at Borough Hall, Sean Fennel computerized the basic framework for this index. His work was of tremendous help in producing the final section of this volume, the Index and Sketches.

At the Office of the Borough President, Anne Marie Winkler generously provided lists of schools and their principals; and Ted Wydrinski tirelessly and eagerly contributed from the lode of maps in the Topographic Division.

PREFACE

This revised edition retains most of the original contents of *Staten Island: A Resource Manual*, and is supplemented by a fuller index that includes additional material on selected topics. Four appendices from the 1964 edition were excised, namely, "Implementing the Social Studies Program"; "Index by Topic"; "Guide to Resources Directory by School Areas" and "The Staten Island Transit Guide Map." The enhancements do not purport to be more comprehensive than the original edition, nor is every topic updated. It was not possible for this compiler to do so at this time. However, if there is sufficient feedback to do so, a future edition may be able to add more, including illustrations. It is hoped that comment will impel a future revised edition.

A publication committee meeting on the contents of the revised *Manual* determined that a 1971 publication, *Black Man on Staten Island*, by Mrs. Evelyn Morris King, should be included. *Black Man on Staten Island* has been edited to include excerpts from a chapter from *Afro-American Census Occupations on Staten Island*. In furtherance of pursuing the current state of diversity knowledge on Staten Island, recent *Staten Island Advance* columns by Michael Pacquette and Maureen Seaberg are recommended.

Other updated topics are:
1. Officially designated city, state and national landmarks
2. All public schools and their original dates of opening
3. Most parochial schools and, where possible, their corporate founding
4. Most private schools and their incorporations
5. Most historical Black churches on Staten Island
6. A few lesser known but historically significant Staten Islanders

Do not look for expanded or revised materials on sports or entertainment. Miss Holden had a few such references in the 1964 edition, but the revision editor did not draw upon the rare sources available mostly in the local newspapers. Hopefully, one day the journalists familiar with these subjects will write such histories, based at least in part on their own articles and expanded interviews on the subject.

BIBLIOGRAPHIC SOURCES

Birnbaum, Alexandra Mayes, editorial consultant. *Birnbaum's Bermuda 96*. New York: HarperCollins, 1995.

Cerullo, Fred, Edward Aspinall and Minko Bennet. *Manuscripts of Exemption and Assessment*. Borough Hall, Department of Finance, Office of Real Property. Various dates.

Clute, John J. *Annals of Staten Island*. New York, 1877.

Directory of the Board of Education of the City of New York. New York, 1910, 1920, 1930 and 1940.

Dolkart, Andrew S. *Guide to New York City Landmarks*. New York: John Wiley & Sons, 1998.

Foord, John. *The Life and Public Services of Andrew Haswell Green*. New York: Doubleday Page and Co., 1913.

Gazetteer of Suburban New York, The Brooklyn Daily Eagle Almanac. Brooklyn, 1897.

Henderson, Dwight Franklin, editor. *The Private Journal of Georgianna Gholson Walker, 1862–1865, with selections from the Post-War Years, 1865–1876*. Confederate Centennial Studies No. 25. Tuscaloosa, Alabama: Confederate Publishing Company, 1963.

Hine, Gilbert, and William T. Davis. *Legends, Stories and Folklore of Old Staten Island*. Part I: *The North Shore*. No publisher, 1925.

Historic House Trust of New York City and City of New York Parks and Recreation. *Historic Houses in New York City Parks*. New York: Historic House Trust, 1992.

Preservation League of Staten Island. *Staten Island Walking Tours*. Staten Island: Privately published, 1986.

Rushe, George. *Your Bermuda*. Bermuda, 1995.

Sachs, Charles L. *Made on Staten Island*. Staten Island: Privately published, 1988.

Selden, William K. *The Legacy of John Cleve Green*. Princeton, New Jersey: Privately published, 1988.

Smith, Dorothy Valentine. *Staten Island: Gateway to New York*. Staten Island: Gateway State Bank, 1970.

Staten Island Advance. Staten Island, New York. Various issues.
Willensky, Elliot and Norval White. *AIA Guide to New York City*, third edition. New York: Harcourt Brace Jovanovich, 1988.

See also bibliographies in original publication: pages 8–9, 15–16, 36–37, 45–46, 79–82, 91, 143–145, 223–227.

INTRODUCTION

At the entrance to the harbor of the City of New York lies Staten Island, the Borough of Richmond. For newcomers to our country, the Island is a first view of America; for returning ocean travelers, it represents "home"; for a quarter of a million New Yorkers, it actually is home. For residents of the other boroughs, the Island's parks and beaches are a retreat from crowded city streets. For the tourist, the Island offers the thrill of a five-cent, five-mile ferry ride across the Upper Bay.

The verdant hills visible from the ferry are symbolic of the rolling countryside which is disappearing all too quickly. Fortunately, a vast acreage of land has been set aside for public parks, so that future generations are assured of wooded areas for bird sanctuaries, ponds and lakes for boating and fishing, and a beachfront for swimming.

Staten Island is surrounded by the waters of Newark Bay and the Kill Van Kull on the north; by the Upper New York Bay, the Narrows, Lower New York Bay, and the Atlantic Ocean on the east; by Raritan Bay on the south; by Arthur Kill (Staten Island Sound) on the west.

Appropriately named "backbone of Staten Island" is a range of hills from St. George to Richmondtown. These include Fort Hill, Pavilion Hill, Ward Hill, Grymes Hill, Emerson Hill, Todt Hill, and Lighthouse Hill. At the intersection of Todt Hill Road and Ocean Terrace is a 409.8 foot elevation that is reputed to be the highest point along the Atlantic coastline between Maine and Florida. This spot was a British lookout during the American Revolution. The range of hills is broken sharply at Concord by a natural cleft between Grymes and Emerson Hills, called "Het Kloven" by the Dutch settlers. Part of the new Clove Lakes Expressway follows this valley.

A beachfront extends from South Beach, near the site of the first permanent settlement on the Island, Oude Dorp, to Tottenville, interspersed with marshland areas, some of which are being reclaimed for parkways and for residential purposes. Marshlands in other sections of the Island also are being reclaimed for expressways and industry.

The Island consists of 38,947 acres (approximately 57 square miles), including several small islands such as Shooter's and Prall's Islands.

1

Among the boroughs of New York City, it ranks third in area. Staten Island is two-and-a-half times the size of Manhattan. Triangular in shape, it is 13.9 miles long from northeast to southwest and is 7.3 miles at its greatest width.

To the shores of this Island have come many generations of people who were determined to make a good life for their families. They have left behind them a record of significant contributions in all fields of human endeavor. Awareness and appreciation of this heritage can come only through knowledge and understanding of past struggles and achievements. Fortunately, many landmarks have been preserved in the Borough of Richmond. These form the link between the past and the present and, because they are tangible, they are meaningful to the pupils in our schools.

This publication traces the growth and development of Staten Island from the time of the Indians to the present day, with some indications of future development. Historic spots and other landmarks, as well as places of special interest, are noted. It is hoped that class visits to these places will motivate and enrich the curriculum as the teacher, with the background material provided herein, relates local history to the social studies program.

To assist the teacher in utilizing this publication two kinds of reference marks are used in the text that follows:

> *Indicates that the person or place so identified is listed in the Resources Directory beginning on page 251.
> ( )   Numbered references in parentheses indicate the titles listed in the bibliography which appears at the end of each chapter.

CHAPTER I

INDIAN LIFE

THE EARLIEST INHABITANTS of Staten Island have been traced back to prehistoric man. Recent discoveries by local archeologists of three Clovis-type projectile points on a site in Rossville definitely prove that the Paleo-Indian lived on the Island from 8,000 to 12,000 years ago. At Bowman's Brook, near Port Ivory, Mariners Harbor, evidences have been discovered of the Lamoka culture dating back to about 3500 B.C. Other archeological findings trace the Staten Island Indians through the Archaic and Woodland Periods, and finally into the Contact Period when the Delawares met the white settlers. Indian burials have been found in Tottenville and Mariners Harbor, but village and camp sites have been located in scattered sections of the Island, particularly in Travis, Greenridge, Woodrow, Huguenot, Silver Lake, and Arrochar.

LENI-LENAPE† CULTURE

When the white man first came to the shores of Staten Island, friendly Indians of the Delaware or Leni-Lenape Nation were established there. *Leni* means "genuine or original" and *Lenape* means "Indian or man" (4), and so they were sometimes called the "original people." They had a culture similar to that of the tribes which inhabited the western end of Long Island. Three bands of the Unami division of the Lenapes lived on Staten Island: Hackensacks on the North Shore, Raritans on the South Shore, and Tappans on the East. They all spoke dialects of the Algonkian language, belonging to the same linguistic stock as the New England Indians. The "totem" or sign of the Unami was the Turtle.

The Staten Island Indians named their settlement *Aquehonga*, which meant "high, sandy banks." At times they called it *Aquehonga Manacknong* (8) meaning "as far as the place of bad woods."

The Leni-Lenapes have been described as having coppery brown skin, straight black hair, dark brown eyes, thick lips, and broad noses.

---

†*Lenni-Lenape* is preferred by some authorities. Webster's dictionary gives *Leni-Lenape* which is used in this publication.

HOMES

They built their homes on the well-drained sandy soil of knolls near the shore or near tidal inlets, if possible close to a spring. These dome-shaped wigwams were about twelve feet high and from ten to thirty feet or more in diameter. Small limbs of trees (often hickory) were set in the ground, arched to form the frame and lashed together at the top with bark rope. This frame was thatched with bark slabs, grass or rush matting, and layered like shingles. Often salt hay from the Fresh Kills meadow was used for this purpose. A hole was left at the top where the poles were fastened together, so that the smoke could escape from the fireplace which was built in a depression in the center of the wigwam. The edges of this smoke hole were daubed with clay as a protection against fire. The doorway was a small round opening at ground level, protected by deerskin or bark. A low bench, covered with cornhusk mats or skins, was built around the inside of the wigwam to be used as a chair or bed (3). Parallel poles were hung overhead for food and clothing. (A diorama at the Staten Island Museum shows a Staten Island village of the Leni-Lenapes.)*

CLOTHING

The Indians depended upon the skins of animals for their clothing. In the summer, the brave wore a loin cloth or breechcloth, perhaps of buckskin. In winter he might add hip length leggings and moccasins to his raiment. A strip of hair was left down the center of the otherwise shaved head, and into this "roach" or cockscomb, one or two feathers were placed. It is important to remember that these Staten Island Indians did not wear large feathered headdresses, as did tribes in other sections of the country. Red, yellow, and black colors ornamented their faces.

A leather skirt was the usual costume of the Indian woman, supplemented by an animal skin over her shoulders in cold weather. Toe bones of deer, bear and wolf teeth, stone pendants, and periwinkle shell beads were used as decorations. The women wore their hair long, sometimes braided.

PLAY

The Leni-Lenape children played games just as do today's children. Outdoors, the boys threw stones, fought, wrestled, and played with blunt arrowheads and toys. They were taught the skills of swimming and fishing with their hands. As they grew older, they learned to use the bow and arrow and the spear for hunting, and to know the ways of nature and the cries of wild animals. In winter they practiced scaling sticks over ice and snow. Girls played with miniature cooking utensils. A favorite game was finding a hidden object under a row of moccasins (3). The children had pet dogs and probably tamed the young bobcats, opossums, and raccoons as do youngsters today, for the skeletons of these animals are sometimes found in the burials of the young.

OCCUPATIONS OF THE BRAVES

The Indian men and women divided their numerous duties. The braves were responsible for protecting the home and providing food. Shad, striped bass, and other fish were caught chiefly in nets stretched in the tide, weighted by grooved pebbles. Oysters and clams were collected with little effort. The woods of Staten Island provided the hunter with deer, bear, muskrat, beaver, bobcat, fox, wolf, opossum, raccoon, rabbit, and wild turkeys, ducks, and geese.

Another important task of the brave was making the dugout canoe, often thirty or forty feet long. After a suitable tree had been selected, a strip of bark about a foot wide was removed and a fire started around the base of the trunk, wet clay being applied about four feet above the ground to prevent the flames from spreading. When the tree had been burned through sufficiently, a crude axe was used for the final felling.

A typical Algonkian
Indian village

Fire was used again to hollow out this single piece of wood, care being taken to saturate the part of the trunk to be preserved. Then stone hatchets and sharp clam shells were employed to scrape out the charred inner portion of the log, leaving a crude but practical means of transportation between Staten Island and the mainland areas.

The Leni-Lenapes made fire by the same methods that Indians used in other parts of the country. The usual way involved friction, accomplished by "twirling a stick between the hands, and pressing its point until it cut into a slab of soft wood and finally produced the temperature of fire" (3). At other times they would strike flint against a piece of pyrite until sparks were generated and ignited the shredded bark or grass tinder (1).

Braves who were skilled in the art made the stone implements used in their daily living. Many such artifacts found on Staten Island are on display at the Staten Island Museum. Among them are knives, spearheads, hammerstones, axes, scrapers for removing fat from skins, drills for making holes in leather and wood, and arrowheads, some of brown jasper and some of deer antlers. Bows usually were made of hickory and strings of animal sinews.

Shells were the source of the wampum beads used for money and for ornamentation. The Indians polished small pieces of shell and then bored holes in the beads so they could be strung on strong thread made of animal sinews. Dark beads were made from the dark purple part of the inside of the clam shell, and white ones from the periwinkles. The beads were sometimes used to decorate the women's skirts and the moccasins. The chief use of beads, of course, was for trade. Loose ones were called *sewan*, while strings or belts of beads were called *wampum*.

OCCUPATIONS OF SQUAWS

The most important duties of the Indian women were the same as those of the modern mother – raising and training the children and keeping the home. One meal a day, usually at mid-morning, was customary. However, the clay or stone pot was always on the fire (10), held there by a stick passing through the holes on either side of the upper rim, so that anyone could eat when he was hungry. Meat was often broiled on spits or roasted in the hot ashes with ears of maize.

Other foods were boiled in clay pots. First, stones were heated and then plunged into the water to hasten the boiling process. Corn had a variety of uses in the diet, some of which we enjoy today, for the Leni-

Lenape squaw made succotash, johnnycake, corn pone, and *sapraen* or mush (10). Fish was also a major part of the diet. The fire had to be fed continuously, so the older women and children were kept busy gathering firewood.

Although the housekeeping chores must have been simple, many additional tasks occupied the squaw. It was she who butchered and skinned the animals, and then cured and smoked the meat. She also ground the corn into coarse flour by pounding the kernels with a stone pestle in a wooden or stone mortar.

The squaw did most of the farming. The brave sometimes helped with the planting by walking ahead, digging holes with a sharp stick. The squaw, following closely, dropped in the seeds or plants and covered them. Later, she cultivated with a simple hoe made of a stone or shell, lashed to a wooden handle. The chief crops were Indian maize, beans, pumpkins, squash, and tobacco.

The woods and fields provided many berries, fruits, nuts, and other wild foods. Among those found by the Leni-Lenape squaws were strawberries, blackberries, plums, cherries, grapes, acorns, butternuts, hickory nuts, Indian turnip, wild mint, wild leek, various cresses, and mushrooms. Some of these still may be found in the woods and fields of Staten Island. Storable foods were placed in pits lined with bark or grasses. These held shelled corn, beans, nuts, and similar foods until the squaw was ready to use them. Later these storage pits often became refuse receptacles.

The women also made wooden bowls and ladles, and willow or bark baskets, and dug the clay used to make the primitive pottery which was hardened by baking in a hot fire.

NATURAL RESOURCES AND TRADE

Staten Island had many natural resources – fertile soil, good fishing, abundant shellfish, a plentiful supply of game, and many natural springs. Artifacts reveal that considerable trading was conducted on the Island as the Indians of other tribes stopped off on their travels along the eastern coast. The Leni-Lenapes traded wampum and fish for flint which was not found locally. (A diorama at the Staten Island Museum shows the Indians trading with visiting tribes.)*

ARCHEOLOGICAL FINDINGS

Archeologists' findings in refuse pits, which sometimes contained burials, reveal part of what we know of Indian life. Within these pits have been found such items as crude drinking cups, ladles, and dishes made from box turtle shells; spoons fashioned from deer skulls and wild turkey bones; primitive musical instruments such as bone or willow flutes and turtle shell rattles; pipes, usually with short, thick tubes made of steatite (soapstone); beaded items made of shells, horns, teeth or quills; and fragments of broken pottery.

BURIALS

The many Indian skeletons found on Staten Island prove that the Leni-Lenapes interred the bodies on their sides, with the "arms and legs bent so that the hands and knees were drawn up near the chin" (7). The body usually faced the east or southeast. A diorama of an Indian burial, including artifacts unearthed in April 1960, is on display at the Staten Island Museum. The Leni-Lenapes believed in a life hereafter, in a "Great Spirit." *Mannetto* was the Lenape word for any supernatural power. The witch doctor, *Shaman,* concocted charms or cast spells over the ill Indian to frighten away the evil spirits (3).

The Leni-Lenapes on Staten Island were basically a friendly people, although "not far advanced intellectually" (7). There was some trading between the colonists and Indians but many tragedies occurred because of misunderstandings and the white man's unfair treatment of the Indian. Consequently there arose a struggle for survival between the Indians and the early settlers, resulting in the Pig War of 1640, the Whiskey War of 1644, and the Peach War of 1655.

The Indians who left Staten Island joined the Delaware Indians in New Jersey, and later moved further west. It is believed that some who are living on the Wisconsin Reservation today can trace their ancestry back to Staten Island Indians.

BIBLIOGRAPHY

1.   "Archeology on Staten Island." *The News Bulletin.* Staten Island Institute of Arts and Sciences, 10:19-21, October 1960.
2.   BAYLES, RICHARD M., ED. *History of Richmond County (Staten Island) New York: From Its Dis-*

covery to the Present Time. New York: L. E. Preston and Co., 1887. P. 48-53.

3.   BOLTON, REGINALD P. *Indian Life of Long Ago in the City of New York*. New York: Schoen Press, 1934. P. 167.

4.   BRINTON, DANIEL G. AND ANTHONY, REV. ALBERT S. *A Lenape-English Dictionary*. Philadelphia: Historical Society of Pennsylvania, 1888. P. 236.

5.   BURGHER, ELLIOTT R. "Folsom Points Found at Rossville, Staten Island." *Proceedings of the Staten Island Institute of Arts and Sciences*. XX: 40-43, Fall 1957.

6.   CLUTE, JOHN J. *Annals of Staten Island: From Its Discovery to the Present Time*. New York: Press of Charles Vogt, 1877. P. 6-7.

7.   LENG, CHARLES W. AND DAVIS, WILLIAM T. *Staten Island and Its People*, Vol. I. New York: Lewis Historical Publishing Co., Inc., 1930. P. 71-84.

8.   MORRIS, IRA K. *Memorial History of Staten Island*, Vol. I. New York: Memorial Publishing Co., 1898. P. 10-19.

9.   RITCHIE, WILLIAM A. *Indian History of New York State. Part I. Pre-Iroquoian Cultures*. Educational Leaflet Series No. 6, Rev. Albany: New York State Museum, 1953. P. 13

10.   RITCHIE, WILLIAM A. *Indian History of New York State. Part III. The Algonkian Tribes*. Albany: New York State Museum and Science Service, n.d. P. 24

11.   SKINNER, ALANSON. *The Indians of Manhattan Island and Vicinity*. Port Washington: Ira J. Friedman, Inc., 1961. P. 64 (Reprint of Guide Leaflet Series No. 41, American Museum of Natural History.)

CHAPTER II

DISCOVERY, EXPLORATION,
AND EARLY ATTEMPTS TO SETTLE

THE DISCOVERY OF STATEN ISLAND is credited to Giovanni da Verrazzano, an Italian navigator, sailing under the French flag, who entered New York Bay in the three-masted *Dauphine* in April 1524.* Friendly Leni-Lenapes guided the ship to safe anchorage near "The Watering Place" (Tompkinsville).*

Verrazzano's report to King Francis I gives us the first known written description of Staten Island. He wrote of his regret "to leave this region which seemed so commodious and delightful, and which we supposed must also contain great riches, as the hills showed many indications of minerals" (6).

No exploration followed Verrazzano's original discovery, and the Lenapes continued to enjoy this region undisturbed.

HENRY HUDSON

Almost 100 years later, in September 1609, Henry Hudson, the English navigator employed by the Dutch East India Company, sailed into the Lower New York Bay and sighted Staten Island.* In the Journal written by Robert Juet, mate of the *Half Moon*, we find reference to the Staten Island Indians and to the land "pleasant with grass and flowers and goodly trees" (6). It is generally accepted that Henry Hudson named the island *Staaten Eylandt* after the governing body of Holland, the States-General.

Hudson rode at anchor in the Narrows* for several days before voyaging up the Hudson River. He traded with the Lenapes, giving them clothes for tobacco, Indian wheat, oysters, and beans. One unfortunate experience is recorded. Hudson sent a group of five sailors to sound the Narrows, but they were attacked by Indians and John Coleman was killed by "an arrow shot into his throat" (6). He is reported to have been buried at a spot called Coleman's Point, Long Island.

After voyaging up the river as far as what is now Albany, Hudson realized that the Pacific Ocean did not lie ahead, and so he returned to the waters of New York Bay. He knew that he had not discovered a route to the Far East, but he also realized that he had found a fertile land, rich with fine furs that could be obtained from the Indians for a few trinkets or beads. As a result of Hudson's explorations, The Netherlands claimed the territory and named it New Netherland.

The Dutch East India Company, although disappointed that Hudson had failed to find a route to the Orient, sent over ships to carry on fur-trading, particularly in the Hudson Valley and on Manhattan Island where some traders had settled before 1613.

DUTCH WEST INDIA COMPANY

The Dutch West India Company, chartered in 1621, governed all the land claimed by Holland until 1664. The company needed settlers to manage the fur trade, and in 1624 sent about thirty families to this section of the New World. Fort Orange was established on the site of what is now Albany. Soon Fort Amsterdam on Manhattan was settled. In exchange for transportation, necessary equipment, and supplies, the settlers were bound to stay in America at least six years, to sell all their furs to the company for export, and not to manufacture anything which was not for their own use. Such terms did not appeal to the Dutch, so many of the first settlers sent over by the Dutch West India Company were French, and were followed by other nationality groups.

Peter Minuit was appointed first Director-Governor of New Netherland and purchased Manhattan Island from the Indians in 1626 for about $24 worth of trinkets (60 Dutch guilders).

"THE WATERING PLACE"

The outward bound ships at this time used to stop at "The Watering Place," now Tompkinsville, Staten Island. Here a fresh spring supplied them with water for their voyage back to Europe. The site of this spot is indicated by a D.A.R. marker in Tompkinsville Park.* See page 12.

PATROONSHIPS

Holland had to find some way to encourage settlers, so the government offered patroonships to wealthy directors of the Dutch West India Company. They were given large tracts of land and were required to bring over farm workers and their families. The patroon was independent of the provincial governor and ruled his little domain as he saw fit. This, of course, proved to be a source of annoyance to government officials throughout the Dutch Colonial Period. Justice was administered by *schouts*, who were the prosecutors, and by *schepens*, who were the judges (17). Both were appointed by the patroon. Like tenant farmers today, the workers for a patroon did not own the land but had to turn over to him a large percentage of the harvest as rent and as payment for any equipment supplied.

"The Watering Place" in Tompkinsville Park

MICHAEL PAUW, THE FIRST PATROON

In 1630 Michael Pauw was granted part of New Jersey (Pavonia, now Jersey City), and all of Staten Island by the Dutch West India Company. His memory is perpetuated in the name of Pauw Street, New Brighton. Pauw purchased the Island from the Indians but made no attempt to colonize the land and relinquished his rights in 1637. So, although Staten Island was under Dutch control, it remained in the hands of the Leni-Lenapes, who numbered about one hundred at that time (3).

DAVID PIETERSZ DE VRIES, SECOND PATROON

Captain David Pietersz De Vries, who previously had founded a colony in Delaware, was the second patroon to receive land rights on Staten Island. In January 1639, he sent a few families to settle near "The Watering Place," now Tompkinsville.*

13

The following year, Director-Governor William Kieft, who had succeeded Wouter Van Twiller, had a distillery set up under the direction of William Hendricksen. Probably the first distillery in America, it was the first on Staten Island, the predecessor of several breweries which have been important as an industry throughout the years.

De Vries' brave colonists were massacred by the Indians in September 1641 in revenge for having been accused wrongfully of stealing some pigs belonging to the settlers. Actually the pigs had been stolen by sailors of the Dutch West India Company when their ship stopped at "The Watering Place." This incident has become known as the Pig War. De Vries, absent from the Island the night of the massacre, did not give up his rights to Staten Island until some time after this event.

CORNELIUS MELYN, THIRD PATROON

In spite of De Vries' prior claim, Cornelius Melyn was granted all of Staten Island except the De Vries Farm, and in 1642 established a colony of about forty settlers near what is now Fort Wadsworth.* A flag was to be raised at this high point to signal to Fort Amsterdam when any ships arrived in the Lower Bay. The following year, Melyn was forced to abandon his colony because of another Indian uprising, during which the houses and cattle were burned and several people killed.

Again, this incident was the result of mismanagement and poor judgment by Governor Kieft and the cruelty of his agents. This has become known as the Whiskey War, because it was while he was at a drinking party in New Amsterdam that Kieft determined to punish the Indians. After fifty or more Indians had been killed, there was a general uprising to avenge the slaughter, resulting in the attack upon Melyn's colony. At the time, the patroon was away at his more comfortable home up the Hudson.

HIS SECOND ATTEMPT AT COLONIZATION

Kieft was recalled in 1643 and Peter Stuyvesant became the new Director-General. Melyn made another attempt to colonize Staten Island in 1650 with a group of about seventy settlers brought over from Holland. The Indians insisted on his buying the land again. Under the command of Captain Adriaen Post, sixteen farms were built and soon became prosperous. Melyn worked hard to build a good colony. Grain and corn grew abundantly on the fertile land. He brought over oxen for ploughing, milk cows, and cattle.

There was a good supply of fish and of wild game – turkeys, geese, snipes, and wood hens. Wolves, foxes, wildcats, bears, beavers, opossums, raccoons, muskrats, rabbits and deer inhabited the woods. Cherry and apple trees had been introduced and wild grapes were plentiful. These early colonists also learned to use the wild foods available in the woods and fields.

They lived in simple one-story houses, built of wood, clapboarded (as is the Voorlezer's House),* with either thatched or boarded roofs. A description of the typical Dutch dress of the period may be found in social studies texts (4).

Unfortunately, Melyn's colony was destroyed completely by the Indians in 1655. This occurred during the so-called Peach War which was caused by the killing of a squaw in New Amsterdam for stealing a peach from the orchard of a Dutch farmer, "one Van Dycke." The Indians avenged her death by an attack on New Amsterdam during which they killed Van Dycke. They were forced to retreat to Staten Island where they destroyed Melyn's colony. This was the last local struggle in which Leni-Lenape Indians participated. Most of them crossed the Kill, withdrawing to New Jersey.

His Surrendering of Patroon Rights
At this time, Peter Stuyvesant was the Director-General of New Amsterdam. There was ill feeling between him and Melyn about the latter's patroonship and independence (12). After the disaster to his colony, Melyn surrendered his patroon rights to the Dutch West India Company for 1,500 guilders, and went with his family to New Haven, under the protection of the English.

OTHER DUTCH COLONISTS
A survivor of the Peach War, Captain Adriaen Post, and a partner of Melyn's, Patroon Van der Capellen, attempted unsuccessfully to revive the Staten Island colony.† However, Dutch Colonial records indicate that there

†Their names are perpetuated in Post Avenue, Port Richmond, and Capellen Street, Huguenot.

was some continuous occupation of Staten Island by one or more brave families from that time on. A treaty of peace was made with the Indian chiefs in 1660, paving the way for successful permanent colonization.

BIBLIOGRAPHY

1. BAYLES, RICHARD M., ED. *History of Richmond County (Staten Island) New York: From Its Discovery to the Present Time*. New York: L. E. Preston and Co., 1887. P. 44-47.
2. CLUTE, JOHN J. *Annals of Staten Island: From Its Discovery to the Present Time*. New York: Press of Charles Vogt, 1877. P. 1-7, 14-41.
3. DU BOIS, THEODORA AND SMITH, DOROTHY M. *Staten Island Patroons*. Staten Island, N. Y.: Staten Island Historical Society, 1961. (May be purchased from the Staten Island Historical Museum, Richmondtown, Staten Island 6, N.Y. for 80¢.)
4. FISHER, MARGARET AND FOWLER, MARY J. *Colonial America*. Grand Rapids, Mich.: Fideler Co., 1960. P. 63-65.
5. HAMPTON, VERNON B. "Staten Island . . . Its Story." *Tercentenary Booklet*. Staten Island, N. Y.: Staten Island Tercentenary Commission, 1961. P. 8-9.
6. LENG, CHARLES W. AND DAVIS, WILLIAM T. *Staten Island and Its People*. Vol. I. New York: Lewis Historical Publishing Co., Inc., 1930. P. 85-104.
7. LIPINSKY, LINO S. *Giovanni da Verrazzano, the Discoverer of New York Bay*. New York, Triggs Color Printing Corp., 1958. P. 20. (Booklet may be purchased at Sales Desk of Museum of the City of New York for one dollar.)
8. McMILLEN, LORING. "David Pietersz De Vries and the First Settlement of Staten Island." *The Staten Island Historian*, II: 25-27, October 1939.
9. ——. "Dutch Had Settlement on Staten Island When New Amsterdam Became a City 300 Years Ago." *Staten Island Advance,** April 25, 1953. P. 6A.
10. ——. "Tompkinsville Site of Water Place." *Staten Island Advance,** September 27, 1949.
11. MORRIS, IRA K. *Memorial History of Staten Island*. Vol. I. New York: Memorial Publishing Co., 1898. P. 20-39, 46-62.
12. O'HALLORAN, JOHN D. "The Patroons of Pavonia and Staten Island." *The Staten Island Historian*, XIV: 11-12, April-June 1953.
13. SANTORA, DANIEL. *Giovanni da Verrazzano, a Short History of His Discoveries*. Staten Island, N. Y.: Staten Island Italian Historical Society, 1949. P. 12 (Copies of this pamphlet were sent to Staten Island schools in 1949.)
14. SANTORO, DANIEL AND RALLO, JOHN A. *Italians – Past and Present*. Staten Island, N. Y.: Staten Island Italian Historical Society, 1955. P. 22-28.
15. STEINMEYER, HENRY G. *Staten Island 1524-1898*. 2nd ed. Staten Island, N. Y.: Staten Island Historical Society, 1961. P. 1-10. (May be ordered from Board of Education listing, *Library Books for Secondary Schools*.)
16. WABEKE, BERTUS H. *Dutch Emigration to North America 1624-1860, A Short History*. New York: The Netherland Information Bureau, 1944. P. 13-60. (May be consulted in Library of Netherland Information Service at 711 Third Avenue, New York City.)
17. WIDDECOMBE, LAWRENCE W. "The Law as It Existed and Was Administered in New Amsterdam 200 Years Ago." *The Staten Island Historian*, XXIII: 3-7, January-March 1962.

*Back issues of *The Staten Island Advance* are on microfilm in the St. George Public Library, Staten Island.

CHAPTER III

THE COLONIAL PERIOD: 1661-1776

DURING THE COLONIAL PERIOD, from 1661 to 1776, the population of Staten Island grew from the first few families to about 3,000 inhabitants, widely scattered over the Island, enjoying a peaceful life on their well-kept farms. This was a fertile land, with clear springs, abundant fishing and hunting, and beautiful woodlands. It provided a good life in which religious freedom was preserved, simple wants were satisfied, and family ties were strong.

FIRST PERMANENT SETTLEMENT AT OUDE DORP

PIERRE BILLIOU

The failure of the patroon system made it necessary to establish another system, whereby the land was given outright to the settlers. In August 1661, a group of sixteen Dutch and French settlers, under the leadership of Pierre Billiou, a Walloon,* applied to Governor Peter Stuyvesant for "Ground Briefs" or land grants on Staten Island. Their request was granted, but not all of the original applicants moved to the Island at that time, some remaining in Brooklyn or Manhattan. Among those who settled were families of Pierre Billiou,* Walraven Luten,† and Thys Barentsen (10).

OUDE DORP*

This little colony, established in August 1661, was the first permanent settlement on Staten Island, and later came to be known as Oude (pronounced "owd") Dorp, which means old village. It was located at what is now South Beach, along the shore end of Ocean Avenue "on the banks of Old Town Creek." The mouth of this creek was closed by a storm about 1730, so the exact location is difficult to ascertain (22). There are plans for a historical marker to be placed at the site to commemorate this early settlement.

BLOCKHOUSE

The Dutch West India Company supplied a small detachment of soldiers to protect this new settlement from the Indians, and a blockhouse was

17

built to which the settlers could flee. This was a protection not granted previous colonists under the patroon system.

FAMILY NAMES OF SOME EARLY SETTLERS

Other families of the original nineteen applicants came to the Island within a few years. Descendants of these early settlers are living on Staten Island today. In the following list appear the name of the settler and the family name of the descendant: Thys Barentsen, Tysen family; Wynant Pieters, Winant family; Johannes Christofels, Christopher family; Gerit Mannaat, Manee family; Nicholas Stillwell, Stillwell family; David d'Amareu, Demarest family; William Britton, Britton family (15).

DIFFERENT NATIONALITIES

The many different nationalities represented in this early colony – the Dutch, French, Belgian, and English – were unified by the common purpose of enjoying religious freedom. This intermingling of various national groups has existed throughout the history of the Island.

ENGLISH SETTLEMENTS ELSEWHERE

During the period of Dutch control of New Netherland, the English had settlements in Connecticut, Long Island, and points south, basing their claims to all northern territory on the explorations of the Cabots. New England had attracted more than 30,000 colonists, but the entire colony of New Netherland had only 10,000 in 1664.

STATEN ISLAND UNDER ENGLISH RULE

In 1664 King Charles II decided to revive the English claims to the Dutch settlement, and granted to his brother James, the Duke of York, all the territory occupied by the Dutch. A British fleet of four frigates was sent to New Amsterdam, and Director-General Peter Stuyvesant was forced to surrender his unfortified colony in September of that year.

OUDE DORP BECAME DOVER

With the end of the Dutch Colonial Period, New Amsterdam became New York. The Duke appointed Colonel Richard Nicholls Governor and one of his first acts was to capture the blockhouse on Staten Island. Oude

Dorp was renamed Dover, and the settlers found themselves under English rule. Staten Island, Long Island, and Westchester were known as Yorkshire. Land patents were given to the original settlers, and many other grants of land were made. One was to Nicholas Stillwell who later became Constable, and one to a Thomas Walton. The Walton-Stillwell House is still standing at South Beach.*

FINAL PURCHASE OF STATEN ISLAND FROM THE INDIANS

Governor Nicholls was replaced by Governor Francis Lovelace in 1668. There were some minor Indian troubles and Governor Lovelace, in the year 1670, found it necessary to purchase Staten Island again from the Indians. This was to be the final purchase, so the Indian boys and girls, as well as the adults, were required to place marks on the deed as a record of the transaction, the Indians claiming no recollection of six prior purchases made by De Pauw, De Vries, Melyn, and others.

TERMS OF THE TREATY

For the last purchase of Staten Island, the Indians received 400 fathoms of wampum, 30 match boots, 8 coats of Durens made up (probably a cheap woolen material), 30 shirts, 20 kettles, 20 guns, a firkin of powder (quarter of a barrel), 60 barrels of lead, 30 axes, 20 hoes, and 50 knives (1, 14).

To symbolize the finality of this transfer of land, the Indians handed over a block of soil and a twig taken from every type of tree growing on the Island, except the ash and the hickory. This Turfe and Twigg deed provided that any member of the original tribe would be permitted "in perpetuity" to cut down ash or hickory trees which were used in basketmaking. A large mural at 30 Bay Street, St. George, portrays this transaction.*

By 1675, there were only a few Indians left on Staten Island, but, according to tradition, some of their descendants still live on the Island.

POPULATION GROWTH

Gradually other settlers came to Staten Island, and by 1670, Nieuwe Dorp (New Dorp) had been settled near the water's edge and Oude Dorp (Old Town) so named to distinguish the two.

Another settlement of this period, shown on an early map, was known as Stony Brook (near the junction of Amboy Road and Richmond Road, New Dorp). By 1695 the population of the Island was divided evenly amongst the English, the French-speaking people, and the Dutch. The latter group settled particularly on the North Shore.

By 1698 the population of the entire Island was 727, about 70 of whom were slaves, who were, for the most part, kindly treated by their masters. Between 1698 and the outbreak of the Revolution, the population quadrupled (1, 14). The following figures reveal this growth:

1698 – 727	1737 – 1,889	1756 – 2,132
1712 – 1,279	1746 – 2,073	1771 – 2,847
1723 – 1,506	1749 – 2,154	1776 – 3,000

Throughout the Colonial Period, therefore, small hamlets developed around the scattered farms, some along the shores, some inland. A study of maps (9) of this period reveals the following names: Old Town, New Dorp, Burying Place (Port Richmond), Great Kills, Smoking Point (Rossville), Stony Brook, Prince's Bay, Billopp's Point, Long Neck (Travis), and Richmondtown. Villages, as such, however, did not develop until after the Revolution, with the exception of Richmondtown.

GOVERNOR LOVELACE AND LAND GRANTS

Governor Francis Lovelace, who had been appointed Governor of New York Province in 1668, ordered surveys made of Staten Island, and lots were laid out on the north, east, and as far south as what is now Great Kills. Jacques Guyon received a large grant of land now known as Oakwood on which he built a home that stood until 1925. The name is perpetuated in Guyon Avenue. Large land grants also were made to the Governor's two brothers, Dudley and Thomas.

GOVERNOR'S MILL

Governor Lovelace started the first water mill on Staten Island where a tidal creek crossed the present Richmond Terrace near Clove Road. This creek became known as Palmer's Run* after John Palmer in 1677 received a patent to the property. Palmer held it for ten years and then deeded it to Governor Thomas Dongan who enlarged the original mill built by

Lovelace, later called Dongan's Lower Mill, and also erected another mill on Clove Road near Post Avenue known as Dongan's Upper Mill. The Lower Mill changed hands several times after the Revolution and finally came into the hands of the Bodine family. Bodine's Creek and Bodine Street took their names from this old family. In 1938 this old mill was demolished. The mill creek, at one time the natural boundary between West New Brighton and Port Richmond, is now carried underground through a culvert.

DUTCH RECAPTURE NEW YORK
The plans of Lovelace to develop Staten Island came to an end in July 1673 when the Dutch captured New York and renamed the colony New Orange. Captain Anthony Colve, the new Governor, appointed Pierre Billiou Sheriff and Magistrate, making him the most prominent Islander at that time.

ENGLISH REGAIN CONTROL
In November 1674, over a year later, the English regained New York. Surveys of the Island and grants of land to settlers continued. By 1679 one hundred tracts of land (about 80 acres each) had been granted by the new Governor, Sir Edmund Andros. An unusually large patent of 932 acres was granted to Christopher Billopp. On this he erected his two-story fieldstone English manor house which was to be the scene of a Peace Conference during the Revolutionary War.*

In 1677 Obadiah Holmes had been granted a patent for the land on which he built the original stone and frame cottage that is now part of the Britton Cottage at New Dorp Beach. More details about this house will be found in the Reference Section.*

STATEN ISLAND IN 1679
A vivid description of Staten Island in 1679 is recorded in the Journal of Jasper Danckaerts (1, 5, 9, 11, 33). Herein he relates his visit to the American Colonies with Peter Sluyter in October 1679. They were two Dutch missionaries, Labadists, belonging to a Protestant group formed in 1672 by Jean Lapide. The following is an actual description of the settlement at Oude Dorp eleven years after it was established: "There were seven hous-

es, but only three in which anybody lived. The others were abandoned, and their owners had gone to live on better places on the Island, because the ground around this village was worn out and barren, and also too limited for their uses." Dankaerts then describes coming to Nieuwe Dorp (now New Dorp) where he "found an Englishman who could speak Dutch." After leaving this settlement, he mentions going "from one plantation to another, for the most part belonging to the French." So we find a happy mingling of Dutch, English, and French, as well as a few friendly Indians living peaceably together on Staten Island in 1679. Dankaerts noted the population as "about a hundred families."

The missionaries continued their three-day journey, and difficult walking it must have been, to "the west point, where an Englishman lived alone, some distance from the road." This was probably the home of Christopher Billopp, previously mentioned.

RELIGION OF THE EARLY SETTLERS

The early settlers on Staten Island, as elsewhere in the Colonies, were a religious people. As early as 1663, the Reverend Samuel Drisius,* minister of the Reformed Dutch Church of New Amsterdam, who could speak in English, French and Dutch, came across the bay to preach in the blockhouse at Oude Dorp, a practice he continued for several years. After his death, other visiting ministers attended to the religious needs of the settlement.

French Church

In 1693 Reverend David de Bonrepos, a resident minister, preached to a congregation of 36 French, 40 English, and 44 Dutch settlers (39). In 1698 this group received a deed to land at Greenridge and a French Huguenot Church was built there. The site of this church is indicated by a State Historical Marker on Arthur Kill Road, north of Richmond Avenue.*

Voorlezer's House

The Dutch had to depend upon a visiting clergyman or "voorlezer" known also as a lay reader. In 1695 they received a lease of land and built the Voorlezer House which, fortunately, has been preserved (31).* This house will be described in the section on education. Hendrick Kroesen, the Voorlezer, lived there and for many years guided the inhabitants as lay reader and as schoolmaster.

CHURCH OF ST. ANDREWS

In 1705 the Reverend Aeneas Mackenzie was sent from England to found the Protestant Episcopal Church of St. Andrew.* While this was being built, services were held at the French Church in Greenridge. In 1712, when St. Andrew's was completed, Queen Anne presented the congregation with a silver chalice and paten which may be seen at the Historical Museum in Richmond.*

The original St. Andrew's was constructed of stone with a Dutch type gambrel roof with flaring eaves and a Christopher Wren steeple. Used as a hospital by the British during the Revolution, the church suffered some damage. The present edifice contains part of the original stone walls which have remained through two fires, one in 1867 and the other in 1872. Each time the church was rebuilt within a year. Many quaint epitaphs may be read today in the tombstones in the adjoining graveyard.* Inside the present St. Andrew's are three tablets – one unveiled in 1908 in memory of Queen Anne, one in memory of the first rector, and one for the fourteen rectors who served the church during the first 200 years of its existence. The English gradually left the French Church to attend St. Andrew's. In later years the little church at Greenridge, without sufficient support, was closed (18).

REFORMED DUTCH CHURCH

Around the beginning of the eighteenth century, as previously noted, the Dutch began to concentrate on the North Shore of the Island (the present Port Richmond section). Wanting their own place of worship, they built the Reformed Dutch Church of the North Shore in 1715 on what is now the site of the Staten Island Reformed Church.* It was a frame, one-story, shingle sided building in the shape of a hexagon, terminating in a high six-sided steeple. Because there were no pews, worshipers brought their own chairs or benches. The men sat near the walls while the women sat in the middle of the room. The sermons were lengthy, and the sleepy worshiper was awakened in time to make his contribution by the bells attached to the velvet collection bags which were on long poles (14). During the Revolution this church suffered severe damage, and in 1780 it was destroyed completely by a windstorm. Plans for the Richmondtown Restoration include construction of the Old Dutch Church in the hexagonal form on property directly across the road from the Voorlezer's House.

The present Staten Island Reformed Church is the third church building erected on the site. On its north side is a cemetery, part of which is the "Burial Place," as it was called at the end of the seventeenth century, and by which the locality was then known.

By 1769, with an increase in population, the Dutch needed a second place of worship and built a Reformed Dutch Church at Richmondtown. This little church was burned by the British as a "Rebel Church" during the Revolution, rebuilt in 1808 and abandoned about 1878. The parsonage of this church, built about 1855, still stands at 74 Arthur Kill Road. It is on the corner of this property that the hexagonal Dutch Church of the North Shore will be reproduced, since no plans have been found for the Richmondtown church.

PRESBYTERIAN CHURCH

Another church built in colonial days was the Presbyterian meeting house built about 1717 at Stony Brook, that section of New Dorp near the intersection of Amboy Road and Richmond Road. This church was used until its members joined the Reformed Dutch congregation in Richmondtown in 1769.

MORAVIAN CHURCH

The Moravian Church at New Dorp, erected in 1763, was the last house of worship to be constructed on the Island prior to the Revolution. This building, formerly used as a church and parsonage, is still standing, and is now the Cemetery office.* It is a Dutch colonial, one-and-a-half story white frame building, with a sweeping roof extended over the long piazza which is supported by built-up square columns. One large room was used as the church, the rest as the home of the minister. Many old epitaphs may be read in the graveyard adjacent to this old building, some predating the erection of the building itself. During the Revolution, English soldiers were buried there. The present Moravian Church was built in 1845 (11).

Original Moravian Church, New Dorp

HOMES

The earliest colonists on Staten Island had to build their homes from materials found there. The first houses, therefore, were simple, one-room cottages, boarded on the inside, clapboarded on the outside, with a thatched roof. Clay mixed with straw was used between the clapboards and the inner wall to provide insulation, according to research done by Loring McMillen, Borough Historian.

After a few years, the settlers built homes of fieldstone, bonded with lime (mortar made by burning oyster shells). Bricks for chimneys and fireplaces were made of clay found beneath the soil. Clay pits may still be visited in the Charleston* region of Staten Island. The stone part of the Walton-Stillwell House at Camp Seaview, South Beach, dates back to the original settlement at Oude Dorp.*

The houses consisted of only one or two rooms, additions being made as needed, resulting in the low rambling houses of the Colonial Period which we see on Staten Island today. Examples of this type of rambling architecture, with approximate dates of original construction are: the Britton-Cubberly Cottage (1678) with low ceilings, hand-hewn beams, wide floor boards, hand wrought hinges, Dutch door, and deep-set windows with sloping sills; the Austen House (1680),* a low rambling stone farmhouse, built by a Dutch merchant as a simple stone cottage; the Billiou-Stillwell-Perine House (19), original section built in 1663, and believed moved from Oude Dorp to present location; the Kreuzer-Pelton House (1720), original stone section at the western end of the house; the Housman House (1730), a typical pre-Revolutionary Dutch house built on the stagecoach route between Long Neck (Travis) and the present Rosebank. Locations of these houses and other details appear in the Reference Section. For a full descrip-tion of colonial homes on Staten Island refer to Loring McMillen's articles on "Staten Island Architecture" which appeared in the *Staten Island Histo-rian*, as noted in Bibliography (29).

The kitchen, with its large open fireplace, was the center of home life, providing heat, light, and cooking facilities. Such kitchens are described in many textbooks (7). An excellent example of a colonial kitchen is dis-played in the Staten Island Historical Museum.

Window panes and windows of the early houses usually were small, since glass had to be imported. Native woods, such as oak, maple, and white pine were used for framework, trim, flooring, and the panelling which came at a later date.

The French and Dutch continued to build the stone or brick house, while the English preferred the frame house. The frame was fitted together on the ground, wooden pegs securing the joints, and when it was complet-ed, the neighbors worked together to raise it into place. A description of a "raising bee" or "house raising" may be found in many books (7). A section of a typical "mortise and tenon" framework is exhibited on the first floor of the Staten Island Historical Museum.

In the simple one or two room cottages, previously described, there was often a garret where the children slept which was reached by a steep stair-way. By the early 1700s, however, larger homes were being built, one and a half stories or two stories, with larger windows and doors, and steeper roofs. Just prior to the Revolution, piazzas or porches were added, supported by columns. In these larger homes, the kitchen was often placed in an addition known as the "ell." This made it possible to have an open hall in the main part of the house, off which were the parlors. The Lake-Tysen House,* erected about 1740, exemplifies this feature. Carpenters began to show their skill in woodwork, mantel pieces, panelling and cupboards. Some fine examples of this handwork may be seen in the homes mentioned or in the "Panel Room" on the second floor of the Historical Museum.*

A few of the wealthier settlers were able to build larger homes at an ear-lier period, but they were not typical. The two-story fieldstone English manor house of Christopher Billopp is the outstanding example of this (6).*

Following is a list of homes built during the Colonial Period which are still standing, but have not been mentioned previously. Locations and

other details appear in the Resource Listing.
(All dates of construction are approximate.)

Lakeman-Cortelyou House (1678) Scott-Edwards House (1730)
Buckeleven-Egbert House (1690) Martling-Cazine House (1730)
Purdy's Hotel (1690) Cropsey House (1750)
Treasure House (1700) Winant House (1750)
Seguine-Britton House (1700) Christopher House (1750)
Woods of Arden House (1720) Wiman House (1760)
Egbert House (1720) Gerritsen House (1770)
Prall House (1720) Neville House (1770)
Brougham Cottage (1720) Decker House (1770)
Holmes-Cole House (1720) Boehm House (1770)

GOVERNMENT

Early in the history of the first permanent settlement at Oude Dorp, the government of New Netherland had selected magistrates from among the settlers. On January 28, 1664, a Court of Justice for Staten Island was established and three judges appointed: David d'Amareu, Pierre Billiou, and Walraven Luten. The Dutch terms *schout* and *schepen* designated "sheriff" and "magistrate."

Gradually Dutch law gave way to English law, and by 1680 the government of the Island consisted of a justice, Richard Stillwell, a clerk, Obadiah Holmes, a constable, Cornelius Corson, and five overseers. This was the typical form of town government under the English. Judicial independence had been decreed in 1675 by the following order: "by reason of the Separacon by water, Staten Island shall have Jurisdiction of it Self and have no further dependence on the Courts of Long Island Nor on their Militia" (11). However, court actually was held in Gravesend, Long Island until 1683.

Soon there were town meetings held on Staten Island just as there were in New England, as required by law of the Colonial Assembly, particularly to hold elections of officials and to mediate problems of the farmers. It might be of interest to note the officials so elected prior to the Revolution: supervisor of the town, assessors, constables, surveyors of highways, damage appraisers, road masters, and overseers of the poor.

GOVERNOR DONGAN

In 1683 Thomas Dongan became Governor of the Province of New York. He declared the Island a separate entity, and it became known for the first time as Richmond County, one of the twelve original counties of New York. It was so named for the Duke of Richmond, Yorkshire, England, brother of King Charles II. The Island was divided into sections, known as North, South, and West Divisions, and Castleton.

Governor Dongan took over about 5,100 acres on the Kill Van Kull, calling it the Manor of Castletown (the origin of the name Castleton Corners and Castleton Avenue). At the same time, Captain Christopher Billopp's original grant was enlarged to 1,600 acres and became the Manor of Bentley (41). So we note the creation of large estates on Staten Island.

Governor Dongan was one of the best of the early colonial governors of the Province and he was closely connected with Staten Island (1). He maintained a hunting lodge on the Island. Walter Dongan, his nephew, and his descendants "kept the name alive on the Island for two centuries" (14). The town of Dongan Hills, Dongan Hall of the Staten Island Academy, and Dongan Street in West New Brighton, near the site of the family home, are still reminiscent of this family. A bronze plaque on a granite boulder has been erected on Richmond Terrace, west of Sailors' Snug Harbor, in memory of Governor Dongan.*

COUNTY SEATS
STONY BROOK

The settlement known as Stony Brook (New Dorp) became the center of government in 1683. By 1700, however, the population of the Island had grown to 1,000, living in widely scattered areas, necessitating a more convenient location for local government.

COCCLES TOWN BECOMES RICHMONDTOWN

The county seat was moved, therefore, in 1729 from Stony Brook to Coccles Town, so named because of the many oyster and clam shells found in the waters of the nearby Fresh Kills, or as some claim, because of the mounds of shells left by the Indians. As the county seat, Coccles Town was renamed Richmondtown, a name with greater dignity (16).

By 1730, this was a typical small colonial village, the only settlement on the Island that could be so described. There were only about a dozen homes in the village, but it was so located at the crossroads that it could be reached easily on horseback or by horse-drawn vehicle from any of the farms or settlements. There were a few inns or taverns for the convenience of stagecoach travelers, a blacksmith shop, a grist mill, and a town dock on Richmond Creek. This creek still flows under the Town Bridge,* the only stone arch bridge left on the Island. By stepping off the modern road which covers the bridge, one can see the arched stonework.

The most imposing edifice then, as now, was the Church of St. Andrew's.* Nearby was the Treasure House* (still standing) built in 1700 by Samuel Grosset, a French Huguenot, who carried on his trade as a tanner, by the adjacent creek. Later, this house was occupied by Stephen Wood, also a tanner, and James Stoutenburgh, a saddlemaker and innkeeper. This stone and clapboard house is worth a visit. A rear view reveals the stonework and original boards. The origin of the name is traced to the story that in 1850 the owner found thousands of dollars worth of British coins hidden in the walls of the old house.

The First County Courthouse was built in 1729 at the corner of the present Richmond and Richmond Hill Roads, court previously having been held at one of the public inns. The "Old Red Jail" was built adjacent to the courthouse, replacing the first County Gaol which had stood on the northeast corner of the present Arthur Kill Road and Center Street. The foundation of this Gaol has been excavated recently.* A whipping post was erected on the hill just beyond St. Andrew's. About 1755 the Cocclestown Inn* was built, where, it is said, Major Andre made his will in 1777. This Inn stood until 1836. The Old Dutch Church was erected in 1769 opposite the Voorlezer's House. Nearby, was the homestead graveyard of the Rezeau-Van Pelt family which can be seen today.* Before the Revolution, a gaoler's house and a County Poorhouse also had been built in Richmondtown.

This little village was to remain the county seat of Staten Island until 1920, and as such will form part of the Richmondtown Restoration (35). More details about this project will be given in the last section of this report.

OCCUPATIONS
FARMING
The early settlers were an industrious group. They used the fine farm land to good avail, cared for their cattle and swine in the excellent pasture land, and took advantage of the abundant fishing provided. Those who could afford it had slaves to help them with the work. A Swedish naturalist, Peter Kalm, who visited on Staten Island in 1748, wrote an interesting account of the farms with their large orchards of apple and cherry trees. His description is reproduced in several local histories (1, 9, 14, 38).

HOME ACTIVITIES
The colonists had to be more or less self-sufficient. Within the home such activities as candlemaking, soapmaking, spinning, and weaving were carried on. Although everyone was a farmer, there were also specialists, even in those early days.

BLACKSMITH
The village blacksmith played a leading role, for he made all kinds of tools and hardware, in addition to the horseshoes.*

THE TANNER
The tanner was also important to the life of the community, as leather was needed for shoes, harnesses, and many other purposes.

THE SHIPBUILDER
For geographical reasons, boat building always has been essential on Staten Island. A pre-Revolutionary shipbuilding yard can be traced back to Richard Lawrence in the area now known as Mariners Harbor.

OTHER SPECIAL TRADES
Other occupations were those of the barrel maker (cooper), shoemaker, miller, carpenter, weaver, stagecoach driver, ferryman, and tavern keeper.

EDUCATION
These first Staten Islanders were very much interested in the education of their children, so the boys and girls were taught at home until church-

related schools came into existence.

The Dutch were among the first to make elementary education universal and their public schools were for all children, regardless of color or religion. The Dutch West India Company specified that a schoolmaster should be sent for each settlement (12).

Voorlezer's House, Richmondtown

The Voorlezer's House, erected at its present location in 1696, is claimed to be "the oldest building still in existence in this country which was built and used as an elementary school" (17). It is believed that there were about twenty such Voorlezer houses built in the Hudson Valley, so Staten Island is fortunate to have the only one remaining. This two-story frame clapboarded building was restored in 1940. The floors and framing are the original. Hand hewn timbers and wooden pegs can be observed. It is thought that the large room on the first floor was used for church services and the upstairs room as a schoolroom. The two smaller rooms, one on each floor, were living quarters of the Voorlezer who had his large kitchen in the basement. The fireplaces were of simple construction.

CURRICULUM

Instruction in a school of this period was in "reading, writing, ciphering, and customary forms of prayer, modesty, and propriety."

SUPPLIES

The voorlezer's equipment, according to Dr. William Kilpatrick, who spoke at the dedication of the Voorlezer's House in 1947, were "a strong hand plak (a disc of wood with a long handle) for naughty pupils, a willow whip, a penknife, a sand box for blotting, a writing desk, pens, a seal, green wax, an ink pot, a bundle of goose quills, parchment, an ink horn to hang on his belt, a brass candlestick, an arithmetic board on which to lay the counters, a Bible, and a Psalm Book."

THE SCHOOL DAY

The school day, from 8 A.M. to 4 P.M., opened with roll call, a morning prayer, a hymn, Scripture reading, followed by catechism, a reading lesson and other formal work. There was a long lunch hour in the middle of the day. Children in the early Dutch schools went every day except Sunday, and half a day on Saturday. The only vacations were St. Nicholas Day (December 6th), Christmas, New Year's Day, Easter, and the day following each.

SCHOOL DRESS

The school dress was typical of the period. Boys wore knee breeches, usually brown or green, jackets with starched white collars, and broad-brimmed hats that matched the outfit. Girls wore long dresses of different colors, aprons, and Dutch caps. It was customary for boys and girls to wear their hats in the classroom, with the boys removing theirs for recitations.

Records indicate that a stone schoolhouse was built in Karle's Neck (New Springville) between 1690 and 1700, still being used almost two hundred years later. A school was also established at Stony Brook. The first rector of St. Andrew's, Aeneas Mackenzie, was responsible for the establishment of several church-affiliated schools, directed by the Society for the Propagation of the Gospel, for the purpose of educating the children of the parish.

TRANSPORTATION

FERRIES

Needless to say, some form of ferry transportation was necessary to the colonists from the beginning. There must have been many private sailing vessels providing such service from the time of the 1661 settlement. From canoes and oar-propelled boats developed small-decked sailing vessels called "periaguas" with two masts, boomsails, and high guard rails. Flat barge-like ferries were used to carry cattle, wagons, horses, stagecoaches, "goods of bulk," as well as passengers. Some of these were propelled by side-wheels worked by horsepower (treadmill arrangement).* Many mishaps occurred because of strong winds, storms, and ice.

During the Colonial Period ten different ferries operated from Staten Island to Manhattan, Long Island, and New Jersey. The ferry houses were taverns also, providing food and lodging for stagecoach travelers who were en route to the southern or northern colonies. The passengers were ferried across the bay, crossed the Island by stagecoach to another ferry, ferried to New Jersey, continuing to Philadelphia by coach. The ferries were from the points indicated below (37).

The numerals on the map correspond to those in the listing.

1. From the Watering Place (Tompkinsville) to New York. (First public ferry – 1708.) Known as Darby Doyle's Ferry about 1769 and as Cole's Ferry during the Revolution. Used by the British.
2. From point near present U.S. Public Health Service Quarantine Station,* Rosebank, to Long Island, crossing the Narrows (1713).
3. Billopp's Ferry from Tottenville to Amboy, New Jersey. (Some historians say the Raritan Indians operated a ferry here as early as 1650. Captain Christopher Billopp began operation in 1709.) Used by stagecoaches.
4. Old Blazing Star Ferry from Blazing Star (Rossville*) across Arthur Kill to Smoking Point, New Jersey (1722-1768). Used by stagecoaches.
5. New Blazing Star Ferry (later, site of Carteret Ferry) from Long Neck (Travis)* across Arthur Kill to Carteret, New Jersey (1757-1836). Used by stagecoaches which traveled from Watering Place (Tompkinsville) along Richmond Turnpike (Victory Boulevard) en route to Philadelphia. Preferred over ferries No. 3 and No. 4.
6. From present foot of Richmond Terrace across Arthur Kill to Elizabethtown Point, New Jersey (1736).
7. Joshua Mersereau's Ferry from present Morningstar Road across Kill Van Kull to present Bayonne, New Jersey (1774).
8. Corsen Ferry from point near Dutch Church (Port Richmond) across Kill Van Kull to Bergen Point, New Jersey (1750). Known as Decker's Ferry during the Revolution and used by the British.

9. The Van Tuyl Ferry from end of present Jersey Street to Manhattan (1749-1774).

10. The Come's Ferry from a point at entrance of Kill Van Kull across to New Jersey and also to Manhattan (1774-1779).

The accompanying map indicates the above ferry routes.

Colonial Staten Island Ferries

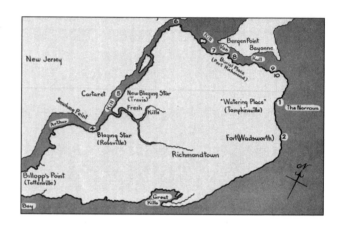

ROADS

The first roads on Staten Island were the Indian trails* which followed the shore, the creeks, and the natural ravines. A D.A.R. marker at Willowbrook Road and Victory Boulevard marks the intersection of two Indian trails, Willowbrook and Blazing Star Trails. As far back as 1679, Jasper Dankaerts mentioned Island roads in his Journal to which reference was made previously. One of these can be traced to the present Old Town Road and Richmond Road, connecting the village of Oude Dorp with the Huguenot settlement at Kleine Kill (Fresh Kills). Records show that more roads were mapped out in 1694, at that time all being laid out in reference to property lines. In 1701 Richmond Avenue and Richmond Hill Road to Coccles Town (Richmondtown) were recorded.

The present Richmond and Amboy Roads were called the King's Road, leading from the Watering Place (Tompkinsville) to Billopp's (Tottenville). This was the first stagecoach route on Staten Island. It was also the road used by the British during the Revolution. The early roads had many twists and turns to avoid natural obstacles (24); some of today's roads, notably Amboy Road, follow these same winding routes.

New Dorp Lane and Old Town Roads were so named in the early 1700s. Some roads were given names of the owners of the property, such as Giffords Lane, Seamans Lane (now Annadale Road), Marshalls Lane (now Huguenot Avenue). Others were named because of natural features, such as Fresh Kills Road (now Arthur Kill Road), and Clove Road (from the Dutch word meaning cleft). Many roads, however, were designated by their destination, such as "Road to Richmondtown" or "Road to Darby Doyle's Ferry." Richmond Terrace, from what is now St. George to the present Port Richmond, was laid out as early as 1705, later becoming part of the Post Road to Philadelphia.

By 1774 more attention was paid to keeping the public highways in good repair, but at best they were like the unimproved dirt roads still in existence on the Island, such as Old Mill Road in Richmondtown.

The highways of the Colonial days were to become the main roads of today except for Hylan Boulevard opened between 1924 and 1927, Drumgoole Boulevard completed in 1939 (originally known as Ramona Boulevard) and the new expressways now under construction.

TRAVEL BY HORSEBACK AND HORSE DRAWN VEHICLE

The only methods of travel on the Island during this period were by horseback and by horse-drawn vehicle. Stages were a common sight on the roads of Staten Island which was an important link in the stagecoach route between New York and Philadelphia.

LANDMARKS

Staten Island is fortunate in having so many landmarks which date back to this Colonial Period. The location and a brief description of many of the old houses appear in the Resources Section of this report. Historical markers are also indicated. The Staten Island Historical Museum has numerous exhibits with actual furniture, household utensils, and equipment dating back to this period. As previously mentioned, a typical kitchen is displayed there.

DUTCH INFLUENCE

Evidences of the early Dutch settlers are few. Some of these exist in the architectural features of the old homes, such as the divided door, the

Dutch oven built toward the back of the fireplace, the fireplace tiles, and the heavy beamed ceilings. Family names and street names can be traced back to the Dutch, such as: Christopher, Cropsey, Cruser, Decker, Egbert, Haughwout, Martling, Post, Prall, Sleight, Van Buren, Vanderbilt, Van Cortlandt, Van Duzer, Van Name, Van Pelt, Vreeland, and Vroom (25).

Other place names of Dutch origin are: Staten Island (Staaten Eylandt); Old Town (Oude Town); New Dorp (Nieuwe Dorp); Kill Van Kull ("kil" – a channel, creek, or river, "kol", a body of water); Arthur Kill ("Achter Kol" – an after river or bay, that is, the bay behind Staten Island); Fresh Kills (Kleine Kill); Great Kills (Groote); Holland Hook; Clove Road and Clove Valley ("Kloven" – a cleft or ravine between two hills); Prince's Bay (named for the Prince of Orange); Robbins Reef ("Robyn's Reft" – Seal Banks). Todt Hill was "Yserberg", meaning Iron Hill, so named for iron deposits found there (36).

FRENCH INFLUENCE

Some French family names and street names can be traced back to the early settlers. Among these are Androvette, Cortelyou, Crocheron, Du Bois, De Puy, Guyon, Joline, Journeay, Laforge, Latourette, Manee, Mercereau, Perine, Poillon, and Seguine (25).

No attempt has been made to describe the costumes, furnishings, customs, and typical family life of the Colonial Period, for this information may be found in many social studies textbooks and local histories (1, 2, 14), in the Historical Museum in Richmondtown, and in the Museum of the City of New York. The purpose of this chapter has been to trace the major developments of the period as they affected the local scene and to report on the landmarks which may be used to vitalize the study.

BIBLIOGRAPHY

1. BAYLES, RICHARD M., ED. *History of Richmond County (Staten Island) New York: From Its Discovery to the Present Time.* New York: L. E. Preston and Co., 1887. P. 53-156, 350-358, 394-396.

2. CLUTE, JOHN J. *Annals of Staten Island: From Its Discovery to the Present Time.* New York: Press of Charles Vogt, 1877. P. 42-83, 204-207, 210-216, 254-259, 262-268, 275-277.

3. COHEN, JOEL. "Dutch Treat on Staten Island." *Our Town,* 2: 12-13, April 1961. (A publication of the Museum of the City of New York.)

4. COLES, ROSWELL S. "The History of a Legend." *The Staten Island Historian,* IX: 9-11, 14-16, April-June 1948. IX: 17-20, 23, July-September 1948.

5. DANKERS, JASPAR AND SLUYTER, PETER. *Journal of a Voyage to New York and a Tour in Several of the American Colonies in 1679-80.* Brooklyn, New York: Long Island Historical Soci-

ety, 1867. P. 140-147.

6. DAVIS, WILLIAM T. *A Short History of the Conference House*. Staten Island, New York: Conference House Association, Inc., 1957. P. 12

7. FISHER, MARGARET AND FOWLER, MARY J. *Colonial America*. Grand Rapids, Michigan: Fideler Co., 1960. P. 9-110.

8. GOODWIN, MAUD WILDER. *Dutch and English on the Hudson, A Chronicle of Colonial New York*. New Haven, Connecticut: Yale University Press, 1919. P. 137-229.

9. HAMPTON, VERNON B. "Staten Island . . . Its Story." *Tercentenary Booklet*. Staten Island, N. Y.: Staten Island Tercentenary Commission, 1961. P. 9-10, 18-19, 21, 47-49, 52-53.

10. HAMPTON, VERNON B. *Staten Island's First Permanent Settlement*. Staten Island, N. Y.: Staten Island Historical Society, 1960. P. 20.

11. *Handbook of the United Brethren's Church on Staten Island, N.Y.* Staten Island, N. Y. 1947. P. 11-13, 37-41.

12. HANKINSON, FRANK AND HAMPTON, VERNON B. *The History of Staten Island Public Schools*. Staten Island, N. Y.: Staten Island Teachers' Association, 1942. P. 3-6. (Mimeographed)

13. LANGDON, WILLIAM C. *Everyday Things in American Life*. *1607-1776*. Vol. I. New York: Scribner's, 1937. P. 18-47, 241-254.

14. LENG, CHARLES W. AND DAVIS, WILLIAM T. *Staten Island and Its People*. Vol. I. New York: Lewis Historical Publishing Co., Inc., 1930. P. 104-164, 430-438, 448-452, 463.

15. ———. *Staten Island and Its People*. Vol. II. New York: Lewis Historical Publishing Co., Inc., 1930. P. 531-539, 609-610, 677-686, 707-708, 721, 734-742, 845-848.

16. MCMILLEN, HARLOW. "Richmondtown: The First 160 Years. Part I. Richmondtown as the County Seat." *The Staten Island Historian*, XXII: 3-5, January-March 1961.

17. ———. "Richmondtown: The First 160 Years. Part III. The Maintenance of Law and Order. Part IV. The Dutch Congregation." *The Staten Island Historian*, XXII: 20-23, July-September 1961.

18. ———. "Richmondtown: The First 160 Years, Part V. The Church of St. Andrew." *The Staten Island Historian*, XXII: 25-28, October-December 1961.

19. MCMILLEN, LORING. "Billiou-Stillwell-Perine House." *The Staten Island Historian*, XX: 21-22, July-September 1959.

20. ———. "David Pietersz DeVries and the First Settlement of Staten Island." *The Staten Island Historian*, II: 25-27, October 1939.

21. ———. "Family Burial Plots Give Way Before Vandals and Weather." *Staten Island Advance*,* October 27, 1949.

22. ———. "First Permanent Island Settlement was Made at South Beach in 1661." *Staten Island Advance*,* January 20, 1950.

23. ———. "How the Dutch Came to Staten Island." *The News Bulletin*, Staten Island Institute of Arts and Sciences "Our Vanishing Landmarks." *The Staten Island Historian*, IX: 28-29, October-December 1948.

29. ———. "Staten Island Architecture." *The Staten Island Historian*, IV: 9-11, 14-15, April-June 1941; IV: 17-20, July-September 1941: V: 25, 27, 32, October-December 1941.

30. ———. "The Voorlezer." *The Staten Island Historian*, VIII. P. 17-19, 22, July-September 1946.

31. ———. "The Voorlezer's House." *The Staten Island Historian*, I: 1-3, 4-8, January 1938.

32. MORRIS, IRA K. *Memorial History of Staten Island*, Vol. 1. New York: Memorial Publishing Co., 1898. p. 32-112.

33. "Nieuwe Dorp Marks One of First White Settlements on Island." *Staten Island Advance*,* April 26, 1941.

34. REED, HERBERT B. "The Ferries of Staten Island." *Tercentenary Booklet*. Staten Island, N.Y.: Staten Island Tercentenary Commission, 1961. P. 24-25.

35. "Richmondtown Restoration." *The Staten Island Historian*, XVII: 11-24, April-June 1956.

36. ROBINSON, MARGARET. "The Dutch Had a Word for It." *The Staten Island Historian*, X: 6-

7, January-March 1949.
37. SCOTT, KENNETH. "The Colonial Ferries of Staten Island." Proceedings of the Staten Island Institute of Arts and Sciences, XIV: 45-58, Fall 1952; XV: 9-31, Spring 1953.
38. STEINMEYER, HENRY G. *Staten Island 1524-1898*. 2nd ed., Staten Island, N. Y.: Staten Island Historical Society, 1961. P. 11-23.
39. VANDER NAALD, CORNELIUS. "History of the Reformed Church on Staten Island." *The Staten Island Historian*, XVI: 1-5, January-March 1955.

*Back issues of *The Staten Island Advance* are on microfilm at the St. George Public Library, Staten Island.

CHAPTER IV

THE REVOLUTIONARY PERIOD: 1776-1783

THE AMERICAN REVOLUTION completely disrupted the peaceful rural life on Staten Island. The proximity of the Island to New York City, at the entrance to the Hudson River, made it an ideal location for British encampments and for troop embarkations to Long Island and New Jersey. Many English and Hessian regiments, each with a distinctive colorful uniform, occupied the Island from 1776 to 1783 (15). Sometimes there were as many as 30,000 soldiers on the Island. The officers were quartered in the taverns and the best homes.

Although sympathetic toward the Crown, the small population of 3,000 Staten Islanders soon found it difficult to meet the demands of the British for food, wood for fuel, and hay and straw for their horses. No important battles were fought on Island soil, but there were many minor skirmishes between the British forces and the Americans who were encamped on the Jersey shore. Plundering and the other ravages of war were common occurrences.

TORY SYMPATHIZERS

More than half of the Islanders were Tories or Loyalists, particularly the wealthy land-owners and members of the Church of England. The Dutch inhabitants and most of the French were sympathetic toward the Patriots. Prominent leaders of the Tory group were Christopher Billopp and his father-in-law, Judge Benjamin Seaman. Several hundred Staten Islanders joined the militia which General William Howe organized and others made financial contributions. Billopp was made a Lieutenant-Colonel of the militia.

When the First Provincial Congress met in New York on May 22, 1775, Staten Island sent five delegates, but no representatives were ordered to the Second Provincial Congress on December 6, 1775 (10). This indicated the Island's sympathy to the Loyalist cause, an attitude both George Washington and General Howe were aware of.

GENERAL HOWE'S ARRIVAL

When General Howe and his 9,000 soldiers disembarked on Staten Island on July 2, 1776, they were accorded a rousing welcome by the citizenry (15). Within a short time, the General's brother, Admiral Lord Richard Howe, also was received graciously when he landed with 20,000 more soldiers on the Island. Military headquarters were set up in New Dorp at the Rose and Crown Tavern on the King's Road (now Richmond Road). It was there that the British officers first read the Declaration of Independence on July 9th. A D.A.R. marker at the intersection of Richmond Road and New Dorp Lane marks the approximate site of the Rose and Crown Tavern.*

FORTIFICATIONS

FORT WADSWORTH

One of the first tasks of the British was to strengthen the fortifications at the Narrows (present site of Fort Wadsworth). From this strategic point, the Indians had watched Verrazzano and Hudson sail into New York Harbor, the early settlers had erected a small blockhouse and signal station, and General George Washington's men had watched for the arrival of the British fleet. From Signal Hill (Ft. Wadsworth)* a rather crude telegraph system had been worked out by the colonists, black and white kegs or large balls being raised on the flagstaff to indicate the approach of the enemy (9).

LOOKOUTS

During the Revolution, the British occupied the defense at the Narrows, and also established lookouts and signal stations on the hills of Staten Island (22). One of these was on the present Grymes Hill,* sometimes also referred to as Signal Hill, the name being perpetuated in Signal Hill Road which begins at Howard Avenue. From this point a clear view of New York Harbor and the Brooklyn shore may be had.* Another elevation used as a lookout was at Ocean Terrace and Todt Hill Road,* the highest point on the Atlantic Coast, which commands a view of Lower New York Bay and Sandy Hook to the southeast, and New Jersey and the Kills toward the north and west.

EARTHEN REDOUBTS

The British built earthen redoubts at various strategic locations throughout the Island. On the hill above Richmondtown, overlooking the salt meadows and Fresh Kills, the Seventeenth British Dragoons (cavalry) and the Queen's Rangers erected three redoubts (11). Lieutenant-Colonel John Graves Simcoe, in command of the Rangers, had headquarters in the Old Latourette House on Richmond Hill (17). Other earth works were built at Fort Hill on the site of the present Fort Hill Circle* near Sherman Lane, New Brighton; at Pavilion Hill,* overlooking the harbor; at the lighthouse hill overlooking Prince's Bay;* and along the shores of the Island facing New Jersey where the American soldiers were encamped, particularly at Holland Hook,* opposite Elizabethtown, New Jersey (10).

HESSIAN ENCAMPMENTS

About 9,000 Hessian troops were stationed in camps on the Island. A large one was at what is now Jersey Street and Richmond Terrace.

EVIDENCES OF OCCUPATION

Many evidences of British occupation have been excavated and are on display in showcases in the Staten Island Historical Museum. They include buttons of various regiments, gun parts, buckles, broken tobacco pipes, coins, bullets, and cannon balls (15).

PEACE CONFERENCE AT THE BILLOPP HOUSE

Christopher Billopp, greatgrandson of the original owner of Bentley Manor, commissioned Colonel of the Staten Island Militia, was assigned to guard the north and west shores against attacks by the Patriots from New Jersey. The Billopp House, built about 1680, was used as a British barracks. It was there, on September 11, 1776, shortly after Washington's defeat in the Battle of Long Island, that a futile peace conference was held. The Continental Congress delegated Benjamin Franklin, John Adams, and Edward Rutledge to confer with Lord Richard Howe, who had requested the parley, and his aide Sir Henry Strachey (3, 4). Howe offered "to extend the royal clemency and full pardon to all repentent rebels who would lay down their arms and return to their allegiance to the King" (1).

The American delegates, however, remained firm in their demands for recognition of the complete independence of the colonies. A large mural in the library of the Staten Island Community College, at 30 Bay Street, St. George, and a smaller one at Borough Hall depict this event.*

The path from the shoreline of Raritan Bay to the Conference House (formerly the Billopp House) which was used by the first peace delegates has been designated as "Liberty Pathway." Plans have been approved for an addition of more than 200 acres to the Conference House Park, extending it along the beachfront of Tottenville as far north as Mount Loretto. The name of Billopp is perpetuated in Billopp Avenue, which will be one of the streets bordering the enlarged park.

A visit to the two-story fieldstone manor house, restored, furnished, and maintained by the Conference House Association, will vitalize the study of the American Revolution.*

SKIRMISHES ON STATEN ISLAND

Since the attempts at peace had failed, the British renewed their efforts to conquer the Continentals. They gained control of New York City, and General George Washington retreated. No attempt will be made in this chapter to trace all of the battles of the Revolution.

Conference House (old Billopp House, as it looks today)

However, some mention will be made of the skirmishes which took place on the Island.

FREQUENT RAIDS

General Hugh Mercer was in command of the Continental Forces in New Jersey opposite Staten Island (1). Frequent raiding parties of British soldiers were sent across the Kills into the encampments of the Patriots who in turn harried the British by striking back whenever they could.

FIRST SKIRMISH AT ST. ANDREW'S CHURCH

In October 1776 an attack was planned upon the British at Richmondtown, but the enemy learned of the Patriots' approach and prepared a defense. Only a few shots were fired, with two soldiers on each side being mortally wounded, and some of the British and Hessians being taken prisoners. All the windows of St. Andrew's Church were damaged. The Patriots escaped back to New Jersey from Blazing Star (Rossville*).

SECOND ATTACK UPON ST. ANDREW'S

In August 1777, another group, under the command of Major Irving, crossed the Kills, landing at Decker's Ferry (opposite Bergen Point) and headed toward Richmondtown. The British retreated to St. Andrew's Church, whereupon the Americans fired at the windows, again breaking every pane of glass, continuing their fire, until the enemy was forced to vacate. British reinforcements routed the Patriots who retreated to the shore. Again several lives were lost on both sides (5). A mural in Borough Hall portrays the skirmish at St. Andrew's.*

GENERAL SULLIVAN'S ATTEMPTED INVASION

General John Sullivan, captured by the British in the Battle of Long Island (August 27, 1776) and later released, organized an unsuccessful invasion of Staten Island on August 22, 1777. This was one of the most important engagements of the Revolution to take place on the Island, and is commemorated by a marker near the Carteret Ferry.* With 1,500 men, Sullivan landed and engaged the British in a series of skirmishes at various points on the Island, capturing more than a hundred prisoners, including two British lieutenant-colonels, and mortally wounding many soldiers.

Sullivan's losses about equalled the enemy's. He was finally forced to retreat to New Jersey when British reinforcements arrived (20). On the grounds of the Conference House is a cannon used to defend Rossville (then Blazing Star) against Sullivan's invasion.*

GENERAL STIRLING'S ATTEMPTED INVASION

During the unusually cold winter of 1779-1780, the ice froze in the Kills solidly enough for troops to march from New Jersey to Staten Island. At his headquarters in Morristown, General Washington planned an expedition to invade Staten Island, and he commissioned General Stirling to carry out the invasion.

On January 14th, with 2,500 men, Stirling crossed on the ice at Elizabethtown Point, marching toward Port Richmond, where the troops divided, some going toward the present New Brighton, and the others toward the end of the present Clove Road in West New Brighton. Tory spies had apprised the British of the American plan and Brigadier-General Cortlandt Skinner's Brigade had ordered reinforcements. After two days, Stirling was forced to retreat to Elizabethtown.

Fascinating descriptions of the various skirmishes are written in considerable detail in Bayles' *History of Richmond County* (1). An interesting account of the capture of Colonel Billopp by the Patriots on two different occasions is given in histories by Leng and Davis (10) and Steinmeyer (18).

REVOLUTIONARY LANDMARKS

Several houses still standing on Staten Island played important roles during the Revolutionary War. The Billopp House or Conference House* already has been mentioned. The Kreuzer-Pelton House* was used as headquarters by Brigadier-General Cortlandt Skinner. Major Turner von Straubenzee, commander of the Hessian mercenaries, was stationed in the Austen House.* It is also claimed that Lord Howe made his headquarters there and that British officers, such as General Knyphausen and General Henry Clinton stayed there (10).

The Billiou-Stillwell-Perine House,* owned by Edward and Ann Perine, was headquarters for Captain John Coughlan. Ann Perine figures in several stories of the period. One legend tells how she outwitted a British soldier who planned to steal her silver shoe buckles (2). Another story centers on the Housman House* which was the scene of a raid by the Jersey "cowboys" who tried, without success, to force Peter Housman, a Loyalist, to disclose where he had hidden his money.

Billiou-Stillwell-Perine House (original section dates back to 1663)

A group of Patriots set up secret headquarters in the Christopher House,* which was built in 1750 and was the home of Joseph Christopher during the Revolution. This house is marked by a D.A.R. tablet. There, at the edge of a swamp which concealed their activities, the Patriots carried on the work of the Committee of Safety, while the British were meeting at Bull's Head Tavern about a mile away. Reports of British activities on Staten Island were sent to General Washington at his headquarters in New Jersey. A plaque on the Staten Island Reformed Church* honors the Mersereau brothers who were active in this work.

Several taverns also are associated with Revolutionary activities on the Island. The Rose and Crown Tavern,* headquarters for General Howe, has been referred to. The Black Horse Tavern,* which stood nearby at the intersection of Amboy Road and Richmond Road, was frequented by the British. The Cocclestown Inn,* built in 1755 in Richmondtown and operated by Richard Cole during the War, claimed fame as the place where Major John André wrote his will June 7, 1777. Three years later, on October 2, 1780, André was executed as a traitor. This famous tavern will be rebuilt as part of the Richmondtown Restoration. The Treasure House, in Richmondtown, used as a tavern during the conflict, was a meeting place for General Howe and the officers and soldiers who were encamped on Richmond Hill.

It is reasonable to believe that any of the pre-Revolutionary houses still in existence on Staten Island can be connected with the War in some way because living quarters were demanded of everyone. Even the Voorlezer's House accommodated some Hessian soldiers. An interesting story concerns Ernst, a Hessian drummer, and a little five-year-old girl, named "Pretty," who are buried in the Rezeau-Van Pelt family graveyard* opposite the Historical Museum (14).

SURRENDER AND DEPARTURE OF THE BRITISH

Although Cornwallis surrendered at Yorktown on October 19, 1781, it was not until December 5, 1783 that Staten Islanders watched happily from the hills as the last of the British sailed through the Narrows (19). The ravages of war had changed the friendly attitude that had been displayed when Howe had arrived in 1776. The final shot of the War was aimed at the fortifications there by a British gunboat. A mural at Borough Hall depicts the Islanders watching the British sail homeward.*

STATEN ISLAND AT THE CLOSE OF THE WAR

Seven years of British occupation had devastated Staten Island. The task before the people was great. Homes, churches, and public buildings had to be rebuilt. The little Old Dutch Church in Richmondtown had been used by the British for fuel. The Reformed Dutch Church in Port Richmond had been damaged during General Sullivan's invasion. St. Andrew's Church needed repairs and the Courthouse, which had been completely destroyed, had to be replaced. Fences, which had been used for firewood by the British, also had to be rebuilt. Cattle needed restocking and forests replanting. Food was scarce, except for the fish in the surrounding waters.

Some of the Staten Islanders who had remained Loyalists forfeited their property and were given new grants in Nova Scotia by the British. Colonel Christopher Billopp and his father-in-law, Judge Benjamin Seaman, Richmond County's last colonial judge, were among those whose property was confiscated. Many Hessian soldiers who had come to love America and the freedom it offered, decided to remain on Staten Island.

BIBLIOGRAPHY

1. BAYLES, RICHARD, ED. *History of Richmond County (Staten Island) New York: From Its Discovery to the Present Time.* New York: L. E. Preston and Co., 1887. P. 157-249.

2. CLUTE, JOHN J. *Annals of Staten Island: From Its Discovery to the Present Time.* New York: Press of Charles Vogt, 1877. P. 84-130, 184-196.

3. DAVIS, WILLIAM T. *A Short History of the Conference House*, Staten Island, N.Y.: Conference House Association, Inc., 1957. P. 12.

4. DAVIS, WILLIAM T. *The Conference or Billopp House, Staten Island, N.Y.* Lancaster, Pa.: Science Press Printing Co., 1926. P. 200.

5. DAVIS, WILLIAM T., LENG, CHARLES W., AND VOSBURGH, ROYDEN W. *The Church of St. Andrew, Richmond, Staten Island – Its History, Vital Records and Gravestone Inscriptions.* Lancaster, Pa.: Science Press Printing Co., 1925. P. 7-74.

6. HAMPTON, VERNON B. "Staten Island . . . Its Story." *Tercentenary Booklet.* Staten island, N.Y.: Staten Island Tercentenary Commission, 1961. P. 11, 14, 18-19.

7. HAUGHWOUT, LEFFERD M. "What a British Lieutenant Thought of Staten Island in 1776." *The Staten Island Historian*, II:6, 8, January 1939.

8. HINE, CHARLES G. *The Story and Documentary History of the Perine House.* Staten Island, N.Y.: Staten Island Antiquarian Society, Inc., 1915. P. 88.

9. KRIST, ROBERT, "Fort Wadsworth." *The Staten Island Historian*, XVIII: 17-18, July-September 1957.

10. LENG, CHARLES W. AND DAVIS, WILLIAM T. *Staten Island and Its People.* Vol. I. New York: Lewis Historical Publishing Co., Inc., 1930. P. 165-204.

11. MCMILLEN, LORING. "The Old Fort Hill." *The Staten Island Historian*, IV:1-2, January-March 1941.

12. ———. "Robertson and His View of the Narrows." *The Staten Island Historian*, II:28, 31-32, October 1939.

13. MORRIS, IRA K. *Memorial History of Staten Island.* Vol. I, New York: Memorial Publishing Co., 1898. P. 144-147, 160-330.

14. "Pretty and the Drummer." *Our Town*, 2:10-13, October 1960. (A publication of the Museum of the City of New York.)

15. SAINZ, DONALD R. "The British Army on Staten Island during the Revolutionary War." *The Staten Island Historian*, VIII: P. 20-24, July-September 1946; VIII:30-32, October-December 1946; IX:6-8, January-March 1948; IX:12-14, April-June 1948; IX:23-24, July-September 1948; IX:32, October-December 1948.

16 SMITH, DOROTHY. "A Diary of the Revolution." *The Staten Island Historian*, IV: 2, 8, January-March 1941.

17. STEINMEYER, HENRY G. "Mettlesome Briton. John Graves Simcoe." *The Staten Island Historian*, XII:9-11, April-June 1951.

18. ———. *Staten Island 1524-1898.* 2nd ed. Staten Island, N. Y.: Staten Island Historical Society, 1961. P. 24-40.

19. ———. *Staten Island under British Rule. 1776-1783.* Staten Island, N. Y.: Staten Island Historical Society, 1949. P. 18.

20. ———. "The Action of August 22, 1777." *The Staten Island Historian*, XV:23, July-September 1954.

21. THOMPSON, ARTHUR R. "Daniel Bissell, American Spy." *The Staten Island Historian*, X:25-27, October-December 1949.

22. WELSH, JOSEPH. "The Telegraph on Staten Island." *The Staten Island Historian*, II:9, 14, April 1939.

Third County Courthouse, Richmondtown

CHAPTER V

THE FEDERAL PERIOD: 1783-1861

AFTER THE REVOLUTION, Staten Island again became a peaceful community, largely dependent upon farming and fishing. There was little money and the small landowners made and grew practically everything they needed. Many of the wealthy British sympathizers had gone to Canada, and their large estates were subdivided. The Islanders were free to develop village life which had been discouraged by the British during the War.

The Post-Revolutionary Period on Staten Island was one of steady growth, although the rate was slow compared to that of Manhattan and Brooklyn. The following census figures reflect the population changes (28):

1783....................	3,500	1830....................	7,082
1800....................	4,564	1840....................	10,965
1810....................	5,347	1850....................	15,061
1820....................	6,135	1860....................	25,492

RESTORATION OF OFFICIAL BUILDINGS

Concern for restoring what had been destroyed and growth in population necessitated the erection of new public buildings in the County Seat of Richmondtown after the Revolution (28). A large inn built in 1820 near the intersection of Richmond Road and Arthur Kill Road (Richmond County Hall) helped accommodate the population growth and afforded facilities for stage coach travelers.

A new courthouse was completed in Richmondtown by 1794 and stood until 1944 when it was destroyed by fire. Foundation stones are still in evidence at Arthur Kill Road near the Treasure House. Until a second County Courthouse could be built, the home of Dr. Thomas Frost was used for court purposes. In the Richmondtown Restoration, the Boehm House* in Great Kills will be moved next to the Voorlezer's House to represent Dr. Frost's home.

The Third County Courthouse,* on Center Street, was built in 1837 and was used until 1920. This building now houses collections of the Historical Museum, particularly firefighting equipment of the old Volunteer Firehouses.

The First County Clerk's and Surrogate's Office was built in 1828 on the corner of Richmond and Arthur Kill Roads adjoining the jail which had been constructed in 1729. These buildings were destroyed by fire in 1895. In 1848 the Second County Clerk's and Surrogate's Office was erected and used until 1920. This is now the Museum of the Staten Island Historical Society which contains a library, costumes, house furnishings, tools, etc., that pertain to the growth of the Island.*

In 1801 the Public Stocks were erected. In 1860 a new jail was built to the rear of the Third County Courthouse, which stood until 1896. It was replaced by a modern jail that was demolished in 1957.

County Clerk's and Surrogate's Office, Richmondtown

REBUILDING FORTIFICATIONS

The fortifications at the Narrows (now Fort Wadsworth), which had been damaged during the Revolution, were restored. By 1808 Signal Hill was protected by Fort Richmond at the edge of the Narrows (present site of Battery Weed), Forts Morton and Hudson on the slopes of the Hill, and Tompkins on the peak of the Hill (26).

With the threat of the impending War of 1812, however, these earthwork defenses were inadequate and Daniel D. Tompkins, Governor of New

York between 1807 and 1817, appropriated $125,000 for the erection of stone fortifications. The new Forts Tompkins and Richmond, built of red sandstone, were completed in 1814, manned, and dedicated with great ceremony. This dedication is depicted in murals at the Staten Island Community College Library at 30 Bay Street and in Borough Hall.*

Fort Tompkins was built in the same style as Castle Williams on Governors Island which is used today as a military stockade. Fort Richmond was half-moon in shape, as is Battery Weed today.

To strengthen fortifications along Lower New York Bay, Fort Smith was erected on the hill at Prince's Bay near the lighthouse on Mount Loretto property.* Much of this hill has been eroded by tides and rain. Bayles says the stones from the blockhouse were used later to construct the present lighthouse, now the residence of the director of Mount Loretto (3).

After the War of 1812, the fortifications at the Narrows were neglected and by 1835 were unfit for use. In 1847 the federal government purchased the military post, tore down the old red sandstone forts and constructed Forts Tompkins and Richmond (known as Battery Weed since 1902). Fort Tompkins is now used as an office building.* The new forts were not completed until 1861 at which time the first troops were garrisoned there.*

GOVERNOR TOMPKINS*
At the close of the War of 1812, Governor Tompkins bought considerable land on Staten Island and built a mansion on Fort Hill, near present Fort Place (3). There he entertained many notables. Tompkins also built a home on St. Mark's Place for his daughter in 1821. Known as Marble Hall, this mansion later became part of the St. Mark's Hotel, and, in 1889, of the Hotel Castleton (29). When Marquis de Lafayette returned to America in 1824 to tour the country, Staten Islanders gave him a hero's welcome at Nautilus Hall, Tompkinsville. Tompkins, who was then Vice-President of the United States (1817-1825), headed the committee. P.S. 15 Richmond, is named the Daniel D. Tompkins School.

SLAVERY
Slavery gradually disappeared on Staten Island after the Revolution, as it did in other parts of New York State. On March 29, 1799, the State Leg-

islature provided "that every child born of a slave within this State after the fourth of July next shall be deemed and adjudged to be born free" (47). Masters were required to register the names of all such children born after July 4, 1800. A fee of 12¢ was charged for each name registered and a fine of $5 was imposed for failure to do so. Slavery on Staten Island was abolished July 4, 1825, two years before abolition in the entire state (28).

Governor Daniel D. Tompkins, long an opponent of slavery, wrote to the New York State Assembly on January 28, 1817 urging that complete abolition be accomplished in this state by July 4, 1827. A facsimile of part of this letter appears in the Official Document Book of the New York State Freedom Train (47). In the same book appears a reproduction of a page from the account book of the town of Southfield, Richmond County, indicating the cost of feeding, clothing, and caring for children of slaves born after the Law of 1799.

COUNTY GOVERNMENT

After the Revolution, Staten Island was still designated as the "County of Richmond," but it was then in the "State of New York," rather than in the "Province of New York." The chief officers were the county judge, sheriff, treasurer, and clerk. Each of the four divisions of the Island (North, South, and West Divisions, and Castleton) had its own supervisor and minor officials. The Supervisors met and decided upon matters affecting the County; the minor officials managed the town affairs.

Design on Borough flag

The design for the seal of Richmond County was ordered by the Court of Common Pleas in 1786 at a meeting in the home of Dr. Thomas Frost (29). In the center were two doves, a large "S" (meaning *Signum*) and "N York." Around the seal was inscribed "Richmond County." This design was adapted on the Borough flag in 1948.*

GROWTH OF VILLAGES

In 1788 official towns were designated with specific boundaries – Northfield, Southfield, Westfield, and Castleton. Within each township were little villages. In 1860, Middletown was created from parts of Castleton and Southfield.

The village of Tompkinsville was developed about 1815, chiefly through the efforts of Governor Tompkins and was named in his honor.* The names of his children are remembered in the street names Hannah and Minthorne. By 1836 Tompkinsville had doubled its population.

The Governor's son, Minthorne, with William J. Staples, purchased land from Cornelius Vanderbilt and his family in 1833 and developed the village of Stapleton. Three years later the village of Richmond was laid out by Henry I. Seaman.

In 1834 Thomas E. Davis formed the New Brighton Association and bought land between Old Quarantine (Tompkinsville) and Sailors' Snug Harbor, renaming the area New Brighton after the well-known seaside resort in England. He planned the streets, constructed Richmond Terrace, and erected many fine homes in the Greek classic style.

On the Island's south and west shores typical American rural communities continued to prosper. By 1835 a village of considerable size had grown up around what had been known successively as The Burying Place, Decker's Ferry, Ryerss' Ferry, and Mersereau's Ferry. The Reverend Brownless of the Reformed Dutch Church suggested the name of Port Richmond, which was adopted (42). Previously known as Blazing Star, Rossville became a thriving village in the 1850s. Cabbages and strawberries grown there were sent by steamboat to New York (22).

Tottenville, known as Bentley, was a fishing village with a few scattered farms. New Dorp continued as a small village devoted to farming. Bloomingview (Huguenot), Long Neck or New Blazing Star (Travis), Great Kills, and Prince's Bay retained their identities as separate communities. In the 1850s Kreischerville (now Charleston) grew up around the brick factory there, just as Factoryville (now West New Brighton) had developed around the factories built there earlier in the nineteenth century.

Other areas also developed, including the Clove Valley* section. In 1832, a New York City merchant, John King Vanderbilt, purchased an 80-acre farm in the Valley and within a few years several large homes were built there by his relatives (60). In the section on homes of this period, it will be noted that other localities on the Island were developed before the Civil War.

In the latter part of the 1700s the families were chiefly descendants of the early Huguenots, Dutch, and English settlers. Each had his own farm, orchard, and woodlot, with nearby salt meadows supplying bedding for the cattle. Before long, however, there was a migration to the Island from different parts of the United States, especially from New England. Immigration from Ireland, because of the potato famine between 1845 and 1847, and from Germany because of the political Revolution of 1848 increased the population. Many of the Germans worked in the breweries and in the dyeing and shipbuilding trades.

Between 1814 and 1861, wealthy bankers and brokers from the East, as well as internationally known figures, came to the north and east shores of Staten Island, and created a cosmopolitan social life previously unknown there. They brought with them many Irish servants who remained on the Island after the demise of their masters.

DEVELOPMENT OF CHURCHES TO 1861

With the increase and diversity of population came the growth of many church organizations. The churches damaged during the Revolution were rebuilt and many new churches organized. St. Andrew's in Richmond-town was repaired around 1787 but had to be rebuilt again in 1867 and in 1872 after two severe fires. Today's Norman-Gothic style edifice, although partially built on the original walls of 1712, bears little resemblance to the first church (20).*

REFORMED DUTCH CHURCHES

The Reformed Dutch Church in Port Richmond, in ruins after the Revolutionary War, was rebuilt in 1786 and again in 1844. This third church, reminiscent of the Greek Revival style of architecture popular in the 1840s, still stands.* A chapel was added in 1898.

In 1808 a Reformed Dutch Church was built on the corner of Center Street and Arthur Kill Road to replace the one destroyed during the Revolution. This was used until 1887. In the Restored Village at Richmond-town, an old Dutch Church in hexagonal style will be reconstructed.

Church of St. Andrew, Richmondtown

In 1820 the Reformed Dutch Church of Tompkinsville was founded at the Quarantine Station. Three years later a church was built in Tompkinsville upon a triangular tract of land given by Governor Tompkins (at Richmond Turnpike, now Victory Boulevard, Van Duzer and Griffin Streets). In 1864 a new building was dedicated at the present location on St. Mark's Place, St. George. Now this is called the Brighton Heights Reformed Church.* At night the illuminated spire is seen from a considerable distance and from the ferry as one crosses Upper New York Bay.

METHODIST CHURCHES

The Woodrow Church,* oldest Methodist Episcopal Church on Staten Island, and one of the oldest in the country, was organized in 1787. It was built by contributions of 87 persons on land given by Abraham Cole. Previously the congregation had been served by Bishop Francis Asbury* and other circuit riders from New Jersey who had preached at the home of Peter Van Pelt (11). The list of original contributors contains the names of families still prominent on the South Shore section of Staten Island.

Among them are: Androvette, Bedell, Cole, Dissosway, DuBois, Journeay, Laforge, Seguine, Sleight, Totten, Winant, and Woglom. These family names are also remembered in street names on the Island. In 1795 Nancy Dissosway presented the Church with a Holy Bible that was printed in 1792 and is still in its possession.

The original church was one-story high, with galleries on two sides and at the end that were reached by stairways. Heated bricks and foot warmers furnished the only heat for the parishioners until stoves were installed about 1822. Men sat on the right hand of the preacher and women on the left. Lightning struck the building in 1832. The present structure was erected in 1842 in the Greek Revival style, with four large columns supporting the roof over an open porch in front. The bell tower was built in 1876.

Woodrow M. E. Church

One of Woodrow's most famous ministers was Rev. Henry Boehm, called Father Boehm, who traveled with Bishop Asbury. A minister for 74 years, he served one year as a pastor of Woodrow (12). During the last years of his life he resided with his granddaughter in a house that is still standing on Arthur Kill Road at the foot of Giffords Lane where he lived to be a centenarian. He is buried on the left of the walk as you enter the graveyard adjoining the Woodrow Church.* Many pioneers of the South Shore section of the Island, including several Revolutionary War veterans, also are buried in this cemetery. The parsonage, still standing, was erected in 1850 and was enlarged in 1861.

Many people walked to church in the early days and as other hamlets developed, parishioners desired more convenient places of worship. This led to the organization of several churches throughout the Island. Methodists in Westfield (Tottenville) met in a Tabernacle on Amboy Road, near Richmond Valley, as early as 1822. In 1841 they erected Bethel Church* on Amboy Road, at its present site, and rebuilt it in 1867. The brick building standing today was erected after a fire in 1886 (18). St. Paul's M.E. Church in Tottenville was organized as an outgrowth of Bethel M.E. in 1856 and a chapel was dedicated three years later. A new church was built in 1883.

In 1802 the Methodist Episcopal Church of Northfield was erected on Richmond Avenue, New Springville. It was replaced in 1849 by the Asbury Methodist Church* which is still standing.

The present Kingsley Methodist Episcopal Church at 186 Cebra Avenue, near St. Paul's Avenue, Stapleton dates its organization back to 1835 when it was incorporated under the name of the Methodist Episcopal Church of Tompkinsville and was served by the Reverend Henry Boehm on the "circuit" plan. A church building was completed in 1838 on property given by Caleb T. Ward. In 1855 a new edifice was erected which became known as Stapleton Methodist Episcopal Church. When this building was remodeled in 1870, the name was changed to Kingsley M.E. Church.

In 1839 the Mariners Harbor Methodist Episcopal Church was dedicated. By 1869 a larger church was needed and this became the Summerfield Methodist Church, now at 100 Harbor Road, Mariners Harbor.

Long Neck (now Travis) also was served by a Methodist Church as early as 1843, although members of the congregation had met previously in the home of John Wood. The Long Neck Chapel at 4117 Richmond Turnpike (now Victory Blvd.) was used until 1868 when it was sold to School District No. 3 of Northfield for a schoolhouse. The incorporation of the present Dickinson Methodist Church dates back to 1865, the building at 3980 Victory Blvd. to 1871.

Trinity Methodist Church, originally called "Pond Church," was erected in 1839 on Pond Road (Jewett Avenue) and Cary Avenue, West New Brighton. In 1853 a new edifice was built on Shore Road (Richmond Terrace) and Dongan Street and renamed Trinity (3). This burned to the ground in 1909 and the church was relocated at the corner of Delafield Avenue and Elizabeth Street, West New Brighton in 1912.

EPISCOPAL CHURCHES

St. John's Protestant Episcopal Church, Clifton (now Rosebank), was founded in 1843, but the cornerstone of the present building was not laid until 1869 (8).*

St. Luke's Episcopal Church on Arthur Kill Road, Rossville, was dedicated in 1844, with a few pews set aside for Negroes from Sandy Ground. Jasper F. Cropsey was the architect. This church had been organized in the home of Colonel William E. Ross in the previous year. The building was demolished in 1961.

The present Church of the Ascension (Episcopal), at 1 Kingsley Avenue, West New Brighton, dates back to 1800 when the Trinity Chapel was built on Richmond Terrace. This was affiliated with St. Andrew's Church until 1819 when it became a separate parish.

St. Paul's Episcopal Church on Richmond Avenue (now St. Paul's Avenue), Tompkinsville, was organized at the Planters' Hotel in 1833. The first church was built on ground given by Caleb T. Ward, after whom Ward Hill was named, and was used until 1861. The cornerstone of the present building at 225 St. Paul's Avenue was laid in 1866.*

Christ Church Episcopal, at 76 Franklin Avenue, was founded in 1849 at a meeting in Belmont Hall, New Brighton. A Gothic style edifice was erected the following year. The present church was consecrated in 1905.

In 1848 Dr. Samuel Elliott, famous eye specialist, erected a church in Elliottville (now Livingston). This was the beginning of St. Mary's Protestant Episcopal Church which was built in 1853 on property given by William Bard at Davis and Castleton Avenues, West New Brighton.

St. Simon's in the Clove Episcopal Church was opened as a mission church of St. John's of Clifton in 1854 and did not become a separate parish until 1955. The first services were held in a little building on Targee Street, Stapleton, then in the unoccupied First Baptist Church which was later moved to Rhine Avenue near Steuben Street, Concord, and then to a site near Clove and Richmond Roads, where a new building was constructed in 1940. This was in the path of the new Clove Lakes Expressway, so in 1960 the present building was erected at 1055 Richmond Road, Concord.

BAPTIST CHURCHES

A Baptist congregation was organized in 1785 but it was not until 1809 that the first Baptist Church was erected on the Island. The "Clove Meeting House" was built on the hillside near the corner of Clove and Richmond Roads. A few gravestones remain at the site, although the building was demolished in 1877.

About 1835 a Baptist Meeting House was built in Fayetteville (now Graniteville) adjacent to the present Hillside Cemetery on Richmond Avenue. The building was demolished after the North Baptist Church was organized. Another Graniteville Baptist Church was erected about 1858. The congregation disbanded in 1882. This building, located on Willowbrook Road near Forest Avenue, became the Graniteville Methodist Church in 1914. It has recently been acquired by a Pentacostal group.

The North Baptist Church, Port Richmond, organized by members of the congregation from the church at Fayetteville, was dedicated in 1843. This is now known as the Park Baptist Church. Some members left this church in 1857, organizing the Mariners Harbor Baptist Church. In 1845 the West Baptist Church was founded in Kreischerville, and in 1860 the South Baptist Church was erected in Tottenville (8).

ROMAN CATHOLIC CHURCHES

The first Catholic Church on Staten Island was St. Peter's Church, now at 53 St. Mark's Place, New Brighton. This was organized in 1839 in a small remodeled factory at Richmond Terrace and Lafayette Avenue, New Brighton. The parish included all of Staten Island and part of New Jersey. Within a few years a church was built on land given by the New Brighton Association. This edifice was dedicated in 1849 and St. Peter's Cemetery was established within a few years. The present St. Peter's Church* was erected between 1900 and 1903.

Prior to the Civil War, three other Catholic Churches served the parishioners on Staten Island – St. Joseph's in Rossville, dedicated in 1851; St. Mary of the Assumption in Graniteville (now Port Richmond), erected in 1853; and The Church of St. Mary on New York Avenue, Clifton (now called Bay Street, Rosebank), organized in 1852.

St. Mary's Church was built in 1857. In 1862 the pastor, Reverend John Lewis, purchased seven acres of land of the Parkinson Estate and laid it out as a cemetery (8). P.S. 46 is adjacent to St. Mary's Cemetery. The first

Catholic Parochial School on Staten Island was organized in St. Mary's Parish in 1853. A new building was erected in 1865 and ten years later had an enrollment of 400 pupils. The present school was built in 1910. Father Lewis served as pastor of St. Mary's for 35 years and is interred near the north entrance of the church.

St. Mary of the Assumption Church, Graniteville (now Port Richmond) was built as a mission church of St. Peter's with the contributions of laborers in the "granite quarries." Later it became a mission church of St. Joseph's in Rossville which it remained until 1877. The present church was erected in 1883.

Before these Catholic Churches were built, it is believed that a priest from Brooklyn conducted services in a frame and stone building standing on Giffords Lane, Great Kills, sometimes known as the Holy Spring House.* The spring still flows in the basement of this little house.

MORAVIAN CHURCHES
The present Moravian Church* in New Dorp was dedicated in 1845. Built in 1763, the original building, which was described in the chapter on the Colonial Period, is now used as the cemetery office. The new building was enlarged in 1955 and 1956.

CHURCH OF THE HUGUENOTS
The Church of the Huguenots was organized in 1849 in Bloomingview (now Huguenot). Two years later the little "Brown Church" as it was known, was built on property given by the Hon. Benjamin P. Prall who was a direct descendant of Pierre Billiou, leader of the 1661 settlement. This little church stood until 1918 when sparks from a train engine set fire to the roof. The present church was erected in 1924 and is known as the Huguenot Reformed Church.

UNITARIAN CHURCH
A Unitarian Church was organized in 1851 at the home of Minthorne Tompkins, son of Governor Daniel Tompkins, and held meetings at the Tompkins Lyceum until a church was erected on Richmond Turnpike (Victory Boulevard) and Cebra Avenue in 1853. The congregation dwindled and in 1865 the building was sold. After a population increase in New

Brighton, the group reorganized and a church building was erected in 1868 at Clinton Avenue and Second Street. It was in this edifice that George William Curtis conducted services in the absence of a preacher.

LUTHERAN CHURCHES

In 1852 St. John's Evangelical Lutheran Church bought a building on Jewett Avenue, previously owned by Trinity Methodist Church. In 1901 a new church building was erected. From the beginning, St. John's Lutheran conducted a parochial school (8). The school was closed in 1908 but reopened in 1952. In 1856 the German Evangelical Lutheran Church in Stapleton (now Trinity Lutheran) was opened. The congregation also maintains a parochial school.

PRESBYTARIAN CHURCHES

As early as 1717 there was a Presbyterian meeting house at Stony Brook, used until 1769. The First Presbyterian Church of Edgewater (now Stapleton), Brownell and McKeon Streets, was organized in 1856 by 26 members. In 1867 this group was joined by the congregation of the Presbyterian Church at Clifton which had been organized by members who had left the Reformed Dutch Church at Tompkinsville (8). The present church on Tompkins Street was erected in 1894.

HOMES

At the close of the Revolution, Staten Island was a community of about 276 homes. However, the growth in population stimulated new construction and different styles of architecture began to appear (41). There was a trend toward the larger two-story house, although the one-story and the one-and-a-half-story building continued. Timber and brick became more popular than the native fieldstone. There were larger windows with fewer and larger panes of glass. Usually there was a full-length veranda in the front, and often in the rear also. The Woodrow House* (1810) on Woodrow Road, south of Arthur Kill Road, Greenridge, is representative of a one-and-one-half-story style with sweeping roof and two verandas.

Later the more ornate doorway appeared. This had side windows and fan lights overhead, and opened into an entrance hall with a staircase leading to the second floor. The Moore House* at 3531 Richmond Road exemplifies this style. This was the second parsonage of St. Andrew's Church, built in 1818 on the site of the first.

The kitchen* continued to be the all-important family room. Cooking was still done in the large open fireplace. Swinging cranes held kettles and pots. The tin "Dutch oven" open on one side to the blazing fire also was popular, as was the brick oven built into the fireplace.

A small cottage of this period is the Beaver Cottage,* built in 1875 on Richmond Road, Dongan Hills (now opposite the Berry Apartments). Another plain cottage is the Finley House in Egbertville, built about 1790 by the Egbert family as their residence and cooper shop. This will be moved to Richmondtown and restored as the Cooper's House.* An interesting feature is the oven which extends outside the house. Nearby on Richmond Road is the Seaver House,* built about 1800, and now being restored by a private owner.

The Simon Swaim House (1760), originally a 90-acre farm along King's Road (now Richmond Road), will be restored as a typical eighteenth century farmhouse in the planned Richmondtown Restoration. Another farm of the 1830s is to be restored around the homestead known as the Decker Farm* on Richmond Hill Road, now owned by the Historical Society. Considerable planting has been done there already.

A typical farmhouse still standing is the Burbank House* (1800) which was erected on Todt Hill Road on land that was once part of the Governor Dongan grant. As the home of Abraham Burbank, supervisor of the town of Castleton from 1793 to 1798, this house is marked with a D.A.R. plaque.

There are several homes along Amboy Road* from Prince's Bay to Tottenville which were built between 1820 and 1860 and are kept in excellent condition. Many of these were erected by oystermen. Other large homes are along Arthur Kill Road* between Rossville and Richmond Valley, and along Victory Boulevard* near Signs Road, Travis.

In the 1830s many homes were built in what was known as the Greek-Revival type of architecture with large columns, some simple Doric, others fluted or paneled. Among these are the Ward-Nixon House* (1830) on Ward Hill; the Tyler House* (1835) in West New Brighton where President Tyler's widow lived for many years; the Biddle Mansion* (1840) in Tottenville; the Tysen House* on Sailors' Snug Harbor property; the Seguine Mansion* (1845), Prince's Bay.

Several other buildings were constructed in this Greek-Revival style or a modification of it. Among those still standing are The Third County Courthouse* on Center Street, Richmondtown; the buildings at Sailors' Snug Harbor* (1831); the original Marine Hospital Buildings* in Clifton (1837); Woodrow M.E. Church;* Staten Island Reformed Church;* the Bennett House* (1837), Richmondtown, now used as a general store; The Stephens House* (1837), Richmondtown, used as a general store for about a century and to be restored as such.

Many wealthy New Yorkers and Southern planters built stately homes in the Greek Revival style along Shore Road (now Richmond Terrace). This became known as Temple Rd. Columbia Hall,* erected about 1835, and the building adjacent to it remain.

Another architectural style popular between 1840 and 1860 was the Gothic type with steep roofs, gables, and carved woodwork (41). Several houses were built in this style in Clove Valley* about 1840. Two were constructed by the Brittons who operated a mill on Britton's Pond which was formed by damming Clove Brook. Ice was harvested there also (36). The house at 1015 Clove Road, built by Henry Britton, is now the home of John Franzreb who operates Clove Lakes Stables.* The home of the late Abraham Britton is across the road at 956. A steep-roofed Gothic cottage stands at 1336 Clove Road at the corner of Schoharie Street, Sunnyside. Just before the Civil War, Captain Allen,* a retired sea captain, lived there (60).

William H. Ranlett, the architect, designed and built several Gothic cottages on Staten Island. He lived in the one that is still standing at 508 Clove Road, West New Brighton (1845). Another on Davis Avenue West New Brighton, erected in 1848, was the home of Dr. Samuel Elliott, and later of Sidney Howard Gay, an abolitionist. The original building of St. Joseph's Hill Academy for Girls, Arrochar, is a house of this type. Built in 1850, it was then known as "Clar Manor." The parsonage of the Reformed Dutch Church on Arthur Kill Road, Richmondtown, erected in 1855, is of this design and will remain as part of the Restored Village. Many churches constructed on Staten Island at this time were influenced by the Gothic style.

The Italian villa style of architecture, featuring a square building with a cupola or captain's lookout on top, was popular on Staten Island between 1845 and 1860 (41). Examples of this are: the Goodhue Home* (1845) on Clinton Avenue, New Brighton (Robert and Sarah Goodhue were among the founders of the Unitarian Church on Staten Island); the Alexander House, summer home of Junius Brutus Alexander, southern cotton grower, now the Richmond County Country Club* on Flagg Place, Dongan Hills; the Wyeth House* on Meisner Avenue, Egbertville, home of Judge Nathaniel Wyeth, Jr., who was a member of the State Legislature; and the Parkinson House* (1854) on Richmond Road, New Dorp, built on the site of the Rose and Crown Tavern,* which was British Headquarters during the Revolution.

Several large, elegant homes were erected on Staten Island before the Civil War. In 1850, Colonel William Ross built a wooden replica of Windsor Castle, in park-like surroundings at Blazing Star (now Rossville). Stained glass windows opened onto balconies overlooking Arthur Kill. This beautiful home, renamed Lyon Mansion, was sold to Governor Lyon of Idaho who died there in 1875 (22). The building was demolished about 1920. Next to the Ross Castle was the Mason Mansion, a 30-room Italian villa style building of great elegance.

In the early 1830s, Major George Howard, who was then Keeper of the Stores at the Quarantine, Tompkinsville, bought 42 acres of land "between Eddy and Louis Street and between Richmond Turnpike (Victory Blvd.) and Howard Avenue (38)." He erected a large home on the Eddy Street corner which he sold a few years later to John Anthon, who, with his son Charles Anthon, gathered historical information on Staten Island which was later published by the Staten Island Institute of Arts and Sciences and is referred to as "Anthon's Notes." Howard then built a house which is still standing on St. Paul's Avenue opposite Hannah Street.

Madame Suzette Grymes, widow of Governor Claiborne of Louisiana, who had married John Randolph Grymes of New Orleans, came to Staten Island in 1836 and erected a beautiful home on the hill which bears her name. The entrance to Grymes Hill at that time was from Richmond Road. She added to her property in 1839 and in 1846, calling her entire estate *Capo di Monte,* meaning "top of the mountain." In 1858 she sold her home to William Butler Duncan, after whom Duncan Road was named (29). Several other beautiful mansions were erected on Grymes Hill,* many of which remain today (15).

Sir Edward Cunard, manager of the Cunard Line, built a large brick Victorian style mansion on Grymes Hill, commanding a view of the waters surrounding New York City, calling his property *Bellevue*, meaning "superb view." His home, erected in 1851, was the scene of many social affairs. As part of Wagner College, this building is now known as Cunard Hall.* Wagner College also purchased the General William Green Ward Home,* built about 1860 and named *Oneata*, a Seminole word meaning "kissed by the dawn" (19). This mansion, located on the West Campus, is the Music Building of Wagner.

At the foot of Grymes Hill, on Clove Road, at the corner of the present Howard Avenue (previously known as Serpentine Road) was the Nichols House, built between 1852 and 1854 and purchased by Mr. Nichols in 1864. Frederick Law Olmsted, designer of Central Park, landscaped this estate, known as *Vale Snowden*. Many rare trees and shrubs planted on the ground remain, as do parts of the stone wall which surrounded the property (29).

HOTELS AND INNS

Several large hotels were erected in the St. George-New Brighton area before the Civil War. The residence of Thomas E. Davis was used as a section of the fashionable Pavilion Hotel* which was on Richmond Terrace, just below St. Peter's Church. Additions were made, including a 200-foot colonnade in front of the building. This was a 300-room, six-story hotel, with a large ballroom that attracted many notables, such as President Martin Van Buren and Henry Clay. Many Southern plantation owners and well-known people from foreign lands frequented the hotel. Wealthy New Yorkers, especially in the summer, came to escape the heat and to enjoy the luxurious facilities. Jenny Lind, the Swedish singer, was a frequent guest there when she was singing at Castle Garden (Fort Clinton, Battery Park). Adelina Patti, who was introduced to America by Max Maretzek, also stayed at the Pavilion. During the Civil War, Confederate officers sent their wives and children there for safety (30). The building was closed in 1900 and was demolished in 1904.

There were several other popular hotels on the Island. The two-story brick Planters' Hotel,* built in 1820, patronized by wealthy Southerners, is still standing at the corner of Bay and Grant Streets, Tompkinsville.

The Patten House was built in 1840 on Richmond Plank Road (now Richmond Road) at the head of New Dorp Lane which was used then as a straight mile race track from that point to the beach (45).

Cunard Home (now part of Wagner College)

The Port Richmond or St. James Hotel at 2040 Richmond Terrace, Port Richmond, was built about 1795 as the private home of Gozen Ryerss who operated the ferry after the Revolution. It was there that Aaron Burr (Vice-President of the United States 1801-1805) lived during the last year of his life, dying there on September 14, 1836. This building stood until about 1944 (39).

Inns also were very popular during this period when the stagecoach was the chief mode of transportation and travelers needed accommodations en route to Philadelphia from New York. Names of many distinguished people are found on the guest lists. Among the inns were Bodine's Inn at Castleton Corners; Butler's Tavern on Morningstar Road, Graniteville; Rossville Hotel (1825) at Blazing Star Ferry; the Oakley House at the foot of the present Rossville Avenue (then Shea's Lane); and the Cocclestown Inn at Richmondtown (1755-1836). A typical inn of this period is preserved in Killmeyer's Hotel* (1859), now Simonson's Tavern in Charleston.

INDUSTRIAL GROWTH

Farming continued to be important on Staten Island after the Revolution. In 1829, James Stuart in *Three Years in North America*, after a visit to the

Island, wrote of "comfortable-looking farmhouses amidst rich valleys and lands and orchards abounding in fruit . . . " and of the "extraordinary quantity of cherry trees" (65).

However a definite pattern of industrial growth began to take shape. During the Revolution, the British had discouraged industries, but after the War the Islanders were free to develop industrial as well as village life. Gristmills, sawmills, and blacksmith shops continued to be as important as they had been during the Colonial Period.

OYSTERING

From the time of the first settlement, oystering had been carried on in Staten Island waters. By 1840 the beds were exhausted, so oyster seed and immature oysters were brought from bays in Long Island and New Jersey, and finally from as far south as Norfolk Bay, Virginia, and Chesapeake Bay, Maryland. These were "planted" at Prince's Bay and in the Kill Van Kull from Mariners Harbor to Port Richmond (25).

Many of the wealthy oyster captains built large two-story colonial type wooden homes with Greek Temple columns along the Shore Road (Richmond Terrace) from Mariners Harbor to Port Richmond facing the Kill. A few of these houses still stand along the Terrace. Often as many as 40 or 50 sloops would be moored in the Kill opposite what came to be known as "Captain's Row."*

The oyster captains from Staten Island sometimes hired Negroes from around Snow Hill, Maryland, to come back with them to prepare the beds and plant the oysters. It was a group of these Negro oystermen and their families who settled in Sandy Ground in the late 1830s or early 1840s. Sandy Ground is a small community bordering on Bloomingdale Road between Drumgoole Boulevard and Arthur Kill Road. During the Civil War oystering* was a thriving business on the Island because it was not possible to get oysters from the South (25).

BASKETMAKING

Basketmaking was carried on during this period by a few men skilled in the craft. The Morgans* were among these craftsmen and built a home in New Springville about 1810. This will be moved to Richmondtown and used as a basketmaker's shop. Many of the oystermen made the baskets they needed in their trade, but others depended upon the local basket-maker. Small baskets were needed also in harvesting the strawberries which were grown on the Island, particularly in Rossville, and shipped to Manhattan by steamboat. Some baskets and tools used in the craft are displayed at the Historical Museum* (23).

FACTORIES

As various industries developed, the rural character of Staten Island began to change. Factories developed on the north and east shores. In 1819, a group of men from Boston started a cloth dyeing factory, Barrett, Tileston and Company, at Richmond Terrace and Broadway, Factoryville (now West New Brighton) which brought many New Englanders to the community who were skilled in this field. This company was reorganized in 1825 as the New York Dyeing and Printing Establishment. In 1850 Colonel Nathan Barrett, uncle of Major Clarence T. Barrett,* started another such factory on Cherry Lane (now Forest Avenue) near Barrett Avenue. This is the location of the Sears Roebuck Store today. Later the two companies merged into the well-known Barrett-Nephews Company.

There were many small industries manufacturing a variety of products. In 1833 a gun factory operated by Joseph Hall was located in New Brighton, between Franklin and Lafayette Avenues, but moved to the Willowbrook section near Victory Boulevard two years later, giving the name of Gun Factory Road. Flour mills, and a wallpaper factory were also developed. The Jewett White Lead Works (later National Lead Company) in Port Richmond dates from 1842. In 1838 the Staten Island Whaling Company, which processed whale oil, began operation. In 1844 the Crabtree and Wilkinson factory (later Irving Manufacturing Company) on Jersey Street began production of silk bandannas and commemorative scarves. The Louis De Jonge Company* started the manufacture of colored, coated, and embossed papers about 1850 in a plant on Richmond Turnpike (Victory Blvd.) and Austin Place. The firm has been located at 330 Tompkins Avenue, Rosebank since 1918.

The Rosebank plant of the New York Paraffin Candle Company came to Staten Island at this time also. Antonio Meucci was a factory superintendent (56). General Joseph Garibaldi, in exile here at Meucci's home, was employed by this factory (10). In 1851 these two men opened a brewery in Rosebank (later known as Bachmann's Clifton Brewery). They lived in a home which has been preserved at 420 Tompkins Avenue.*

Jewelry boxes were manufactured in Graniteville until the 1950s, the last owner being Louis Ettlinger and Sons. A carriage and wagon factory was built in Richmondtown in the 1850s by Marsh and Nolan and will be restored as part of the Richmondtown Village.

USE OF NATURAL RESOURCES

Natural resources of the Island resulted in some industrial development at this time. The trap rock (erroneously called granite) in an area from the plaza of Bayonne Bridge to Victory Boulevard and Travis Avenue created the Staten Island Granite Company, organized in 1841. Trap rock for road and wall building was quarried there until 1896.

Natural clay gave rise to several firms which were engaged in brick-building by 1840. In 1854 Balthasar Kreischer, who had migrated here from Germany, began making firebrick for furnaces, stoves and ovens (1). This business continued in the family until the 1930s. The American Brick Company and Dolan Brick Company on Arthur Kill Road (around Fresh Kills section) also made common brick.

The Atlantic Terra Cotta Company* on Arthur Kill Road, Tottenville (at Atlantic Railroad Station) made terra cotta building ornaments until the firm closed during the 1930s.

Some open iron mining activities were undertaken in the areas of Todt Hill, Ocean Terrace* and at the southern end of Jewett Avenue, about the year 1833. This activity is remembered in the street name of Iron Mine Drive. The iron was used in the manufacture of red ochre paint and also as flux to be mixed with other ores. Many rocks containing iron ore are found on Staten Island today, some being used in rock gardens of the homes.

A rather ingenious use of a natural resource was the crushing of quartz pebbles from the beach sands at Tottenville by a sandpaper factory, operated by James Pike Gage near the shore at Page Avenue in the early 1860s. Horses were used to drag a millstone which crushed the pebbles. The finished sandpaper was shipped out from nearby docks (35).

Ice harvesting on many of the Island ponds was another lucrative industry. Clove Lakes (then Britton's Mill Pond), Silver Lake (before it became a reservoir), Crocheron's Pond at Bulls Head, Winant's Pond and

Killmeyer's Pond were among those used for this purpose. Large blocks of ice were marked out, sawed, and stored in icehouses. One icehouse stood at the present location of Clove Lakes Park Restaurant until it burned in 1920 (58).

BREWERIES

Breweries have been an important part of the industrial scene on Staten Island for a long time. Before the Civil War one of the largest was Bechtel's Brewery* in Stapleton, at the head of Broad Street founded in 1853 by John Bechtel who sold it to his son, George, in 1865. Another was the Constanz Brewery established in 1852 by August Schmid. In 1875 this became Monroe Eckstein's Brewery, Manor Road, Four Corners, opposite Todt Hill Houses.

Records indicate that a Captain Thomas Lawrence had a distillery in New Brighton before 1815. He built a home on the southwest corner of Westervelt Avenue and Shore Road which later became the Belmont Hotel. This was razed in 1900.

OTHER OCCUPATIONS

The shopkeeper had his role in community life and there were many small general stores in the areas of densest population. Harness making and horseshoeing continued to be important trades as they had been during the colonial period. Shipbuilding also continued to flourish.

GAS MANUFACTURE

Plans for the manufacture of gas on Staten Island date back to 1855, but it was not until April 1857 that gas flowed through the mains to thirty customers. By August 1860 seventeen miles of mains had been laid and 350 customers were served. The manufacturing plant was located near Townsend's Dock, Clifton. The first mains were laid to Factoryville (West New Brighton), then to Port Richmond, branching off to Richmond Turnpike (Victory Blvd.) and Serpentine Road (Howard Avenue), and finally along Clove Road. The Civil War halted further extension of service. In 1863 gas lighting was installed on the *Westfield* and *Northfield* ferries. Gas receivers were filled at the gas company and carried to the boats each day. Street lighting by gas did not come to Staten Island until 1865.

BURNING OF QUARANTINE

Community action has often been aroused on Staten Island. An example of this was the burning of the Quarantine hospitals, first at Seguine's Point, Prince's Bay in 1857, and then at Tompkinsville the following year (40).

The citizenry became alarmed over the spread of yellow fever. As immigrants stopped at Quarantine (near present site of St. George Coast Guard Base), victims of this dread disease were removed from the ships and hospitalized on the Island. Men who worked on the docks were free to return to their communities and homes, and consequently the epidemic spread to the general populace (40).

A large group of incensed citizens met and determined their course of action. They descended upon Quarantine, broke down the walls, removed the patients, and then burned the buildings. The Governor of the State sent militia to the Island, and the county had to pay for the property destroyed.

Later the State built two artificial islands off South Beach, Hoffman and Swinburne Islands,* and transferred the Quarantine Hospitals there. These islands finally were abandoned in 1937.

NEWSPAPERS

Several newspaper attempts were started before the Civil War. The first were chiefly literary, but they gradually carried more local news. According to Leng and Davis, the earliest newspaper on Staten Island was the *Richmond Republican*, dating back to 1827 (28). This was edited by Charles Baldwin who had offices on Griffin Street, Tompkinsville, but was printed in Manhattan. Four years later William Hagadorn became the owner and changed the name to *Richmond County Republican* and then added to the title *Saturday Morning Advertiser*. By 1833 the name had been changed to *Richmond County Free Press*. William Hagadorn's son, Francis L., became editor and proprietor of the first newspaper which was printed on the Island. This was the *Richmond County Mirror* which lasted from 1837 until 1839. Other attempts were the *Sepoy* (1859), the *Staten Islander*, the *Richmond County Gazette*, and *Richmond County Sentinel*. Copies of these old newspapers have been microfilmed and may be seen at the Staten Island Institute of Arts and Sciences Library.*

In 1849 Francis Hagadorn and Company established an independent mail route, called the Staten Island Express Post, because of dissatisfaction with the Post Office services. Mail boxes were located at various places where the *Staten Islander* was sold. Letters were collected by post riders and delivered to destinations on Staten Island or taken to connecting expresses such as Boyd's City Dispatch Post or Adams and Wells Expresses. Elliott Burgher* gave a collection of Staten Island Express Covers of the period from 1850 to 1860 to the Historical Museum (7).

COMMUNICATIONS

During the earlier periods, messages had been sent from Signal Hill (Ft. Wadsworth) to Manhattan by means of a crude system of black and white kegs or large balls on a flagstaff. By 1801 this had been replaced by a sem-aphore station there, a system of movable arms on a pole. At one time there were ten such arms, each signifying a different numeral, and operated by rope and pulley. Information on the names of ships arriving and their car-goes was relayed from Sandy Hook, New Jersey to Staten Island and then to a building in Bowling Green Park, Manhattan (50, 51). This system was used to ensure docking facilities.

The magnetic telegraph, first used between Washington, D.C., and Bal-timore, May 24, 1844 was introduced on Staten Island in June 1860. The lines crossed under Kill Van Kull from Bergen Point, New Jersey to Port Richmond, and along the shore to Quarantine (Tompkinsville). The cost was 25¢ for the first 10 words and 20¢ for each additional 10 words. During the Civil War the lines were extended to Tottenville and under the Arthur Kill to Perth Amboy, New Jersey (69).

INSTITUTIONS

Several large institutions, built on Staten Island before the Civil War, are rendering service today. Four of them were related to the care of seamen and their families.

SEAMEN'S RETREAT

In 1831 New York State purchased forty acres of land in the present Clifton area to build a Seamen's Retreat for ill and disabled seamen. At that time a state tax was imposed upon all seamen entering the Port of New York and placed in the Seamen's Retreat and Hospital Fund. This practice continued until about 1881. The original three-story hospital building, completed in

1831, has been demolished. However, the granite buildings facing Bay Street, erected in 1837, in Greek Temple style, are being used for the Outpatient Clinic of the U.S. Public Health Service Hospital.*

The City of New York took over control of the Seamen's Retreat in 1878 and leased the property to the Marine Hospital Service (now the Public Health Service) five years later. In 1903 the federal government purchased the property. In 1935 the main part of the new hospital known as the Marine Hospital was completed, facing Vanderbilt Avenue. When it opened, it was the tallest building on Staten Island, the center tower rising to 160 feet from the ground. Since then additional wings have been added. The present bed capacity of 839 is in sharp contrast to the original facilities for 34 patients in the Seamen's Retreat in 1831.

SAILORS' SNUG HARBOR

In 1833 Sailors' Snug Harbor* opened in New Brighton as a home for "aged, decrepit, and worn-out seamen," under the provisions of a will executed in 1801 by Alexander Hamilton for Captain Robert Richard Randall. The income from leasing Randall's 21-acre farm, bounded by 5th Avenue, 10th Street, 4th Avenue and 8th Street, Manhattan built this retirement home and will continue to maintain it. The main building erected in 1833 in Greek Revival style is now the administration building, one of five dormitories facing the Kill Van Kull (49). Throughout the years about fifty other buildings were constructed on the large acreage, formerly the David Houseman Farm. Originally a large farm including a dairy herd was maintained at the Harbor, but this was discontinued many years ago. Now there are many flower gardens, large trees, a fish pond, fountain, and greenhouse around the well-cared for grounds of 30 acres. A bronze statue of Captain Randall,* the work of Augustus St. Gaudens, occupies a prominent position on the front lawn. A little church built in 1855 is still used for services on Sundays and for daily meditation. Many facilities are available for the men in the hobby and craft shops, in the library, in the Recreation Hall and Music Hall. At one time as may as 1,000 seamen resided at Sailors' Snug Harbor, with several men in a room, but social security and pension plans have decreased the need for the facilities provided by Captain Randall, so that now only 325 men reside there, each with his own room.

MARINERS' FAMILY HOME

Aged women relatives of seamen have been cared for since 1854 in The Mariners' Family Home* at 119 Tompkins Avenue, Stapleton on property adjacent to the Old Seamen's Fund and Retreat Hospital. This Victorian type mansion was built with State funds, but is maintained by voluntary contributions. "The Family" now consists of about 20 members, but at one time as many as 60 women resided there.

SOCIETY FOR SEAMENS' CHILDREN*

The Society for Seamen's Children was organized in 1846 and opened a home in Port Richmond for the care and instruction of needy children of seafaring men. The following year it moved to Stapleton, but soon outgrew the facilities there. In 1850, therefore, it leased land from Sailors' Snug Harbor, adjacent to St. Vincent's Hospital, and erected a large four-story home on Castleton Avenue. This housed the children for many years. Now the Society places children in foster homes. The building, remodeled, is used by the Staten Island Mental Health Society.

COUNTY POOR HOUSE

A County Poor House was established in 1829 on Manor Road (that section presently called Brielle Avenue). This is now part of the Sea View Hospital and Home.*

Before 1829 the aged poor had been boarded in private homes at the expense of the County. Some historians claim that a building in Richmondtown, originally built as the Gaoler's House was referred to as the "County House" in 1792 and later as the "Poor House." This was demolished in 1827.

SAMUEL R. SMITH INFIRMARY

At the beginning of the Civil War there was need for medical assistance for dependents of men who had been called into service. Through the efforts of the Richmond County Medical Society, particularly Dr. William C. Anderson, the first voluntary hospital on Staten Island was opened in 1861 as a dispensary "for the Indigent and suffering sick" in a building at the corner of Bay Street and Union Place, Stapleton. This was named the Samuel R. Smith Infirmary* in memory of Dr. Samuel Russell Smith

(1801-1851) who had lived at 85 Hannah Street, Tompkinsville, and brought patients to his home for treatment rather than traveling over bad roads to visit them. A Ladies' Auxiliary was founded in 1863 to raise money for the hospital and in the following year the Infirmary was moved to a site near the present parking lot of the Medical Arts Building (on the north side of Tompkins Avenue, now St. Mark's Place). Ralph Waldo Emerson is reported to have been a speaker at the opening of this Infirmary which was to serve the sick poor, no provisions being made for the patient who could afford to pay. The Women's Auxiliary has supported hospital activities since that time supplying linens, china, glass, and funds for many services. The growth of the Staten Island Hospital will be described in a later section of this report.

EDUCATION

After the Revolution, greater educational opportunities were provided by the villages throughout the Island.

It is interesting to observe that three Islanders were appointed to the First Board of Regents of the University of the State of New York, established in 1784 – Abraham Bancker, John C. Dongan, and Hermanus Garrison. The next Island representative was George William Curtis,* after whom Curtis High School was named, who served in this capacity from 1864 to 1892. This representation from the Island indicates a very definite public interest in education which has continued to the present day.

Several private schools were organized before the Civil War, most of them short-lived. A church-attached school was Reverend Peter J. Van Pelt's Seminary on Richmond Terrace, near Richmond Avenue, opened in 1802 as a "seminary of learning." In 1812 he established what was probably the first Sunday School in the country. A Thomas Fardon had a boarding school for boys in Tompkinsville, and a Mrs. Reed had a Seminary for Young Ladies on Griffin Street, Tompkinsville (in 1829 known as Coddington's). About 1823 the Castleton House Academy for "young gentlemen" was established about two and a half miles from Tompkinsville (20).

Records show that there was a schoolhouse in the Tottenville-Rossville section in 1769 which was probably the forerunner of the Rossville District School dating back to 1796. The New Springville School (then Karle's Neck) erected around 1700 was enlarged in the early

1800s (demolished in 1890). In the 19th century it was known as District School No. 2, Northfield accommodating forty children (near the site of old P.S. 27 on Richmond Avenue).

There was also a public school in Castleton Corners as far back as 1784, located on Manor Road (near the site of old P.S. 29 which later became old P.S. 35). The 1889 building is now used as The Elim Gospel Tabernacle. Another schoolhouse, run by a Terrance Reilly, was at the intersection of Richmond Avenue and Richmond Terrace, Port Richmond. In a report of 1802, four other schools were named – Indian Hill (between Eltingville and Annadale), Smoking Point (near Rossville), Woodrow and Bentley.

In 1812 a school district was created in each of the four towns of Northfield, Southfield, Westfield, and Castleton, with a superintendent of schools in charge of the entire Island.

There was a school in Tompkinsville in 1815, in which Governor Daniel D. Tompkins showed a great interest, and one in Westfield (Tottenville) in 1822.

Henry Martin Boehm* (son of Reverend Henry Boehm) was a schoolmaster in the Southfield School District No. 3 between 1840 and 1860, becoming Richmond County School Commissioner in 1860. His school was on Fresh Kills Road (Arthur Kill Road), Greenridge, near Richmond Avenue and later in the house on Arthur Kill Road and Gifford's Lane, Greenridge.

Portions of Schoolmaster Boehm's diary, reproduced in the *Staten Island Historian* make fascinating reading, particularly the section dealing with specific rules and regulations (64).

The year 1842 saw the dawn of the Public School System of New York State, providing free education for all children. Prior to this date the schools of New York City were under the Public School Society, a philanthropic organization established in 1805. Gradually the District Schools or Ward Schools disappeared. Prescribed courses were set by the State and qualified teachers were required. Harmon B. Cropsey became the first County Superintendent of Richmond in 1842, with 19 schools and 20 teachers under his supervision. These, except one, were one-room schoolhouses with all grades.

The school day of 1842 included scripture reading, arithmetic lessons, reading, geography, penmanship, spelling, dictation, and singing. The centennial of the state school system was celebrated in 1942. At that time, a typical classroom session was conducted at the Voorlezer's House.*

In 1845 a district school on Richmond Road near Van Duzer Street was in existence. By 1853, there were schools, not only in New Brighton, West New Brighton, Tompkinsville, Westfield (Tottenville), and Stapleton, but also in Old Place, New Springville, Newton (Great Kills), Bloomingview (Huguenot), Garretson (Dongan Hills, opposite the site of the present firehouse), Chelsea and Rossville (on the present City Yard on Rossville Avenue). A one-room stone schoolhouse stood on the property now occupied by the Mohlenhoff farm on Victory Blvd., Travis. The West New Brighton school was on the site of the present 1568 Richmond Terrace, but later was moved to Elizabeth Street and Cary Avenue.

There are few records available which give information about Staten Island schools prior to 1861. Mr. Frank Hankinson, former Superintendent of Schools on Staten Island, and Dr. Vernon B. Hampton, retired teacher, did research in this area in 1942 (14). Research carried on by Dr. Hampton disclosed that on September 20, 1861 a group of 36 teachers of the Island's 47, held a meeting presided over by Henry M. Boehm, the County School Commissioner, and founded the Richmond County Teachers' Association.

TRANSPORTATION

Before the Civil War, stages operated between the various ferry landings and also into the interior of the Island. There were stages between Vanderbilt's Landing and Richmond and from Hillyer's Corners (near Richmond) to New Springville, Bulls Head, and Graniteville.

ROADS

Roads were still unimproved dirt roads or plank roads, some retaining the names by which they had been known before the Revolution. King's Road became Richmond Plank Road between Vanderbilt's Landing and Rossville. Tollgates and tollhouses were established along the way to defray the cost of this improvement (2). One of these was at the intersection of Vanderbilt Avenue and Richmond Plank Road. Toll was one to five cents according to the distance traveled. Another tollhouse* stood at Fresh Kills Road (Arthur Kill Road) and Shea's Lane (Rossville Avenue) (2).

Richmond Turnpike (Victory Blvd.), an important link in the stagecoach route to Philadelphia, was improved from Quarantine (Tompkinsville) to the New Blazing Star Ferry (Travis). Clove Road ran only
from Shore Road (Richmond Terrace) to Richmond Plank Road. Manor
Road continued as an important thoroughfare, as it had been earlier.

A toll bridge over the Fresh Kills at Greenridge was built by the Plank
Road Company about 1850. This made traveling easier from the west
shore to the east and south shores (from New Springville section to
Greenridge). The county built another bridge in 1896. The present bridge
was constructed at the same site in 1931.

Stagecoach and travelers (mural in Richmond Borough Hall)

SAILING VESSELS

Commodore Cornelius Vanderbilt, founder of the Vanderbilt fortune, had
a fast sailboat operating between Manhattan and Staten Island in 1810.
However the success of Robert Fulton's invention of the steamboat soon
improved ferry transportation to and from the Island.

STEAMBOATS*

Through the efforts of Governor Daniel D. Tompkins, the Richmond
Turnpike Company was incorporated in 1816. Steamboat service between
Quarantine (Tompkinsville) and Whitehall Street, Manhattan, replaced
the sailing vessels known as "periaguas" (29). The *Nautilus* went into ser-

vice in 1817, making four trips daily. Stagecoaches traveled along the Turnpike from Quarantine to the New Blazing Star Ferry.* Safely across the Kill Van Kull, the coaches continued through New Brunswick and Princeton to Trenton, across the Delaware River to Pennsylvania, and by way of Bristol to Philadelphia. One coach or chaise made the entire trip, the horses being changed en route. The advent of the steamboat shortened the trip between New York and Philadelphia from two days (three in winter) to twelve hours.

Cornelius Vanderbilt held the controlling interest in the Richmond Turnpike Company from about 1828. However, he had competition from the Tompkins and Staples Ferry from Tompkinsville and the People's Ferry from Stapleton (Townsend's Landing) to Liberty Street, Manhattan. In 1853 the two ferry companies merged with the Turnpike Company, under the name of the Staten Island and New York Ferry Company, with a fleet of five single-ended steamboats, remaining in existence until 1864 when the company was sold to the Staten Island Railway Ferry Company. These ferries left from Whitehall Street and made three stops on Staten Island – Tompkinsville, Stapleton, and Vanderbilt's Landing at Clifton.

Other steamboats operated from points on the North Shore to Pier 18, North (Hudson) River, stopping at Elm Park, Port Richmond, Factoryville (West Brighton), Snug Harbor, and New Brighton seven times a day. Steamboats plying between Keyport, New Brunswick, and Perth Amboy, New Jersey, and Robinson Street, Manhattan, stopped at Tottenville, Rossville, and Chelsea once a day (4).

Ferry service also continued under various ownerships between Port Richmond and Bergen Point, New Jersey (52); between Port Richmond and Manhattan; between Tottenville and Perth Amboy, New Jersey and between Long Neck (Travis) and Carteret, New Jersey.

RAILROADS

June 2, 1860 marked a new era in transportation on Staten Island with the advent of the first steam railroad, an enterprise of Commodore Cornelius Vanderbilt and his associates. The wood-burning locomotive pulled passenger cars from Vanderbilt's Landing (Clifton) to Tottenville. Five trips a day were made during the week, and three on Sunday. They connected with the new double-ended side wheelers, *Northfield*, *Middletown*, and

Westfield which ran hourly between 7 A.M. and 6 P.M. The Staten Island Railroad Company purchased the ferry to Manhattan in 1865, combining these two transportation methods.

PERSONALITIES CONNECTED WITH STATEN ISLAND

About 1836, Dr. Samuel MacKenzie Elliott, the eminent eye specialist, purchased property around Bard Avenue and Richmond Terrace. Within ten years he had built some of the grey square stone houses still standing in that section, then called Elliottville (now Livingston), which became quite a literary colony. This was the Dr. Elliott to whom James Russell Lowell, Henry Wadsworth Longfellow, N. P. Willis, and other famous men came for treatment.

To him also came Mrs. Francis George Shaw. Finding the climate agreeable, Mr. Shaw bought property between Bard and Davis Avenues, north of Henderson Avenue. He was a prominent philanthropist and civic leader, serving as a trustee of the Seamen's Retreat (now U.S. Public Health Service Hospital) and of the S. R. Smith Infirmary (Staten Island Hospital). After the Civil War, Mr. Shaw was influential in the establishment of the Staten Island Savings Bank which opened in 1867. All the Shaws were abolitionists. A daughter, Mrs. C. R. Lowell,* widowed by the Civil War, tried the first plan of organized charity on the Island (16). Another daughter was married to George William Curtis, noted editor.

Francis Parkman, also a patient of Dr. Elliott, lived with the Shaw family for two years. His *Conspiracy of Pontiac* was published when he was a Staten Island resident (13).

Staten Island often has been a quiet retreat for literary figures who have written glowing descriptions of its natural beauty. Judge William Emerson, county judge of Richmond from 1841 to 1843, lived in that section now called Emerson Hill, Concord, then known as Dutch Farms. He was visited by his brother, Ralph Waldo Emerson,* and many friends, including Henry James, father of the novelist of the same name. Henry David Thoreau came to Staten Island as a tutor for the children of Judge Emerson. In a letter of 1843 he wrote: "the whole island is like a garden and affords very fine scenery." He spoke of the beautiful cedar, gum, tulip, peach, and cherry trees and of the woods of honeysuckle (28, 63). In another letter, he spoke of the beautiful sight from Madame Grymes' house looking into the Harbor. Grymes Hill and Emerson Hill still afford excellent views of the New York Harbor.

Prior to the Civil War and during the struggle, some well-known abolitionists were active on the Island (13). Among them was Sydney Howard Gay who lived in a cottage in West New Brighton. This little home was used as a station on the Underground Railroad, aiding runaway slaves to escape to Canada. During the War, Gay was the managing editor of the *New York Tribune*. His writings helped the success of the Republican Party and Lincoln's election in 1860. Among the prominent men who visited at the Gay home were John Greenleaf Whittier, James Russell Lowell, and William Lloyd Garrison. Other abolitionists who lived on the Island were Albert Oliver Willcox and his sons. Mr. Gay's daughter, Mary Otis Gay, married one of the Willcox sons (13). After the War, Gay became editor of the *Chicago Tribune*, but returned to Staten Island in 1872 to live on Davis Avenue, West New Brighton, until his death in 1888.

George William Curtis, famous essayist, editor, and lecturer, came to Staten Island in 1856. His novel *Prue and I* was written in his home at 234 Bard Avenue where he lived with his wife, the daughter of Francis George Shaw. This was the old Shaw Homestead and is still standing at the corner of Bard and Henderson Avenues.* Curtis' praises of Staten Island were many. Perhaps the most famous is "God might have made a more beautiful spot than Staten Island, but He never did." Curtis was interested also in politics and became a delegate to the Republican National Convention in Chicago which nominated Lincoln. During the 1863 "draft riots," Curtis hid Wendell Phillips and Horace Greeley, both ardent abolitionists, in his Bard Avenue home to protect them from the angry mobs. He and Sydney Howard Gay were very close friends.

Curtis was a prominent figure in the Unitarian Church on Staten Island, often occupying the pulpit in the absence of the pastor. Curtis High School was named after him, as were Curtis Avenue, Curtis Court, Curtis Place and P.S. 19, Richmond.

Two well-known artists also made their home on Staten Island before the Civil War. One of these was William Page* who came to the Island in the 1840s and lived in an octagonal house on Page Avenue, Richmond Valley. He was famous as a portrait painter. Jasper Francis Cropsey who lived at 1922 Arthur Kill Road, was the "first Staten Islander to attain international reputation in art." He was a landscape artist and also an architect of note (59, 27).*

Home of George William Curtis

Frederick Law Olmsted (1822-1903), one of the first landscape architects, made his home in Eltingville, Staten Island, from 1848 to about 1860 in the Woods of Arden House near Hylan Boulevard. Olmsted turned the property into a wheat farm and also planted many fruit trees there. During a trip to Europe in 1850 he ordered 5,000 trees which he planted around his Eltingville home (5). Two Cedars of Lebanon and many other unusual trees stand today as a tribute to Olmsted's interest in agriculture and landscaping. He is best known as the designer of several parks, including Central Park, Manhattan; Prospect Park, Brooklyn; Fairmount Park, Philadelphia; and Franklin Park, Boston. The Woods of Arden House has a most interesting history dating back to 1700.*

Commodore Cornelius Vanderbilt (1794-1877) was born on Staten Island, began his interest in transportation in a small sailboat venture, became a railroad magnate and millionaire, and maintained an interest in the Island, contributing to many philanthropies. The Vanderbilt home was in Stapleton, not far from the site of the present Paramount Theater.* His oldest son, William H. (1821-1885) was left the bulk of his father's estate, a sum of 90 million which he was able to double before his death. He had a successful farm on the site of the present Miller Field. The Vanderbilt name is remembered in the beautiful Vanderbilt Mausoleum which overlooks Moravian Cemetery,* in the name of Vanderbilt Avenue, Clifton and in the many charities to which members of the family contributed.

Captain Jacob Hand Vanderbilt,* locally known as Captain Jake, brother of Commodore Vanderbilt, owned a large mansion on the hill above Clove Valley on the site of the Augustinian Academy. His property was adjacent to that of Sir Edward Cunard. Captain Jake was in command of a steamboat at the age of eighteen, and rose to the presidency of the Staten Island East Shore Railroad and Ferry (3). He was well-known on the Island for his fast trotting horses.

BIBLIOGRAPHY

1. ABBOTT, MABEL. "Kreischerville: A Forgotten Chapter in Staten Island History." *Proceedings of Staten Island Institute of Arts and Sciences*, XI: 31, January 1949.
2. ——. "The Old Tollhouse at Rossville." *Proceedings of Staten Island Institute of Arts and Sciences*, XI: 70-73, April 1949.
3. BAYLES, RICHARD M., ED. *History of Richmond County (Staten Island) New York: From Its Discovery to the Present Time*. New York: L. E. Preston and Co., 1887. P. 250-273, 326-368, 397-444.
4. BETANCOURT, B. C., JR. "Staten Island Steam Ferries." *The Staten Island Historian*, XVI: 9-13, April-June, 1955.
5. BOYLE-CULLEN, MARGARET. "The Woods of Arden House." *The Staten Island Historian*, XVI: 25-27, October-December 1953. XV: 4-8, January-March 1954. XV: 13-15, April-June 1954.
6. BUCK, WILLIAM J. "The Staten Island Rapid Transit Railway Company." *Tercentenary Booklet*. Staten Island, N.Y.: Staten Island Tercentenary Commission, 1961. P. 27.
7. BURGHER, ELLIOTT R. "The Staten Island Express Post." *Proceedings of Staten Island Institute of Arts and Sciences*, XI: 44-49, January 1949.
8. CLUTE, JOHN JACOB. *Annals of Staten Island From Its Discovery to the Present Time*. New York: Press of Charles Vogt, 1887, P. 131-136, 259-267, 270-300, 310-333.
9. COLE, ROSWELL S. "Some Effects of Physical Geography on the Culture of Staten Island." *The Staten Island Historian*, V: 2, 6-7, January-March 1942.
10. CULICETTO, PETER J. "General Joseph Garibaldi." *Tercentenary Booklet*. Staten Island, N. Y.: Staten Island Tercentenary Commission, 1961. P. 51.
11. HAMPTON, VERNON B. "Francis Asbury on Staten Island." *The Staten Island Historian*, IX: 1-4, January-March 1948.
12. ——. "Henry Boehm, Centenarian: His Life and Staten Island Ministry." *The Staten Island His-*

torian,XX: 25-30, October-December 1959.

13. ———. *Staten Island's Claim to Fame*. Staten Island, N.Y.: Richmond Boro Publishing and Printing Co., 1925. P. 44-45, 58-78, 83-85, 127-134, 139-142, 150-152, 154-169.

14. HANKINSON, FRANK, and HAMPTON, VERNON B. *The History of Staten Island Public Schools*. Staten Island, N. Y.: Staten Island Teachers' Association, 1942, P. 1-7.

15. HINE, CHARLES G., ED. *History and Legend of Howard Avenue and Serpentine Road, Grymes Hill, Staten Island*. Staten Island, N. Y.: Hine Brothers Printery, 1914. P. 80.

16. HINE, CHARLES G., and DAVIS, W. T. *Legends, Stories and Folklore of Old Staten Island. Part I. The North Shore*. Staten Island, N. Y.: Staten Island Historical Society, 1925. P. 140.

17. HOLLE, HENRY A. Dr. "Quarantine." *Tercentenary Booklet*. Staten Island, N.Y.: Staten Island Tercentenary Commission, 1961, p. 20.

18. HUBBELL, ARTHUR Y. *Prominent Men of Staten Island, 1893. (Columbus Centennial)*. New York: A. Y. Hubbell, 1893. P. 67-73, 133-145.

19. JACOBSEN, ANITA K. "The Ward Family: Grymes Hill." *The Staten Island Historian*, VI: 10-11, 16, April-June 1943.

20. JESSUP, PIERSON D. "237 Years of a House of God." *The Staten Island Historian*, X: 9-11, 14-15, April-June 1949.

21. KOLFF, CORNELIUS. "The Naming of Greenridge." *The Staten Island Historian*, II: 1-3, 7, January 1939.

22. ———. "The Time of Rossville's Glory." *The Staten Island Historian*, IV: 22, 24, July-September 1941.

23. KOLLMER, BURTON A. "Staten Island Baskets." *The Staten Island Historian*, I: 4, January 1938.

24. ———. "The Candle Maker of Blood-Root Valley." *The Staten Island Historian*, III: 2, 7-8, January 1940.

25. ———. "The Yesterday of the Oysterman." *The Staten Island Historian*, III: 17, 19, 23-24, July 1940.

26. KRIST, ROBERT. "Fort Wadsworth." *The Staten Island Historian*, XVIII: 17-18, July-September 1957. XVIII: 25-28, October-December 1957.

27. LEASON, PERCY. "Jasper F. Cropsey." *Proceedings of Staten Island Institute of Arts and Sciences*, 10: 49-52, October 1944-May 1946.

28. LENG, CHARLES W., and DAVIS, WILLIAM T. *Staten Island and Its People*. Vol. I. New York: Lewis Historical Publishing Co., Inc., 1930. P. 205-272, 456-461, 467, 475, 482-484.

29. LENG, CHARLES W., and DAVIS, WILLIAM T. *Staten Island and Its People*. Vol. II. New York: Lewis Historical Publishing Co., Inc., 1930. P. 580, 589, 592-594, 611-635, 643-653, 687-701, 708-714, 729, 758-760, 925.

30. MAGRUDER, HERBERT T. "In the Heyday of the Pavilion Hotel." *The Staten Island Historian*, XII: 9, 14-16, April-June 1951.

31. MCMILLEN, HARLOW. "Richmondtown: The First 160 Years – Part II. Richmondtown as the County Seat, 1782-1837." *The Staten Island Historian*, XXII: 13-14, April-June 1961.

32. ———. "Richmondtown: The First 160 Years – Part VI. The Residents of Richmondtown. The Tradesmen." *The Staten Island Historian*, XXIII: 1-3, January-March 1962.

33. McMILLEN, LORING. "Clove Lakes, Made by Man, Years Ago Was a Little Boy's Old Swimming Hole." *Staten Island Advance*,* October 28, 1949.

34. ———. "First Ferryboats to Manhattan Had Terminal in Stapleton." *Staten Island Advance*,* October 10, 1949.

35. ———. "Gage's Sandpaper Factory, Tottenville." *The Staten Island Historian*, III: 9, 11, April 1940.

37. ———. "Ice Was Once Cut on Island Ponds, Then Stored for Summer Use." *Staten Island Advance*,* April 7, 1950.

38. ———. "Major George Howard and His Little Memoir." *The Staten Island Historian*, XIX: 6-7, Jan-

uary-March 1958.

39. ———. "Port Richmond Hotel." *The Staten Island Historian*, VII: 25, 27, October 1944-December 1945.

40. ———. "The Quarantine." *The Staten Island Historian*, XIV: 9-11, April-June 1953.

41. ———. "Staten Island Architecture." *The Staten Island Historian*, V: 1, 3, 8, January-March 1942. V: 25-27, 31-32, October-December 1942. VI: 17, 19, 24, July-September 1943. VI: 25, 27, 30, October-December 1943.

42. ———. "250 Years of History in Port Richmond." *Staten Island Advance*,* September 1, 1953.

43. ———. "Willowbrook Used to Power 2 Mills." *Staten Island Advance*,* May 8, 1950.

44. MORRIS, IRA K. *Memorial History of Staten Island.* Vol. 2, New York: Memorial Publishing Co., 1898. P. 1-48, 129-159, 170-171, 190-196, 216-227, 232-234, 281-282, 292-299, 304-318, 321-325, 375-386, 412-428, 468-475.

45. ———. "The Old Patten House." *The Staten Island Historian*, IV: 9, 15-16, April-June 1941.

46. "New York Ferryboats." *American Heritage*, X: 26-31, 78, October 1959.

47. New York State Freedom Train Commission. *Official Document Book, N.Y.S. Freedom Train.* Albany, N. Y.: 1949. P. 40.

48. OLWIG, ROBERT A. "The Press on Staten Island." *Tercentenary Booklet.* Staten Island, N.Y.: Staten Island Tercentenary Commission, 1961. P. 28.

49. "Our Host. The Sailors' Snug Harbor." *The News Bulletin,* Staten Island Institute of Arts and Sciences, 10: 2-4, September 1960.

50. REED, HERBERT B. "Communications on Staten Island." *The Staten Island Historian*, XVI: 13-15, April-June 1955.

51. ———. "Communications on Staten Island." *Tercentenary Booklet.* Staten Island, N.Y.: Staten Island Tercentenary Commission, 1961. P. 22.

52. ———. "Port Richmond Bergen Point Ferry." *The Staten Island Historian*, XX: 15-16, April-June 1959. XX: 23-24, July-September 1959.

53. ———. "Staten Island Horsecars and Their Successors, Trolleys." *The Staten Island Historian*, XIV: 1-4, January-March 1953.

54. ———. "The New Blazing Star Ferry." *The Staten Island Historian*, XXII: 30, 32, October-December 1961. XXIII: 7-8, January-March 1962.

55. ———. "The Ferries of Staten Island." *Tercentenary Booklet.* Staten Island, N.Y.: Staten Island Tercentenary Commission, 1961. P. 24-25.

56. SANTORO, DANIEL, and RALLO, JOHN A. *Italians – Past and Present.* Staten Island Italian Historical Society, 1955. P. 40-59.

57. SMITH, DOROTHY V. "A Small Restoration." *The Staten Island Historian*, XVIII: 28-29, October-December 1957.

58. ———. "Ice-Harvesting on Staten Island." *The Staten Island Historian*, I: 17-18, 20, July 1938.

59. ———. "Staten Island Artists." *The Staten Island Historian*, II: 17-19, 24, July 1939.

60. ———. "The Clove and Its Valley." *The Staten Island Historian*, XVII: 25-27, July-September 1956.

61. ———. "The Staten Island Dyeing Industry." *The Staten Island Historian*, V: 9-10, 14, April-June 1942.

62. STEINMEYER, ELLINOR B. "Kreischerville Clay Works." *The Staten Island Historian*, II: 17, 23-24, July 1939.

63. STEINMEYER, HENRY G. *Staten Island 1524-1898.* 2nd ed., Staten Island, N.Y.: Staten Island Historical Society, 1961. P. 41-60.

64. STODDARD, CHARLES C. "A Staten Island Schoolmaster." *The Staten Island Historian*, VII: 1-2, 8, January-March 1944.

65. STUART, JAMES. "Three Years in North America." *Tercentenary Booklet.* Staten Island, N. Y.: Staten Island Tercentenary Commission, 1961. P. 53-55.

66. TURK, RICHARD J., JR. "Emerson Hill." *The Staten Island Historian*, XXI: 13-14, April-June 1960.
67. TYLER, JOHN. "Oystermen of Sandy Ground." *The Staten Island Historian*, XIX: 13-14, April-June 1958.
68. WELSH, JOSEPH J. "The Gas Industry." *The Staten Island Historian*, II: 22, July 1939.
69. ———. "The Telegraph on Staten Island. *The Staten Island Historian*, II: 9, 14, April 1939.

*Back issues of *The Staten Island Advance* are on microfilm in the St. George Public Library, Staten Island.

Chapter VI

CIVIL WAR PERIOD: 1861-1865

THE CIVIL WAR affected the social and economic life on Staten Island. Business with the South terminated and financial difficulties resulted. However, the oystermen on the Island became wealthy during this period because the southern supply of shellfish was cut off and the demand for local oysters doubled the normal price. The large hotels were busy also, particularly the Pavilion Hotel and the Planters' Hotel,* as many Southerners sent their families there for safety.

CAMPS

It was on the Island, where there was ample space, that various regiments were assembled in at least fourteen different army camps before being sent to other parts of the country (9).

Camps Washington and Arthur occupied the site of the Old Quarantine Station at Tompkinsville which had been burned by the citizens in 1858. At New Dorp, Camps Vanderbilt, Yates, Lafayette, and Sprague were set up. Camp Scott was at Stapleton, Camp Leslie at Clifton, Camp McClellan at Factoryville, and there were others at various points along the East and North Shores (1, 9). It takes little imagination to realize how all these training camps must have disrupted the otherwise tranquil life of Staten Island.

Chester A. Arthur, who later became the 21st President (1881-1885), was responsible for outfitting the New York Militia. It was he who selected Staten Island as an ideal spot for organizing troops. He was appointed Inspector General of the State Militia and later became Quartermaster General.

VOLUNTEERS

In the first wave of enthusiasm, many young men responded to the call for volunteers from Richmond County. A bounty of fifty dollars was given to each volunteer. Large sums of money were subscribed by citizens for this purpose and also for the care of dependent families of the soldiers (1).

CONSCRIPTION AND DRAFT RIOTS

As the War continued, draft quotas were set, and serious riots occurred in July 1863 in Richmond County, as well as in Manhattan, to protest the Federal Conscription Act of March 1863 (12). Mobs, completely out of hand, seized muskets from Tompkins Lyceum on Van Duzer Street, Stapleton, and other drill rooms, set fire to homes and stores, and attacked innocent Negroes who were living on McKeon Street, Stapleton. They also burned the car barns of the Staten Island Railroad at Vanderbilt's Landing, Clifton. Property damage amounting to about $20,000 were paid by the County after claims were investigated by the Board of Supervisors.

It was during these "riots" that Wendell Phillips, abolitionist and orator, and Horace Greeley, editor of the *New York Tribune*, found refuge in the home of George William Curtis on Bard Avenue.* Local historians describe these draft riots in detail (1, 12, 13).

As it became increasingly difficult to fill the draft quotas, it was necessary to increase the bounty paid to each volunteer to two hundred dollars. A like sum was offered also to any person able to procure a volunteer. It was possible for a young man to circumvent the draft by a payment of three hundred dollars. Many Islanders availed themselves of this alternative under the Conscription Act. The County, itself, to avoid further rioting, agreed to pay the money or to provide substitutes for draftees who had been called. This method of filling the draft quota left Richmond County in heavy debt at the end of the Civil War (1).

Between 1861 and 1864, 2,279 Staten Islanders volunteered or were drafted. About 180 were mortally wounded or died as a result of war injuries or illnesses. Several Civil War Memorials have been erected on the Island. One of the largest is a marble shaft at Bethel Cemetery, Tottenville.*

STATEN ISLAND FERRIES IN THE WAR

Staten Island ferries played an important role during the Civil War. In December 1861 the Government purchased four ferries, the *Clifton*, the *Westfield*, the *Southfield*, and the *Hunchback* for use as gunboats and troop carriers (2).

The *Westfield*, flagship of the Union Forces, ran aground during the Battle of Galveston Bay in January 1863. Unable to get the flagship afloat, despite the efforts of the *Clifton* to do so, the Union Forces blew her up.

Later the Confederates salvaged the main shaft of the *Westfield* and made a "60-pounder rifled gun" which eventually found its way to the Annapolis Naval Academy gun-park (2).

The *Clifton* participated in several engagements before running aground at Sabine Pass, Texas, in September 1863. Later a second Staten Island ferryboat named the *Clifton* was purchased by the Government and commissioned as a naval gunboat. The *Southfield*, flagship of the Union vessels at the time, sank April 1864 (2).

Bayles reports that President Lincoln enlisted the aid of Commodore Cornelius Vanderbilt in combating the success of the ironclad *Merrimac*. The Commodore sent his large, well-appointed steamboat, the *Vanderbilt*, up the James River in search of the *Merrimac*, but was unsuccessful in the search. He then loaned the boat to the Government for the duration of the War (1).

THE NARROWS FORTIFICATIONS

The fortifications at the Narrows, begun in 1847 by the Federal Government, were completed by August 1861 and troops from the 5th Regiment New York Volunteers Artillery were garrisoned there. On November 7, 1865 the United States War Department ordered the name of the post changed from Fort Richmond to Fort Wadsworth* in memory of Brigadier General James S. Wadsworth who was killed in the Battle of the Wilderness, Virginia, May 6, 1864 (8).

MILITARY LEADERS

Several famous Civil War military leaders came from Staten Island and others resided there after the conflict. Major General Francis Channing Barlow, a hero at Gettysburg, Yorktown, and other battles, had been a private tutor with a family on Grymes Hill before the War. He frequently visited the Island thereafter, and in 1867 married Ellen Shaw, daughter of Francis George Shaw, the philanthropist mentioned in the previous chapter. His name is remembered in Barlow Avenue, Eltingville (6).

Major General Richard Delafield was appointed Colonel of Engineers at Ft. Wadsworth in 1863 when the fortifications at the Narrows were being strengthened. He lived on Bard Avenue, West New Brighton. Delafield Place, West New Brighton and Delafield Avenue, Port Richmond commemorate the name (6).

Major General Joseph G. Totten, a Tottenville resident, Chief Engineer of the U.S. Army, directed the building of forts along the Eastern Coast from 1838 until his death in 1864. Totten Street and Tottenville are named after this family (6).

Rear Admiral Andrew E. K. Benham, the first Annapolis appointee from Staten Island, played an active part in naval engagements along the Eastern Coast during the Civil War. Later he became commander of the Lighthouse Department on Staten Island (present Coast Guard Base at St. George). As a young man, Benham was a student of Henry Boehm of Greenridge. His family home was the Benham Mansion on Arthur Kill Road, Greenridge, now in ruins. The name Benham is perpetuated in Benham Boulevard, Eltingville (6).

Other leaders who came to live on the Island included Rear Admiral John Drake Sloat, commander of the Pacific Squadron during the Mexican War, who lived on Richmond Terrace, New Brighton, between Franklin and York Avenues, from 1861 until his death in 1867 (6).

Another was General Ely S. Parker, Iroquois Indian of the Seneca Tribe, called "Old Seneca" by Mark Twain. He was a Colonel of the Engineers during the War, military secretary to General Ulysses S. Grant, and later Commissioner of Indian Affairs. Parker lived with his family at the Pavilion Hotel in New Brighton (6).

Major General Thomas L. Crittenden, Union general, lived in Annadale until his death. Crittenden Place, Port Richmond, is named after him (6).

Major General John C. Fremont lived in New Brighton after his retirement. He had commanded the forces in the western districts of the country during the Civil War, and was appointed Governor of the Arizona Territory in 1878. Fremont was the first Republican candidate for President of the United States in 1856. It was at the First National Headquarters of the Republican Party at Bay Street and Simonson Avenue, Clifton, that he learned of his defeat. Fremont Avenue, Grant City, commemorates the name (6).

Major Clarence T. Barrett was a prominent Staten Island citizen after his services in the War. He was a landscape architect, county police commissioner, superintendent of the poor, school trustee, president of Barrett, Nephews and Company, and a trustee of Smith's Infirmary. Barrett lived on

Broadway in West New Brighton in a home owned by Colonel Harden which was demolished in 1930 when the Staten Island Zoo was built. His name is perpetuated in the name of Barrett Park, West New Brighton, and by a statue in the park southeast of Borough Hall (6)*

Mathew B. Brady, noted Civil War photographer, visited on Staten Island, but it is doubtful that he ever resided there, although legend claims that he lived on Grymes Hill (3).

OTHER PERSONALITIES PROMINENT DURING CIVIL WAR

As indicated at the end of Chapter V, there was a group of ardent abolitionists on Staten Island during the War. The families of Francis George Shaw, George William Curtis, Sidney Howard Gay, and Albert Oliver Willcox were the most famous. As managing editor of the *New York Tribune* from 1862 to 1866, Gay was able to influence public opinion. His home was used as a station on the Underground Railroad (7).

Another prominent literary and political figure was Hon. Erastus Brooks (1815-1886). As newspaper correspondent and eloquent speaker, he stirred men to enlist to preserve the Union. He was elected a New York State Senator in 1853, State Assemblyman in 1878, and was a gubernatorial candidate of the Know-Nothing Party in 1856 (7). Brooks lived on the corner of Forest Avenue and Clove Road. Some of the trees on this property, now part of Clove Lakes Park, were planted on the Brooks Estate.* Brooks Pond, in the Clove Lakes chain, perpetuates his name.

Tyler House

Between 1851 and 1861 John Tyler, who had been President of the United States from 1841 to 1845, was a frequent visitor at the home of his mother-in-law, Mrs. Juliana Gardiner. The Gardiner Mansion, now called the Tyler House,* built about 1835, still stands at 27 Tyler Avenue, east of the junction of Clove Road and Broadway, West New Brighton. It is a fine example of the Greek Revival type of architecture with four large fluted columns on the portico. After the President's death in 1862, Mrs. Tyler brought her family to her mother's home where they lived for fifteen years. Some of the Tyler children went to school on the Island. Mrs. Tyler, a Southerner, was sympathetic towards the Confederate cause. A story is told about the confiscation of a Confederate flag by a group of young Island boys who had learned that the symbol was hidden in the Gardiner Mansion (7). P.S. 45, Richmond was officially designated "The President John Tyler School" in 1959 (4).

CHURCHES

For the most part, life went on as usual during the War Period on Staten Island. Children went to school, fathers worked, mothers carried on their household tasks, and they all worshiped together on Sundays. A few new churches were erected during these years.

St. Patrick's Roman Catholic Church in Richmondtown was dedicated in 1862 as a mission church of St. Joseph's in Rossville. Previously, services had been conducted at the Washington Hotel which was on Arthur Kill Road, just north of the brook between St. Andrew's Church and the Treasure House, and then at 256 Center Street. The original church building, still standing, was renovated and redecorated for its centennial celebration in 1962. Although St. Patrick's will not be within the Restored Village of Richmondtown, the exterior has been whitewashed to carry out the colonial atmosphere.*

St. Rose of Lima opened in 1864 as a mission church of St. Peter's R.C. Church in a small building on Castleton Avenue and Roe Street, Factoryville (West New Brighton). As a separate parish in 1875, a new brick church and school were erected. The present building at 981 Castleton Avenue was dedicated as the Church of the Sacred Heart in 1899. A new school was built in 1917 on North Burgher Avenue, New Brighton.

EDUCATION

As noted in the chapter on the Federal Period, Henry Martin Boehm† was elected School Commissioner of Richmond County on November 6, 1860, succeeding a David A. Edgar. Assuming office on January 1, 1861, Commissioner Boehm recorded in detail all his visits to schools. A photostatic copy of his diary kept between January 1, 1861 and February 21, 1862 has been made available by Dr. Vernon B. Hampton. The records show the Commissioner's visits to the 24 district schools, some of which he indicated as still under the "rate bill system" which supplemented the funds received from the State, assessing the parents in proportion to the number of children they sent to school. The system was abolished by the New York State Legislature in 1867 because, although the charge was small, it prevented some children from receiving schooling.† The State apportioned money to the various school districts in relation to the number of children between the ages of 5 and 15 residing therein. Each town was required to raise by taxes an amount of money equal to that provided by the State.

During the Civil War Period and until 1898, Staten Island was divided into five townships, each with several district schools. On the following page is a list of the 24 schools visited by Commissioner Boehm. Those marked with an asterisk were under the "rate bill system."

St. Patrick's R. C. Church

† Cubberley, Ellwood. *Public Education in the United States.* Rev. ed. Cambridge, Mass.; Houghton Mifflin Co., 1934. P. 198-205.

Town of Northfield
District School:
No. 1 – Richmond*
No. 2 – New Springville (new building about 1821) (school on that site since early 1700s)
No. 3 – Long Neck (Linoleumville)
No. 4 – Graniteville* (Port Richmond) (built 1855)
No. 5 – Mariners Harbor*
No. 6 – Port Richmond Village (later Free School No. 6)
No. 7 – Near Mallet's Mill (Summerville) (near site of present toll booth of Goethals Bridge)
No. 9 – Wach Oaks (Watchogue)
Town of Southfield
District School:
No. 1 – Clifton (Rosebank)
No. 2 – Near New Dorp* (Bayles records this school as in Concord) (1)
No. 3 – Head of Giffords Lane (Bayles records this as in New Dorp) (1)
Town of Westfield
District School:
No. 1 – Richmond Valley*
No. 2 – Bloomingview (Huguenot)
No. 3 – Fresh Kills (Greenridge)
No. 4 – Rossville
No. 5 – Tottenville*
No. 6 – Lemon Creek (Pleasant Plains) (built 1852)
No. 7 – Between Rossville and Tottenville* (Kreischerville – built 1856)
Town of Castleton
District School:
No. 1 – Four Corners (Manor Road) (School on that site as far back as
    1784)
No. 2 – Factoryville (West New Brighton)
No. 3 – New Brighton (school built in 1843 – a free school – Boehm
        Mentioned need of a new school in 1861 and by 1886, No. 4 had
        been added in New Brighton, now Tompkinsville)
Town of Middletown
District School:
No. 1 – Tompkinsville (site of P.S. 15)
No. 2 – Stapleton (erected 1855 – became Union Free School No. 2)
No. 3 – Near New Dorp (Boehm indicated this as near Joseph Egberts –
        Morris records that Joseph Egbert lived on corner of Richmond
        Road and Liberty Avenue, Dongan Hills. This, then, must have
        been the old school on Richmond Road, near foot of Four Corners
        Road, Garretson's)

VOLUNTEER ORGANIZATIONS

During the Civil War many volunteer groups were organized on Staten Island to care for the needy and to supply the encamped soldiers with clothing, bandages, blankets, and similar items. Typical of these were the "Mariner's Harbor Soldiers' Relief Society," the "Ladies' Relief Society of

New Springville," and the "North Shore Soldiers' Aid Society at Factoryville" (1). As reported in Chapter V, the Samuel R. Smith Infirmary (now Staten Island Hospital) also served community needs.

Finally, peace came to this war-torn country and Richmond County resumed its tranquil way of life and prepared for future growth.

BIBLIOGRAPHY

1. BAYLES, RICHARD M., ED. *History of Richmond County (Staten Island)New York: From Its Discovery to the Present Time.* New York: L. E. Preston and Co., 1887. P. 273-319, 342-345, 592.

2. BURGHER, ELLIOTT R. "Ferryboats That Went to War." *Proceedings of Staten Island Institute of Arts and Sciences,* XII: 43-48, January 1950.

3. COLE, ROSWELL S. "Mathew B. Brady." *The Staten Island Historian,* VIII: 10-12, April-June 1946.

4. HAMPTON, VERNON B. "Intimate Associations of John Tyler and Julia Gardiner Tyler with Staten Island." *The Staten Island Historian,*XX 17-20, July-September 1959.

5. ——. "Staten Island . . . Its Story." *Tercentenary Booklet.* Staten Island, N. Y.: Staten Island Tercentenary Commission, 1961. P. 11-13.

6. ——. *Staten Island's Claim to Fame.* Staten Island, N. Y.; Richmond Borough Publishing and Printing Company, 1925. P. 49-50, 73-75, 96-104, 106-108.

7. HINE, CHARLES G., and DAVIS, W. T. *Legends, Stories and Folklore of Old Staten Island. Part I. The North Shore.* Staten Island, N. Y.: Staten Island Historical Society, 1925. p. 50-54, 69-79.

8. KRIST, ROBERT. "Fort Wadsworth." *The Staten Island Historian,* XVIII: 20, July-September 1957.

9. LENG, CHARLES W., and DAVIS, WILLIAM T. *Staten Island and Its People.* Vol. I. New York: Lewis Historical Publishing Co., Inc., 1930. P. 275-299.

10. ——. *Staten Island and Its People.* Vol. II. New York: Lewis Historical Publishing Co., Inc., 1930. P. 816, 951, 963, 1003-1005.

11. MORRIS, IRA K. *Memorial History of Staten Island.* Vol. 2. New York: Memorial Publishing Co., 1898. P. 324-325, 387-407.

12. REEKSTIN, WILLIAM F. "The Draft Riots of July 1863 on Staten Island." *The Staten Island Historian,* XIX: 27-30, October-December 1958.

13. STEINMEYER, HENRY G. *Staten Island 1524-1898.* 2nd ed. Staten Island, N.Y.: Staten Island Historical Society, 1961. P. 61-66.

14. WELSH, JOSEPH. "The Telegraph on Staten Island." *The Staten Island Historian,* II: 14, April 1939.

CHAPTER VII

PERIOD OF EXPANSION: 1865-1898

THE POPULATION of Staten Island grew steadily after the Civil War as the following figures indicate:

1865	28,209	1890	51,693
1870	33,629	1898	65,000
1880	38,950		

However, this growth did not keep pace with that of other suburban communities in the New York City area.

GROWTH

With the industrial development on the Island after the War, many people came to work in the factories. Immigrants, particularly from the southern part of Europe, became railroad and industrial workers. The economy of the Island began to depend upon manufacturing and commerce rather than upon agriculture as it had previously.

Hundreds of wealthy families built large mansions and villas on the Island. Fashionable hotels and fine bathing beaches with clean unpolluted waters attracted visitors. This was a wooded island of scenic beauty, offering opportunities for quiet home life and excellent facilities for recreation. Many athletic and social clubs were formed. Had transportation been adequate, undoubtedly the growth of Staten Island would have been more dramatic during these years immediately prior to consolidation. The following pages will describe various phases of expansion.

LOCAL GOVERNMENT AND SERVICES

The concentration of population continued to be along the shores of the Island, and the officially designated towns remained the same as described in the chapter on the Federal Period – Northfield, Southfield, Westfield, Castleton, and Middletown.

COUNTY GOVERNMENT

Under a system of County Government, each of these five townships elected a member of the governing Board of Supervisors which chose its own president. The following officers were elected by the people at a general election: school commissioner, surrogate and county judge, district attorney, sheriff, county clerk, treasurer, and four coroners (41). The seat of this County Government was in the County Courthouse and in the County Clerk's and Surrogate's Office, both in Richmondtown.* Stages met the train at Court House Station (now Oakwood Heights), conveying the passengers to the County Seat.

TOWN GOVERNMENT

Each town also elected "four justices of the peace, board of assessors, tax collector, town clerk, three excise commissioners, four constables, sealer of weights and measures, and highway commissioners" (41). Until 1890 there was no secret ballot. The captains of the various election districts distributed the ballots.

INCORPORATED VILLAGES

In 1866 New Brighton, Edgewater, and Port Richmond became incorporated villages, followed by Tottenville in 1869. Edgewater included what is now known as Tompkinsville, Stapleton, and Clifton. When a section was incorporated into a village, it no longer was considered within the town of which it had been a part, but had its own local government, with elected officers, such as board of trustees, health officer, clerk, treasurer, and engineer.

Many other areas became unincorporated villages, but they were governed by the town or incorporated village of which they were a part. Some of these were Richmondtown, Rossville, Kreischerville (now Charleston), Travis, Garretson (now Dongan Hills), New Dorp, Giffords (now Great Kills), and Mariners Harbor.

VILLAGE HALLS

In 1871 the Village Hall was erected in New Brighton which was then the largest village on the Island. Between 1875 and 1882 this Victorian structure on Lafayette Avenue also housed the police station. At present the building is used as the Medical Health Center.*

In 1889 the Edgewater Village Hall was built in Washington Park (now called Tappen Park, Stapleton). This two-story red brick building, also Victorian in style, remains as a landmark.* Municipal Court and City Magistrate's Court were held in these Village Halls until the new courthouses were erected.

POLICE PROTECTION

In 1867 Richmond County was protected by a police force which was part of the County of New York, but three years later it became a separate police district with its own Board of three Police Commissioners, fifty police officers and a Captain, with headquarters at 19 Beach Street, Stapleton. A second police station was at 1590 Richmond Terrace, West New Brighton, and another on Arthur Kill Road, near Main Street, Tottenville (still standing).* A unit of mounted policemen was organized about 1895 with a substation at Rockland and Forest Hill Roads, New Springville. This unit moved to New Dorp in 1899.

Stapleton Village Hall

FIRE PROTECTION

More volunteer fire companies were organized to supplement those which had been formed before the Civil War. It is reported that there were 33 such units on the Island in 1886 (10). A complete list of these companies is recorded by Leng and Davis (33, 34). Two volunteer units still serve their immediate communities in 1963 – the Oceanic Hook and Ladder Company at 4010 Victory Boulevard, Travis, dating back to 1881 and the Richmond Engine Company in Richmondtown organized in 1903.*

Before the turn of the century most of the fire-fighting equipment was pulled to the fires by the volunteer members, so it was necessary to have more units than needed today with our modern equipment. The source of water for these handpumpers was a nearby creek or cistern, for this was before the day of the fire hydrant. By 1896 there were some horse-drawn fire engines. The Third County Courthouse on Center Street in Richmondtown houses a very complete collection of fire-fighting equipment and other relics from the days of the early volunteer firemen.*

FEDERAL GOVERNMENT INSTALLATIONS
FORT WADSWORTH
The Fort at the Narrows continued to be the chief defense of New York Harbor. Between 1892 and 1901 the property was extended from 90 acres to 226 acres, fortifications were modernized and strengthened and living quarters for the soldiers stationed there were made more comfortable. Many private estates in nearby Arrochar were taken over by the Government during the Spanish-American War period.

STATEN ISLAND LIGHTHOUSE DEPOT
In 1886 the Staten Island Lighthouse Depot under the Lighthouse Service began functioning at the site of the present St. George Coast Guard Base of the United States Coast Guard. Prior to that time, the offshore lightships were based there, as they are today. Various aids to navigation, such as buoys, were and still are repaired and maintained at St. George. In those early days mineral oil was used for lighting the lamps in the buoys and the cans and boxes for carrying this fuel to the buoys were manufactured at the Staten Island Depot (45).

UNITED STATES QUARANTINE SERVICE
The U.S. Quarantine Service* has been at its present location in Rosebank (Bay and Nautilus Streets) since 1873. This large acreage was purchased from the estate of William B. Townsend, after whom Townsend Avenue was named, with the understanding that no detention hospital would be erected there. Vessels were boarded by quarantine officers, and passengers or crew members with quarantinable diseases were taken immediately to Hoffman Island* (abandoned in 1927) or Swinburne Island (abandoned in

1928). Burial grounds were at Seguine's Point (site of Wolfe's Pond Park). In the 1890s the Public Health Service, then the Marine Hospital Service, was given the responsibility of administering the Quarantine laws. However it was not until 1921 that New York State turned over the Quarantine Station at Rosebank to the U.S. Government (24).

DEVELOPMENT OF CHURCHES

The churches which had been organized before 1865 continued to serve their parishioners. Some congregations erected new and larger edifices. New organizations also appeared (27). Reference should be made to previous chapters, as only new churches will be indicated.

METHODIST CHURCHES

Grace Methodist Episcopal Church* was organized in 1867 by a group from the Trinity Methodist Church of West Brighton, and a chapel was erected on Heberton and Castleton Avenues, Port Richmond. One of the founders was Read Benedict,* who owned a large estate known as "Ravenhurst" between Manor and Jewett Avenues, Westerleigh. Fire ruined the Benedict home in 1931 (37). In the auditorium of Grace Church is a bronze tablet in memory of Read Benedict and his wife. In 1895 the Chapel was destroyed by a fire and a new Gothic style edifice of dark brick with terra cotta trim was erected and dedicated in 1897. This is the present church. Services were held in the public school nearby (old P.S. 20) until the new church was completed. In 1886 the parsonage was built, and the present Sunday School building facing Castleton Avenue was dedicated in 1922.

St. Mark's M. E. Church, still standing on Amboy Road, Pleasant Plains, was dedicated in 1872 and rebuilt in 1892 (33). Previously, meetings had been held in an old schoolhouse to accommodate the Methodists of the area who found it too far to travel to Woodrow, the mother church, or to Bethel in Tottenville.

There were also several other Methodist churches, particularly the Rossville African Methodist Episcopal Zion Church on Bloomingdale Road, Bogardus Corners (Sandy Ground) and the St. John's African Methodist Episcopal Zion Church in Edgewater incorporated in 1875 (33).

Episcopal Churches

In 1865 the Episcopal Church of the Holy Comforter at 76 Old Amboy Road, Eltingville, was erected. This frame edifice, built in English Gothic style, was designed by Richard Upjohn, the architect of the famous Trinity Church in Manhattan. It is now known as St. Alban's Protestant Episcopal Church (4).*

In 1869 the cornerstone was laid for the beautiful St. John's Episcopal Church at 1331 Bay Street, Rosebank (then called New York Avenue, Clifton). An earlier church had been founded in 1843 nearly opposite the present church. The spires of this edifice can be seen by all ships as they come through the Narrows. Arthur Gilman, architect for the State Capitol in Albany and the Equitable Life Building in Manhattan, and a resident of Howard Avenue, designed St. John's Church.* Built of rose-colored granite from Connecticut in the English Gothic style of architecture, it has lovely stained glass windows that merit a visit (4). One of these is a memorial to Dr. John T. Anderson, formerly of the nearby Quarantine Station. The study in the large rectory adjacent to the church, built in 1862, was furnished by Mrs. Cornelius Vanderbilt (4).

St. John's
Episcopal
Church

The cornerstone of St. Paul's Episcopal Church at 225 St. Paul's Avenue, Stapleton, was laid in 1866, an earlier church dating back to 1835. This new edifice of gray traprock, built in English Gothic style, was consecrated in 1870. It was erected by the Honorable Judge Albert Ward as a memorial to his only sister, Mary Mann Ward, and became known as St. Paul's Memorial Church.* The rectory of similar architecture was built in 1865.

St. Stephen's Episcopal Church at 7516 Amboy Road, Tottenville, was organized in 1872 as a mission of St. Luke's Church in Rossville. Services were held in private homes and in other buildings until the present church was completed in 1887.

BAPTIST CHURCHES

In 1871 the North Baptist Church of Port Richmond was remodeled, an addition erected, and the name changed to the Park Baptist Church, still standing at 130 Park Avenue, Port Richmond. In 1881 a Negro mission church was started and ten years later St. Phillip's Baptist Church was erected for the congregation.

The First Baptist Church of New Brighton was organized in 1884 and used the Unitarian Church on Clinton Avenue until its own building was erected in 1897 at the corner of Hamilton and Westervelt Avenues where it stands today.

CATHOLIC CHURCHES

The Catholics of the Island were served by the four churches opened before the Civil War and the two erected during the Conflict.

The Church of the Immaculate Conception was incorporated in 1887, having been a chapel of St. Mary's R.C. Church for five years. The present church building on Targee Street, Stapleton was started in 1908.

Our Lady Help of Christians Church was built in 1898. Prior to 1890, Catholics in Tottenville had to walk to St. Joseph's Church in Rossville to attend services. When the Catholic families in the area had increased from twelve to about fifty, property was purchased on William Street (now Yetman Avenue) at the corner of Arrent Street (now Craig Avenue). This property was sold in 1892 and the congregation met in the Eureka Fire House on Arthur Kill Road and Butler Avenue (since demolished). The first school of the parish was built in 1910, and a new school was erected in 1955. Until 1916 the parish extended from Tottenville to Eltingville. In that year a small hall was rented on Huguenot Avenue, Huguenot. This eventually became the parish of Our Lady Star of the Sea, Huguenot.

MORAVIAN CHURCHES

The second Moravian Church to be organized on Staten Island was the Castleton Hill Moravian, which met in old P.S. 29, Richmond, on Manor Road for five years until its building on Richmond Turnpike (now Victory Boulevard) was dedicated in 1873.

The Great Kills Moravian Church was established in 1886 in a small chapel on Amboy Road. From 1884 to 1886 services had been held in a schoolhouse in Giffords, as Great Kills was called. The present church on Hillside Terrace was built in 1895.

The parsonage of the New Dorp Moravian Church, built in 1880 at 1256 Todt Hill Road, was the gift of William H. Vanderbilt, son of Commodore Cornelius Vanderbilt. The beautiful Vanderbilt Mausoleum* to the rear of the Moravian Cemetery was completed in 1886. This was designed in Romanesque style by Richard M. Hunt, noted American architect. Within are interred the remains of the members of the Vanderbilt family who gave so generously to the Moravian Church and to charities on Staten Island, as well as elsewhere in the country.

LUTHERAN CHURCHES

The two Lutheran Churches organized prior to the Civil War continued to serve the members of their congregations. Three others were organized before consolidation. In 1881 the St. Peter's German Evangelican Lutheran Church was formed in Kreischerville, meeting in a chapel of St. John's Methodist Episcopal Church in the same community. Balthasar Kreischer, manufacturer of firebricks in this locality named for him, erected at his own expense a new building for St. Peter's Church which was opened in 1883. The building on Arthur Kill Road was later used by a Hungarian congregation.

The history of Zion Lutheran Church at 77 Bennett Street, Port Richmond, may be traced back to 1894 when the congregation met and planned for a building on Avenue B, Port Richmond. This was started in 1895 and opened on Christmas Day 1900 (33). The cornerstone for the present

Gothic style brick edifice was laid in 1921 and dedication ceremonies held in 1926.

Our Savior Lutheran Church now located on Bard and Forest Avenues was organized about 1893 as the Zion Scandinavian Evangelical Lutheran Church. The name was changed to Our Saviour Lutheran to avoid confusion with the other congregation. A wooden building was erected on Nicholas Avenue, Port Richmond, which served the congregation until 1929 (33). The new brick edifice was completed in 1958 although services had been held in the church basement since 1929.

PRESBYTERIAN CHURCHES

Prior to the Civil War the First Presbyterian Church of Edgewater had served the Island community. A new edifice was completed in 1894.

Calvary Presbyterian Church* was organized in 1872. The original wooden building, erected on land donated by Mrs. Sarah J. Bement, was destroyed by fire in 1892. The present church at Castleton and Bement Avenues, West New Brighton was erected in 1894.

When the church at Sailors' Snug Harbor was demolished, Calvary received five beautiful stained glass windows. Reverend Gerald Huenick, Pastor of Calvary, reports that the ceremonies for the dedication of the first group of windows were televised over WPIX, the first live television program broadcast from Staten Island. Thomas W. Harland, skilled artisan, will be remembered for the notable work he did on the stained glass windows at Calvary as well as in many other Island churches.

CONGREGATIONAL CHURCH

The Immanuel Community Church was incorporated in 1902, but its origin dates back to 1895 when the Deems Memorial Chapel on Jewett and Maine Avenues was erected. This nondenominational church was named in memory of Dr. Charles Deems, a Brooklyn minister, who had been a leading figure in the National Prohibition Camp Grounds Association that developed the Westerleigh area. This Chapel was the original building around which Immanuel Union Church* has been built. It was one of the first nondenominational churches in the United States (46). Additions were made in 1916 and 1956. The names connected with the early church appear in a section on Prohibition Park.

SYNAGOGUES

In 1887 the Congregation B'nai Jeshurun was formally organized and a building fund started. Four years later the synagogue at 199 Victory Boulevard, corner of Pike Street, Tompkinsville, was opened for services. This became the mother synagogue for others which were to follow as the Jewish population grew in the twentieth century (18).

RANDALL MEMORIAL CHURCH

The handsome Randall Memorial Church was built in 1892 on the grounds of Sailors' Snug Harbor. With its beautiful dome and square fluted pillars, it resembled St. Paul's Cathedral in London. The floors of marble were laid out in the form of a Greek cross. It was a sad day for Staten Islanders when this edifice was razed because of the prohibitive cost of necessary repairs. Fortunately, some of the stained glass windows have been preserved in Calvary Presbyterian Church as previously reported.

HOMES AND RESIDENTIAL GROWTH

Beautiful homes and estates with wide lawns and attractive gardens were common along the north and east shores of Staten Island during this period. Shade trees grew to immense proportions and some of these are still standing as testimony of this day of large mansions. Green banks sloped gently toward the shore where many wealthy families had bathing houses and boat houses.

Other large estates were developed in the hill areas, now known as the Country Club Grounds, Emerson Hill, Grymes Hill, and Lighthouse Hill. A few estates will be mentioned as representative.

One of the largest was "Effingham," owned by the southern cotton grower, Junius Brutus Alexander, in the late 1800s. This property is now part of the Richmond County Country Club grounds. The large three-story brick house was enclosed by one of wood "with an air space between" (5). On the beautifully landscaped grounds were a brick stable, a coach house, and many other small brick buildings, some of which are still standing. The Alexander Home is now the clubhouse of the Country Club.*

Another vast estate overlooking Dongan Hills was the Cromwell Estate, home of George Cromwell, Staten Island's first Borough President. Known as "Far View Farm," the Victorian mansion was built as a summer home by Henry B. Cromwell, father of George, just before the Civil War. Here the elder Cromwell, founder of the Cromwell Steamship Lines, raised thoroughbred horses and cattle. Upon their father's death in 1864, George and his brother Henry B. Jr., inherited considerable property in the area and subsequently added to their holdings. By 1897 the Cromwells owned almost the entire hill now known as the Country Club grounds. They continued to raise choice Jersey cattle and Hackney horses. Their mother married the Honorable Charles L. Benedict, Judge of the U.S. District Court, who also lived on the hill (35). The Cromwell name has been given to Cromwell Circle (on the hill), Cromwell Avenue in Dongan Hills, Cromwell Recreation Center (Pier No. 6, Tompkinsville, under the jurisdiction of the Parks Department), and to P.S. 38, Richmond, which is called the George Cromwell School. The Benedict name is remembered in Benedict Place on the hill. Part of the property was subdivided into plots for real estate development in 1936 and the remainder developed after "Far View" was torn down in 1945. This is known as the Country Club section of Dongan Hills, an area noted for its beautiful homes and gardens.

On Richmond Hill Road, now Lighthouse Hill,* was the Meissner Estate of twelve acres with a large Victorian house still standing (31). Part of this property was sold to the United States Government for the Lighthouse in the early 1900s. The only other houses then on the Hill were the Latourette House,* present Golf Course Field House, built in 1830; the Keppler House, now part of the Eger Norwegian Home for the Aged; and the Judge Nathaniel J. Wyeth House still standing (referred to in the chapter on the Federal Period). Today Lighthouse Hill is covered with lovely modern homes. One of the principal streets leading up the hill is called Meisner Avenue.

Another hill area was Fort Hill. Here was the beautiful home of Daniel Low,* friend of Lafayette. Alan Seeger, famous poet who lived on Staten Island during his boyhood and attended Staten Island Academy, composed a poem entitled *The Old Low House, Staten Island* (34). Daniel Low Terrace was named after the prominent citizen who was a great benefactor to Staten Island and whose descendants have continued in his path. Before moving to the Fort Hill area, now a fashionable residential section, Low had lived in a large residence near Ft. Wadsworth. This became the home of the Von Briesen family, after whom the adjacent park is named.*

Many beautiful homes were erected in the lowlands also. One of these was "Beechlawn" built by Colonel Richard Penn Smith about 1877 on Clove Road between St. Peter's Cemetery and Martling Avenue, West New Brighton. Colonel Smith was the youngest colonel in the Civil War, participating in most of the important battles, including Antietam and Gettysburg (4). He moved to Staten Island after the Conflict and bought seventeen acres on which he erected his mansion that became the Actors' Home in 1902. Colonel Smith made a fortune in the wholesale coal business after he discovered that small coal, which had been discarded up to that time, could be utilized in producing steam. A parking lot for the Staten Island Zoo will remove the last vestiges of "Beechlawn" – the stairway that led to the entrance and the foundation stones, still visible in June 1962.

Colonel Stebbins, Parks Commissioner of New York City in 1873, erected a castle-like building on his property bounded by York and Franklin Avenues, Van Buren and Buchanan Streets. Stebbins Avenue is named after the Colonel.

A large private estate of Louis T. Hoyt, a Wall Street broker, extended from Castleton Avenue to Forest Avenue and from Bard Avenue to Randall Manor, bounded by a high stone wall. Hoyt Avenue is reminiscent of this family.

Sir Roderick Cameron, of the Australian Steamship Line, had an unusually large estate in park-like surroundings near the Grasmere lake which bears his name (34). The house was still standing in the 1920s, but has been demolished since then. However, the remodeled gatehouse stands near the intersection of Steuben Street and Fingerboard Road. The mansion, known as "Clifton-Berley," was the scene of many gay social events in the late 1800s. Interesting newspaper accounts may be consulted on the microfilm files at the Staten Island Museum.* Cameron and Roderick Avenues and Cameron Lake remind us of this vast estate.

Several large homes were erected in the Arrochar section of the Island in the 1870s and 1880s, many of them standing today. It was William M. MacFarland who named this area after the hills of Arrochar in Scotland. MacFarland Avenue bears his name. P. S. 39, Richmond, is known as the Arrochar School.

Fox Hill was the name given by Lewis Henry Meyer to his estate near the area which is now known as Fox Hills* (4). Meyer was the first president of the Staten Island Savings Bank when it was organized in 1866. A large community of high-rise apartments providing for 6,000 families in the middle-income bracket has been planned for this area according to the May 10, 1962 *Staten Island Advance*. It is of interest to note that one of Staten Island's greatest promoters, Erastus Wiman, in the latter part of the 1800s had an ambitious plan for this Fox Hills area off Vanderbilt Avenue. He dreamed of providing $2,500 homes for wage earners whose annual incomes averaged $1,200 to $1,800. This plan for low-income housing never materialized, but it is an indication of the foresight of Erastus Wiman about whom we shall read later.

The family of President Theodore Roosevelt owned a large colonial mansion on the left side of Signs Road, not far from Richmond Avenue, New Springville, opposite Crocheron's Grist Mill. The ownership of the property passed from Roosevelt's grandfather to his father and it is believed that the President visited this country home as a boy (21). Later the building was used as a private school. Much of the New Springville Park (including the Wildlife Refuge) was Roosevelt property.

Large homes were built also by oystermen* in the area from Prince's Bay to Tottenville. Many of these are exceptionally well-kept today by appreciative residents, some of whom are descendants of the original owners.

There were elegant homes overlooking Upper New York Bay in the St. George area – along Stuyvesant Place, St. Mark's Place, Westervelt Avenue, and Daniel Low Terrace. Many had private tennis courts and all were beautifully landscaped. Curtis High School and McKee Vocational and Technical High School occupy the sites of former mansions. A few of these old houses remain, but they are gradually being demolished to make way for modern apartment houses. Two houses of the Benziger brothers remain, one at the corner of Westervelt and Benziger Avenues, and the other on Daniel Low Terrace and Fort Place, now a convent for the Sisters of St. Paul. The Benziger family continues to maintain a Manhattan firm that sells religious articles.

Developments around Livingston, along Richmond Terrace, and on Grymes Hill have been reported in a previous chapter. The beautiful old mansions on Grymes Hill that belong to Notre Dame College* today were once the homes of the wealthy and the scenes of a gay social life.

Along with the influx of the wealthy, there was general immigration from southern Europe, as improvements on the railroad brought gangs of Italian laborers to the shores of Staten Island. Many of them settled in the Tompkinsville area. Great numbers of laborers also came to work in the small factories. This created a housing demand that was solved by the building of tenements and of small cottages.

It was during this period that certain nationalities developed little communities such as the French in Grant City, Italians in Rosebank, Scandinavians in Port Richmond, English and Scottish in Livingston, Polish in Linoleumville, and Germans in Stapleton.

There were simple Victorian houses built in scattered areas throughout the Island as more people moved to the area. Many of these, with their typical Mansard roofs, are noted in the Tompkinsville, St. George, and Port Richmond sections.

COMPANY HOUSING

Another development in housing was the erection of homes for employees of industrial plants. The Crabtree and Wilkinson Company, makers of silk bandannas, built two-story frame attached houses, known as The Cottages, for their employees. Another row of four-story brick buildings on the west side of Jersey Street was known as Holtcamp Row. Balthasar Kreischer also built homes for the employees of his brick factory. Three of these were still standing in January 1963.

LOCAL NAMES

Throughout the residential growth on Staten Island, specific sections within a community have been given local names. Among these is the name of Hamilton Park, New Brighton, named by Richard Hamilton who, during the Civil War Period, erected sixteen homes on his property bounded by York, Prospect and Franklin Avenues, and Buchanan Street. He fenced in the entire area, leaving two entrances on the Franklin Avenue side.

Some sections were named because of a natural feature, such as Duck Pond, a section in New Brighton. Actually there was a pond in the area around Jersey Street and York and Brighton Avenues. However, a larger section extending to the present Goodhue Playground was so-called. During the Cleveland campaign in 1888 a local Democratic Club used the symbol of ducks swimming in a pond on a political banner that was raised on Jersey Street.

PROHIBITION PARK

An area that developed before 1898 was Prohibition Park, now Westerleigh. After the Civil War there was a nationwide movement for prohibition resulting in the formation of the Prohibition Party in 1869. In 1887 the National Prohibition Campground Association acquired a wooded tract of twenty-five acres, bounded by the present Watchogue Road and Demorest, Maine and Wardwell Avenues (46). This became a summer resort for members of the movement, similar to the Methodist Camp at Ocean Grove, New Jersey. The entrance to the Park was at Maine and Jewett Avenues. A large auditorium, known as University Temple, with a seating capacity for 4,000 was constructed at Fiske Avenue and the Boulevard. This building burned in 1903. Varied programs were presented, chiefly lectures and sermons on science and religion. Lots were sold to people throughout the country. Streets were laid out in the area and named for the "dry" States of our nation (Maine, New York, Ohio, Virginia) and for Prohibition Party Presidential candidates (Livermore, Bidwell, Fiske, Woolley). Hotels and boarding houses were constructed to accommodate guests – the Park Hotel with a capacity for 500, the Villa, and the Grove House. Many cottages were built and within a short time large residences were erected which remain as imposing homes of today. On the southwest corner of Maine and Jewett Avenues stands the home of the Reverend Doctor William H. Boole, one of the founders of the community and a well-known evangelist.

Other leaders in the movement were Ella Boole, the minister's wife, who later became a leader in the W.C.T.U.; Reverend Charles Deems for whom the Deems Chapel, the Deems Literary Society and Deems Avenue were named; and Dr. Isaac Funk whose firm at that time was working on the Funk and Wagnalls Standard Dictionary (19). It is said that the editorial staff of this notable work lived in the house on Waters and St. John Avenues.

Within a few years the Immanuel Union Church* was founded to serve the needs of the community. Dr. Charles Rawson Kingsley was pastor from 1894 until 1933. His wife, Florence Morse Kingsley, was editor of the children's page of the *Ladies' Home Journal* and the author of thirty-two books, chiefly about New England home life. Among the best-known of her books are *Titus, A Comrade of the Cross*, and *The Transfiguration of Philura*. Mrs. Kingsley died in 1937 at the age of 78 in her home at 116 Kingsley Avenue, formerly the Jewett Homestead.

The Westerleigh Collegiate Institute which will be referred to under *Education* was organized in 1895 so that the children of the Park could get a good education (19). Dr. Kingsley was the first headmaster of the school, as well as pastor of the new church. P. S. 30, Richmond, was organized within the Villa Hotel which it soon outgrew. Then the National Prohibition Society gave the land for the present P. S. 30, the site of the old Park Hotel. That part of P. S. 30 was dedicated in 1905.

Westerleigh Park* today, bounded by Maine, Willard, Neal Dow, and Springfield Avenues, is part of the original 15-acre park that was used for band concerts and lectures. A bandstand in the center is reminiscent of this earlier period in Westerleigh's development. Mr. John Pollock states that this little part was "the first parcel of land (on Staten Island) donated to New York City for park purposes" (46).

Gradually other people, not associated with the Prohibition Movement, moved into the area, and a real estate development took over. Now this is a well-developed community.

HOTELS

After the Civil War, the shorefront around New Brighton became a haven for the wealthy, as the resort hotels gained in popularity. A beautiful view and fine clean bathing beaches attracted many distinguished visitors from all over the world.

The Pavilion Hotel,* previously mentioned, was the scene of many gay balls and parties. Old Staten Island newspapers on microfilm give us glimpses of these events.* The old hotel closed in 1900 and was torn down four years later.

Another famous hotel was the 400-room St. Mark's, built in 1876 at 125 St. Mark's Place, opposite Curtis High School. This was the site of

Marble Hall, built by Governor Tompkins for his daughter. In 1889 the Hotel Castleton* was erected at this same location. It was completely destroyed in a spectacular fire in 1907 and never rebuilt. The Castleton Park Apartments now occupy this site.

A smaller hotel known as Belmont Hall was at the corner of Westervelt Avenue and Shore Road (Richmond Terrace). This stood until about 1900.

There were many other hotels in various parts of the Island to accommodate visitors who came to enjoy the recreation that Staten Island offered. Some of them will be mentioned in the following paragraphs.

RECREATION

After the Civil War, there was an awakened interest in physical health and body-building which lead to the formation of many athletic clubs throughout the country, particularly among the wealthy (40).

STATEN ISLAND ATHLETIC CLUB

The first one to be organized on the Island was the Staten Island Athletic Club in 1877. Among the original members was Frederick Janssen, founder of the sporting goods firm of that name. At first the group met in a boat club at the foot of Franklin Avenue, New Brighton, then leased property at Bement and Henderson Avenues, and in 1885 purchased an estate at Bement Avenue, overlooking the Kill Van Kull at a point often referred to as "The Cove" because of the indentation of the shore line. The large home of G. W. Campbell was used as the clubhouse.

Track, high jumping, bicycling, and rowing were the first activities which interested the S.I.A.C. and several championships were held by members (40). Later, lacrosse, tennis, baseball, and football were added and a large grandstand erected to accommodate the spectators. A boat-house was built on Kill Van Kull at the foot of Bement Avenue. Gradually the social life of the Club became more important than the athletic events for which it was founded and in 1894 it disbanded. The grounds were used later for the annual Richmond County Fair and for Curtis High School football games before the Athletic Field was built. Mr. McMillen, Borough Historian, notes that the first games of the S.I.A.C. "were held in 1877 on the New Dorp Trotting Track, a half-mile dirt track which lay south of Richmond Road and east of New Dorp Lane" (40). In the same newspaper article

McMillen reports that Frederick W. Janssen had described a "three hour trip by horse and wagon," presumably from New Brighton to New Dorp.

STATEN ISLAND CRICKET AND BASEBALL CLUB

The Staten Island Cricket and Baseball Club, organized in 1872, played its first game at Camp Washington, the present location of the Baltimore and Ohio Railroad freight yards in St. George. When the North Shore railroad was planned, the club purchased the Delafield Estate in Livingston between Davis and Bard Avenues, near the Staten Island Athletic Club. The Delafield mansion was used as the clubhouse from 1886 to 1931 when the city bought the property. Annual cricket matches were played between American teams and English, Canadian, and Australian teams. Among the Staten Island players were Eugenius H. Outerbridge, after whom the Outerbridge Crossing was named and Randolph St. George Walker. There were also an excellent tennis court and an archery range on the property. Tennis became a more popular sport than baseball and in 1906 the name of the club was changed to the Staten Island Cricket and Tennis Club, retaining that title until 1931 when it became the Staten Island Cricket Club. Cricket matches are still held at the city-owned Walker Park,* as this property is now known, named in memory of Randolph St. George Walker, Jr., casualty of World War I.

TENNIS CLUB

Lawn tennis was a very popular sport towards the end of the 19th century and the courts on Staten Island were considered the finest in the East, attracting visitors from near and far. In 1874 Mary Ewing Outerbridge, sister of Eugenius H. Outerbridge, introduced the game to Staten Island. Bringing some tennis equipment from Bermuda, she influenced the Staten Island Cricket and Baseball Club to set up a grass court on their property at Camp Washington. This was the first lawn tennis court in the country and the scene of the first national tennis championship tournament in the United States in 1880 (9). Many nationally known tennis champions played there and names such as Grace and Ellen Roosevelt, cousins of Franklin Delano Roosevelt, were prominent in the local press. The Roosevelt girls won the first national doubles championship in 1890 at the new location of the Staten Island Cricket and Baseball Club. After her marriage to Appleton Clark, an insurance broker, Grace lived at 326 Westervelt Avenue, New Brighton.

The Clifton Tennis Club was organized in 1876 off New York Avenue (Bay Street), Clifton, but soon moved to Valley Street, Arrochar where it was active until the property was taken over for the Verrazzano-Narrows Bridge approaches in 1960.

Tennis courts were laid out also on the parade grounds in the quadrangle at Fort Wadsworth.* This hard court was home court for Henry W. Slocum, Jr., national tennis champion in 1887.

There were tennis courts at private schools such as St. Austin's* and on many private estates such as General Ward's "Oneata" on Grymes Hill.* Photographs taken by Alice Austen, noted woman photographer, on display at the Historical Museum, have captured the spirit of the tennis enthusiasts of this period.

BOAT CLUBS

Several boat clubs were organized on the Island, attracting many off-Islanders. Among them was the New York Canoe Club with headquarters near the present site of the American Docks. This was the first canoeing club to be established in America. The New York Yacht Club was in Rosebank. The building still stands behind the Austen House, at the east end of Maryland Avenue (56). In Stapleton, there was the Corinthian Yacht Club. The Staten Island Yacht Club had its anchorage in Kill Van Kull, near the Staten Island Athletic Club. Others were the Clifton Boat Club and the Staten Island Rowing Club. Canoeing and rowing were popular in the Bay, in the Kills and in the many lakes of the Island. It must have been a pretty sight to observe all the small craft surrounding the Island. Many pilots lived in Stapleton, so pilot-boats mingled amongst the canoes, rowboats, sailboats, yachts, and sailing vessels of the oystermen.

BASEBALL

Baseball was popular on Staten Island towards the close of the 19th century, and several big league players were Staten Island boys (43). The Metropolitans of the National League, who later became the New York Giants, were brought to the Island by Erastus Wiman, playing their home games at St. George (6).

FOX HUNTING

Fox hunting and riding the hounds was another favorite pastime of the wealthy. In 1888 the Richmond County Country Club was established at Little Clove Road and Ocean Terrace, Sunnyside. Six years later the club moved to its present location on Flagg Place, Dongan Hills, buying the summer home of Junius Brutus Alexander as its clubhouse.* Among the organizers were Clarence Whitman and Eugenius H. Outerbridge. Fox hunting and riding the hounds gave way to golf, tennis, and social gatherings. Recently a swimming pool was added to the facilities offered. The old coachhouses of the Alexander Estate remain.

OTHER RECREATIONAL ATTRACTIONS

One of the favorite summer resorts on Staten Island was Silver Lake, known as Fresh Pond until about 1850. Attractions were a large hotel and dance pavilion on the wooded shores of the lake. Boating, fishing, and picnic grounds brought many to this picturesque spot (now part of the water supply system). In the winter, ice was harvested at Silver Lake as well as at other ponds. These local ponds were used for swimming in the summer.

Clambakes were featured at many places along the shore. Several breweries such as Bechtel's in Stapleton and Eckstein's on Manor Road provided picnic grounds and dancing.

SOUTH BEACH

South Beach attracted visitors from across the Bay with its bathing beach, shooting galleries, dance pavilions, vaudeville shows, and small hotels. In 1886 this area began to develop as a summer resort comparable to the Coney Island of today. By 1890 ferries ran from Whitehall Street, Manhattan, and from Fort Hamilton, Brooklyn, to a pier at South Beach at a fare of ten cents. It is reported that on a single Sunday as many as 100,000 visitors came by boat or train as entire families came for outings (66).

MIDLAND BEACH

Midland Beach opened in 1896, accessible by a trolley from Richmond Road. Soon another trolley operated between the two beaches. At Midland, two bandstands offered concerts and a large Casino provided excellent vaudeville entertainment. A scenic railroad and ferris wheel were added features. It was, however, the bathing that was the chief attraction at both beaches (68). The recent Parks Department development of these two areas has removed the last vestiges of the gay resorts.

FISHING

Fishing was another form of recreation. Weakfish, blackfish, porgies, and flounder abounded in the waters surrounding Staten Island and fishermen came in great numbers to enjoy this sport. Peteler's Hotel at New Dorp Beach and many other hotels along the South Shore offered picnic grounds and restaurants for fishermen and bathers.

CYCLING

Cycling* was popular on the Island. It is reported that the first velocipede with iron-tired wheels appeared on Staten Island in 1868. Gradually this "boneshaker" grew in popularity and schools were opened to instruct riders. The "high-wheeler" with rubber tires was fashionable between 1870 and 1890. After the modern bicycle with two wheels of like size was developed in 1884, bicycling became so popular on Staten Island that thousands came on weekends during the 1890s and the early 1900s (48). Many shops rented bicycles which were very expensive at that time.

YOUNG MEN'S CHRISTIAN ASSOCIATION*

It is interesting to note that there was a YMCA program on the Island in this period before consolidation. It had originated in small headquarters in Stapleton as early as 1857. Ten years later the North Shore YMCA was formed, meeting at Trinity M.E. Church. Within five years the group had its own building at 1590 Richmond Terrace, West New Brighton. An East Shore Branch was founded in 1883, meeting in Tompkinsville near the site of the present Tompkinsville Park. The program was abandoned on Staten Island in the early 1900s because of disinterest. However, a unit in Fort Wadsworth continued until 1922 (57). Only recently has the YMCA program been reactivated on the Island.

GERMAN CLUB ROOMS

A building that played a leading role in the cultural and recreational life of Staten Islanders from the latter part of the 19th century until World

War I was the German Club Rooms built on the corner of Van Duzer and Prospect Streets, Stapleton* in 1874 on the site of the old Tompkins Lyceum. It was used for balls, entertainments, concerts, lectures, and political campaigns. During World War I the name was changed to the Stapleton Club Rooms. This old landmark was completely destroyed by fire in 1932 (65).

INDUSTRIAL EXPANSION

The period from 1865 to 1898 was one of great industrial expansion on Staten Island as elsewhere in the country. However, some of the earlier occupations remained important to the economic life of the people.

FARMING

Farming continued to be a leading occupation after the Civil War. In 1886 there were over 300 farms, growing such crops as white potatoes, Indian corn, oats, wheat, rye, buckwheat, and sweet potatoes (72). In the Rossville section, strawberries, asparagus, and cabbage were raised. Milk, butter, cheese, and wool were also produced. Much of the produce was hand-packed into large wagons that were driven to market in Manhattan or Jersey City. This was the beginning of "truck farming" that was carried on extensively in the 20th century around Graniteville, Bull's Head and New Springville sections. A few such farms exist today. David J. Tysen, 2nd had a large tomato farm and canning factory in New Dorp near Tysens Lane.

In the 19th century, before the period of farm mechanization, horses were used behind simple ploughs. Many German and Italian immigrants worked as farmhands. Farm tools* typical of this era are displayed in the Historical Museum.

OYSTERING

Oystering* also continued as a profitable industry. By 1880 about 150 families on Staten Island depended upon the oyster trade for their livelihood. Since the local "beds" were exhausted, oysters were brought from bays around Long Island, Virginia, Maryland, "refreshed" by the waters of the Passaic and Raritan Rivers and then taken to wholesale market at the foot of West 10th Street, Manhattan. Oyster grounds for the planting of oyster seed and the raising of oysters were off Prince's Bay, Rossville, and

Mariners Harbor. Negro oystermen lived at Sandy Ground. Wealthy planters resided along the Shore Road (Richmond Terrace), Mariners Harbor as reported previously, and also in Tottenville, Pleasant Plains, and Rossville. Clamming was also successful during this period, providing a livelihood for some families along the South Shore.

SHIPBUILDING

Another industry that has been important on Staten Island since colonial times was shipbuilding. Many of the boats used by the oystermen – catboats, sloops, schooners, yachts – were built on the Island. Numerous shipyards for building and repairing were located along the waterfront, particularly in Tottenville, where in 1886 there were at least eight actively engaged in this work (34). Some evidences of these boatyards remain along the shore.* Other shipbuilders were busy along the North Shore, in the Port Richmond-Mariners Harbor area.

OLD FACTORIES

Prior to the Civil War, the industrialization of Staten Island had begun. During this latter period, some factories, described previously, continued to prosper and others were developed.

Among those that had been organized before the Conflict and continued in business were: Hall's Gun Factory, adding hardware to its products in the 1870s; Jewett White Lead Works, reorganized in 1882; the Crabtree and Wilkinson Factory, reorganized as the Irving Manufacturing Company at 67 Jersey Street in 1881, makers of dress linings, tarlatans and other summer goods (71); Louis Ettlinger and Sons, manufacturers of jewelry boxes; Marsh and Nolan Carriage Factory; B. Kreischer and Sons, manufacturers of firebrick;* American Brick Company; Atlantic Terra Cotta Company;* Bachmann's Brewery, Bechtel's Brewery; and Eckstein's Brewery (formerly Constanz). None of these industries exist today.

However, the Louis De Jonge Company,* organized in 1847, manufacturers of fancy papers, is still in business. It is considered the oldest paper-finishing plant in the United States (36). The firm moved from Victory Boulevard to Tompkins Avenue, Rosebank in 1918.

In 1895 Barrett Nephews Company,* which had been operating a plant on Cherry Lane (Forest Avenue), as described in the chapter on the

Federal Period, bought out the New York Dyeing and Printing Establishment at the foot of Broadway, West New Brighton. The new firm was called Barrett, Nephews and Company-Old Staten Island Dyeing and Cleaning Establishment. Today only a small creek remains as a reminder of the large Factory Pond which was the source of water supply for the industry. Later the firm became a dry cleaning plant, moving from the Island in the 1930s, but existing today in Manhattan (29).

NEW FACTORIES

The largest industrial plant on the Island in the latter part of the 19th century was C. W. Hunt Company,* founded in 1872. It was located along the Kill Van Kull at Shore Road (Richmond Terrace) and Van Street, West New Brighton (28). Charles Wallace Hunt (1841-1911) came to Staten Island in 1868 and established a retail coal business near Shore Road and Broadway. There is still a coal office at this location. Being of inventive nature, Hunt soon worked out a mechanical way of unloading coal from barges or railway cars to storage bunkers or coalyard bins, a process then performed by hand. He also invented the grab bucket (known as the clam shell), automatic railway cranes, the pivotal bucket carrier and many other devices operated by steam engine. Altogether Hunt had 147 patents. At the Island plant he manufactured this machinery which was installed in most of the ports of this country and abroad and in the U.S. Navy coaling stations. Hunt built a home on the southwest corner of Barker Street and Woodruff's Lane, West New Brighton. In 1899 he purchased the McNamee mansion on Howard Avenue, Grymes Hill. Unfortunately, C. W. Hunt did not protect his inventions, and failure came to him as his patents expired and other companies started manufacturing the machines he had invented. A detailed description of Hunt's inventions is given in an article in the *Staten Island Historian* (8).

The first linoleum factory in the United States was built in 1873 on 300 acres in Long Neck, renamed Linoleumville (now Travis). The American Linoleum Manufacturing Company erected its wooden buildings at the end of Richmond Turnpike (Victory Boulevard). These were replaced nine years later by brick buildings, the chimneys of which remain.* The factory, operated by Joseph Wild and Company, employed at its peak 700 persons. A night shift was needed to fill the orders for linoleum, and in

120

1882 this plant became one of the earliest users of electricity on Staten Island. Steamboats carried the finished product to Manhattan. David Melvin, who became superintendent of the factory in 1874, invented the process now used in making inlaid linoleum (34). Melvin and Wild Avenues are reminders of this once prosperous industry which remained in operation until the late 1920s. For a brief time the Sandura Linoleum Company kept the plant going. In 1930 the community changed its name to Travis, by which it had been known earlier.

The Windsor Plaster Mills of J. B. King and Company, known locally as King's Plaster Mill, built a plant in 1876 on the present site of the U.S. Gypsum Company* which has been located there since 1924. From the time of the sailing vessels, gypsum rock had been brought from Nova Scotia as ballast. It was Jerome King who saw the possibility of grinding the rock and selling the calcined plaster of paris. The Staten Island plant was his second organization for this purpose. A severe fire completely ruined the one-story frame building in 1885. A larger building was erected, but this also burned in 1901, and had to be rebuilt. A report on current production of the U.S. Gypsum Co. is given in the next chapter.

In 1881 the S. S. White Company,* which had been founded in Philadelphia by Dr. Samuel Stockton White, merged with the Johnston Brothers, a dental firm at Seguine's Point, Prince's Bay, that had been in business since 1865. The new firm incorporated under the name S. S. White Dental Manufacturing Company (70). The factory at that time manufactured artificial teeth, dental instruments, appliances, and dental chairs. The plant consisted of two brick buildings, two wooden ones and a dock for the sailing vessels. The Johnston home on a bluff south of the plant is now occupied by the Marist Fathers.* The industry as it exists today is described in the next chapter.

In 1884 a group of German chemists built the International Ultramarine Works at the foot of Johnson Avenue, Rossville, near the Arthur Kill. A royal blue dye called ultramarine was manufactured from the clay found in the area. Homes for the plant officials were erected on the grounds. When the U.S. entered World War I this property was confiscated by the government under the Alien Property Act and the buildings became idle. In 1947 they were bought by the Onyx Chemical Company, manufacturers of textile dyes (55). This plant was closed in 1963.

Another chemical company which came to Staten Island just prior to consolidation was the Standard Varnish Works which moved from Long Island to 2600 Richmond Terrace, Mariners Harbor in 1895. This large paint manufacturing plant merged with the Toch Brothers Chemical Company in 1924, becoming the Standard-Toch Chemicals, Inc.

Unexcelled Manufacturing Company,* makers of fireworks, began operations in Graniteville in 1887 with 4 buildings and 20 employees. By 1930 it had grown to 167 buildings and 200 employees. The firm is no longer in existence. Some of the buildings have been converted into private homes. Other manufacturers of fireworks on the Island were Charleton's on Cherry Lane (Forest Avenue) near Willowbrook Road and Pain's Fireworks at the foot of Alter Avenue, Dongan Hills.

The Rubsam and Horrmann Atlantic Brewing Company was established at 191 Canal Street, Stapleton in 1870. The tower clock has long been a landmark. Destroyed by fire in 1930, the tower was replaced in 1936. In 1953 the Company was purchased by Piel Brothers* which continued operations until 1963.

Many other firms were established before consolidation. One of these was the Dean Linseed Oil Works on the Shore Road (Richmond Terrace), Port Richmond, started in 1869, which later became known as the American Linseed Company (34). Another was a silk factory in Tottenville opened by Owen Howard Barnard in 1890 (34). Barnard Avenue, Tottenville, is a reminder of this family name.

Staten Island also had its own wagon and carriage factories. Among them were "Brown's Carriage Manufactory" on Richmond Terrace near Taylor Street, West New Brighton, established in 1866, which later became the Richmond Storage and Warehouse Van Company; "Marsh and Nolan" on Richmond Road in Richmondtown; and "Lemers" on Cary Avenue and Clove Road on present site of Blue White Laundry. Old newspaper advertisements give vivid descriptions of the products of these factories.*

Livery stables rented riding horses and carriages and met passengers at the ferry just as taxis do today. Facilities for boarding horses were also offered at these stables. Among the best known were Finley's Livery Stable on Monroe Avenue at the foot of Benziger Avenue, Tompkinsville (building now occupied by a small factory); Charles Baezler's Livery Stable at 139 Bay Street, Tompkinsville (building now owned by Rosebank Storage Warehouse, Inc.); Brown's Rapid Transit Livery Stable on Shore Road, near Taylor Street, West New Brighton, affiliated with Brown's Carriage Manufactory; and O'Leary's Stables, not far from the Pavilion Hotel in New Brighton.

There were also several small dairies on the Island. A representative one was the Meadow Brook Dairy founded in 1887 at 94-98 Canal Street, Stapleton.

The American Dock and Trust Company was established by Alfred J. Pouch in 1872 as a warehouse terminal for storing cotton and other merchandise, continuing this operation until the present.

QUARRYING AND MINING

Quarrying continued at Quarry Hill (site of Bayonne Bridge Plaza) and at Victory Boulevard (then Richmond Turnpike) and Signs Road, Travis. Traprock quarried there can be seen in retaining walls in many sections of the Island.

Iron mines at Todt Hill and at Meiers Corners (north side of Richmond Turnpike and Jewett Avenue), as described previously, continued to operate until the 1880s. Perhaps the most extensive operation was the surface mining carried on by the Richmond Mining Company in the present Westerleigh section (58). The iron ore was sold to smelters to be used with other ores as flux. The operation was discontinued because of shipping expenses.

About 1876 approximately 80 tons of fibrous serpentine, an inferior quality of asbestos, were mixed on Pavilion Hill.* This was a short-lived venture because of the poor grade of the mineral. Pieces of this fibrous serpentine are found on the hill areas today.

ICE HARVESTING

Ice harvesting on the Island ponds prospered as homes and breweries were supplied with this local product. A large icehouse was built on Silver Lake in the 1860s by a William Brady. Later this business was operated by the Franzreb family until about 1902. In 1897 the Richmond Ice Company consolidated the many small ice dealers and leased the ponds at Concord, Silver Lake, and the three in the Clove Lakes chain. A large icehouse was erected the following year on Martling's Pond (one of the Clove Lakes).

An article in *The Staten Island Historian* describes this industry which flourished until artificial ice was manufactured (62).

BANKING INDUSTRY

With industrial expansion and population growth there was a need for banking institutions. An early attempt had been made by a Richard D. Little to establish a bank in Port Richmond, a venture which lasted only four years (34). It was not until 1866 that the first successful banking institution was organized on the Island (34). This was the Staten Island Savings Bank in Stapleton which at the time had space in the Village Hall. Now it has its own building at the corner of Beach and Water Streets and three branches.

In 1885 the Bank of Staten Island was organized in Tompkinsville, but soon moved to Bay Street, Stapleton. This bank has changed ownership several times and is now a branch of the First National City Bank of New York, with another office in the Port Richmond Shopping Plaza area.

The First National Bank of Staten Island was founded in 1886 in New Brighton and moved to Bay and Canal Streets, Stapleton, in 1897. In 1905 it became a branch of the Corn Exchange Bank of New York. Now it is known as the Chemical Bank New York Trust Company. Another branch is at 24 Bay Street, St. George.

The Richmond County Savings Bank also was organized in 1886, with Monroe Eckstein, owner of Eckstein's Brewery, as its first president. The offices were in the Odd Fellows Hall, Richmond Terrace and Broadway, New Brighton. This bank is now located at Castleton Avenue and Taylor Street with branches in Great Kills and Port Richmond.

In 1898 the Staten Island National Bank and Trust Company, originally called the Port Richmond National Bank, was organized in Port Richmond. This later became part of the Chase Manhattan Bank with five Staten Island branches.

Just before consolidation, several building loan and savings associations were organized. Such institutions have played a major role in the development of Staten Island, by their encouragement of homebuilding. Among the early ones was the Staten Island Building and Loan Association which has since then merged with the New Brighton Savings and Loan Association and has three branches. The Richmond County Federal Savings and Loan Association* was organized in 1881 as Richmond County Building and Mutual Loan Association, its original investors being employees of the S. S. White Dental Manufacturing Company. The main office was at 190 Main Street, Tottenville. This has recently been designated as a branch office and the main office has been transferred to Great Kills.

BUSINESS FIRMS

Several other Staten Island firms that were well-established in this period before consolidation remain in business today. Among them are: the Bedell Funeral Home, organized in 1841; Steers and Steers Funeral Home, established in 1842; Weitzman's Photo Shop in existence since 1872; Feist and Sons, stonecutters, organized in 1875; and Grimshaw Confectionery Co., in business since 1876 (35). Addresses of the above are given in the telephone directory.

There were many small neighborhood stores at this time, but there was also door-to-door selling. The peddler and his horse-drawn wagon were a common sight and sound, as he cried out his wares. Dry goods, oysters, meat, bread, vegetables, and many other items were peddled in this manner. Peddlers with horse and wagon were seen on Staten Island into the first quarter of the 20th century (61).

PHOTOGRAPHY

Local historians of any area have been aided in their research by the work of photographers* who have preserved visual records of old homes, people and events. This has been true on Staten Island also. One of the earliest photographers whose pictures have been preserved in the Historical Museum was Charles F. Hoyer who had a studio in the Planters' Hotel at Bay and Grant Streets, Tompkinsville, before 1859.* John Loeffler took over this studio in 1860, joined later by his son August, remaining in business over 50 years. Mr. Raymond Fingado, a curator at the Historical Museum, reports that John Loeffler was the first Staten Island photographer to use flash powder for indoor and night work (17).

John E. Lake was a traveling photographer with a studio at 79 Shore Road (Richmond Terrace), Elm Park from 1870 to 1890. He traveled about the Island by horse and wagon, carrying his photographic equipment with him (17). Another well-known early photographer on the Island was Isaac Almstaedt, whose work also has been preserved.

Recognition came late for Alice Austen,* now considered to have been one of the foremost woman photographers. Her story will be told in the next chapter. A study of her excellent photographs reveals the social life of the Island during the latter part of the 19th century and the early years of the 20th.

UTILITIES

It was during the last two decades of the 19th century that utilities developed on Staten Island to give greater comfort to its citizens.

Gas

It was noted previously that gas was introduced for home lighting on the Island immediately prior to the Civil War by the Richmond County Gas Light Company. After the War more mains were laid on Todt Hill Road and on many side streets, extending the service to hotels and to more homes. Gas lights appeared on the streets of Stapleton and Tompkinsville in 1865 and in New Brighton in 1874. During a depression period in the 1870s many householders returned to the use of kerosene oil lamps, for gas was expensive to produce. More efficient types of gas lamps were developed to encourage the use of gas.

In 1884 the Staten Island Gas Light Company, previously organized in 1855, was reincorporated and built a plant on Willow Avenue, Clifton, next to the Richmond County Gas Light Company. The two firms soon merged, one producing the gas and the other distributing it.

After the invention of the incandescent bulb in 1879 gas for home lighting gradually gave way to electricity. In the 1890s gas ranges for cooking were introduced into the homes of Staten Island.

A relic of early gaslight days, erected in the latter part of the 19th century, stands on Post Avenue (near P.S. 19, Richmond). This is a small church-like building with two stained glass windows.* Mr. Frederic H. J. Rider, of the Brooklyn Union Gas Company, relates the story of two elderly ladies who refused to allow the Gas Company to erect a gas holder on their property, but consented to the erection of this "church-like building" to house the "governor."

Electricity

In 1882 the American Linoleum Manufacturing Company introduced electricity for illumination in its Travis plant. By strange coincidence, the huge modern Con Edison generators are located on Victory Boulevard directly across from the site of the old Linoleum plant.

Three years later George Bechtel installed electricity in his brewery on Richmond Road (that section now known as Van Duzer Street), Stapleton. Soon his home and greenhouse were illuminated (50).

However, it was the great promoter, Erastus Wiman, who made Staten Islanders aware of electricity in 1886. He installed a private power plant at St. George to illuminate his Staten Island Amusement Park there and his Erastina Park at Mariners Harbor, scene of the Buffalo Bill Wild West Show. Power lines were strung on telegraph poles along the railroad right of way (60).

When Wiman's spectacular venture failed in 1887 he sold the electric generators to the Edison Electric Illuminating Company which started to provide street lighting on Staten Island. By 1888 the villages of Edgewater and New Brighton were lighted. Gradually, streets in other villages were illuminated and electricity was brought into the homes. By 1892 the Livingston Power Plant was erected along the Kill Van Kull at the foot of Davis Avenue. This landmark was demolished in 1963.

Several small electric companies entered the field but by 1897 all of these had been consolidated into the New York and Staten Island Electric Company (50). This name was changed to the Richmond Light and Railroad Company in 1902. In 1923 the Staten Island Edison Corporation purchased the electric business, selling out to Con Edison in 1950.

Water

In the 1880s private water companies began to supply water through mains for the first time. Prior to that, the source of water was pumps, wells, and cisterns (61). The Staten Island Water Supply Company was organized in 1879 to furnish water to the North Shore area from Richmond Turnpike to Arthur Kill. Through a system of pumping stations, water was pumped from artesian wells in West New Brighton to a reservoir on top of Fort Hill, and then distributed through mains to Staten Island users. The Company also sold water to factories and refineries in New Jersey.

The Crystal Water Supply Company was organized in 1883 to supply the area from Richmond Turnpike to Lower New York Bay as far south as New Dorp. The pumping station* was in Clove Valley and a reservoir near Four Corners. A large tank was erected on Grymes Hill.*

The South Shore Water Company, formed in 1889, furnished water to a part of the South Shore and the Dongan Hills Water Company, organized the following year, supplied the area around Dongan Hills.

The Tottenville Water Works, constructed in 1897, supplied the Tottenville-Prince's Bay section. All of these companies were acquired by the city in 1909 and Staten Island was serviced by the Board of Water Supply of the City of New York.

COMMUNICATIONS

Telegraph

Although the telegraph system was extended to Staten Island before the Civil War, it was not until the 1880s that the entire island was served. In 1877 the system was extended from Bergen Point across Kill Van Kull to Port Richmond, thence to Clifton, Richmond, Rossville, Tottenville, and to Amboy (74).

By 1882 the Western Union Telegraph Company had offices in Stapleton, Tompkinsville, New Brighton, and the Quarantine Station. In 1898 there was also Postal Telegraph service on the Island with an office at Quarantine. A 65-foot tower there was used to send information on arrival and departure of ships. The tower's use was discontinued in 1937 (74).

Telephone

Staten Island was the scene of telephone experimentation as early as 1850. In that year Antonio Meucci came to the Island soon after his arrival from Italy. In his homeland he had been successful in transmitting voices over wires connected to batteries to produce the needed electricity. He continued further experiments at his little house in Clifton (now Rosebank) where he lived with Garibaldi.* Meucci filed a caveat (application for a patent) in 1871 but was unable to obtain the patent because of financial difficulties (59). In the meantime Alexander Graham Bell was experimenting and announced his invention of the telephone in 1876. Friends of Meucci aided him in unsuccessful attempts to prove his claim to prior invention of the instrument.

Three years after Bell's invention, the Staten Island Telephone Exchange Company was organized with Erastus Wiman as president (33). Only local service was provided. The first central office on the Island was opened in the rear of the old post office building at 369 Richmond Terrace, New Brighton. Soon a second telephone exchange was opened in Port Richmond. In 1883 underwater cables were laid across Kill Van Kull to Bayonne, connecting Staten Island with Elizabeth, Newark, and Manhattan. In that same year the New York and New Jersey Telephone Company bought out the interests of the Staten Island Telephone Exchange Company and extended lines throughout the Island (49). The Staten Island Telephone Company was a subsidiary of the larger organization. In 1896 the New York Telephone Company took over the telephone service on the Island.

In the 1890s other exchange offices opened in Tompkinsville, West New Brighton, New Dorp and Tottenville. The old Tompkinsville building, now vacated, stands on St. Mark's Place, near Victory Boulevard.* The earliest telephone poles presented a different appearance from those of today. Each line from an individual subscriber was attached to the cross arms of the poles leading to the central office. Now large cables carry many lines, more than half of them underground. The old phones with the hand cranks are a far cry from the newest models distributed by the New York Telephone Company today.* Details of later development of the telephone system are given in the next chapter.

Newspapers

There had been several newspaper ventures before the Civil War, most of which were short-lived. However, the *Richmond County Gazette*, which had started in 1859, continued under different ownerships. It consolidated with the *Richmond County Sentinel* in 1882, appearing semi-weekly. Issues from 1859 to 1902 are on microfilm in the Library of the Institute of Arts and Sciences.* The *Staten Island Leader* began publication in 1866 and continued into the 20th Century (34).

In 1886 the *Richmond County Advance* was founded by John Crawford, Jr., as a weekly paper appearing on Saturdays. In 1910 it became a semi-weekly and in 1918 a daily called the *Daily Advance*. It was not until 1921 that it became the *Staten Island Advance* which is the Island's only daily newspaper. Crawford started his weekly publication in a small building on Broadway, near Henderson Avenue, West New Brighton, where he also did job printing (36). In 1913 a new building was erected at 1267 Castleton Avenue, which housed the *Advance* until its beautiful modern plant was opened in 1960.*

The *Staten Islander*, which was a competitor of the *Advance* for many years, was founded as a weekly in 1889, although an earlier venture had this same name. The Staten Islander Building* still stands in Tompkinsville at the junction of Bay Street and Central Avenue (called Pershing Square). The paper became a daily in 1926 and was discontinued in 1928. Microfilmed issues are in the Library of the Institute.

A Tottenville weekly newspaper was started in 1881. Originally named the *Westfield Times*, it later became the *Staten Island Transcript* in 1899 and then consolidated with the *South Shore Times* in Great Kills, becoming the *Times-Transcript* with offices in both towns. Later a new building was erected at 5389 Arthur Kill Road, Tottenville. This publication, carrying only South Shore news, appeared until 1962 as the *Staten Island Transcript and Westfield Times*. The Institute has copies from 1927 to 1941 on microfilm.

Before consolidation there were many other newspaper attempts, some of them political organs, others printed in the German language. Old newspapers remain as one of the finest sources of firsthand information about people, community growth, and social and economic problems. Therein is found a clear-cut picture of any given period of a community's development.

INSTITUTIONS

In the previous chapter, four institutions which cared for seamen and their families were described. These continued to serve the Staten Island community in this period of expansion. During the late 1800s the name of the Seamen's Retreat was changed to the U.S. Marine Hospital (7). On the grounds of Sailors' Snug Harbor the bronze statue of Captain Robert Randall* was unveiled in 1884 and the Randall Memorial Church, described in the section on churches, was erected in 1892. The services rendered by the Mariners' Family Home and the Society for Seamen's Children continued as before.*

S. R. Smith Infirmary*

Before consolidation Staten Island's first voluntary hospital grew through the generosity and service of many benefactors. In 1870 the S. R. Smith Infirmary, which had opened in 1861, moved to 85 Hannah Street at the corner of Van Duzer Street, Tompkinsville. This had been the residence of Dr. S. R. Smith. Five years later the first Charity Ball was held for the benefit of the little hospital, Erastus Wiman lending his showmanship talents to the affair. This Ball has been an annual social event and fund-raising activity since 1875.

In 1887 Dr. George W. Frost gave the hospital six acres of ground on Castleton Avenue. Many benefactors gave liberally and construction began. Two years later the "tower" building was opened as the new S. R. Smith Infirmary (34). George William Curtis presided at the laying of the cornerstone. This original building of the present Staten Island Hospital is used for offices, clinics, and interns' quarters.

The growth of the Hospital has depended not only upon the generosity of those who could afford large monetary contributions, but also upon the service of the Women's Auxiliary. In the very beginning this group donated fruit, vegetables, linens, clothing, and other necessities. Gradually its services were extended. An early secretary of the Auxiliary was Mrs. Thomas Melville, wife of the Governor of Sailors' Snug Harbor, sister-in-law of Herman Melville, author of *Moby Dick*.

A two-year training school for nurses was opened in 1894 at the S. R. Smith Infirmary. In 1943 the training school became affiliated with Wagner College. By 1898 the first voluntary hospital on the Island had grown to the extent that private as well as charity patients could be cared for.

County Poorhouse

The county poorhouse as previously described continued at the same location. Records indicate that poor administration existed about 1873 and Commissioner Josephine Shaw Lowell,* of the State Board of Charities, daughter of Francis George Shaw, met with the supervisors concerning the need for improvements in the poorhouse (34). Subsequent change of officials brought about better conditions.

SOCIETY FOR THE PREVENTION OF CRUELTY TO CHILDREN

In 1880 the Richmond County Society for the Prevention of Cruelty to Children was incorporated. George William Curtis was active in this organization which by 1897 had moved from smaller quarters to a large house at 118 Castleton Avenue, opposite Staten Island Hospital. Part of this building remains as a private residence. This agency which sheltered neglected and delinquent children closed its doors in 1949. After Richmond was incorporated into the City of New York, the Board of Education supervised the education of these children.

STATEN ISLAND DIET KITCHEN

Another charitable organization was the Staten Island Diet Kitchen* which was incorporated in 1882 "to furnish nourishing food for the needy sick to be given free upon presentation of a written requisition from a physician" (34). Its first quarters were at 18 Broad Street, Stapleton. Later it moved to Van Duzer and Grant Streets and eventually restricted its service to distribution of milk.

MOUNT LORETTO

In 1882 Father John C. Drumgoole purchased a large acreage of farmland in Prince's Bay, Staten Island to care for homeless newsboys who had been sheltered previously at a Mission on Lafayette Street, Manhattan. The Sisters of St. Francis, Third Conventual, were established to minister to the needs of the children. Also known as the Mission of Immaculate Virgin, the institution has grown far beyond its original purpose. A large beautiful edifice, the Church of S.S. Joachim and Ann, was erected. A statue of Father Drumgoole reminds the visitor of the founder of Mount Loretto* which now cares for over 900 boys and girls (from ages 6 to 18) from broken homes. The boys are housed in modern dormitories and the girls in buildings on the Raritan Bay side of Hylan Boulevard. Many educational and vocational opportunities are offered by both the School Board of the Catholic Archdiocese of New York and the New York City Board of Education which has established P.S. 611 and P.S. 612 there. Until 1961 a herd of 110 dairy cattle was cared for on the grounds (37).

The lighthouse which had been constructed in 1868 was closed by the U.S. Government in 1925 and purchased by the Mission as a residence for the Director.

St. Michael's Home

Another institution for dependent Catholic children is St. Michael's Home, at 1380 Arthur Kill Road, Greenridge, which opened in 1884, under the direction of the Presentation Sisters, with 60 children. Since 1945 the Sisters of Mercy have cared for the children who have been placed there. The home has facilities for 144 boys and 136 girls between the ages of 3 and 17.

Day Nurseries

It is also interesting to note that three Day Nurseries were started on Staten Island before consolidation. Among them were the New Brighton or Evelyn Bridgman Day Nursery at 72 Cleveland Street, named in memory of Mrs. Edward C. Bridgman who had been a benefactor of many Island charities; the Stapleton Day Nursery at 96 Wright Street, founded in 1895; and the Port Richmond Day Nursery founded in 1897, now under the direction of the Staten Island Mental Health Society, Inc., and located at 166 Lockman Avenue, Mariners Harbor.

EDUCATION

With the population growth came the need for more and larger schools on Staten Island. A study of *Beer's Atlas* of 1874 and *Robinson's Atlas* of 1898 reveals the locations of schoolhouses in Richmond County. Twenty-five schools were shown on the earlier map and twenty-nine on the 1898 map. A few of these were the one-room schoolhouses visited by Commissioner Boehm during 1861 and 1862. Some were new buildings on the same sites, and others were in new locations. Dr. Vernon B. Hampton has had these schools indicated on a 1945 map of Staten Island which also shows the buildings existing as of that date. It is interesting to find that many of the present-day buildings are on the original sites of 1874 and 1898.

Dr. Hampton notes that of the 29 schools in 1898, 18 of them were graded (22). Three high school departments were organized in the local common schools (16). Port Richmond High School was organized in the Union Free School in Port Richmond in 1881, the Tottenville High School Department in 1882 and the Stapleton High School Department in 1886. These all offered two-year courses (23).

Referring back to the list of schools reported during the Civil War Period, we find District School No. 4, New Brighton, added to the town of Castleton in 1871. The original tablet of this old schoolhouse is on the wall of the first floor hall of P.S. 16 on Daniel Low Terrace (formerly Madison Avenue), Tompkinsville, which was erected in 1896 and is scheduled to be demolished soon. On the floor of the entrance are tiles reading "Castleton No. 4." District School No. 8, Seaside (now Eltingville) was added to the town of Westfield. District School No. 4, Middletown, on Manor Road, one-half mile north of Rockland Avenue was built in 1872 (42), and District School No. 9, Port Richmond, was added to Northfield.

George Egbert, late member of Local School Board 54 from 1902 to 1957, recalled attending school in 1868 in the Baptist Church on the side of Emerson Hill at the corner of Clove and Richmond Roads. Soon a two-room school was built at the corner of Vanderbilt Avenue and Richmond Road, near Mary Street, a predecessor of P.S. 12 which was erected on a site nearby (15).

The following chart locates the public elementary schools on the Island in 1874 and 1898. Reference to the section on education during the Civil War Period will reveal the District School numbers of most of these buildings.

NORTHFIELD

LOCALITY	1874	1898	1963
Richmondtown	Richmond Hill Rd., opposite Old Mill Rd.	same	P.S. 28 –1908, new site; addition 1937; to be replaced
New Springville	Old Stone Rd. (Richmond Ave.) opposite Asbury Meth. Church	new bldg., same site 1898; P.S. 17 erected there; now demolished	Served by – P.S. 42 built 1926
Willow Brook	Forest Hill Rd. and Rockland Ave.	not shown	Served by – P.S. 30 – 1904; additions 1928, 1940
Long Neck	4117 Richmond Turnpike; had been Long Neck Chapel	diagonally opposite at No. 4108. 1st floor built 1880; 2nd floor added 1897	P.S. 26 – same site as in 1908, now Travis; bldg., 1903
Graniteville	none shown	Richmond Ave., near Forest Ave., built 1894	P.S. 22 – new site 1914; additions 1930, 1955
Old Place	north side Forest Ave. between North-field and South Aves.	new building across the street, 1895; became P.S. 24	Served by – P.S. 22
Mariners Harbor	none shown	Christopher, Mer-sereau and Andros; became P.S. 23 (1895)	P.S. 44 (1926, 1956)
Port Richmond	Heberton Ave. and New St., site owned since 1842	new bldg. 1890; additions	P.S. 20 – same site; 1890 bldg. still used; new bldg. 1914
West New Brighton	not shown	Greenleaf Ave. fur-ther east than present bldg. 1889	P.S. 19 – new site 1930; additions 1953
Port Richmond (outskirts)	not shown; built 1873 Quarry Hill; opposite St. Mary's Cemetery	same location; bldg. erected 1897	P.S. 21 – same location (Elm Park) bldg. 1905
Chelsea	Chelsea Rd. near South Ave.	Chelsea Rd. near Bloomfield Rd.; was old P.S. 25	Served by – P.S. 26

SOUTHFIELD

Clifton (Rosebank)	not shown on map; some historians claim school at N.Y. Ave. (Bay St. and Cliff St.)	new bldg. 1896; now called 161 Hylan Blvd.	P.S. 13, old bldg. still used; new build-ing 1906
New Dorp	east side Mill Rd. near Ebbitts St.	same as 1874	P.S. 41 – new bldg. and site – 1925; addi-tions – 1937, 1949

LOCALITY	1874	1898	1963
New Dorp	not shown	old P.S. 9, built 1894, 8th St., near Beach Ave., later used as police precinct	P.S. 41
Concord	not shown; Mr. Egbert remembered school at Vanderbilt Ave. and Richmond Rd. (75)	Steuben St. and Rhine Ave., built 1894, P.S. 12	P.S. 12; new bldg. 1900; old bldg. still in use
Great Kills	Amboy Rd., near Giffords Lane	new site; new bldg. 1898; P.S. 17	P.S. 8 – same site as 1898; new bldg. 1918; additions 1938, 1952

WESTFIELD

Richmond Valley	west side Amboy Rd. Near railroad and Rich. Valley Rd.	new site; Weiner St.; old P.S. 2 built 1896, demolished	Served by – P.S. 1
Bloomingview (Huguenot)	west side Amboy Rd. opp. Kingdom Ave., site owned since 1873	same site; old P.S. 5, built 1895, demolished	new P.S. 5 built 1930 Kingdom and Desius Ave.
Fresh Kills (Greenridge)	Arthur Kill Rd., opp. Muldoon Ave., site owned since 1851,	same site; school built 1868, enlarged 1905; was old P.S. 7, demolished	Served by – P.S. 42 Richmond Ave. and Augusta Ave. built 1926
Rossville	Rossville Ave. (site of City Yard) few blocks southeast of 1901 site	same as 1874 (old P.S. 6 built 1901 – new site, closed 1945)	Served by – P.S. 4
Tottenville	school on Amboy Rd. and Wood Ave.; another on Amboy Rd. and Satterlee St.	both replaced by 1878 bldg. on Summit St.; site owned since 1873	P.S. 1 – same location 1878 bldg. still in use; new bldg. 1907
Lemon Creek	northwest side railroad, near Sharrott Ave.	new site – Latourette St., built 1894; addition 1900	P.S. 3 – old bldg. still used, 1959 bldg. adjacent
Kreischerville (Charleston)	Arthur Kill Rd., north side Claypit Rd.	new location, few blocks south on Arthur Kill Rd. erected 1896	P.S. 4 – 1896 bldg. still used; additions 1906 and later
Seaside (Eltingville)	not shown	added by 1886 not on map cited by Bayles	P.S. 42

CASTLETON

Four Corners	498 Manor Rd.	site of old P.S. 29 erected in 1889, later used as old P.S. 35; now used as church	P.S. 29 new site, 1581 Victory Blvd., erected 1921; additions 1941, 1952

LOCALITY	1874	1898	1963
Factoryville (West New Brighton)	Eliz. St. and Cary Ave. building still stands	not shown	P.S. 18, Broadway built 1890, add. 1904, still used; to be replaced by new bldg. on adjacent site
New Brighton	Prospect Ave.; in 1871 on York Ave.	new bldg. erected 1898; P.S. 17	same bldg. still used, to be replaced at new site as P.S. 31
New Brighton (now Tompkinsville)	Madison Ave. (now Daniel Low Terr.) erected 1871	new bldg. same site erected 1896; P.S. 16	1896 bldg. still used; additions 1905, 1925; to be replaced
MIDDLETOWN			
Tompkinsville	St. Paul's Ave. and Grant St., built 1855	new bldg. same site 1897	P.S. 15; 1897 bldg. still used
Stapleton	Broad St., built 1855, additions 1876, 1885	same site, new bldg. 1896; old P.S. 14, demolished 1962	P.S. 14, 100 Tompkins Ave., built 1950
Garretsons (Dongan Hills)	east side Rich. Rd. foot Four Corners Rd.	new bldg. on Jefferson Ave.	P.S. 11 on site of 1898 bldg.; new bldg. 1921; addition 1931
Egbertville	Manor Rd., about 1/2 mile north of Rockland Ave., built 1872	converted to residence, destroyed by fire	P.S. 10 and 28
Egbertville	not shown	Richmond Rd. and Rockland Ave. built 1894	P.S. 10, 1894 bldg. still used

Children now attending school in the buildings that were erected before 1898 might be led to an appreciation of some of the architectural features of these edifices which differ so greatly from the schools of today. Particularly interesting are the facades of these buildings with their ornamentation and the tablets on both the exterior and interior.*

Bayles states that there were 7,289 students in the 28 public schools on Staten Island in 1886 and a faculty of 125. The largest of these schools was Middletown's District School No. 2 on Broad Street, Stapleton with an enrollment of 1,284 pupils. There were about 1,000 additional pupils in private schools (4).

Several private schools were organized before consolidation when wealthy families lived on Staten Island. Among them was Professor Anton G. Methfessel's School on Van Duzer Street, Stapleton. The Methfessel Institute (later known as the Edgewater Institute) specialized in the teaching of foreign languages (33). St. Austin's Episcopal School for boys was established in 1883 in the Garner House* (now part of St. Vincent's Hospital) at the corner of Bard and Castleton Avenues, continuing until about 1898 when it moved to Connecticut. St. Austin's Place nearby is a reminder of this school. In 1883 the Brighton Heights Seminary for Girls opened on St. Mark's Place (opposite the Brighton Heights Reformed Church).

The Staten Island Academy and Latin School was established in 1884 in the building on Van Duzer Street which had been used previoulsy by Professor Methfessel's School. The Professor was the first President of the Board of Trustees of the new Academy. The school provided instruction from kindergarten through high school. A new building was opened in 1896 at the corner of Stuyvesant Place and Wall Street, St. George, which is used now for the Upper School.* The Lower School is located on Todt Hill Road, Dongan Hills in what was formerly the Stettinius Mansion,* now known as Dongan Hall.

Another private school was that of Professor John M. Hawkins located at Clinton and Prospect Avenues, on the estate of Nicholas Muller.* Later this became the home of the old Arden School, and then was used by the Staten Island Division of Manhattan College. St. Peter's Senior High School for boys now occupies this property. There was also a school operated by a Professor Koch on Grant Street, Tompkinsville (33).

In 1895 the Westerleigh Collegiate Institute, accommodating 200 pupils, was established on a site now bounded by New York Place, College Avenue and Maine Avenue (46). The first headmaster was Reverend Doctor Charles R. Kingsley after whom Kingsley Avenue was named. The Institute had an excellent scholastic standing and attracted students from great distances. Both academic and commercial courses were offered. A fire in 1903 completely destroyed the building in Westerleigh. Thereafter classes were held for several years at the Staten Island Club House on Richmond Terrace in New Brighton and later in the Pavilion Hotel nearby. The school was discontinued about 1913.

Mrs. Anna Harriet Leonowens, who had been governess to the children at the Court of Siam, also had a private school for young children on Richmond Terrace and Tompkins Place, West New Brighton.

Three Catholic Churches operated parochial schools during this period. They included St. Peter's, New Brighton, and St. Mary's in Rosebank, both established in 1853, and St. Rose of Lima, West New Brighton (now the Sacred Heart School), organized in 1876. St. John's Lutheran also had a church-affiliated school.

TRANSPORTATION

The chief problem during the period following the Civil War was inadequate transportation facilities. Ferry service was poor and sometimes even hazardous. The *Westfield* exploded at the Whitehall Street slip in 1871, resulting in more than fifty deaths and 200 serious injuries (34). Service on Staten Island itself was limited also.

STAGECOACHES

Horse-drawn stages continued to serve the interior localities on the Island, one operating into the early 1900s between Port Richmond and Linoleumville (Travis). Other stagecoach routes were between Vanderbilt's Landing (Clifton), and Castleton Corners; between New Dorp and Greenridge through Richmondtown; between Huguenot and Rossville; between Port Richmond and Richmondtown; from West New Brighton railroad station to Castleton Corners and from Columbia Street (Clove Road) and Richmond Terrace to Mariners Harbor (51). People walked great distances to reach means of transportation.

The wealthier families had their private carriages. It must have been a picturesque scene at the ferry terminal to see these well-kept horse-drawn vehicles awaiting the return of the ladies and gentlemen from Manhattan. Reminders of that day are stone blocks or stepping-stones used for alighting from carriages,* and hitching posts which are found today in some neighborhoods. The Historical Museum owns a collection of horse-drawn vehicles that are shown and used for special occasions and will at some future time be on permanent exhibition in Richmondtown.

ROADS

Staten Island roads prior to 1890 were among the worst in the State (33). Most of them were narrow dirt or clay roads with the exception of a few like Richmond Terrace and Richmond Turnpike (Victory Boulevard) and some privately owned streets which were in better condition (76). Broken stone and water-bound macadam were used in attempts to improve road conditions. By 1894 it was reported that the county had 30 miles of macadam. This attracted many bicyclists.

In the section on *Roads* during the Federal Period, a toll bridge over Fresh Kills was mentioned. This gradually deteriorated until it was unsafe and the County Supervisors contracted for a new bridge that opened in 1896. The opening celebration at which the Mount Loretto band played is described in an article in *The Staten Island Historian* (63).

HORSECARS

Horsecars first appeared on the streets of Manhattan in 1832, but it was not until 1867 that the Staten Island Horse Railroad Company began operation, carrying passengers along the shore from Vanderbilt's Landing to Fort Wadsworth. At first the ties were made of light pine placed a few inches into the ground, spiked with thin rails. Later the rails were laid on heavy beams that rested on cross-ties (51). Gradually lines were extended to Tompkinsville, to Port Richmond, and finally to Holland Hook,† Mariners Harbor to connect with the new Elizabeth Ferry. The carfare was ten cents until the competition of the North Shore Railroad from Elm Park to Clifton reduced it to five cents. These horse-drawn vehicles operated on single tracks, with passing switches at intervals. There were several changes in ownership because of mismanagement and insufficient revenue. By 1887 the Staten Island Belt Line Railroad Company has assumed control and made extensive improvements including installation of stoves in the cars which had been unheated until that time (51).

Passengers changed from the East Shore to the North Shore Line at a junction in Tompkinsville near Arietta Street (Victory Boulevard) and Minthorne Street, where the stables and car barns were located. The East Shore Trolley ran along the shore from Ft. Wadsworth to Tompkinsville along New York Avenue (now Bay Street) and the North Shore Line went up Arietta Street and Richmond Turnpike to Brook Street, down through Jersey Street and along Richmond Terrace to Bodine's Creek at the foot of Columbia Street (Clove Road) (25). Trolleys ran on an hourly schedule. During the winter when the tracks were covered with snow, sleighs were hitched to the horses to render service.

---

† Name traced to a Henry Holland. Sometimes incorrectly spelled as Howland Hook.

The Richmond County Railroad Company, organized in 1885, operated a horsecar line from the Stapleton Ferry Landing, through Stapleton to Richmond Road, thence to Foley's Grove,* later called Robin Hood Park, Concord (25). Another route was from West Brighton Ferry Landing up Broadway to Castleton Avenue, to Columbia Street, along Manor Road to Eckstein's Brewery (building still standing opposite Todt Hill Houses) (67). These two routes were sold to the Staten Island Midland Railroad in 1890, which gradually extended service from St. George to the County Courthouse in Richmondtown. A branch of this line went through Clove Road to Port Richmond, and another from Grant City to Midland Beach. This trolley railroad became electrified in 1895 and was reorganized as the Midland Electric Railroad Company (51). Car barns were erected at Richmond and Clove Roads, Concord. It is interesting to note that the routes of the old horsecar lines are for the most part the routes of the Transit Authority buses on the Island today.

ELECTRIC TROLLEYS*

The first electric trolley car, with overhead wires and a long flexible arm on the roof contacting the circuit, started operation in 1893 from Bergen Point Ferry, Port Richmond, along Richmond Terrace to Jewett Avenue, along Jewett Avenue to Prohibition Park (now Westerleigh). Ownership of this line changed several times. Later it was taken over by the Midland Electric Railroad Company (52).

In 1895 the Staten Island Electric Railroad Company took over the route of the horsecars from Mariners Harbor to Clifton and gradually extended the following routes: from Ft. Wadsworth to South Beach; up Castleton Avenue to Clove Road, down to Richmond Terrace; along Richmond Terrace from Brook Street to Clove Road, Sunnyside; from Port Richmond to Bulls Head; to Holland Hook connecting with a scheduled ferry service to Elizabethport; from St. George through Tompkinsville to West New Brighton over the route followed by the Staten Island Belt Line Railroad Company (54). A repair shop was built on Brook Street in 1895 for the electric cars. This building is now used by the Sanitation Department.*

FERRIES

The ferries from Manhattan stopped at Tompkinsville, Stapleton, and Clifton (Vanderbilt's Landing) until 1886 at which time St. George became the terminus for both the ferries and the railroad. The ferries of that period were double-ended side-wheelers with an enclosed cabin on the main deck and an open deck above. They were named for the townships – *Northfield, Southfield, Westfield, Middletown.*

Ferries also ran from landings on the North Shore at Elm Park, Port Richmond, West Brighton, Snug Harbor, and New Brighton to Whitehall Street, Manhattan, until the St. George terminal was constructed. Fare was ten cents and ferries ran hourly from 6:30 A.M. to 7:30 P.M. making the ten-mile trip in one hour.

In 1867 the Staten Island Railroad Company began operating a ferry between Perth Amboy and Tottenville. The sidewheeler *Maid of Perth,* placed in service that year, operated until 1905 when it was scrapped (53).

Several other ferries also operated during this period. A steam ferry between Port Richmond and Bergen Point, New Jersey, began service in 1876, continuing until 1945 under several different owners. At that time the steam ferries were replaced by diesel-propelled ferries which remained in operation until the line closed in 1961. Thus ended a ferry service that dated back to the 17th century and throughout the years had employed all kinds of vessels.

Staten Island Ferry Terminal at Manhattan

Steam ferry* service also existed between the Island and Elizabethpoint, New Jersey, from 1896 until 1932. At that time diesel ferries were introduced, operating until 1961 when this line also ceased operation.

Ferries crossed between St. George and Brooklyn during this period. The St. George to 69th Street, Brooklyn line continues in operation today.

The Blazing Star Ferry from Travis to Carteret, New Jersey, had ceased running in 1836. However, a launch service was inaugurated about 1873 to serve the needs of the employees of the American Linoleum Company who lived in New Jersey.

RAILROAD

The steam railroad had been in operation from 1860 between Vanderbilt's Landing (Clifton) and Tottenville, a distance of 13 miles. In 1880 the Staten Island Rapid Transit Railway Company, newly organized subsidiary of the Baltimore and Ohio Railroad, gained control of both the railroad and the Manhattan ferry (previously operated by the Staten Island Railroad Company). The tracks were extended from Clifton to Tompkinsville in 1884. Part of the new route was on a trestle over the water which at that time came as far as Bay Street. Since then the land has been filled in. Finally, a tunnel was constructed under the grounds of the Lighthouse Department (present Coast Guard Base), and the tracks completed to St. George in 1886, making this the terminus of all transportation routes. A new ferry terminal with two large slips was constructed in that year at the foot of Hamilton Avenue, and a terminal was completed at Whitehall Street, Manhattan, three years later. A North Shore Route opened between St. George and Arlington in 1887 and a line to South Beach was completed in 1892 (11).

A railroad bridge across the Arthur Kill from Holland Hook to Elizabeth was completed in 1889. This was the first connecting link between the Island and the mainland, making it possible to transport coal and freight directly from New Jersey to the railroad yards in St. George. In 1959 this bridge was replaced by the longest vertical lift railroad bridge in the world.

PERSONALITIES

ERASTUS WIMAN*

Transportation on Staten Island improved during the 1880s largely through the efforts of Erastus Wiman (1834-1904) who envisioned the great future growth of the Island. A Canadian by birth, Wiman came to Manhattan to manage a commercial agency and soon made Staten Island his home. He was a businessman and a promoter who allied himself with William Pendleton, manager of the North Shore Ferry and Robert Garrett, President of the B & O Railroad. Wiman became vice-president of the Staten Island Rapid Transit Company and also president of the Staten Island Telephone Exchange Company.

He secured control of Vanderbilt's "country road" railway line between Clifton and Tottenville, the East Shore Ferry and the North Shore ferries. Then he decided upon one terminus for all these facilities at a point nearest to Manhattan, naming the locality St. George, after George Law, prominent engineer who lived on Grymes Hill (26). It was Wiman who persuaded the Government to allow the railroad tunnel to be built under the Lighthouse Maintenance Depot. He also extended the North Shore Railroad route to Elm Park and the line to South Beach which paved the way for a new resort there. Wiman is credited with the idea of connecting Staten Island to New Jersey by means of the railroad bridge which became a reality in 1889.

To encourage people to come to the Island and to use the transportation facilities he had provided, Wiman organized the Staten Island Amusement Company, of which he was president (75). He erected a large three-story casino with a seating capacity of 5,000 at a cost of $35,000 at the St. George waterfront on the site of the present B & O freight yards. There he built a giant illuminated fountain powered by a central electric generator and presented spectacular productions such as the *Fall of Babylon* (38). He engaged Cappa's Seventh Regiment Band to entertain the visitors. During the day the Metropolitan Baseball Club (later the New York Giants) and a Canadian lacrosse team played at this St. George amusement area.

To Erastina* (now Mariners Harbor), Wiman brought Buffalo Bill and his Wild West Show in 1886 which attracted thousands of people to the Island (12). Annie Oakley, the sharpshooter, the Indian braves and squaws and all the animals in the show disembarked at a Stapleton dock and proceeded to Erastina. Staten Islanders were astonished at the sight and filled the grandstands which seated 10,000. Wiman had arranged parking space for 2,000 carriages. An article in *The Staten Island Historian* describes this venture and states that an estimated "two million visited the show" (64).

Wiman's spectaculars were short-lived, however, and he lost money – his own and that belonging to others. The Edison Illuminating Company (of which Wiman was a director) purchased his electric generators in 1887 and provided the first electric street lighting on the Island. In the following year Wiman tried to revive his show, renaming it *The Fall of Rome*, adding more girls and a herd of elephants, but this, too, lost money (67).

Erastus Wiman owned several homes on Staten Island. One was at 287 St. Mark's Place, opposite McKee Vocational and Technical High School. This large mansion later became the Staten Island Club and more recently was used as the Elks Club until 1959 at which time the Elks purchased the Bowne Mansion* in Greenridge. The old building was demolished in 1963. Wiman's summer home was in Great Kills. The present Meadowbrook Inn on Russell and Wiman Avenues (with an entrance on Hylan Boulevard) is built around this old house.* Wiman also owned the Woods of Arden House where Frederick Olmsted had lived between 1848 and 1860, as mentioned previously, and where Dr. William C. Anderson, physician at Smith's Infirmary grew unusual vegetables in the late 1860s for patients' diets. Wiman opened this mansion as Arden Inn and gave theatrical performances on the beautifully landscaped grounds. In 1893 Wiman wrote a book entitled *Chances of Success*. Unfortunately he did not live to see many of his dreams of Staten Island's inevitable development materialize, for he was indeed a man "ahead of his time." Erastine Place, Mariners Harbor, Wiman Place, Rosebank and Wiman Avenue, Great Kills were named in his memory.

WILLIAM H. VANDERBILT

Reference was made to William H. Vanderbilt (1821-1885), son of Commodore Cornelius Vanderbilt, in the chapter on the Federal Period. Some evidences of the Vanderbilt Farm remained until the early decades of the twentieth century, including the house, the stables, the tower, and the dock. This property on New Dorp Lane, southeast of Hylan Boulevard, is now occupied by the U.S. Government. It was on this farm that the children of William H. Vanderbilt were born. They attended school in the little schoolhouse on Mill Road with the children of the Tysen, Lake, Guyon, and Johnson families (44). The name of William H. Vanderbilt is linked with ferry and railroad transportation on the Island after the Civil War. After the Commodore's death in 1877, this eldest son, William, became president of the New York Central Railroad and held controlling interests in other railroads in the United States and Canada. He built an elegant mansion on Fifth Avenue at Fifty-first Street, Manhattan. Some of the Vanderbilts on Staten Island today trace their ancestry back to this family. The name is remembered by associations reported elsewhere and in the name of P.S. 14, Richmond, officially designated as *The Vanderbilt.*

WILLIAM WINTER

After the Civil War, literary figures continued to be part of the local citizenry. George William Curtis, mentioned under the Federal Period, actively participated in community affairs until his death in 1892. A close friend of Curtis was William Winter* (1836-1917), poet, essayist, and dramatic critic on the *New York Tribune,* who came to the Island in 1879. Many of the literary greats such as Henry Wadsworth Longfellow, Oliver Wendell Holmes, and Thomas Bailey Aldrich visited the Winter home, as did famous actors and actresses, such as Edwin Booth, Joseph Jefferson, Ellen Terry, Richard Mansfield, Helena Mojeska, Julia Marlowe and producer-managers Augustin Daly and David Belasco (21). The Winter family lived at 17 Third Avenue (now 146 Winter Avenue) in the Fort Hill section of the Island in a house that still stands. The name of William Winter is kept alive by the Arthur Winter Memorial Library at the Staten Island Academy, St. George, which he gave in memory of his son who was killed in a sledding accident on Staten Island in 1887, and by the name of Winter Avenue. Among William Winter's published books are *Shakespeare on the Stage,* in three volumes, and *Life and Art of Richard Mansfield* (77).

BILL NYE

Edgar Wilson Nye, known as Bill Nye (1850-1896), was a famous humorist and lecturer who lived in a large residence on Third Avenue (now Winter Avenue), New Brighton in the 1880s. He wrote several humorous books, including *The Comic History of the United States,* containing cartoons. Nye was also a columnist on the *Staten Island Advance* (21).

NATURALISTS – WILLIAM T. DAVIS AND OTHERS

Staten Island has been the home of several noted naturalists and scientists. Perhaps the most famous of these was William T. Davis who was born in 1862 at the home of his grandfather, John C. Thompson. The Thompson property was bounded by Hyatt Street, Tompkins Avenue (now St. Mark's Place) and Stuyvesant Place, St. George. At an early age William T. Davis* moved to 146 Stuyvesant Place near the corner of Hyatt Street. His interest in nature was deepened by the influence of men like Augustus Radcliffe Grote, naturalist; Arthur Hollick and Dr. Nathaniel Lord Britton,‡ noted botanists; and John J. Crooke, naturalist and mining engineer, whose name is remembered by Crooke's Point, Great Kills Beach.

When only seventeen, Davis met Charles W. Leng, who shared his interest in entomology. Both of these men became students of local history and in 1930 published a four-volume history, *Staten Island and Its People*, which is considered the most authoritative complete history of the Island. Three years later a fifth volume appeared (33, 34, 35, 36, 37).

In 1881, Hollick, Davis, Britton, Leng, Edward C. Delevan, Jr., and nine others formed the "Natural Science Association of Staten Island." The following year they housed their collection in the Village Hall* at Lafayette and Fillmore Streets, New Brighton, with Davis as the curator. This was the beginning of the Staten Island Institute of Arts and Sciences (47). In 1905 the Public Museum was moved to the top floor of Borough Hall. Later it was quartered in the Norvell House at the corner of Hyatt Street and Stuyvesant Place where the Children's Program of Lectures was started.

Finally the present Museum Building was opened in 1918 and nine years later a second floor and attic were added. Many of Davis' carefully arranged collections are housed in the attic where he had worked on them. Davis' scrapbooks and *Natural History Notes* in longhand are in possession of the Institute (20).

‡ In 1879 Britton and Hollick published *The Flora of Richmond County.*

William T. Davis became recognized as an international authority on the cicada known as the 17-year locust which most recently emerged in May 1962. He wrote many treatises on natural science subjects. His little volume, *Days Afield on Staten Island*, first published in 1892, records his impressions and findings during his nature walks around the Staten Island countryside, often with Charles W. Leng or with Louis P. Gratacap (14).

Davis influenced many young Staten Island men to follow careers in natural science. Among the "Davis boys," as they were called, were Alanson Skinner (1886-1925) who became a world-known American Indian archeologist; Carol Stryker, first curator of the Staten Island Zoo; James Paul Chapin, famous ornithologist and Congo explorer; and Howard Cleaves, wild animal photographer and lecturer. The latter two are still very active in their chosen fields.

The name of William T. Davis will not be forgotten. The Wildlife Refuge in New Springville perpetuates his name.* Public lectures on natural science subjects are given several times a year as Davis Memorial Lectures, utilizing a fund he left to the Staten Island Insitute of Arts and Sciences at his death in 1945. He also bequeathed property to the Institute and to the Historical Society. When Davis was president of the Staten Island Historical Society in 1930 he paid off the mortgage on the Billiou-Stillwell-Perine House, now owned by the Society. The new P.S. 31, Richmond, built to replace P.S. 17, will be named the William T. Davis School. An excellent biography of Mr. Davis has been written by Mabel Abbott, Staten Island author (1).

One of the naturalists who influenced William T. Davis was Augustus Radcliffe Grote (1841-1903) who was also a poet and composer. As a child, he lived on Rockland Avenue, near Manor Road. Later he became director of the Museum of the Buffalo Society of Natural History but returned to Staten Island about 1880, living near Franklin Avenue, New Brighton (34).

Another naturalist who affected the growth of the Staten Island Institute was Louis Pope Gratacap (1851-1917) who resided on Pelton Avenue. He was the author of several scientific books, a skilled photographer and a geologist. He became Curator of Mineralogy and Conchology at the American Museum of Natural History and supervisor of the Morgan Collection of gems (2).

HISTORIANS

John J. Clute was one of the first historians on Staten Island to publish a book as the result of his research. He wrote for Staten Island newspapers and then published the *North Shore Advocate*. He was also a justice of the peace and a surveyor, laying out many of the streets in Factoryville (West New Brighton), Concord, and Grant City. His history, *Annals of Staten Island From Its Discovery to the Present Time*, was published in 1877.

Ten years later, another local historian, Richard M. Bayles, published a larger volume than his predecessor's, *History of Richmond County (Staten Island) New York: From its Discovery to the Present Time* (4).

Ira K. Morris (1847-1921) was the author of a two-volume *Memorial History of Staten Island* which appeared in 1898 (44).

ARTISTS

Of the artists who lived on Staten Island during the period following the Civil War, the best known was the landscape painter, Frederick W. Kost (1861-1923). He resided on the Island between 1867 and 1900. His father was the proprietor of Richmond County Hall and later operated the German Club Rooms. Kost was educated in Commissioner Boehm's school in Greenridge, the Methfessel Institute, Cooper Union, and the Academy of Design, where he was influenced by George Inness. In the 1880s he studied in Europe (32).

MUSICIANS

Max Maretzek (1821-1897), famous operatic manager and conductor lived in Pleasant Plains from about 1850 until his death in 1897. He devoted his life to bringing the best opera to America. At his home he entertained many notables (30). Maretzek Court, near St. Louis Academy, is named after him.

Madame Bernice De Pasquali (Dolly James), who became a Metropolitan opera star, lived on Bay Avenue and Richmond Terrace. As a young girl, she attended the Mariners Harbor public school and sang in the choir of St. Mary's Church, Port Richmond, in the 1890s. Madame De Pasquali toured Europe, Canada, other foreign countries and finally sang at the Metropolitan Opera House in New York in 1909 – the first American-born and American-trained singer to achieve that honor (21). At one time she sang opposite the famous Enrico Caruso.

OTHERS

It was during this period of time that General William Green Ward and his wife were entertaining at their beautiful mansion, "Oneata,"* which has been referred to previously. This large residence on Grymes Hill with its fine woodwork and large French doors that open on the long porches is a reminder of the Civil War General. Among the well-known visitors to the General Ward Estate was General Ulysses S. Grant, who at one time considered retiring to Staten Island. The Garner House,* now part of St. Vincent's Hospital, was selected as a possibility. Unfortunately, Mrs. Grant came to visit on a damp day in 1876 when the mosquitoes infested the area, and she decided against living on the Island (21).

Staten Island became the home of Thomas Jefferson Griffin (1834-1867), a naval engineer who supervised the construction of iron-clad steamers such as the *Monitor* during the Civil War Period, working under Captain John Ericsson, the Swedish inventor of the "iron-clad" (37). Griffin lived on Castleton Avenue between Dongan Street and Clove Road, West New Brighton, near the old home of Governor Thomas Dongan. During his few years on Staten Island (1865-1867), Griffin was active in the community. He died of yellow fever in Panama while working for the Peruvian Petroleum Company (13).

The Faber Brothers, John Eberhard and Lothar W., of the Eberhard Faber Pencil Manufacturing Company, lived for many years along the Shore Road (Richmond Terrace) in Port Richmond, near the site of the present Parks Department Faber Pool. Faber Street is also reminiscent of the family (34).

Ward House (now part of Wagner College)

150

The great Shakespearean tragedian, Thomas W. Keene, resided in the remodeled Bodine Inn (built in 1770) at the corner of Manor Road and Richmond Turnpike (Victory Boulevard). He died at Smith's Infirmary (Staten Island Hospital) in 1898 (21).

Many other people who were part of the Staten Island scene between 1865 and 1898 have been mentioned in other parts of this chapter. No attempt has been made to compile a complete list. Rather, representatives from various walks of life have been noted.

CONSOLIDATION

There had been a movement toward consolidation of various sections in the New York area as early as 1868 (33). Finally, in 1889, Andrew H. Green presented to the State Legislature a bill providing for a commission to consider the values of consolidation. David J. Tysen urged Green to include Staten Island in the plan. The commission that became duly appointed presented to the Legislature a bill which called for submitting the question of consolidation to the voters (41). At a general election, the majority voted for consolidation. The bill creating Greater New York with its five boroughs was finally passed by the State Legislature in 1896. A charter, drafted by a committee on which George M. Pinney, Jr., represented the Island, was submitted to the State Legislature in February 1897. At the first election under the new charter, in November 1897, George Cromwell, Republican, became the first president of the Borough of Richmond, taking office on January 1, 1898.

Thus all village and town governments were abolished and Staten Island became part of the City of New York. The five townships of Castleton, Middletown, Northfield, Southfield, and Westfield were designated as Wards 1 to 5 in that order. These Wards remain today as our political divisions for election purposes. The general area encompassed within each township is shown below:

1. Castleton – New Brighton, Factoryville (West New Brighton), Elliottville (Livingston), Centreville (Four Corners)
2. Middletown – Tompkinsville, Stapleton, Egbertville, Todt Hill, Emerson Hill, Grymes Hill (south side Victory Boulevard)
3. Northfield – Port Richmond, Mariners Harbor, Graniteville,

Chelsea, Long Neck (Travis), New Springville

4. Southfield – Clifton, Rosebank, New Dorp, Richmond, Giffords (Great Kills), Concord, Seaside (Eltingville) (southeast side of Richmond Road and Amboy Road to Harold Avenue, Annadale)

5. Westfield – Tottenville, Kreischerville (Charleston), Rossville, Richmond Valley, Pleasant Plains, Annadale, Bloomingview (Huguenot), Fresh Kills (Greenridge)

The view of the Island as seen from the ferry about the year 1898 has been described by a local historian as one of wooded hills and fine residences with the steeple of the old Reformed Church, the Hotel Castleton and the towers of the Smith Infirmary (now Staten Island Hospital) marking the skyline (69).

The 20th century was to bring a change to the Island under consolidation. The next chapter will trace the many developments which have taken place. The wooded hills and fine residences around the St. George area have disappeared. The large hotels have been demolished. The towers of the Staten Island Hospital have been obscured completely by tall buildings. Only the steeple of the Brighton Heights Reformed Church stands out as it did in 1898, but now brightly illuminated at night, as though proudly proclaiming its heritage.

BIBLIOGRAPHY

1. ABBOTT, MABEL. *Life of William T. Davis.* Ithaca, N.Y.: Cornell University Press, 1949. P. 321.
2. ——. "Our Literary Soil." *The News Bulletin.* Staten Island Institute of Arts and Sciences, 11:104-107, May 1962.
3. *Art Work of Staten Island* (published in twelve parts). Chicago, Ill.: W. H. Parish Publishing Co., 1894.
4. BAYLES, RICHARD, ED. *History of Richmond County (Staten Island) New York: From Its Discovery to the Present Time.* New York: L. E. Preston and Co., 1887. P. 319-325, 333-338, 342-348, 400-401, 403-404, 420-423, 427-428, 432-444, 449-468, 500-502, 586-606, 611-613, 647-650, 660-677, 686-693, 709-718, 722-741.
5. BEATTY, LUCY A. "Recollections: Effingham." *The Staten Island Historian,* XVII:1-2, January-March 1956.
6. "Big League Games Here." *Staten Island Advance,** 75:C2, March 25, 1961.
7. BOWDEN, DR. JOHN N. "Shipping Firms Supported Marine Hospital." *Staten Island Advance,** 75:D16, March 25, 1961.
8. BRINLEY, C. COAPES. "Charles W. Hunt, Pioneer Industrialist." *The Staten Island Historian,* XVII:2-5, January-March 1956.
9. ——. "Staten Island, the Home of American Lawn Tennis." *The Staten Island Historian,* XV:9-

10, April-June, 1954.

10. BRITTAIN, PHILIP J. "Firemen Literally Ran to Fires 75 Years Ago." *Staten Island Advance,** 75:E2, March 25, 1961.

11. BUCK, WILLIAM J. "The Staten Island Rapid Transit Railway Company." *Tercentenary Booklet.* Staten Island Tercentenary Commission, 1961. P. 27

12. "Buffalo Bill Show Drew Over Million Visitors," *Staten Island Advance,** 75:E6, March 25, 1961.

13. DALE, IDA D. "Thomas Jefferson Griffin: Superintendent of Iron Clads." *The Staten Island Historian,* XI:25-28, October-December 1950.

14. DAVIS, WILLIAM T. *Days Afield on Staten Island.* 2d. ed. Lancaster, Pa.: Science Press Printing Co., 1937. P. 122.

15. EGBERT, GEORGE L. "The Early Decades." *The Staten Island Historian,* XIV:27-31. October-December 1953.

16. ENDRESS, ERWIN. "Few Went to High School in Simpler Days of 1886." *Staten Island Advance,** 75:A6, March 25, 1961.

17. FINGADO, RAYMOND C. "Photography on Staten Island." *The Staten Island Historian,* 1:2-6, January 1940.

18. FINK, RABBI LEON, and EHRLICH, MAXWELL. "They Paved Way for Synagogues." *Staten Island Advance,** 75:E6, March 25, 1961.

19. FUNK, CHARLES EARLE. "Prohibition Park, Staten Island." *The Staten Island Historian,* XIII:17-24, July-September 1952.

20. GASTEYER, CARLIN. "Highlights of the Institute's History." *The News Bulletin.* Staten Island Institute of Arts and Sciences, 11:45-47, December 1961. 11:56-58, January 1962.

21. HAMPTON, VERNON B. *Staten Island's Claim to Fame.* Staten Island, N.Y.: Richmond Boro Publishing and Printing Co., 1925. P. 72, 76-78, 144, 147, 154-160.

22. HANKINSON, FRANK, and HAMPTON, VERNON B. *The History of Staten Island Public Schools.* Staten Island, N.Y.: Staten Island Teachers' Association. 1942. P. 7-9. (Mimeographed)

23. HOGBEN, MAURICE DENZIL. "Public Secondary Education in U.S.: A Perspective. (Staten Island in the Eighties and Nineties. II From High School Departments to High Schools, 1881-1904)." *The Staten Island Historian,* XXI:1-12, January-March 1960.

24. HOLLE, DR. HENRY A. "On Guard Against Disease." *Staten Island Advance,** 75:D-12, March 25, 1961.

25. "Horsecar Lines Had Problems." *Staten Island Advance,** 75:E8, March 25, 1961.

26. "How Did St. George Get Its Name?" *Staten Island Advance,** 75:D14, March 25, 1961.

27. HUBACH, REV. FRED. G. "Let's See If You Can Find Your Church in '86." *Staten Island Advance,** 75:D14, March 25, 1961.

28. "Hunt's Plant Known Worldwide." *Staten Island Advance,** 75:A13, March 25, 1961.

29. "Island Boasted 2 Dyeing Plants." *Staten Island Advance,** 75:E10, March 25, 1961.

30. JACOBSEN, ANITA K. "Max Maretzek, Staten Islander." *The Staten Island Historian,* V:17-18, 23-24, July-September 1942.

31. JESSUP, MARGUERITE C. "Growing Up In Richmondtown." *The Staten Island Historian,* XII:17-19, 22-23, July-September 1951.

32. LEASON, JEAN. "Frederick W. Kost, Staten Island Artist." *Proceedings of the Staten Island Institute of Arts and Sciences,* XI: 50-55, January 1949.

33. LENG, CHARLES W., and DAVIS, WILLIAM T. *Staten Island and Its People.* Vol. I. New York: Lewis Historical Publishing Co., Inc., 1930. P. 250, 301-335, 439-499, 505-508, 515, 517-520.

34. ———. *Staten Island and Its People.* Vol. II. New York: Lewis Historical Publishing Co., Inc. 1930. P. 578-579, 617-637, 668-672, 761-764, 777-779, 802-806, 820-834, 857, 873, 896, 977.

35. ———. *Staten Island and Its People.* Vol. III. New York: Lewis Historical Publishing Co., Inc. 1930. P. 9-10, 18-20, 119-120, 174-178, 188-189. 193-195.

36. ———. *Staten Island and Its People.* Vol. IV. New York: Lewis Historical Publishing Co., Inc.,

1930. P. 392-393, 466-472, 474-475, 477-485.

37. ———. *Staten Island and Its People.* Vol. V. New York: Lewis Historical Publishing Co., Inc., 1933. P. 89-91, 120, 284-287.

38. "Lighted Fountain Highlight of Vast Amusement Center." *Staten Island Advance,* 75:C6, March 25, 1961.

39. "Linoleum Plant Bloomed in Travis 75 Years Ago." *Staten Island Advance,* 75:E12, March 25, 1961.

40. McMILLEN, LORING. "Great Teams Fielded by S.I.A.C." *Staten Island Advance,* 75:C2, March 25, 1961.

41. ———. "Villages, Towns of Old Island." *Staten Island Advance,* 10B, April 26, 1952.

42. MEADE, PATRICK H. "Eighteen Seventy-two Schoolboy." *The Staten Island Historian,* XVI:20-21, July-September 1955.

43. MORRIS, CHARLES V. "Athletes and Athletics – Staten Island's Claim to Fame." *Tercentenary Booklet.* Staten Island, N.Y.: Staten Island Tercentenary Commission, 1961. P. 42-46.

44. MORRIS, IRA K. *Memorial History of Staten Island,* Vol. II, New York: Memorial Publishing Co., 1898. P. 134-140, 191, 193-196, 200, 208-209, 221-223, 235-237, 254-258, 338, 358-360, 367-374, 429-430, 440-446, 461-467, 471-475, 482-487.

45. NICHOLS, CAPTAIN FRED F. "They Lighted the Lamps with Oil." *Staten Island Advance,* 75:D19, March 25, 1961.

46. POLLOCK, JOHN, JR. *Our Heritage.* Westerleigh, Staten Island, N.Y.: Immanuel Union Church, 1960. 46 p. (Mimeographed)

47. POWELL, MILDRED S. "It Was 'Bugs Davis Society' in '86." *Staten Island Advance,* 75:B14, March 25, 1961.

48. REED, HERBERT B. "Bikes, Bloomers, and Boulevards." *The Staten Island Historian,* XXXII: 17-19, July-September 1961.

49. ———. "Communications on Staten Island." *The Staten Island Historian,* XVI:14-15, April-June 1955.

50. ———. "Electric Industry on Staten Island." *The Staten Island Historian,* XV: 15-16, April-June 1954. XV: 20-21, July-September 1954.

51. ———. "Staten Island Horsecars and Their Successors, Trolleys." *The Staten Island Historian,* XIV:1-4, January-March 1953, XIV: 12-14, April-June 1953, XIV:17-18, July-September 1953.

52. ———. "Staten Island's Trolley Railways." *The Staten Island Historian,* XV:25-28, October-December 1954, XVI: 5-7, January-March 1955.

53. ———. "The Tottenville-Perth Amboy Ferry." *The Staten Island Historian,* XXI:33-34, October-December 1960.

54. REIFSCHNEIDER, FELIX E. "Staten Island Trolleys." *The Staten Island Historian,* XXI: 6-8, January-March 1951.

55. REYCRAFT, JACK. "Old Ultramarine Works a Bustling Plant Again." *Staten Island Advance,* October 2, 1947.

56. RICHMOND, JOHN P. "Yachting in Richmond County." *Tercentenary Booklet.* Staten Island, N.Y.: Staten Island Tercentenary Commission, 1961. P. 23.

57. ROBINSON, HARRY H. JR. "YMCA Active in '86." *Staten Island Advance,* 75:E6, March 25, 1961.

58. SAFFORD, RAYMOND. "Iron Mining on Staten Island." *The Staten Island Historian,* II:10-11, 14-15, April 1939.

59. SANTORO, DANIEL, and RALLO, JOHN A. *Italians – Past and Present.* Staten Island, N.Y.: Staten Island Italian Historical Society, 1955. P. 40-47.

60. SHAKESHAFT, HAROLD I. "Advance Saw Electricity Come to Island." *Staten Island Advance,* 75:D13, March 25, 1961.

61. SHERIDAN, GEORGE, as told to Helen J. Adams. "New Brighton: A Recollection." *Staten Island*

*Advance,** 75:B6, March 25, 1961.

62. SMITH, DOROTHY. "Ice-Harvesting on Staten Island." *The Staten Island Historian,* I:17-18, 20, 23, July 1938.

63. STEINMEYER, HENRY G. "Bridge Celebration, 1896." *The Staten Island Historian,* X:1-4, January-March 1949.

64. ———. "Drums Along the Kill Van Kull." *The Staten Island Historian,* XII:1-3, January-March 1951.

65. ———. "Fall of a Curtain." *The Staten Island Historian,* XIII:25, 29-30, October-December 1952.

66. ———. "South Beach: The Resort Area." *The Staten Island Historian,* XIX:17-22, July-September 1958.

67. ROBINSON, HARRY H., JR. "YMCA Active in '86." *Staten Island Advance,** 75: Historical Society, 1961.P. 67-79, 125-127.

68. ———. "Too Late the Phoenix." *The Staten Island Historian,* XV:1-3, January-March 1954.

69. STODDARD, CHARLES C. "Fifty Years Ago." *Proceedings of the Staten Island Institute of Arts and Sciences,* II:1-7, October 1948.

70. TALBOT, JAMES M. "History of the S.S. White Dental Manufacturing Company." *Proceedings of the Staten Island Institute of Arts and Sciences,* XI:95-99, April 1949.

71. "Textiles Made by Irving Co." *Staten Island Advance,** 75:E-19, March 25, 1961.

72. "364 Farms on Island in 1886." *Staten Island Advance,**75:E6, March 25, 1961.

73. UHLER, W.P. "Sailing Vessels Docked at S.S. White Plant." *Staten Island Advance,** 75:B14, March 25, 1961.

74. WELSH, JOSEPH. "The Telegraph on Staten Island." *The Staten Island Historian,* II:9, 14, April 1929.

75. "Wiman: He Remade the Island." *Staten Island Advance,** 75:D13, March 25, 1961.

76. "You'd Get Lost on 1886 Roads." *Staten Island Advance,** 75:D18, March 25, 1961.

77. YOUNG, ROBERT, JR. "William Winter on Staten Island – 1879-1917." *Proceedings of the Institute of Arts and Sciences,* XVI: 40-45, Spring 1954.

CHAPTER VIII

THE COSMOPOLITAN PERIOD: SINCE 1898

THE INCORPORATION OF Richmond County into Greater New York brought many changes as the Island "emerged from a rural town and country community into a municipality" (53). Loring McMillen, Borough Historian, has named the years from 1898 to the present time the Cosmopolitan Era.

POPULATION GROWTH

In 1898 the population of the Island was concentrated in villages along the North and East Shores and in some localities in the South Shore area, a pattern which has been followed through the years. Improved transportation, attractive real estate developments and industrial growth during the twentieth century have stimulated a gradual increase in population as shown by the following table:

1898 – 65,000	1930 – 158, 346	1954 – 210,000
1900 – 67,021	1940 – 174,441	1957 – 212,000
1910 – 85,969	1945 – 184,000	1960 – 222,000
1920 – 116,531	1950 – 191,555	1962 – 234,045[1]

In 1900 the population of the Island was 1.9 percent of the total population of New York City. By 1957 the proportion had increased to 2.7 percent (16) and by 1962 to 3.1 percent.[2] Although there was a period of rapid growth between 1910 and 1930 this was surpassed by the rate of expansion established between 1957 and 1962. Further growth is anticipated after completion of the Verrazzano-Narrows Bridge* in 1964.

In 1962 the greatest density of population was in the area on the Northeast Shore (St. George, New Brighton, Tompkinsville, Stapleton, Rosebank). Next in density was the South Beach, New Dorp, Great Kills, Eltingville area, followed closely by the section around Port Richmond and

[1]Estimated by U.S. Post Office Department, St. George, October 1, 1962.
[2]Chamber of Commerce, June 5, 1962.

Mariners Harbor. The South Shore – Tottenville, Pleasant Plains, Charleston, Rossville sections – remained the least thickly populated (16).

MUNICIPAL GOVERNMENT AND SERVICES

The consolidation in 1898 brought an end to incorporated villages and county government. Staten Island was divided into the five political divisions designated as Wards. (These were identified at the end of Chapter VII.)

The office of the Borough President replaced the Board of Supervisors which had governed prior to consolidation. The first Borough President was George Cromwell who held the office from 1898 to 1913 (46). He organized the government of the borough and chose qualified citizens to assist him as commissioners of the various departments (57). Through the years that followed, the powers of the Borough Presidents were decreased gradually by several charter revisions. Under the Revised Charter of 1938 most of the appointive privileges were transferred to the Mayor who selected the commissioners for the entire city. Superintendents in each Borough Department were Civil Service appointees.

The Borough President continued to appoint the Commissioner of Borough Works until this position was eliminated under the charter revision effective January 1, 1963. The president retains the power to appoint the members of his cabinet.

BOROUGH PRESIDENTS, 1898 TO 1963
The following have served as Borough President of Richmond:

George Cromwell	Republican	1898 to 1913
Charles J. McCormack	Democrat	1914 to 1915‡
Calvin D. Van Name (91)	Democrat	1915 to 1921
Matthew J. Cahill	Democrat	1922 (Jan. to July)‡
John A. Lynch	Democrat	1922 to 1933
Joseph A. Palma	Fusion	1934 to 1945
Cornelius A. Hall	Democrat	1946 to 1953‡

| Edward G. Baker | Democrat | 1953 to 1954 |
| Albert V. Maniscalco | Democrat | 1955 to 19– |

‡Died in office.

It is not the purpose of this report to explain the structure and operation of the government of the City of New York (43, 61). Books on this subject appear in the Board of Education *List of Textbooks*.

JUDICIAL SYSTEM

For the most part, the judicial system of the Island remained as it had been before consolidation, with the offices of the county judge and surrogate, the district attorney, the county clerk, the public administrator and the commissioner of jurors. However, the courts presided over by the justices of the peace were superseded by the Court of Special Sessions, the Municipal Court and Magistrates' Court (90). In 1931 the judge-surrogate position became two separate positions (52). On September 1, 1962 a new centralized state court system went into effect as provided by an amendment to the State Constitution. Under reorganization the County Court system has been replaced by the Supreme Court which consists of a Civil Court and a Criminal Court. Newspaper articles have explained this system (12, 13, 23).

The Third County Courthouse* in Richmond (built in 1837) continued to serve the borough until 1920 when the new Greek temple style courthouse was opened in St. George. In this County Courthouse* at St. George are the Supreme Court, the new Criminal Term of the Supreme Court, the Surrogate's Court (a probate court), and the offices of the District Attorney. Until September 1, 1962 the Court of Special Sessions was housed there also. Currently it is located in the Magistrates' Courthouse in Stapleton as part of the Criminal Court.

The West New Brighton Municipal and Magistrate's Courthouse* was opened in 1929, followed a year later by a Municipal and Magistrate's Courthouse in Stapleton.* With reorganization, the two Municipal Courts merged under the title of Civil Court and are now located in West New Brighton. The Magistrate's Court and Court of Special Sessions became merged as the Criminal Court located in Stapleton.

In 1931 a new Domestic Relations Courthouse,* including Children's Court and Family Court was opened. This is now part of the statewide Family Court which handles all family matters except divorce actions and adoptions. P.S. 44, in Mariners Harbor, was named in honor of Judge Thomas Cyril Brown (1876-1938), who as the first resident justice of the Domestic Relations Court on Staten Island displayed an unusual interest in the welfare of children (46).

CIVIC CENTER AT ST. GEORGE

Borough President Cromwell planned the Civic Center at St. George, which had become the terminus for the railroad and ferry through the efforts of Erastus Wiman. This was the natural political center, Richmondtown being too distant from Manhattan. An imposing Borough Hall, facing the Ferry Terminal, was erected between 1904 and 1906. Prior to that time, the Richmond,* a building still standing at the corner of Richmond Terrace and York Avenue, New Brighton, was used as temporary headquarters by Cromwell and his staff. At that time this five-story office and apartment building was the largest on the Island.

By 1905 a new Ferry Terminal had been built with viaducts leading from Richmond Terrace. This was destroyed by fire in 1946. Five years later the present larger terminal was opened.*

Other Buildings in the St. George Area
In addition to the Borough Hall and Courthouse the following buildings have been erected in the St. George-New Brighton-Tompkinsville area:

Curtis High School – Hamilton Ave. and St. Mark's Place	–1904
St. George Library – 10 Hyatt Street	–1907
Staten Islander Building – 150 Bay Street	–1914
120th Police Precinct Building – 78 Richmond Terrace	–1917
Museum of the S.I. Institute of Arts and Sciences – 75 Stuyvesant Place	–1918
St. George Theatre Building – 25 Hyatt Street (Houses theatre and business offices)	–1928
Staten Island Medical Arts Building – 100 Central Avenue	–1931
St. George Post Office – 45 Bay Street	

(Houses a U.S. Civil Service Office, an area office of the

F.B.I. and area headquarters of U.S. Customs Bureau)   –1932

Richmond Health Center – 51 Stuyvesant Place

(Houses Health Department and Library of the Staten

Island Institute of Arts and Sciences)   –1936

Department of Welfare Building – 95 Central Avenue   –1951

Richmond Building – 350 St. Mark's Place

(In addition to business offices, houses Tax Dept. and

Department of Water Supply, Gas, and Electricity)   –1962

Staten Island Office of the N.Y. State Motor Vehicles*

Department – 450 St. Mark's Place   –1962

Other office buildings are located along Bay Street and along Richmond Terrace. In 1958 a large Municipal Parking Lot was opened on Central Avenue, St. Mark's Place, and Hyatt Street.

POLICE DEPARTMENT

Under consolidation, the Richmond County Police became part of the Police Department of New York City. In 1898 there were about 66 men on the force. In 1962 there were approximately 500 police officers on Staten Island, including superior officers, detectives and members of the Youth Squad. Special squads investigate accidents, radar teams control traffic, and Manhattan members of the narcotic squad are called upon when needed. Several mounted policemen* are assigned to the Island and their horses are stabled in Sunnyside. The 120th Precinct Building and Island Headquarters in St. George was erected in 1917 and the Tottenville 123rd Precinct Station House in 1922. The New Dorp 122nd Precinct, which had been housed in old P.S. 9 since 1934, was relocated in a new building on Hylan Boulevard between Grant City and New Dorp during the early part of 1963. In addition to the stationhouse at New Dorp, a "second building will house the emergency service squad, the accident investigation squad and garage facilities for all vehicles operating in the borough" (30).

FIRE DEPARTMENT

It was not until 1905 that the New York City Fire Department began to serve Staten Island. Modern firehouses have gradually replaced the stations of the Volunteer Fire Companies which numbered 57 in 1905. Of the 6 Volunteer Companies* still active in 1929, only 2 remained in 1963. A firehouse was opened in June 1960 on Richmond Road at Summit Avenue, New Dorp.* A building on Richmond Avenue at Lamberts Lane in Graniteville was under construction in 1963. When this is completed it is expected that the two volunteer firehouses will be closed. Fire Commissioner Edward Thompson has stated that 10 sites have been selected for construction of new facilities on Staten Island as they are needed (88). A $1.25 million Fire Communications Center* was opened on February 26, 1962 on Slosson Avenue at the edge of Clove Lakes Park. This replaced the Fire Alarm Telegraph Bureau that had been located in Borough Hall. The new building is equipped with the latest electronic and signal devices, and has a "radiation fallout-proof" sub-basement area housing emergency equipment (88). All fire alarms are received there and orders are transmitted to the Island's 16 firehouses and two volunteer companies.

SANITATION DEPARTMENT

In 1901 the New York City Department of Street Cleaning assigned two sweepers to the Borough of Richmond to clean the improved pavements. Gradually services were extended and garbage was collected. A large stable was built in 1904 on Swan Street, Tompkinsville, to house the equipment of the Street Cleaning Department. This barn, representative of the period in which it was erected, is now used by the Department of Sanitation (44).*

OTHER CITY SERVICES

Staten Island receives the same services from the various city departments as do the other four boroughs. Therefore, this report will include only those activities which relate to problems of the Island.

Soon after the consolidation, installation was started on a system of sanitary and storm sewers as a necessary health protection. This has not kept pace with population growth but it is hoped that under the new charter adequate facilities will be provided to prevent unsanitary conditions.

Early in the 1900s the waters surrounding Staten Island became polluted, but it was not until 1950 that sewage disposal plants were erected in Port

Richmond and in Oakwood. Dr. Natale Colosi, professor of bacteriology and public health at Wagner College, stated in 1962 that about 80% of the sewage entering the surrounding waters was treated compared with only 40% in 1935. Water pollution, particularly in Raritan Bay, remains a problem as hundreds of outlets discharge municipal and industrial wastes into the Bay. Treatment plants are needed at these various outlets.

Air pollution is a serious problem on Staten Island. Causes involve industries, heating equipment, incinerators, automobiles, and landfills. Committees of prominent citizens have been striving for air pollution abatement for many years. New York City has created the Department of Air Pollution Control which checks violations and approves commercial heating equipment and incinerators. Literature on the subject may be obtained from the Department at 15 Park Row, Manhattan (5). Mobile units that take air samples often track down sources of pollution.

The control of natural streams is a problem related to the post-World War II building boom. Numerous brooks, springs, and man-made lakes had provided ice and water power in the past. However, in building they often are enclosed in drain pipes of inadequate size and rerouted indiscriminately, causing flooding in some areas. After heavy rains, this condition can be observed in many localities.

INTERNATIONAL CONFLICTS

During the Cosmopolitan Era, three major wars have occurred, in addition to the Korean Conflict. The Spanish-American War began April 21, 1898 and ended in a Peace Treaty on April 11, 1899. During this period the defenses at Ft. Wadsworth were strengthened and a fort constructed at Ward's Point,* Tottenville to guard the entrances to New York Harbor. Many naval vessels were anchored off Tompkinsville and a chain was stretched across the Narrows. Many Staten Islanders volunteered for service, a recruiting office being established at Tynan's Hall, Stapleton (a building now occupied by the Volunteers of America). After the War, the Joseph S. Decker Camp No. 20, of the United States War Veterans, joined this national veterans' organization which combined the many groups of Spanish-American war veterans that had been formed throughout the country. The Staten Island group urged the erection of the "Hiker" monument near Borough Hall, St. George (44). This has since been removed to Tompkinsville Park.* In 1912 a monument was erected in Bethel Cemetery,* Tottenville to honor Joseph S. Decker, in whose memory the Staten Island Camp had been named. On Veterans' Day 1962, the last living charter member of the Decker Camp participated in official ceremonies.

Borough records indicate that there were 5,000 Staten Islanders in uniform during 1917 and 1918, and that 21,000 men and women were in the armed services during World War II (52). In almost every community on the Island tablets or plaques have been erected to honor those who served their country. In 1920 Dr. Louis A. Dreyfus and his wife, Berta, gave the land now known as Hero Park on Victory Boulevard and Louis Street to commemorate those who gave their lives in the First World War. A bronze tablet of dedication was placed on a large glacial boulder called Sugar Loaf Rock* which is situated in the center of the Park. Each Memorial Day appropriate ceremonies are held at this spot that was once a favorite play area for children. Richmond Turnpike was renamed Victory Boulevard after the Armistice of 1918.

INDUSTRY DURING THE WAR PERIOD

Many local industries played important roles during the two World Wars. During World War I, Downey's Shipyard in Mariners Harbor (employing about 10,000), Standard Shipbuilding Company on Shooter's Island in the Kill Van Kull (employing about 8,000), and Staten Island Shipbuilding Company (on the site of Bethlehem Steel Company's Mariners Harbor yard) constructed vessels for the government. It was at the Townsend and Downey Shipyard on Shooter's Island that the yacht *Meteor* had been built for Kaiser Wilhelm II in 1902. This company ceased operations about 1906. The yard was taken over by the Standard Shipbuilding Company at the beginning of World War I and was active until about 1920 (48).

During World War II, Downey's Shipyard and Brewer Dry Dock Company were engaged in a program of building, converting, and repairing ships for the government. Many destroyers were constructed at the Bethlehem Steel Corporation's shipyard which employed over 10,000 people. Employment was at an all-time high and attracted many off-Islanders.

Industrial plants participated in the defense program during the Second World War. The S.S. White Dental Manufacturing Company supplied United States Army Camps with dental supplies and equipment, manufactured flexible shafting for airplanes and tanks, and made many small parts for the government. This company still has government contracts. Nassau Smelting and Refining Company also aided in the war effort by reclaiming nonferrous metal scrap from the Navy Yards and Army Depots to be used in war machinery. Many small machines shops were activated. Men and women were trained for defense jobs under a War Industries Training Program conducted by the New York City Board of Education in various high schools.

STATEN ISLAND TERMINAL OF ARMY'S NEW YORK PORT OF EMBARKATION
During the Second World War and the Korean Conflict of 1950 the municipal piers along the east shore (Tompkinsville to Clifton) were taken over by the Army and Navy for troop embarkation and for the shipment of tanks, guns, vehicles, food, and other essentials. Wounded personnel, disembarked there, were removed by ambulance to Halloran General Hospital. Prisoners of war also arrived at the Terminal.

HOSPITALS DURING THE WARS

During World War I the Fox Hills Base Hospital was established for the wounded soldiers who were disembarked at the piers in the Stapleton area. The frame barracks erected between Rosebank and Grasmere in an area that is now divided by Hylan Boulevard had a bed capacity of 3,000. These buildings were used until 1933. During World War II barracks were constructed nearby on the Targee Street side of the railroad tracks. They were used for troop cantonment as the men awaited their orders. After the War, the barracks became a Federal Housing Project. Today only the chimneys remain.* Recent newspaper articles report plans for high-rise apartments to be built at this site.

Halloran General Hospital, named for Colonel Paul Stacey Halloran of the U.S. Medical Corps, was opened in 1941 in buildings that had been completed for a state hospital for mentally deficient children. This facility cared for the wounded soldiers over a period of ten years. It was the largest Army hospital in the country at that time. German prisoners of war were used in laboring jobs and in some technical positions for which they were fitted. After the buildings were returned to state jurisdiction, Willowbrook State School was opened there.

In 1942 the Federal Government leased Seaside Hospital and the other buildings belonging to St. John's Guild at New Dorp Beach. These all became known as the Staten Island Area Station Hospital and cared for the sick and wounded soldiers from units stationed on Staten Island and also for the dependents of men in the armed forces. Most of the buildings have been demolished. The remaining ones were used as a private nursing home for the aged until January 1963.

THE ARMORY

The Armory * on Manor Road near Martling Avenue was erected in 1926 on a site that had been used as early as 1912 to stable the horses for Troop F, a cavalry unit belonging to Squadron C, Brooklyn, of the New York State Guard (44). After World War I, Captain William H. Morris of Troop F returned home determined to secure an Armory for his troops. It is now used as a drill hall by Troops B and C of the First Reconnaissance Squadron of the 101st Armor of the New York State Guard. Within are several displays, including firearms and colorful guidons of various troops.

OTHER ACTIVITIES RELATED TO THE WAR EFFORT

Staten Islanders were active in Liberty Loan campaigns and in Red Cross projects, as were Americans throughout the country. During World War I, Mary Otis Willcox, daughter of Sidney Howard Gay, prominent Islander during the Civil War Period, headed the Red Cross activities, organizing a membership of 18,000 (44). Her husband, William G. Willcox became President of the Board of Education of the City of New York. P.S. 48 in Concord is named after him. During the Second World War, Mr. Samuel A. Turvey was the Chapter Chairman.

FEDERAL GOVERNMENT INSTALLATIONS

FORT WARDSWORTH*

The development of the fortifications at the Narrows has been traced in the preceding chapters. As a coast artillery post this installation was one of the country's strongest defenses.

In 1902 the name "Battery Weed" was given by the War Department to Fort Richmond, the stone fort that is still at the edge of the water. This was to honor Captain Stephen H. Weed, 5th U.S. Artillery, a Brigadier

General of the U.S. Volunteers who had been killed in the Battle of Gettysburg July 2, 1863 (41).

Fort Wadsworth was utilized during World Wars I and II and during the Korean Conflict both for defense purposes and for training. Colonel Rowan, former commanding officer of the Post, has described these activities briefly (76).

Between the two World Wars new barracks, administration buildings, the Parade Ground, and roads were constructed at the Fort as the Army Engineers were assisted by civilians under the program of the Works Progress Administration and the Civilian Conservation Corps (41).

The activities at Fort Wadsworth during World War II are reported fully in an article in *The Staten Island Historian* (41). In 1954 the military post became the launching site for "Nike," the "supersonic anti-aircraft guided missile" increasing the importance of the fortifications. In 1962 these missile units were transferred from the Fort. In June 1963, the Second U.S. Army Corps which had been stationed at Camp Kilmer, New Jersey, was moved to Fort Wadsworth.

Considerable property at the Island post was confiscated for the anchorage and approaches for the Verrazzano-Narrows Bridge. Soon the bridge traffic will be zooming over this important historic military installation (66).

MILLER FIELD*

In 1919 the U.S. Government purchased the former estate of William H. Vanderbilt at New Dorp from George W. Vanderbilt (44). The Vanderbilt Mansion was not razed until 1936. The stables which had been used for the well-known Vanderbilt horses were still standing in 1926, but have since been demolished.

The government field, originally used as an Aero Defense Station, was named in memory of Captain James E. Miller who was the first American aviator killed in action in World War I (41). It became an emergency landing field and a training area for the New York National Guard Units. During World War II prisoners of war were sent to this installation before being assigned to concentration camps.

In 1946 Miller Field became the repair center for the Army in the Greater New York area, a motor transport pool, and later an ordnance depot. Now the 215-acre field is "used chiefly by an aircraft maintenance unit of the First Army, operating as a sub-installation of Fort Wadsworth" (86). The civilian mechanics repair aircraft in a large double hangar near the beachfront.

U.S. COAST GUARD-ST. GEORGE BASE*

The Lighthouse Service at St. George was transferred to the Department of Commerce on July 1, 1903. In 1939 the Bureau of Lighthouses was merged with the U.S. Coast Guard, a branch of the Treasury Department. As a unit of the 3rd Coast Guard District, the depot at St. George soon thereafter became home port for Coast Guard cutters which had been based previously at Pier 18, Stapleton. These cutters are used as patrol boats, as weather ships, and as rescue vessels. About 1954 Ellis Island was closed and the Coast Guard personnel stationed there was transferred to St. George.

The services carried on by the Lighthouse Depot at St. George since 1886 have been continued, with modern equipment. Buoy lights now are supplied with tanks of acetylene gas or are operated by giant storage batteries (38, 64). Such aids to navigation (totaling over 500) as buoys, fog signals, lightships, etc., are still repaired and maintained at the base. Five buoy tenders are in constant service. A full explanation of the activities of the U.S. Coast Guard St. George Base appeared in a newspaper article written by Captain F. F. Nichols (63).

The lighthouses which are under the jurisdiction of the 3rd Coast Guard District include the Sandy Hook Lighthouse erected in 1764, Robbin's Reef Lighthouse* (originally built in 1839 and rebuilt in 1883), Richmond Light on Lighthouse Hill, erected about 1907, New Dorp Light behind Moravian Cemetery, and Elm Tree Beacon at the foot of New Dorp Lane on Miller Field property, rebuilt in 1939. The last three maritime beacons listed are the range lights which guide the ships into Ambrose Channel off Sandy Hook. The beam of light is directed toward Ambrose Lightship, a floating lighthouse since 1823. The present *Ambrose*, built in 1952, is the sixth ship to occupy that station.

The story of a woman lighthouse keeper who cared for Robbin's Reef Lighthouse* from 1886 to 1919 appeared in a recent issue of *The Staten Island Historian* (71).

U.S. Quarantine Station*

The establishment of the U.S. Quarantine Station in Rosebank in 1873 was described in the previous chapter. In 1921 the U.S. Government assumed control of the station (including Hoffman and Swinburne Islands), formerly administered by the State of New York. It is now under the jurisdiction of the U.S. Public Health Service.

Public Health Officers and agricultural inspectors board vessels coming into the Port of New York as they continue through the harbor without stopping. Smaller vessels and those without doctors aboard anchor off Quarantine while the passengers and crew are checked for quarantinable diseases – cholera, plague, relapsing fever, smallpox, typhus, and yellow fever (34) – and for other communicable diseases. A yellow flag is flown while the Public Health Officer is aboard (38).

Swinburne and Hoffman Islands, created artificially in 1872 as centers for persons with quarantinable diseases, were abandoned for such purposes in 1927 and 1928. A Merchant Marine training school was established on Hoffman Island in 1938 and prepared merchant seamen until it closed in 1946. Several years ago Bernard Baruch purchased both islands from the Federal Government and gave them to the city for recreational use (14). Present plans call for construction of a bulkhead around the two islands and filling in the shoal area between with rock taken from excavations for the water tunnel now being built between Brooklyn and Tompkinsville. This mile-long island off South Beach would be added to the Park System of New York City. It has been proposed that two 18-hole golf courses be constructed there (65).

DEVELOPMENT OF CHURCHES

In the earlier sections of this report, the growth of churches on Staten Island has been given in detail. Most of the churches organized before 1898 are still active, and many of the original buildings are still used.

As the population grew during the twentieth century, additional churches of all religious denominations were organized and new buildings erected. According to the Staten Island Chamber of Commerce, there are more than 130 churches on the Island today, including about 90 Protestant churches, 34 Roman Catholic churches, and 7 synagogues. There are also churches belonging to the following denominations: Pentecostal,

Seventh Day Adventist, Mennonite, Greek Orthodox, Assembly of God, Christian Science, Congregational, Evangelical Free, as well as of other non-denominational groups.

Of the 34 Catholic churches on the Island today, only 8 had been organized before consolidation, and of the 7 synagogues and temples of the Jewish faith, only one had been built (15).

PROTESTANT CHURCHES

In the early 1900s St. Mary's Episcopal Church* on Castleton and Davis Avenues, West New Brighton, which had been organized in 1848, erected a new parish house, chapel, rectory and cloisters adjacent to the church. A severe fire in 1947 completely destroyed the church which was rebuilt the following year in the early English Gothic style.

The Reformed Church of Huguenot Park,* organized in 1849, is significant from a historical as well as an architectural viewpoint. In 1924 the new church building was dedicated as a national monument to the Huguenot settlers of our country. Memorial pillars and windows in the church commemorate Pierre Billiou and other early settlers of Staten Island. Ernest Flagg, noted architect who lived on Staten Island, designed the edifice which was built of serpentine rock quarried on Todt Hill.

ROMAN CATHOLIC CHURCHES

In 1899 the parish of Our Lady of Good Counsel* was established and purchased its present church building which had been erected five years earlier as a convent for an order of cloistered nuns. The Augustinian Academy for boys was established there, functioning from 1899 until 1926 except for a two-year period between 1919 and 1921.

St. Peter's Church* in New Brighton, the oldest Catholic parish on the Island, organized in 1839, completed its present building between 1901 and 1903. The Cardinal's Tower is a familiar landmark as one crosses on the ferry from Manhattan. At night the lighted cross on top of the tower can be seen from a distance (29).

Of architectural interest is the original St. Clare's Church in Great Kills erected in 1921. This was the first Catholic church on the Island built in Colonial style.

OTHERS

A list of churches may be compiled from various sources, such as: Staten Island Telephone Directory; a Saturday edition of the *Staten Island Advance*; the Staten Island Division of the Protestant Council at 57 Bay Street, St. George; the Catholic Information Center at 1190 Castleton Avenue, West New Brighton; the Jewish Community Center at 475 Victory Boulevard, Tompkinsville.

Several new church buildings are planned to serve the growing communities of the Island. Among these is a new synagogue now being erected on Forest Avenue, West New Brighton by the Temple Israel Reform Congregation. A modern Gothic edifice is planned for All Saints Episcopal Church at 2329 Victory Boulevard, Willowbrook to replace its Mariners Harbor building that was destroyed by fire in 1958. The Unitarian Church of Staten Island will build on property near Todt Hill Road and Ocean Terrace.

HOMES AND RESIDENTIAL GROWTH

Towards the end of the nineteenth century and the beginning of the twentieth, social colonies in New Brighton and West New Brighton started to decline as families moved away. As industry came to the New Jersey shore opposite Staten Island, both the air and the surrounding waters became polluted, making this section of the Island less attractive for homes and hotels. The Baltimore and Ohio freight yards added to the undesirability of the location for residential purposes.

19TH CENTURY MANSIONS

The mansions of the nineteenth century had been built during a period when wealthy families with many servants lived on the Island. As wealth declined and retinues of servants disappeared from the social scene, many of the larger mansions served other purposes.

One of these was Fox Hill Manor, the home of Lewis Henry Meyer, built about 1840 on an 18-acre wooded tract along Fingerboard Road. In 1911 this became Mount Manresa, now the oldest laymen's retreat house in the country. Part of the property has been taken for the Clove Lakes Expressway. The old mansion is scheduled for demolition. A large new retreat house will replace the former landmark (100).

Colonel Richard Penn Smith's home, built about 1877, on Clove Road, West New Brighton, bordering on Martling's Pond, became the Actors' Home in 1902. Many well-known retired actors and actresses resided there until 1923 when the Actors' Fund purchased property in New Jersey (44). The Island home remained standing until 1938. In 1963 this property was acquired by the City for a parking lot.

St. Dorothy's Academy, a Catholic school for boys and girls, at 1200 Hylan Boulevard, Old Town, was once the home of the Italian banker, Tocci. Later this beautiful Italian villa was purchased by Pio M. Goggi* who manufactured American champagne in the Italian tradition at his winery on Van Duzer Street, Stapleton (48).

The David Latourette House, dating back to 1836, was taken over by the City of New York in 1927 as the clubhouse of the Latourette Golf Course (48). Other mansions were acquired by institutions and will be mentioned in the section devoted to that phase of community service.

LARGE HOMES OF THE TWENTIETH CENTURY

Several large homes were built during the twentieth century. One of the most unusual was that erected by William Horrmann* in 1910 on Grymes Hill at a point 320 feet above sea level. Atop the mansion Horrmann built a "crow's nest" making the height of the house 120 feet (32, 47). From the observation tower (440 feet above sea level) the horizon line can be seen in all directions. This building, reminiscent of castles along the Rhine River, is now the Motherhouse of the Sisters of Presentation who staff several parochial schools on the Island.

Another large home erected on the hills at the turn of the century is the large fieldstone house, nearly 100 feet square, built by a Henry Decker of Todt Hill. It was constructed almost entirely of native stone that was found on the surrounding ten acres of land. It is reported that many of the fittings in the house were imported from Europe (48).

Later Decker's daughter and her husband, Dr. John Randall, Sr., occupied this home, now the residence of the Lahr family.

On Hylan Boulevard, Great Kills, is a beautiful mansion built early in the 1900s by Henry Salomon, a hair net manufacturer, who was founder and first commodore of the Richmond County Yacht Club (formerly called Yvette Yacht Club). The building is now a funeral home.

Among the large mansions on Grymes Hill, overlooking the water, is that of the late Louis A. Stirn (78 Howard Avenue) who died in 1962 at the age of 98. He was a silk importer who is credited with bringing the seed of the mimosa (silk tree) from China to Staten Island. Now hundreds of these graceful trees add beauty to the Island as they flower during the summer months (46).

REAL ESTATE DEVELOPMENTS

Throughout the Island large estates were subdivided and smaller homes were erected. Real estate developers acclaimed the advantages of Staten Island as a residential community, laid out streets and advertised widely. In the early 1900s plans were made to develop the beach area around Huguenot, but the company went bankrupt. Similar attempts were unsuccessful in the 1930s. Some entrance pillars to streets laid out at that time are still visible, although the sidewalks are overgrown with weeds. This area is within the boundaries of the urban renewal project recommended by the City Planning Commission in 1962.

During the late 1920s and the early 1930s the hills on Staten Island were developed. Cornelius G. Kolff subdivided property on Emerson Hill, giving the area its name, developed the section between Bay Street and the Narrows known as Shore Acres, and started a development on the South Shore called Woods of Arden. About this time Lighthouse Hill was developed by a Mr. Platt who purchased a large acreage there and envisioned an artists' colony. He and his wife had purchased the Meissner Estate and lived in the old house which is standing today.

Sections around New Dorp and Midland Beach were developed by James Watson Hughes. His widow contributed funds for the New Dorp Public Library as a memorial to her husband who had been a community leader. This colonial style brick building, known as the James Watson Hughes Memorial Library,* opened as a sub-branch of the New York Public Library in 1928.

Joseph Springstead promoted the growth of the Great Kills area and in 1926 built the first modern office building on the South Shore.

Ole O. Odegaard has planned several developments of custom-built homes on Staten Island over a period of more than fifty years (46). Among them are Forest Heights, Manor Heights Park and more recently Ravenhurst Park (named for the home of Read Benedict).*

173

In the late 1920s Peter Larsen, an Island builder, began what is known today as development building. He also constructed the first four-family duplex houses on the Island. By erecting a hundred or more homes, although of different designs, on a single tract of land, Larsen cut down the cost, thereby encouraging home ownership (47). Other developers throughout the Island followed this pattern. One can observe the growth of such developments today, as large unused tracts of land are acquired and one and two family homes are erected. Information about current building projects can be obtained from the local newspaper, *The Staten Island Advance*, from the Staten Island Chamber of Commerce, and from the Staten Island Real Estate Board.

Some of the other early developers on the Island and the sections that they developed before 1930 were:

David J. Tysen, 2nd	– one of the earliest developers on Staten Island – the New Dorp section (46)
Charles Durkee	– Durkee Manor, Grasmere (47)
Walter Reno Watson	– New Dorp Gardens (46)
Albert P. Semler	– Grant City (46)
Max Bache	– Hylan Boulevard sections from Dongan Hills to Great Kills (46)
Horatio J. Sharrett	– Deere Park, Todt Hill (46)

RANDALL MANOR
Until 1927 Sailors' Snug Harbor owned the section of the Island now known as Randall Manor,* named for the benefactor of the large institution. In 1927 the corporation sold the Harbor Woods (from Henderson Avenue to Forest Avenue) to a building corporation which began to erect a number of residences there. One of the fresh ponds that formerly attracted fishermen, known as Allison Pond,* is now under the supervision of the Parks Department.

HOME OWNERSHIP
From its earliest development, Staten Island has been a community of home owners. According to the April 1960 Federal Census 60.4% of Island families owned their homes. This figure is somewhat higher today, several thou-

sand new homes having been erected in the last two years. The modern homes on Staten Island are varied in design. No one style predominates. Some houses are built today with architectural features of the Colonial and Federal periods. This is evident in sweeping roofs, tall columns, and characteristic doorways. On Emerson Hill is an unusual home with walls of glass. On Lighthouse Hill is a modern pre-fabricated house designed by the late Frank Lloyd Wright, the noted architect. Built in 1959, this was the first Wright pre-fabricated home to be constructed in the East.

APARTMENT HOUSES

It was late 1920s and early 1930s that apartment houses began to appear on Staten Island, particularly in the St. George-New Brighton-Silver Lake areas (48). In 1951 an F.H.A. project of 416 apartments was erected on Howard Avenue, Grymes Hill. The following year the Grymes Hill Manor Estates, garden apartments, were opened. Garden type apartments known as Carolina Gardens, were built on Hylan Boulevard between New Dorp and Oakwood.

HIGH-RISE APARTMENTS AND COOPERATIVE APARTMENTS

Today new high-rise apartment houses are beginning to dot the skyline. The tallest residential structure on the Island (Parkview House) can be seen from the ferry slip at Manhattan. At the present time these apartments are located in areas close to St. George, but plans have been filed for apartment houses in scattered sections of the Island. A few cooperative apartment houses also have been constructed.

PUBLIC HOUSING

Seven public housing projects have been erected on Staten Island and one was under construction in 1963 (58). They are:

1. Edwin Markham Houses (Federal Project)
   Richmond Terrace and Broadway, Port Richmond
   Completed June 1943 – 360 apartments
2. South Beach Houses (City Project)
   Lamport Boulevard and Kramer Street, South Beach
   Completed March 1950 – 422 apartments

3. Todt Hill Houses (City Project)
   Manor Road and Schmidts Lane, Castleton Corners
   Completed June 1950 – 502 apartments
4. General Charles W. Berry Houses (City Project)
   Richmond Road and Seaver Avenue, Dongan Hills
   Completed October 1950 – 506 apartments
5. Mariners Harbor Houses (Federal Project)
   Lockman Avenue and Grandview Avenue, Mariners Harbor
   Completed August 1954 – 607 apartments
6. Stapleton Houses (State Project)
   Broad and Hill Streets, Stapleton
   Completed 1962 – 693 apartments
7. West Brighton Plaza (Federal Project)
   Castleton Avenue and Broadway, West New Brighton
   Completed 1963 – 400 apartments
8. Richmond Terrace Houses (Federal Project)
   Richmond Terrace and Jersey Street, New Brighton
   Under construction in 1963 – 489 apartments

RESIDENTIAL LAND USE

A survey conducted by the Department of City Planning in 1959-1960 revealed that of the 38,947 acres on Staten Island only 4,851 acres or 12.4% of the total area was used for residential purposes. The Department of Census reported 65,156 housing units in 1960. Inevitably much of the vacant land on the Island, 33.4% of the total acreage, will be developed for homes. It is hoped that zoning laws will protect the suburban atmosphere of the borough.

GARDENS

Many Islanders are proud of their gardens and often open them to the public under the sponsorship of local garden clubs. An outstanding garden, which can be seen as one drives along Ocean Terrace, is that of Albert C. Fach, a former Staten Island District Attorney. Situated near the highest point on the Island, Fach's home commands a panoramic view of New Jersey. Each Christmas Mr. Fach displays a Nativity scene on his property, with life-size figures, a stable and live animals.

HOTELS

During the early part of the twentieth century the large, fashionable hotels in the St. George-New Brighton area disappeared. The Belmont Hotel was torn down in 1902, the Pavilion Hotel* was demolished in 1904, and the Hotel Castleton* was destroyed by fire in 1907. A few smaller hotels remained in the St. George-Tompkinsville area.

Other hotels attracted people to the South Shore. The largest of these was the Terra Marine Inn at Huguenot Beach, a 150-room hotel completed in 1908. The well-known Staten Island architect, James Whitford, Sr. designed this three-story hotel, with a ballroom overlooking the Lower Bay. It was built originally to accommodate prospective buyers of building lots in a Huguenot Park development project. The popularity of the hotel waned when the company went bankrupt in 1911. However, Islanders frequented the spot which was operated under different management until 1923. This landmark was demolished about 1948.

Smaller hotels were popular for outings, clambakes, and picnics, favorite forms of recreation before the automobile offered other opportunities for enjoyment. Many of these hotels were near the railroad stations between Grant City and Tottenville. A typical one was that of Albert P. Semler who built his hotel around 1910 adjacent to the park and picnic grounds he had started in the 1890s (46). Located near the Grant City railroad station, this building, with its cupola was a familiar landmark.

In addition to the hotels at South Beach and Midland Beach there were smaller ones at the other beaches along the South Shore. The Casino at Boehm's Hotel, New Dorp Beach, was well-known as a training camp for boxers. This building was demolished in 1953.

Other hotels were located on main thoroughfares, such as the Atlantic Inn on Richmond Road, Grant City which was the scene of social affairs until a few years ago. The building is now a funeral home. The Oakwood Park Hotel (later known as Oakwood Arms) was built about 1896 at the corner of Amboy Road and Clarke Avenue. This was considered a very fashionable spot until the 1920s. It was used as the Elks Clubhouse between 1925 and 1942 and was razed five years later.

RECREATION

Modern inventions such as the automobile, the motion picture, radio, and television had their impact upon the types of recreation on Staten Island as they did elsewhere in the country.

However, many Island residents have continued to take advantage of the opportunities offered by an area that provides boating, fishing, swimming, ball playing, horseback riding, and many other outdoor activities.

SPORTS AND ATHLETICS

Interest in athletics has remained high on the Island. As previously reported, baseball was first played at St. George in the late 1880s. Many local business firms sponsored baseball teams, particularly prior to World War I. One well-known team was the Siscos, sponsored by the Staten Island Shipbuilding Company. This team played at Sisco Park, Port Richmond, site of the present Weissglass Stadium* which is used for baseball, football, wrestling, and auto racing. The Alaska Baseball Team played at Alaska Park which is the site of West Brighton Plaza, opposite Public School 18. Baseball continues to be popular as evidenced by the high school interscholastic teams, the many Little League teams, and teams sponsored by business firms. However, the game does not have the semi-professional status it had on Staten Island until about twenty years ago.

Football

Football also achieved great popularity on the Island. A Stapleton team, known as the Stapes, was one of the original members of the National Football League (56). Thompson's Stadium, the site of the Stapleton Houses today, was the scene of local football clashes between the Stapes and the West Brighton Indians and the Elm Park Imperials. Professional football teams have been replaced by interscholastic teams. A detailed account of athletes and athletics from 1900 to 1950 appeared in the *Staten Island Tercentenary Booklet* (56). Local newspapers devote considerable space to present-day sports activities on the Island.

Golf

Golf tournaments were held on Staten Island as long ago as 1878 on the Harbor Hills Golf Links in New Brighton. Since the early part of the twentieth century, the Island has had several large golf courses. Among the first ones were: The Fox Hill Golf Course,* off Vanderbilt Avenue and

Targee Street; Tysen Manor Golf Course,* between Hylan Boulevard and Mill Road and New Dorp Lane and Tysens Lane, which lasted until 1938; Mayflower Country Club Golf Course, in Huguenot, built on a 147-acre tract in 1928, later known as the South Shore Golf Course.

Now the Parks Department maintains public golf courses at Latourette and Silver Lake Parks. The Richmond County Country Club Golf Course is privately owned.

During the late 1920s and early 1930s many "Tom Thumb" or miniature golf courses were opened. One has been maintained under the same ownership until the present time. In 1962 it was relocated on an adjacent site on New Dorp Lane near Hylan Boulevard.

Horseback Riding

Horseback riding is still a favorite form of recreation on Staten Island and bridle paths are provided by the Department of Parks in Clove Lakes Park and in Latourette Park. Several stables and riding academies are in operation. The largest of these, Clove Lakes Stables,* offers hayrides in the summer and fall and horse-drawn sleigh rides in the winter.

Bowling and Swimming

Bowling is popular on Staten Island. Several large bowling centers have been constructed in various sections of the borough.

Several private swim clubs have been organized on the Island. The pools are preferred to the polluted waters which have been eroding the beachfronts.

Boat Clubs

In the preceding section of this report, several yacht and boat clubs were noted, most of which no longer exist. Among new groups formed during the twentieth century were the Bentley Yacht Club (active from 1905 until World War I, and reorganized in 1931), the Prince's Bay Yacht Club, the Ocean Yacht Club in Stapleton, and the Richmond County Yacht Club of Great Kills. A more recent club is the Prince's Bay Boatman Association organized in 1934 and active today. In August 1962 the 17th annual national Thistle class sailing championships were held in Raritan Bay off Great Kills.

All types and sizes of pleasure boats are moored at the marinas in Great Kills Harbor* and at Lemon Creek,* Prince's Bay. The interest in boating on Staten Island is very high. The Power Squadron gives courses in small-boat handling.

RECREATIONAL ATTRACTIONS

Some of the Island's recreational areas that were popular during the late 1800s continued to attract crowds in the early part of the new century.

Silver Lake Park*

Silver Lake Park remained a favorite spot until the reservoir was built in 1917. The Silver Lake Hotel became Raisch's Casino after the death of John Franzreb, previous owner, in 1902. Many Island organizations sponsored dances there. Swimming, boating, fishing and ice skating were enjoyed on the Lake. At that time the only body of water there was the South Basin. The present North Basin, close to Forest Avenue, was a marsh which was converted into another section of Silver Lake after the City of New York purchased the property for a reservoir.

During the depression days of the 1930s theatrical performances were given at Silver Lake during the summer by the Federal Theatre Project. The audiences sat on the grassy slopes of the eastern side of the Lake just as present day audiences flock there Wednesday nights during the summer months to enjoy open-air concerts staged by the Staten Island Musicians' Society Band.

South Beach

In the early 1900s Happyland at South Beach was one of the most famous amusement parks along the East Coast. It was similar to Luna and Steeplechase Parks at Coney Island. Thirty thousand people attended the opening day on June 30, 1906 (82). Happyland had large hotels, many concessions, a theatre featuring variety acts, and a large swimming pool. However, since it depended upon week-end off-Islanders, it was a financial failure within three years. Bathing became unsafe because of sewage and oil. A raging fire swept through the entire beach area in 1917 and again in 1929. Each time the amusement area was rebuilt. In the years that followed, fires continued to ravage the South Beach section. Tirelli's carousel, built in 1912, was a favorite of the children until it closed in the 1950s.

The Federal Government began construction of the Franklin Delano Roosevelt Boardwalk* in 1935. It now extends from Ft. Wadsworth to Miller Field. South Beach is under the jurisdiction of the Department of Parks. In addition to the beachfront area there are also facilities for handball. Seaside Boulevard, recently completed, connects this beach with the adjoining Midland Beach.

Midland Beach

Another Island summer resort popular along the Atlantic Coast was Midland Beach, often attracting thousands of visitors on a single day. Many came on excursion boats that ran directly from Manhattan and Newark (89). Originally owned by the Midland Railroad Company, the beach was sold to the Hincliffe family. Several hotels, a large amusement park, bathhouses, free movies, band concerts, a long fishing pier, and a fine boardwalk made Midland Beach a gala resort. For many years Daniel W. Leonard was the manager. During the 1920s several large fires destroyed the amusement area and although attempts were made to rebuild Midland Beach it never regained its former popularity. Now the Parks Department maintains the beach area which has bathing houses, play areas and a boardwalk. During the summers 1961 to 1963 dance band concerts were given for young people, sponsored jointly by the Parks Department and Consolidated Edison.

Ward's Point

Another excursion spot before World War I was situated at Ward's Point,* Tottenville. This had been the site of a fort during the Spanish-American War. The fort was removed after the War and resort buildings erected. A hotel, bathing beach, picnic area, and carousel attracted crowds who came from New Jersey and Manhattan by steamboat. A fire in the 1930s destroyed most of the buildings. Erosion has changed the physical features of the Point, but it is still an interesting place to see.

COUNTY FAIR GROUNDS

In 1905 the new County Fair Grounds* were established in Dongan Hills on the site now occupied by the General Charles W. Berry Houses (52). County fairs had been held on Staten Island since the early 1800s. In the 1860s the Richmond County Agricultural Society had fairs on its club grounds, now part of Miller Field. In the late 1890s fairs were held on the field of the Staten Island Athletic Club at "the Cove," West New Brighton. With the gradual disappearance of farms in the twentieth century, County fairs at the Dongan Hills Fair Grounds became part of the Island's history. Around 1928 the half-mile race track was used for greyhound or whippet races and for sulky races.

PUBLIC PARKS

Long before consolidation citizen committees on Staten Island had urged that land be acquired for parks. In 1898 there were only three public parks – Westerleigh Park, Port Richmond Park (now called Veterans Park) and Washington Square (now called Tappen Park) in Stapleton – all small neighborhood parks, still in use as sitting areas. In 1902 the Committee on Parks of the Staten Island Chamber of Commerce recommended that 3,500 acres of parkland and 210 acres of playground should be set aside (45).

It was not until the early 1920s, however, that extensive lands were acquired for park purposes. The gift of Hero Park by Dr. and Mrs. Louis A. Dreyfus inspired new interest in parks on the Island. Since that time 5,140 acres have been designated as park areas, representing 13.1% of the total acreage of the borough. Plans call for the acquisition of another 2% of the land.

The parks of Staten Island were developed in the 1930s as part of the vast program of expansion of the park system of New York City. The position of Commissioner of Parks was created in 1934 to replace the individual borough commissioners. Each borough has its own director.

Today the parks on Staten Island provide innumerable kinds of recreational facilities to meet the needs of the community. These include golf at Latourette and Silver Lake; boating at Clove Lakes and Willowbrook Parks; a boat basin at Great Kills Marina; tennis at Silver Lake and Walker Parks; bridle paths at Clove Lakes and Latourette Parks; swimming at Wolfe's Pond, Great Kills Park, South Beach and Midland Beach; fishing at Willowbrook Park, in Martling's Pond (part of Clove Lakes Park), and at the beach parks; and a cricket field at Walker Park.* Picnic areas and sports areas are provided in several parks. Pamphlets listing all city parks and their facilities may be obtained from any borough office of the Parks Department (60). The annual report of the Parks Commissioner which describes the development of the park system and the reclamation of marshlands may be secured from the Manhattan office of the Department at 64th Street and Fifth Avenue, New York, 21 (59). A recent publication of the Staten Island Institute of Arts and Sciences describes in detail several of the park areas on Staten Island, noting the natural features that can be observed (92).

Playgrounds, Swimming Pools and Recreational Centers
The Department of Parks provided playgrounds in centralized locations, in the various housing projects, and adjacent to some of the schools (60). Several playgrounds, constructed in the 1930s, were called War Memorial Playgrounds and bear the names of World War I heroes.*

Two outdoor swimming pools also are maintained by the Department. The Faber Pool in Port Richmond, which opened in 1932, was named for the Faber family, pencil manufacturers, who were interested in athletics and lived near the site (44). The Joseph H. Lyons Pool in Tompkinsville which opened in 1936 was named in honor of the organizer and first commander of the Staten Island Post No. 563, Veterans of Foreign Wars and also Richmond County commander of the American Legion.

Pier 6 at Tompkinsville became George Cromwell Recreation Center, in memory of Staten Island's first Borough President, when it was taken over by the Parks Department in 1936. A full recreational program is conducted for young people and adults. Occasionally exhibits and dances are held there.

Goodhue Center, supported by the Children's Aid Society, with financial assistance from the Community Chest and Council, maintains a recreational program for boys and girls of all ages. The center is housed in the home of the late Robert and Sarah C. Goodhue,* 304 Prospect Avenue, New Brighton, which was built about 1845. A swimming pool and playground are on adjacent property on Lafayette Avenue.

Recreation centers are also provided for the youth of the community by the P.A.L., by church groups, and by the Board of Education.

THEATRE

In the early 1900s stock companies were popular throughout the nation. The Richmond Theatre located on Thompson and Brook (now Wright) Streets, Stapleton, provided this form of entertainment from 1906 until about 1912 (81). Then the newer media of the silent film attracted patrons to several small moving picture houses in the neighborhood. The Richmond Theatre had been the old German-American gymnasium known as Turn Hall, built in 1890 (81). The theatre later became a moving picture house. The building was destroyed by fire in the 1950s. In the 1920s stock company performances were revived in the Liberty Theatre in Stapleton for several years and vaudeville shows were presented in the Ritz and Palace Theatres.

At one time the Island supported about twenty movie houses. Today there are five theatres and one drive-in. Some of the earliest were the Harbor in Mariners Harbor, the Star in New Brighton, the New Plaza in West New Brighton, the Empire in Port Richmond (still in existence), the Bijou and the Park in Stapleton. In 1922 a local pharmacist erected a moving picture house on New Dorp Lane which has been converted into an electrical appliance store (48).

The Isle Theatrical Corporation purchased the New Dorp Theatre and later built the present Lane Theatre across the street. Organized by three brothers, Charles, Lewis, and Elias Moses, this company erected a chain of theatres in the 1920s, the Liberty in Stapleton (now a bowling center); the Paramount (1920) in Stapleton; the Ritz (1924) in Port Richmond; the Strand (1926) in Great Kills; the Stadium in Tottenville; the Capitol in West New Brighton. Of these six, only the Paramount and the Ritz are still used as theatres. The Victory Theatre in Tompkinsville, built about 1925, closed in 1961.

The Paramount Theatre* on Bay Street, Stapleton, is located on land formerly owned by Cornelius Vanderbilt, father of Commodore Cornelius Vanderbilt. The old homestead was razed to make way for the present theatre. In 1961 the Paramount was redecorated and the projection and sound equipment improved.

The St. George Theatre,* Staten Island's largest and newest, was built in 1930 and decorated in ornate fashion (48). Staten Island's first Drive-In Theatre opened in 1948 on Richmond Avenue, Greenridge with accommodations for 650 cars. This was the first drive-in theatre constructed in the City of New York.

GERMAN CLUB ROOMS

The German Club Rooms, mentioned in the preceding section, continued to be the scene of banquets, charity balls, receptions, concerts, and entertainments. Among the groups which performed on the large stage was The Comedy Opera Club of Staten Island, organized in 1903, which presented operettas by Gilbert and Sullivan and by others (80). Throughout the century amateur theatrical groups have appeared from time to time in different sections of the Island, a few lasting over a period of years. Local newspapers report current efforts.

STATEN ISLAND JEWISH COMMUNITY CENTER*

The Staten Island Jewish Community Center at 475 Victory Boulevard, Tompkinsville, dedicated in 1929, has an extensive recreational and educational program for both children and adults. In 1963 the building was renovated completely and enlarged, thereby increasing its facilities. Two nursery school rooms are included in the new building.

YOUNG MEN'S CHRISTIAN ASSOCIATION*

The early development of the YMCA on Staten Island was reported in the preceding section. Interest in re-establishing the program on the Island was awakened in the 1940s. The Staten Island Branch of the YMCA was organized in 1947 with small headquarters at 36 Richmond Terrace, St. George. Limited activities were conducted in various communities. In 1952 the program was expanded with the acquisition of a 2¹/₂-acre plot of land, including a century old homestead, opposite the Staten Island Zoo. The present modern building at 613 Broadway, erected in 1956, with its gymnasium, swimming pool, and lounge, offers a recreation program for all ages. The organization is seeking to acquire acreage on the South Shore for a day camp.

RICHMOND DAY CENTER

Volunteers on Staten Island work in conjunction with the Department of Welfare of the City to provide recreational activities for people 55 years of age or older. The Richmond Day Center for Older People offers activities at the Berry Houses, at the Stapleton Houses, and at Sailors' Snug Harbor.

SCOUTING

The William H. Pouch Staten Island Scout Camp* offers facilities for Boy Scouts in all boroughs. In 1949, 100 acres of woodland off Manor Road were added to the existing Short Term Camp of 50 acres and the name was changed to honor the former Staten Islander and prominent leader of Scouting in New York City, William H. Pouch. Flagg Pond, which was formerly part of the estate of the late Ernest Flagg, well-known architect, was renamed Lake Ohrbach to honor Nathan M. Ohrbach, Manhattan merchant and leader in Scouting. A large amphitheater on the property is named in memory of the late Mrs. Louis A. Dreyfus who was a benefactor.

Adjacent to the Pouch Camp is Camp High Rock,* a 58-acre camp operated by the Girl Scout Council of Greater New York. The proposed Richmond Parkway will divide the two camps. High Rock is used for day hikes, for overnight troop camping, for a short term camp and for a summer camp program. The first Girl Scout troop on Staten Island dates back to 1914 (51). Now there are 15 senior troops (ages 14 through 17), 91 intermediate troops (ages 10 through 13) and 77 Brownie troops (ages 7 through 9).

CAMPFIRE GIRLS

The Staten Island Council of Campfire Girls was organized in 1912 (48). A year-round recreational program is offered for girls between the ages of 7 and 17.

MUSIC AND ART

Through the twentieth century there have been many groups on Staten Island that have been interested in music and art. The local newspaper reports the activities of the current groups. A few of the larger organizations will be mentioned.

The Staten Island Community Concert Association, part of the national organization, has been presenting performances on the Island since 1951. Annually a series of three or four concerts by outstanding symphony orchestras and internationally known musical artists is given, usually at the Paramount Theatre. One of the Community Concert artists is Eileen Farrell, Metropolitan opera star, who is a Staten Island resident.

The Richmond Opera Company was organized in 1958 by a group of music lovers on Staten Island who were interested in bringing professional operatic performances to the Island. Over a period of four years they brought many fine artists to the stage of the St. George Theatre. The annual Opera Ball, a fund-raising project, was reminiscent of the gay social life Staten Island enjoyed many years ago. It was announced at the close of the 1962 season that the program had not been self-sustaining. Future plans were indefinite.

Among the other groups are the Staten Island Symphony Society, the Staten Island Choral Society, and the Wagner College Glee Club. The College Glee Club tours the country and also offers a few concerts for the public on the campus.

Art

The Staten Island Institute of Arts and Sciences has stimulated local artists to use their talents and to display their work. Each September an outdoor art exhibit is held at Sailors' Snug Harbor, followed by an exhibit in the Staten Island Museum. The Institute also encourages art appreciation. Exhibits on the second floor change frequently. The Art Rental and Sales Gallery offers members the opportunity to rent or purchase original works of art.

Staten Island Council of Arts

In June 1962 the Staten Island Council of Arts, a citizens' committee, was organized as a coordinating agency to help promote artistic and civic improvement in the borough. The group represents educational, cultural and community service groups.

MUSEUMS AND LIBRARIES

The Staten Island Historical Society which had been founded in 1856 was reorganized in 1900 by prominent Staten Islanders, among whom were Rev. Wilbur Fiske Wood, who was elected president of the Society; Ernest Flagg, architect; Ira K. Morris, historian; David J. Tysen, developer; E. C. Bridgman; Judge Nathaniel J. Wyeth; George Cromwell and Calvin D.

Van Name, borough presidents. They met in the historic Fountain House* which had been erected about 1670, according to Morris (57). There British officers were entertained during the American Revolution. The house was remodeled in 1899 by Mr. Justis J. Smith, a well-known New England architect, and remained an interesting landmark until 1935 when it was demolished. The firehouse on Richmond Road, New Dorp, occupies the site of the old homestead.

It was fitting that the Historical Society met in the Fountain House because one of its primary objectives was to preserve historic landmarks. Another aim was to collect historic material pertaining to the Island.

In 1920 the Stony Brook Association merged with the Historical Society. Ira K. Morris became president and Cornelius G. Kolff became secretary. Two years later the new organization joined with the Staten Island Antiquarian Society, meeting at the Perine House (now known as the Billiou-Stillwell-Perine House)* which had been purchased by the Antiquarian Society in 1915. William T. Davis* became president of the Staten Island Historical Society, a position he held until 1939. Many gifts relating to the history of the Island were acquired throughout the years.

In 1934 the borough president of Richmond turned over to the Staten Island Historical Society the old County Clerk's and Surrogate's Office (built in 1848) to be used as a museum. Borough President Palma appointed Loring McMillen as Borough Historian to replace Charles W. Leng who had held the honorary position since 1922 (19). This office, created by state legislation in 1919, is still held by Mr. McMillen. The museum, staffed by volunteer workers, is one of the finest local historical museums* in the State of New York. The Parks Department maintains the physical plant and the grounds of both the museum building and the Third County Courthouse* across the street which houses special collections.

The volunteers gather all kinds of historical material which they catalog and prepare for exhibit. A fine library has been assembled and is available for research. The Society issues an eight page quarterly, *The Staten Island Historian*, and also publishes leaflets and books from time to time. A restored village of Richmondtown has been planned to show the growth of a typical American village during the 17th, 18th, and 19th centuries. Details of this Richmondtown Restoration will be discussed later.

STATEN ISLAND INSTITUTE OF ARTS AND SCIENCES

The early history of the Staten Island Institute of Arts and Sciences* was given in connection with William T. Davis in the preceding section. Today this organization is one of the most active cultural groups on the Island, offering activities of interest to all ages. Various adult sections include archeology, art, astronomy, handcrafts, music and natural history. The Education Department schedules lectures for school classes and field trips to the William T. Davis Wildlife Refuge.* A Saturday morning Junior Museum Program is offered also. The Institute sponsors a series of nature lectures annually in memory of Mr. Davis. These are open to the general public. In-service courses for teachers are conducted each year at the Museum, as well as other courses of more general interest. A publication, *The News Bulletin*, is printed monthly for distribution to members of the Institute (27).

The growth of the public museum as part of the Institute of Arts and Sciences has been traced. The Museum at 75 Stuyvesant Place has both permanent and changing exhibits. The first floor is devoted to the natural sciences, the second floor to art. Photographic exhibits are often displayed in the basement auditorium. A research library is located in the Richmond Health Center building at 51 Stuyvesant Place.

JACQUES MARCHAIS CENTER OF TIBETAN ART*

Another museum that attracts many people to Staten Island is the Jacques Marchais Center of Tibetan Art on Lighthouse Hill overlooking Richmondtown. The museum building, erected in the style of a Tibetan temple, houses the private oriental Buddhist art collection of the late Mrs. Harry Klauber (known professionally as Mme. Jacques Marchais). This building was dedicated in 1947, just prior to her death. Earlier she had erected a library for her large collection of oriental literature. In recent years Tibetan monks have visited the Center and praised the work of Mme. Marchais in preserving Tibetan art and literature. Beautiful gardens built into the hillside enhance the charm of the Center. In 1962 and 1963, an in-service course for teachers was conducted in the library.

THE STATEN ISLAND ZOO

The Staten Island Zoo* is operated both by the City of New York which furnishes cost of maintenance and operation and by the Staten Island Zoological Society which provides exhibits and conducts various programs. When this zoo opened in June 1936, it was hailed as "the first educational zoo in the United States." The late Carol Stryker, previously mentioned, was the first curator. Dr. Patricia O'Connor, zoo veterinarian, is the only woman in the country to hold such a position.

The reptile collection at the Staten Island Zoo is considered one of the finest in the world. The rattlesnake collection of 36 species is unsurpassed. Carl Kauffeld, a Staten Islander, has been curator of reptiles since 1936. Other sections of the zoo house birds, mammals, and tropical fish.

Educational programs and monthly lectures for members of the Staten Island Zoological Society are conducted in the auditorium.

Adjacent to the Zoo is Barrett Park.* This seven acres of land was left to the City of New York by the late Mrs. Edward T. Hardin with the stipulation that a park be established and named for her brother-in-law, Clarence T. Barrett* and that it should be used for "other than merely playground purposes."

LIBRARIES

The first branch of the New York Public Library on Staten Island was opened in Tottenville in 1904 through the efforts of three local organizations, including the Philemon Society, which is still active. Andrew Carnegie had offered funds for library buildings to small communities in the United States and the citizens of Tottenville had applied for this aid. Prior to that time, there had been a public library in Tottenville on Johnson Avenue, formed by the Tottenville Association in 1899, with a stock of 230 books. Earlier efforts have been described in a newspaper article (83). The Port Richmond Branch Library opened in 1905 and the Stapleton and St. George Branches in 1907.

Today Staten Island is served by the St. George Library Center, twelve branch libraries, and a bookmobile. A new branch in Meiers Corners will replace the Todt Hill Houses facility in late 1963. All branches have special programs for children and adults. The first public music lending library in New York City opened at the St. George Regional Public Library in 1952.

CONSERVATION EFFORTS

The wooded areas of Staten Island are disappearing fast as the bulldozers make way for homes and industry. Native wildflowers, song birds, and small mammals also vanish when their natural habitats are destroyed. Fortunately, on the Island, there have been groups and individuals interested in conservation. The expansion of public parks on Staten Island has assured permanent protection of natural woodland.

BIRD SANCTUARY – WILDLIFE REFUGE

Through the efforts and generosity of William T. Davis, who has been referred to several times, a 51-acre bird sanctuary was created in New Springville in 1933. This was maintained jointly by the National Audubon Society and the Parks Department of the City of New York (50).

The area was enlarged to 260 acres and established by the Parks Department in 1956 as the William T. Davis Wildlife Refuge.* Guided field trips are conducted over the nature trails that have been laid out in the Refuge (92). The Spring 1957 issue of the *Proceedings of the Staten Island Institute of Arts and Sciences* was devoted to a report on the botany of the area.

It is of interest to note that Theodore Roosevelt's grandfather had a country home on land that is now part of the Refuge. The property remained in the Roosevelt family until 1878.

THE FEDERATION OF WOMEN'S GARDEN CLUBS*

Eleven women's garden clubs on the Island belong to the Federated Garden Clubs of New York State. These groups have stimulated amongst adults and children an interest in gardening and in conserving natural flora. They maintain a colonial garden on the grounds of the Billiou-Stillwell-Perine House.* Flower shows and garden walks are annual events. In 1962 the Staten Island District, Federated Garden Clubs of New York State adopted the daisy as a motif for its seal. Ten years earlier this flower had been chosen as the official borough flower by a poll conducted by the *Staten Island Advance*.

MEN'S GARDEN CLUB OF STATEN ISLAND

A group of Island men who were interested in gardening and conservation founded the Men's Garden Club of Staten Island* in 1950, as an affiliate of the national organization of Men's Garden Clubs of America. This civic-minded organization planted and has continued to care for the orchard at the Decker Farm in Richmondtown, and has assisted in landscaping the grounds of such buildings as the YMCA, the Staten Island Mental Health Society Center, and the Staten Island Hospital. The men hold two flower shows annually at the *Staten Island Advance* building. These are open to the public.

STATEN ISLAND ARBORETUM

A 75-acre section of the Wagner College campus has been designated as the Staten Island Arboretum.* Trees and shrubs are to be planted and labeled. Many of the existing old trees have been marked. Eventually the woodland area will be opened and native plant life protected there. Ultimately the Arboretum committee plans to aid homeowners in the selection and care of trees.

STATE CONSERVATION DEPARTMENT

The New York State Conservation Department provides a marine fisheries protector to enforce the state fishing laws and a game protector to enforce the laws governing the protection of bird and animal life on Staten Island (24).

OTHER ORGANIZATIONS

The Staten Island Federation of Sportsmen's Clubs* coordinates the common interests of various sportsmen's clubs on the Island. One of these, the Andrew E. Zimmer Fish and Game Protective Association,* conducts classes in conservation, boat handling, compass and map reading, and hunter safety in its New Springville headquarters.

THE ROLE OF THE NEWSPAPER

Over a period of many years the local newspaper, *The Staten Island Advance*, carried a column by Lee A. Ellison, who died in 1962. These articles entitled *Walks with Nature* awakened the interest of Islanders in the conservation of the natural beauty which is fast disappearing.

INDUSTRIAL EXPANSION

As the population continued to increase, new industries were attracted to Staten Island which offered the advantages of adequate labor supply, availability of large tracts of land at a reasonable price, proximity to markets in the metropolitan area, a navigable waterfront, and freight connections to various parts of the country.

In 1900 there were about 60 different industries, employing about 8,000 people. In 1962, according to the Staten Island Chamber of Commerce, there were about 215 industries, with 9,879 employees.

FARMING

With the turn of the century, farming began to decline on the Island. Contributing factors were air pollution, increased land evaluation, and labor problems. In the early 1900s the Cortelyou brothers found it more lucrative to sell salt hay to the truck farmers to protect their crops from frost than to raise their own crops (47). In 1935 there were still about 35 truck farms, but in 1962 that number had dwindled to about 12. These farms which produce vegetables for Manhattan markets are centered around the New Springville-Travis section. Several of them are owned and operated by Greek farmers. Modern machinery and agricultural methods are used, including overhead irrigation. Produce is loaded on special trailers that are pulled into the fields by tractor and then transferred to trucks. Cauliflower, cabbage, celery, lettuce, escarole, kohlrabi, beans, beets, broccoli, carrots, endive, radishes, and squash are the chief crops. The largest and most typical truck farm is operated by the Crampanis family on Richmond Avenue.

Many of the truck farmers turned to flower growing in greenhouses which eliminated the problem of air pollution (48). The Mohlenhoff farm on Victory Boulevard, Travis, which has been in the family since 1910, is the best example of this, The raising of flowers was started in 1928 (46). Gradually the vegetable crops became less important and more greenhouses were constructed. Chrysanthemums, tulips, iris, poinsettias, cinerarias, and bedding stock are grown for market. An unusual type of farm on the Island is Gericke's Organic Farm on Arthur Kill Road.

Dairy Farms
There have been several dairy farms on Staten Island, but none exist

today. In 1899 Julius Weissglass founded the Weissglass Dairy (now the Weissglass Gold Seal Dairy Corporation). He started with 12 cows, 40 ducks and 120 chickens on a 50-acre farm near Bulls Head that had belonged originally to the Simonson family. This was the period when milk deliveries were made by horse-drawn milk wagons along dirt roads. One of the Weissglass milk wagons can be seen at the Clove Lakes Stables.*

Now the sons of the founder own several creameries in upstate New York. The milk is transported to the Island in modern stainless steel tank trucks. It is then pasteurized and bottled at the Mariners Harbor plant on Forest Avenue. Gold Seal Ice Cream was added to the products in 1941. A large clock at the corner of the plant was unveiled in 1951 in memory of the founder who died in 1946. The Weissglass name is perpetuated in the name of the stadium in Port Richmond where many sports events are held.*

Prasse's Goat Dairy and Farm

Prasse's Goat Dairy and Farm at 535 Bloomingdale Road has supplied goat's milk for the New York City area since 1935. Mr. Prasse started to raise Nubian goats as a hobby in 1933, but two years later his dairy was certified for milk sales. Goat's milk, which is easy to digest and is helpful in certain stomach and intestinal disorders, can be bought only with a doctor's prescription. The Prasses sold their business in 1961. The new owners also raise strawberries and asparagus which were important crops in this area a century ago.

CLAMMING AND OYSTERING

Clamming and oystering* were important occupations along the South Shore, particularly in Pleasant Plains and Tottenville, during the early 1900s. Oystering continued to prosper on Staten Island until about 1910 when the waters of New York Harbor became polluted from industrial waste, from shipping, and from sewage. When typhoid fever was traced to Staten Island oysters, the Department of Health condemned the oyster beds in 1916. Clamming was also prohibited.

About 1940 the clam beds were approved again. Very often 50 or 60 men would venture forth in small boats from South Shore harbors. However, during World War II the waters again were condemned. The Prince's

Bay Clam and Oyster Association became reactivated in 1961 after eight years of inactivity and is urging the reopening of Raritan Bay for clamming. The United States Public Health Service, the New York City Health Department and the shellfishing unit of the New York State Conservation Department determine whether clamming may be resumed.

SHIPBUILDING

There were many small boatyards for building and repair along the Arthur Kill in and near Tottenville during the period when clamming and oystering were the principal occupations in that locality. The Ellis Shipyard built large schooners. Other yards bore the names of their owners – Brown, Butler, Rutyan, Latourette (48). Some of the old docks are still visible.

Brewer Dry Dock Company

Large shipyards developed along the north shore of the Island. One of the earliest was Brewer Dry Dock Company on Richmond Terrace in Mariners Harbor, founded in 1899. At one time this was one of Staten Island's largest industrial plants, employing over 1,000 men. During the 1930s the firm built ten Department of Sanitation barges (47). Most of the work now is of a repair nature, such as the annual overhauling of the city-owned ferries and other harbor craft.

Bethlehem Steel Company

The Mariners Harbor yard of the Bethlehem Steel Company is located on a site that was used as a shipyard by R. C. Decker as early as 1853. Other shipyard companies operated there in later years. Some of the owners of the Burlee Drydock Company of Port Richmond started a shipyard at this site for the construction of wooden vessels in 1906. The following year they named the firm the Staten Island Shipbuilding Company. By 1906 a foundry was added and steel ships were built. During World War I this plant had government contracts. In 1929 ownership changed to the United Drydock Company which became United Shipyards Inc. in 1936. Two years later Bethlehem Steel purchased the Mariners Harbor yard. During World War II the Navy acquired part of the property and contracts were awarded to Bethlehem for construction of destroyers and for conversion and repair work of other warships. At one time over 10,000 people were employed at the shipyard. After the War, steel barges and other harbor crafts were constructed there. In 1951 three Staten Island-Manhattan ferries were completed at Bethlehem. Now only the foundry and propeller shop are in operation. There, huge propellers are made for tankers and destroyers that are constructed in other shipyards.

Milliken Brothers – Downey's Shipyard

Milliken Brothers' Structural Iron Works and Rolling Mill, originally founded in 1857, erected a large plant near Elizabeth Ferry, Holland Hook in 1903. This Staten Island factory was one of the world's largest manufacturers of steel products. After the steel trusts were formed, Milliken Brothers dissolved in 1917 (45). The plant was converted into Downey's Shipyard which had large government contracts during World War I. In 1927 this property was the site of the Bellanca Aeroplane Corporation.

Ship Repair and Salvage Companies

There have been many ship repair firms in business on the Island since the turn of the century. McWilliams Drydock at the foot of North Burgher Avenue, West New Brighton, was well-known, but is no longer in operation. Among those still active are Great Lakes Dredge and Dock Company, O'Brien Brothers Shipyard Corporation, Moran Towing Corporation, and Caddell Dry Dock and Repair Company. Merritt, Chapman and Scott Corporation, based at Pier 22, Clifton, has been in the salvage and ship construction business since 1860.

PIER FACILITIES ON THE EAST SHORE

The American Dock Company was founded in 1872 by Alfred J. Pouch. The property includes Piers 1 through 5 along the Upper Bay from Victory Boulevard to the Coast Guard Base. For many years the Isthmian Steamship Line and the United States Line used the facilities of the American Dock Company. Pier 4 is leased by the Universal Terminal and Stevedoring Corporation.

In 1962 Webb and Knapp, Inc., a Manhattan real estate firm, purchased the American Dock Company properties. In November of that year the firm announced plans for five high-rise luxury apartment houses.

Pouch Terminal

Pouch Terminals Inc., with 1,000-foot deep-water piers, No. 19, 20, 21 at Clifton, has been retained by the Pouch interests which founded the organization in 1916. Pier 19 is used by the Barber Line and Pier 21 by the K. Line (Kawasaki), both of which engage in Far East trade. Between 1949 and 1959, the Booth Steamship Line leased Pier 20. In September 1962 the Sabre Steamship Line, which also handles Far East cargo, took a long-term lease of Pier 20. Pouch Terminal has excellent warehouse facilities and direct rail transportation. An interesting list of foreign products and points of origin can be compiled by checking local newspaper articles reporting ship arrivals. A recent check revealed the following: rubber, jute, kopak, and tin from the Far East; zinc from Africa; automobiles from Japan; fiberglass sailboats from the Netherlands; cocoa from West Africa; talc from Italy.

Pier Development by the City of New York

Deep-water piers were built by the City of New York along the Tompkinsville-Stapleton waterfront between 1921 and 1923, during the administration of Mayor John F. Hylan. However, there was little return on the City's investment and for years the piers were referred to as "Hylan's Folly." It was not until the Free Port was established in 1937 that the waterfront showed marked activity. During World War II, the municipal piers were used by the Army and Navy as the New York Port of Embarkation. In recent years shipping activities have increased. Plans have been announced by the Marine and Aviation Department for a large-scale waterfront development project (84).

The New York Foreign Trade Zone

The New York Foreign Trade Zone in Stapleton was established in 1937 and operated by the City of New York for one year. In 1938 a private corporation, the New York Foreign Trade Zone Operators, Inc., began operating the Zone under the supervision of the Department of Marine and Aviation. About 150 persons are employed there (99).

This was the first of the five Foreign Trade Zones in the United States. Originally four piers were used, No. 12, 13, 15, and 16. Now operations are confined to Piers 15 and 16. Cargoes from all over the world are discharged at the piers, duty free, stored in the warehouses, resorted, repacked, sometimes assembled, and re-exported. At one time tobacco for cigar wrapping was stored and auctioned there. The Baltimore and Ohio Railroad operates freight cars directly to the piers.

Among the commodities that are brought to the Staten Island Free Port are: watches for assembly, canned meat, various metals, leather, coffee, chemicals, "cork from Portugal, pepper from Colombia, diamonds from South Africa, cuckoo clocks from Germany, nuts from Brazil, and talc from Italy" (99).

During World War II the facilities were taken over by the Army, but the operations were resumed in 1945. The area is fenced in and guarded by Customs Port Patrol Officers and guards assigned by the Zone Operators.

In passing, it is interesting to observe that Erastus Wiman had urged a free port on Staten Island in 1888. It was largely through the efforts of Cornelius Kolff that the enterprise became a reality.

Other Firms Connected with Shipping
Other firms have been organized on the Island because of the navigable waterfront. An interesting recent one is the Standard Boat Company, a division of Rando Dock, Inc., at 1483 Richmond Terrace, West New Brighton, which began operations after World War II as a ship supply firm. Three lighters are used to deliver supplies to shipping agents, ship owners, and chandlers (96). Iron works, engine and boilerworks, ship chandlers, and marine towing companies are among others that are listed in the Telephone Directory and by the Staten Island Chamber of Commerce.

SOME FACTORIES BEFORE 1898 ARE STILL ACTIVE
A few firms that were founded before consolidation are still in operation. Louis De Jonge Company,* now located in Clifton, was organized before the Civil War in Manhattan. The firm is one of the nation's leading manufacturers of fancy gift papers (47). Baltimore and Ohio freight cars come in on a siding to bring in raw materials and to transport the finished product.

The S.S. White Dental Manufacturing Company,* which moved to Staten Island in 1881, manufactures both dental and industrial products at its Prince's Bay plant. These include dental instruments, dental equipment, medical gasses, and dentifrices. The new Airdent Unit for painless extraction is assembled there. The Island plant, which employs about 800 men and women, also manufactures cream-whipping gas mixtures, molded plastics and flexible shafting for industrial purposes. It has complete chemical and metallurgical laboratories. During both World Wars the company had many government contracts and was honored by the War Department for excellence in war production. The early development of the plant was traced in the preceding section of this report. This firm is one of the places visited by teachers in the in-service community course.

Jerome B. King's Plaster Mill in New Brighton, organized in 1876, was purchased by the United States Gypsum Company* in 1924. The Staten Island plant, with about 500 employees, is one of the U.S. Gypsum's 54 plants. Five modern ships are used to transport the gypsum rock from Windsor, Nova Scotia to the New Brighton dock where it is unloaded by conveyor belt to storage bins and silos (35, 36). The fireproof sheetrock wallboard which is manufactured from the processed gypsum is used extensively in present-day construction. Other products are plaster, paint, and partition tiles. A recent improvement at the plant at 561 Richmond Terrace is the new warehouse on the opposite side of the Terrace with a conveyor to move the finished products from the factory to storage, thereby relieving the traffic bottleneck caused by the previous method of loading the huge trailer trucks that distribute Gypsum products throughout the metropolitan area. Baltimore and Ohio freight cars service the plant. The community course members visit this firm also.

Standard Varnish Works moved to Staten Island from Long Island in 1893. In 1924 the business merged with the Toch Brothers Chemical Company, operating under the name Standard-Toch Chemicals Company, Inc. In 1961 Montgomery Ward & Co. mail order house purchased the firm which it manages as a subsidiary under the name Standard T Chemicals. The plant manufactures protective paints, lacquers, paint-inks, and insulating compounds for wires. Its products have been used on the *Queen Mary*, on Manhattan skyscrapers, and by such companies as Singer, Eastman Kodak, General Electric, and Continental Can. This Mariners Harbor firm has a complete chemical laboratory for research and experimentation.

MANY STATEN ISLAND FACTORIES CLOSED DURING THE DEPRESSION YEARS
During the depression years many industrial plants on Staten Island were forced to close. This affected the communities that depended upon these factories for employment. Many families moved away and in some instances progress in the communities became static.

The largest firm to disband was the C.W. Hunt plant in West New Brighton which had been founded in 1872. Its operation was explained in detail in the preceding section of this report.

The Barrett Nephews Company* (Old Staten Island Dyeing and Cleaning Establishment), which can be traced back to 1819, moved its dry cleaning plant to Manhattan where it still operates. The American Linoleum Manufacturing Company, which had been established in Linoleumville (now Travis) in 1873, closed its large factory that had at one time employed 700 persons.

The brick factories that had prospered before 1898 and in the early 1900s also discontinued operations during the depression years of the 1930s. They included the Kreischer plant in Kreischerville (now Charleston), the American Brick Company, and the Dolan Brick Company in the Fresh Kills area. The Atlantic Terra Cotta Company of Tottenville, manufacturers of building ornaments, also closed.

Another firm which failed at this time was the Irving Manufacturing Company, founded in 1881 in the Crabtree and Wilkinson factory, which manufactured textiles at 67 Jersey Street, now Richmond Terrace.

A smaller firm, which employed a number of Tottenville residents, was the Tottenville Hat Works on Johnson Avenue which closed about 1927.

INDUSTRY ON STATEN ISLAND TODAY
Fortunately for Staten Islanders, several large industries opened plants which have continued to prosper. The largest of these is the Staten Island plant of Procter and Gamble Manufacturing Company* which began operations in Mariners Harbor in 1907. The organization had been founded in 1837 in Cincinnati by a candlemaker from England, William Procter, and a soapmaker from Ireland, James Gamble. From 11 buildings on 77 acres, the Island plant has grown to 64 buildings on 125 acres. Most of the property, known as Port Ivory, is reclaimed marshland. The number of employees has increased from 400 to 1,500.

Ivory soap was the first product made at the plant (97). A Crisco factory was added in 1926. Gradually soap powders, synthetic detergents, cleansers, and prepared bake mixes have been added to the list. A by-product of the industry is glycerin which is sold to drug, cosmetic, and chemical firms (98). The P & G factory has direct rail connection with the Baltimore and Ohio Railroad and has access to the Goethals Bridge which connects with the New Jersey Turnpike.

The third largest firm on the Island is the Nassau Smelting and Refining Company* which opened its plant in 1900 as the Tottenville Copper Company. It had been founded in 1884 by Benjamin Lowenstein, a German immigrant who opened a small shop to buy and sell scrap metals. His business soon expanded to include smelting operations, and by the turn of the century needed a larger plant. It was at this time that Lowenstein moved to Staten Island. He overcame many adversities through two business recessions. In 1931 the Western Electric Company purchased the Tottenville Copper Company and renamed the firm Nassau Smelting and Refining Company (26). This plant, with about 650 employees, is the leading salvage unit of the Bell Telephone system, reclaiming non-ferrous metals from obsolete telephone equipment. Products are shipped by trailer truck or by the Baltimore and Ohio Railroad. Plans have been announced for a huge expansion program. This firm is visited by the teachers as part of the in-service course on utilization of community resources.

Ansbacher-Siegle Corporation,* 92 Chestnut Street, Rosebank is one of the leading manufacturers of fine pigments in the country. Its products are used in industrial paints, in printing inks, and in cosmetics. The large fireproof factory was constructed in 1909 as G. Siegle Corporation, the first color factory in the United States to use German processes. A large fence was built around the five acres of property and an 18-room Bavarian manor-type mansion was constructed on Tompkins Avenue for the plant manager. Other homes were built for the executives, as well as a large stable for riding and carriage horses. The house in which Garibaldi* had lived was moved to its present location on the opposite side of Tompkins Avenue. During World War I the property of this firm was taken over by the Alien Property Fund and American interests acquired the plant and formulae. In 1929 it combined with the Ansbacher Corporation of

Brooklyn which had manufactured insecticides. The firm has large chemical laboratories, its own power plant, and water supply from artesian wells.

The Wallerstein Company* opened its Staten Island chemical plant in Mariners Harbor in 1918 on the site of the old Mersereau farm. Today, with 400 employees, it is one of the country's largest producers of enzymes and enzyme chemicals. These products are used in such industries as meat packing, food processing, baking, textiles, tanning, brewing, drycleaning, and pharmaceuticals (22). At one time the firm made Bosco Milk Amplifier, a chocolate syrup reinforced with vitamins and minerals. In 1957 Wallerstein became affiliated with Baxter Laboratories, Inc. Experimentation and research is carried on in a modern chemical laboratory. This firm is also visited by teachers during the in-service course on community resources.

The Gulf Oil Corporation* acquired 700 acres of land near the Goethals Bridge Plaza in 1928. Swampland was reclaimed and storage tanks erected. Ocean-going tankers bring petroleum products from Texas and South America into Gulfport where they are stored in more than 100 tanks and distributed to customers in the metropolitan area as needed. Staten Island is also a pipeline terminal. From Gulfport, barges carry products to cities in the New England states.

Mobil Oil Company constructed its terminal at Port Socony along the Arthur Kill, Charleston, in 1934. Much of this property is also reclaimed land. During World War II, Port Socony was the terminal of the "Little Big Inch" pipeline which brought oil from the Middle West to the East for our combat ships. Today Socony-Vacuum tankers discharge crude oil, gasoline, and other petroleum products to the huge storage tanks along the Arthur Kill. From that point barges transport the crude oil to a Brooklyn refinery and other products to places in the New York area. Local Mobil dealers receive their supplies directly from Port Socony by truck. About 80 persons are employed at the terminal (8).

Louis Marchi and Company, Inc., located on Front Street in Stapleton, is one of the largest manufacturers of wax artificial fruit in the United States. Mr. Marchi, the founder, was a sculptor who started this business in Manhattan in 1924 after he had retired. In 1943 the firm moved to Staten Island where it now employs 50 persons.

One of the newest industries on Staten Island is the Chivers Book Binding Company* at 20 Clifton Avenue, Rosebank, facing the Narrows. This company, established in Brooklyn in 1909, came to the Island in 1955. It is well-known for its rebinding of library books and prebinding of new volumes. The Picture Cover Bindings, Inc. was established within the same building in 1936. This firm manufactures the colored buckram covers for library bookbinders throughout the country.

Uniforms by Ostwald, Inc.* moved to Staten Island from Manhattan in 1945. At its modern plant on Richmond Terrace, New Brighton, 300 employees manufacture about 1,500 band uniforms each week for musical bands throughout the nation. The firm makes the military headdresses, shakos, for the West Point band. The new Richmond Terrace housing project is being constructed around the plant which has recently expanded.

Another color plant on the Island is the Magruder Color Company, Inc. at 2385 Richmond Terrace, founded in 1927. Dry colors for the printing ink and paint industries are manufactured at the Elm Park plant which has about 10 employees.

Elm Park is also the site of a new building erected in 1961 by the Narva Labs, Inc., manufacturers of perfume, perfume oils, and flavoring for food products. Before moving into the new plant on Granite Avenue, near Wallerstein's, the firm had been located in Stapleton.

An interesting business born of a hobby during the depression of the 1930s is that conducted by the Howat family on Hopping Avenue, Tottenville. Mr. Howat had been chief chemist at the Atlantic Terra Cotta plant, previously mentioned, and when his services were terminated he turned his hobby of making porcelain figurines, vases, and modern art reproductions into a business which has been most successful. Ceramic costume jewelry was added to the products. Some of the Howat pieces are in the contemporary ceramics collection at the Metropolitan Museum of Art.

There are several greenhouses and garden centers on Staten Island. One of the largest is the Richmond Floral Company* in Richmondtown (48). This company and its predecessor have been growing flowers on the Island for over 60 years. Since 1930 it has specialized in the production of orchids for the wholesale cut flower market throughout the United States and abroad.

As in any other community there are many bakeries in the borough. The oldest is Holtermann's Bakery on Arthur Kill Road. The original business was started in 1879 by Claus Holtermann in Richmondtown (47). The son and grandchildren of the founder now operate the firm at a different location and maintain door-to-door delivery as well as a retail store. Another large bakery is Buda Bakers* on Richmond Road, Grant City. This plant may be visited. Arrangements usually can be made for local groups to visit smaller neighborhood bakeries.

A survey of any school neighborhood will show many retail businesses and other small manufacturing plants, some of which may be visited by making special arrangements. The Island has a number of firms making dresses, trousers, blouses, and hats.

Other Firms That Have Closed

Some firms in operation before consolidation prospered during the early part of the Cosmopolitan Period but have since ceased operation. Among these was the Empire State Woven Label Company, Inc. which was organized in 1892 and remained in business at 386 Clove Road, West New Brighton until 1960. Woven labels were designed and manufactured in the brick building that is now known as the Columbian Lyceum. Others were Bechtel's and Eckstein's Breweries and several fireworks factories. Henry Pain's Factory on Alter Avenue, Dongan Hills made flares for the Signal Corps during the first World War. After the War the plant manufactured fireworks until it closed in 1927.

The Rubsam and Horrmann Atlantic Brewing Company, founded in 1870, remained in operation until Piel Brothers, Inc.* purchased the firm in 1953. Underground springs continued to supply the water needed for this industry. Employing about 375 persons, the Staten Island plant produced and distributed Piel's Light Beer and Trommer's Red Label Beer. In September 1962 Piel Brothers, Inc. became a subsidiary of Drewrys Limited U.S.A., Inc. of South Bend, Indiana. In November 1962 the company announced that the brewery would terminate its operations in January 1963 and would offer the plant for sale (25).

The International Ultramarine Works operated its Rossville firm between 1884 and 1917, as noted in the preceding section of this report. The Onyx Chemical Company purchased the old buildings in 1947 and there manufactured chemicals used in processing and finishing textiles, and in germicides and fungicides. This company closed its Staten Island plant in January 1963.

Several large firms were organized during the twentieth century, but are no longer in business. Among these was the L.A. Dreyfus Company plant in Clifton which was established about 1906. There, Dr. Louis A. Dreyfus* manufactured a "synthetic compound basic to the chicle industry" (40). East Indian guttapercha was brought in to Pier 23 by cargo ships and the manufactured products were transported either by ship or by the Baltimore and Ohio Railroad. A larger concrete building was completed in 1917. The business was continued several years after the founder's death. Since then a number of other companies connected with the rubber industry have used this Dreyfus building. The last occupant was the Geschwind Foam Rubber Company which closed its Staten Island plant in 1962 to consolidate with its Brooklyn factory. This firm manufactured rubber cushions and pillows. On the former site of Barrett Nephews Company dry cleaning establishment in West New Brighton, Albert D. Smith and Company manufactured window shade cloth, industrial tape, and book cloth from 1947 until it closed in 1962 when the West Brighton Plaza (housing development) was completed. Charles D. Durkee operated a large marine hardware factory in Grasmere near the railroad as late as the 1940s (47). The building is occupied now by the Brooklyn Union Gas Company.

BANKING INDUSTRY

The early development of banking institutions on Staten Island was traced in the preceding section of this report. Those mentioned are still in existence, most of them under other names. The current trend is for local banks to merge with large Manhattan banks, to open more branches, and to establish drive-in service.

Savings and loan associations have increased in number, giving great impetus to homebuilding on the Island. A list of banks and savings and loan associations appears in the Telephone Directory. Many of the institutions have erected beautiful modern buildings within recent years and are active in community endeavors.

UTILITIES

The early development of utilities on Staten Island was described in the preceding section. During the 20th century the services have been extended to keep pace with the growth in population.

Gas

In 1901 the New York and Richmond Gas Company was incorporated and soon effected a merger with the Richmond Gas Light Company and the Consumers' Gas Light Company. In the early 1900s street illumination by gas was replaced by electricity. Gradually gas lighting in the homes gave way to electricity. Gas cooking became popular in the first decade of the new century and recently gas heating has gained favor among householders.

Gradually gas lines were extended to various sections of the Island. It was not until 1922 that Grant City and New Dorp were serviced. Distribution to outlying communities of the South Shore has occurred only within the last few years.

In 1949 natural gas, which has replaced artificial gas, was brought to the Island through great transcontinental pipelines from Texas. These pipelines span the Arthur Kill from Linden, New Jersey to Gulfport, continue across the Island and then pass under the Narrows to Brooklyn. In 1957 the New York and Richmond Gas Company merged with the Brooklyn Union Gas Company which serves the Island today (75).

Electricity

By 1898 the existing small electric companies on Staten Island had been consolidated into the New York and Staten Island Electric Company and service had been extended to all parts of the borough. In 1902 the company was purchased by the Richmond Light Company which also acquired the electric street railway property of the Staten Island Electric Railroad Company. The new company, known as the Richmond Light and Railroad Company, serviced the Island until the Staten Island Edison Corporation took over in 1923. Ownership changed to Consolidated Edison* in 1952.

In 1947 the first Arthur Kill generating station was completed to supplement the Livingston* plant that had been built in 1897 and had become inadequate for modern demands. The second Arthur Kill power plant in

Travis went into service in 1959. These two stations, known as Arthur Kill 1 and Arthur Kill 2, supply power for Staten Island and for some areas in Brooklyn. Twin high-voltage cables under the Narrows connect the Staten Island plant and the Hudson Avenue plant in Brooklyn. Plans were announced by Con Edison in February 1962 for the installation of a high voltage line over the Arthur Kill from Travis to the Linden station of the Public Service Electric and Gas Company of New Jersey. Both electric companies belong to the interconnecting electric system by which utility companies may purchase power from each other. A $2.9 million substation, scheduled for completion in February 1963, is located near Hylan Boulevard in Rosebank (on site of Fox Hill Area Hospital). The other area substation, called Fresh Kills, is at Travis. It is at these area substations that power is reduced and passed to unit substations where voltage is reduced lower for consumption (95). All of these unit substations are attractively landscaped.

Con Edison has completed an atomic energy power plant at Indian Point on the Hudson. A brochure explaining this project is available from the company.

Water

In 1909 the City of New York acquired the private companies that had been supplying water to the Island residents since the 1880s. Water was obtained from driven wells, and pumped from stations in various sections of the borough. The largest of these pumping stations* is still in operation on Lincoln Avenue near Hylan Boulevard, Grant City. Another is at Victory Boulevard and Ontario Avenue, Sunnyside.

Staten Island is now supplied with water from the Catskill water system. Between 1915 and 1917 the first pipeline was laid under the Narrows between Brooklyn and the Island, carrying water to Silver Lake Reservoir which is 185 feet above sea level. In 1923 a second siphon was laid. These two pipelines deliver about 35 million gallons daily. Silver Lake Reservoir,* with a storage capacity of 440 million gallons, acts as an equalizing reservoir to maintain pressure for those sections of the Island less than 228 feet above sea level. Areas of greater elevation are served by high water pressure generated at the Clove Pumping Station.* A new automatic pumping station to relieve the pressure shortages in the Annadale-Rossville-Tottenville area was completed in 1961 at 535 Woodrow Road.

To augment the Catskill Water Supply six other pumping stations draw water from artesian wells. Chlorination takes place at all these stations, as well as at Silver Lake.

In February 1962 excavation was started on the shaft for the new aqueduct under the Upper Bay that will connect Staten Island to a Catskill shaft in Brooklyn, The shaft, near Hannah and Bay Streets, will be sunk to a depth of 950 feet. The four-mile tunnel, scheduled for completion in 1965, will be constructed through bedrock, unlike the present pipelines that were laid in the mud of the channel bottom. It has been proposed that the excavated rock be used to construct a bulkhead to enclose the shoals around Hoffman and Swinburne Islands and that the area then be filled in to create one island for recreational purposes.

The new aqueduct will have the capacity to deliver 300 million gallons of water daily, almost ten times the present supply. Underground storage tanks, with a capacity of 100 million gallons, will be constructed at Silver Lake, replacing the present reservoir and eliminating the sea gull pollution. The reservoir area will be used for recreational purposes under the jurisdiction of the Parks Department (54). The Island is assured of an adequate water supply by the Board of Water Supply, the agency responsible for the tunnel construction. The Department of Water Supply, Gas and Electricity maintains the facilities.

COMMUNICATIONS

Telegraph

Staten Islanders are provided with telegram, cablegram, and radiogram service through the Western Union Telegraph Company which has an office on Bay Street, St. George.

Telephone

The early development of telephone service on the Island has been traced. New services that were introduced into the other boroughs in the 1900s ultimately appeared in Richmond. Early in the twentieth century the old crank-handle telephone was replaced by a more modern instrument. In 1949 Staten Island received its first dial telephone. Since then dial service has been extended throughout the Island and customers can dial directly to most of the large cities of the nation. Several new telephone buildings have been erected since World War II. A receiving station for the company's mobile radio-telephone network is located on Bogert Avenue, Todt Hill (near the highest point on Staten Island). Messages from ships and vehicles with radio-telephone service come through the automatic equipment in the little red brick building which looks like a typical home in the community.

In October 1962 the district manager of the St. George office of the New York Telephone Company* reported about 65,000 subscribers on the Island. He predicted 7,000 more customers by 1965. This is a sharp contrast to the 900 subscribers in 1896.

Newspapers

Early newspaper ventures have been described. Many of these have been preserved on microfilm by the Staten Island Institute of Arts and Sciences. Some of the newspapers continued to appear in the present century as indicated previously (45). Today the *Staten Island Advance* is the borough's only daily newspaper. It was established as a weekly in 1886, became the *Daily Advance* in 1918, and the *Staten Island Advance* in 1921 (47). Guided tours are conducted through the modern air-conditioned plant at 950 Fingerboard Road, Grasmere, which opened in 1960.* The paper has a daily circulation of over 52,000.

Post Office

In 1917 the existing 24 post offices on Staten Island were consolidated with the General Post Office, except Richmondtown which as the county seat remained a separate office. When the county seat was shifted to St. George in 1920, centralization of the entire Island mail service was completed, and all Staten Island mail was sent from Manhattan to the General Post Office which was then located in the Hugot Building at 36 Richmond Terrace (87). In 1932 the new St. George Post Office and Federal Building* was opened. There all mail is sorted for the eleven other classified postal stations or carrier stations.

Movie Industry

In the early 1900s several movies were filmed on the Island. Among them were many chapters of the series, *Perils of Pauline*, starring Pearl White.

Fred Scott's Farm* on the south side of Sand Lane, westward as far as Hylan Boulevard, South Beach was the scene of location. Some of the wagons and carriages from "Scotts Ranch" have been preserved. Sequences were also filmed at Brady's Pond, Grasmere and at Graham Beach. Civil War scenes in D. W. Griffith's production, *Birth of a Nation*, were filmed in the Fox Hills area.

The well-known Hollywood actress, Mabel Normand, often visited her parents on Staten Island (29).

Today it is not uncommon to see cameramen shooting scenes on the Island for the moving pictures or television screen. Recently the Decker Farm was used as background.

INSTITUTIONS

Of the four institutions founded on Staten Island before the Civil War to care for seamen and their families, three still serve their original purpose.

U.S. PUBLIC HEALTH SERVICE HOSPITAL

The U.S. Public Health Service Hospital* was founded in 1831 as the Seamen's Retreat. The early history of this institution was described in the section on the Federal Period. In 1903, the federal government purchased the property for $250,000, after having leased it annually since 1883. The 1837 buildings facing Bay Street were enlarged in 1912.

The present main building facing Vanderbilt Avenue was completed in 1935 and the two six-story wings added in 1942. On July 1, 1951 the name of the institution was changed from the Marine Hospital to its present designation. In that same year psychiatric service was offered in three remodeled wards and the outpatient service and admitting area were established in the buildings which had been erected in 1837. The Clifton hospital is the largest medical surgical U.S. Public Health Service Hospital in the country. With a bed capacity of over 800 the hospital provides care for American and foreign seamen, U.S. Coast Guard personnel, Federal Civil Service employees injured in line of duty, immigration cases, cadets at State Maritime Academies, and members of the armed services.

SAILORS' SNUG HARBOR

Sailors' Snug Harbor* on Richmond Terrace, New Brighton continues to serve aged seamen as it has since 1833. This institution was described in the section on the Federal Period. Today a modern geriatric program is carried on for the residents (90).

MARINERS' FAMILY HOME

The Mariners' Family Home which has cared for aged women relatives of seamen since 1854 still operates in its original building.

SOCIETY FOR SEAMEN'S CHILDREN*

The Society for Seamen's Children now places the children of seamen and others who need foster care in private homes. The building on Castleton Avenue, originally used as a home for the children, is the headquarters for the Staten Island Mental Health Society.

STATEN ISLAND HOSPITAL

The name of the S.R. Smith Infirmary was changed officially to the Staten Island Hospital* in 1917. The history of this first voluntary hospital on Staten Island has been described in the preceding section. Throughout the years its services have continued to expand. The present bed capacity is 258 plus 53 bassinets. In 1958 the new wing of the hospital was opened. Generous benefactors have made possible the growth of this institution from the time that Dr. George W. Frost gave the land on which it stands. The first automobile ambulance was donated by Mrs. Louis A. Dreyfus in 1913. A gift from the late Mr. David J. Tysen made possible the Tysen Residence for Nurses in 1926. This building is used now by student nurses of Wagner College School of Nursing during their last two years. As a community hospital, the institution depends upon the support of many people. The service of the Women's Auxiliary has been notable and present-day members in many instances are members of families who have been active hospital workers for decades.

ST. VINCENT'S HOSPITAL

In 1903 the Sisters of Charity of St. Vincent de Paul of New York purchased the Garner Estate on Bard and Castleton Avenues, West New Brighton and opened a 50-bed hospital there. A training school for nurses was founded the following year, continuing until 1921. In 1930 a five-story brick building, with a sixth floor central pavilion and a tower, was opened. A Department of Psychiatry was added in 1960, affiliated with the Staten Island Mental Health Society, and a Cobalt 60 unit was installed for cancer treatment. In October 1961 the new Cardinal Spellman Pavilion was dedicated, bringing the bed capacity of St. Vincent's Hospital* to 323. A new School of Nursing was opened in September 1961. In November 1962 St. Vincent's Hospital opened the first center on the Island for premature infants. The Garner House,* built in 1853, is now used as the convent.

The founder of the order of the Sisters of Charity of St. Vincent de Paul in Emmitsburg, Maryland was Mother Seton, who had been born Elizabeth Bayley. Her father was Dr. Richard Bayley who served as a health officer at the old Quarantine Station on Staten Island, died of yellow fever there and was buried in St. Andrew's Cemetery,* Richmondtown. Mother Seton's nephew was a pastor at St. Peter's R.C. Church in 1846, later becoming Archbishop of Baltimore.

RICHMOND MEMORIAL HOSPITAL

The development of the Richmond Memorial Hospital, Dreyfus Foundation is an interesting story of the steady growth of a voluntary hospital supported by a community. In a converted frame farmhouse on Prince's Bay Road, Prince's Bay, Richmond Memorial Hospital opened in April 1920 with a 25-bed capacity. As the population on the South Shore of Staten Island increased, the need for a larger hospital arose.

In 1929 a three-story brick addition with a 48-bed unit (South Wing) was built through the generosity of Mrs. Louis A. Dreyfus and South Shore citizens. Again in 1935 Mrs. Dreyfus financed the building of the North Wing of the hospital which brought the total bed capacity to 101. The Board of Directors voted to honor their benefactress by changing the name of Richmond Memorial Hospital, Dreyfus Foundation.† As more demands were made upon its facilities, and as advances were made in modern medical practice, an expansion program was planned in 1955, resulting in the new air-conditioned wing built in 1956-57, which increased the bed capacity to 152. This present New Wing of the hospital was made possible through federal funds in addition to financial support of South Shore citizens and businesses. The additional floor on top of the North and Central Wings, which was completed in 1962, brought the latest in medical service to the delivery room, nurseries, and the x-ray department. As the South Shore continues to grow, expanded hospital facilities will be necessary.

DOCTOR'S HOSPITAL*

Sunnyside Hospital on Little Clove Road was opened as a private hospital in 1940. In the path of the Clove Lakes Expressway this 43-bed institution was demolished in October 1962. To replace this facility, sixty Staten Island doctors had a modern three-story building erected on Targee Street, opposite P.S. 48, at a cost of $1.5 million. Known as Doctors' Hospital, with a bed capacity of 116, it opened in 1963.

SEA VIEW HOSPITAL AND HOME*

Sea View Hospital on Brielle Avenue opened in 1913 under the supervision of the Department of Hospitals of the City of New York as a sanatorium for 900 patients. At one time this was the largest tubercular hospital in the world with 65 buildings and a bed capacity of more than 2,000. It has its own refrigeration and generating plants. In 1914 an annex to P.S. 30 was opened there for the many children who were patients. In 1939 a Children's Hospital building was erected with a 250-bed capacity.

With the advance in medical science, tubercular cases decreased until Sea View Hospital was no longer needed. In 1961 it was closed for TB patients. However, there is service available for Staten Islanders who might be stricken with the disease. On the grounds is Richmond Boro Hospital for contagious and communicable diseases of children.

Across the road from Sea View Hospital is the Farm Colony, which opened at its present location about 1829 as the Richmond County Almshouse. About 1903 this facility was transferred to the City Department of Public Charities and was designated as the New York City Farm Colony (44). In 1928 it came under the supervision of the Department of Hospitals.

At the present time Sea View Hospital and the former Farm Colony are administered as one under the direction of the Department of Public Welfare, operating under the title Sea View Hospital and Home. There both the aged poor and the aged who can afford to pay are cared for. The former Children's Hospital is the Geriatrics Hospital.

213

ST. JOSEPH'S BY-THE-SEA

For many years a children's hospital known as St. Joseph's-by-the-Sea was operated by the Sisters of Charity of St. Vincent de Paul in a mansion formerly owned by Charles M. Schwab who was president of United States Steel Corporation and Bethlehem Steel Company. This property along the shores of Raritan Bay at Huguenot had been designed as a seaside resort known as Arbutus Beach about 1900 (70). Cornelius Kolff was one of the directors of this short-lived enterprise. Arbutus Lake* is within the property and the name of Arbutus Beach is still used. The Sisters of Charity used the estate as a convalescent home for the New York Foundling Hospital. A steamboat with a capacity for 2,000 carried children on trips to the beach. The mansion is now used as a convent for the Sisters of Charity. Plans were announced in July 1962 for the erection of a Catholic high school for girls on the grounds. This will be called St. Joseph's-by-the-Sea High School.

SEASIDE HOSPITAL

Another convalescent hospital for children was the Seaside Hospital at New Dorp Beach, which had been established in 1886. Until the 1920s the children were brought there in the Floating Hospital of St. John's Guild, a familiar sight to Staten Islanders as it lay at anchor about a half-mile off shore. After that the children were sent directly to the hospital by welfare organizations until the institution closed in the 1940s. St. John's Guild still operates a floating hospital from Manhattan during the summer months.

During World War II some of the buildings of the former Seaside Hospital were used by the Federal Government as the Staten Island Area Station Hospital. In 1952 they were converted into a privately operated nursing home for the aged, known as Seaside Nursing Home. This facility closed in January 1963.

SEA BREEZE HOME

Sea Breeze Home at 4600 Hylan Boulevard opened in 1904 as a summer home for tubercular children. The property was purchased in 1920 by the Association for the Improvement for the Conditions of the Poor, a forerunner of the Community Service Society (10). It became a summer rest camp for mothers and their children who came for a two or three week's vacation from the crowded areas of New York City. In 1927, 55 acres of the original 70 acres were sold. Rehabilitation of the outdated camp facilities, many of them World War I wooden barracks, would have been too costly, so the program on Staten Island was closed in 1959. An investment group purchased the 15-acre site in 1961 but has not disclosed its plans for the shorefront property.

MOUNT LORETTO

Mount Loretto,* the largest child care institution in the United States, was described in the preceding section. Modern buildings are replacing the original structures.

ST. MICHAEL'S HOME

St. Michael's Home in Greenridge was described also in the preceding section. This institution cares for about 300 children from ages 3 to 17.

BETHLEHEM CHILDREN'S HOME

The Bethlehem Children's Home which had been founded in 1886 at College Point, Long Island, opened its building at 375 Fingerboard Road, Arrochar, about 1917. This institution now cares for about seventy children from age six through high school.

WILLOWBROOK STATE SCHOOL*

Willowbrook State School, under the jurisdiction of the Mental Hygiene Department of the State of New York, is a state hospital for the care and treatment of mentally handicapped children. It is the largest institution of its kind in the country. A community mental health clinic is maintained also, offering out-patient treatment to both children and adults.

During World War II the U.S. Army used the buildings as Halloran General Hospital, previously mentioned. Later this became a Veterans' Hospital. Gradually the buildings were returned to the State between 1947 and 1951. In October 1947 twenty patients entered Willowbrook State School (6). Now there are more than 6,000 patients there Employees number about 2,000.

The institution started a school for practical nurses in September 1961. During the one-year course, training is received at Richmond Memorial Hospital and at Sea View Hospital and Home.

EGER LUTHERAN HOME

Several large private homes on Staten Island have become service institutions. One of these was the Keppler House, built before 1898 on Richmond Hill (now Lighthouse Hill). An interesting story about this old house was disclosed recently by Amey Aldrich, sister of Chester Aldrich who owned the property between 1908 and 1924 (2). Mr. Aldrich and a partner purchased the three-story Keppler home, gradually buying additional property until 40 acres had been acquired. In 1909 they opened a convalescent home for boys between the ages of 12 and 20, calling it Aldrich Farm. During World War I, when nurses were unavailable, children from Manhattan were brought to the Farm for picnics. In 1924 the property was sold to the Eger Lutheran Home,* an institution founded in Brooklyn by a Carl Michael Eger. The newly located institution for Norwegian men and women over 65 opened in Egbertville (off Rockland Avenue) in 1926. The Keppler house is still used. A new brick building was constructed in 1956.

SWEDISH HOME FOR AGED PEOPLE

Another institution that occupies a fine old mansion is the Swedish Home for Aged People* at 20 Bristol Avenue, Sunnyside. This building was the home of Commodore Cornelius Vanderbilt's daughter, Alitia, who married L. B. La Bau. La Bau Avenue commemorates this family.

Other homes which have been converted for institutional use have been noted under *Homes, Recreation,* or *Education.*

DAY NURSERIES

The Staten Island Mental Health Society sponsors the Mariners Harbor Day Nursery at 166 Lockman Avenue. City funds assist this program. The Department of Welfare and the Staten Island Child Care Association operate the Edwin Markham Child Care Center at the new Stapleton Houses. Formerly this community service was offered at the Edwin Markham Houses.

EDUCATION

In 1898 Staten Island had 29 district schools, each with a Board of Trustees who selected the teachers. With consolidation, however, these schools came under the jurisdiction of the New York City Board of Education of which William H. Maxwell was the first Superintendent of Schools.

Hubbard R. Yetman (1847-1924), who had settled in Tottenville soon after the Civil War, became the first Borough Superintendent of Schools in Richmond County (1898-1905) with offices in Stapleton (57). He had two borough associate superintendents to aid him. Yetman Avenue in Tottenville commemorates this man who had been teacher, justice of the peace and state assemblyman, as well as school superintendent.

The second Borough Superintendent of Richmond County was Darwin L. Bardwell (1905-1913) (46). P.S. 29 honors his name. In 1909 the title was changed to District Superintendent and in 1926 to Assistant Superintendent. Frank Hankinson was Assistant Superintendent of Staten Island schools from 1926 to 1937. P.S. 50 commemorates his name (46).

Four presidents of the Board of Education of the City of New York have been Staten Islanders: William G. Willcox (name given to P.S. 48), Anning S. Prall (name given to J.H.S. 27) (29), Ellsworth B. Buck (who became a Congressman), and Andrew C. Clauson. Ralph R. McKee, after whom McKee Vocational and Technical High School was named, was a vice-president of the Board of Education. William H. Ettinger, who had been a teacher on Staten Island, became Superintendent of Schools of the City of New York (28).

Of the twenty-nine school buildings that were in existence in 1898, twelve are still in use. The following list is arranged according to date of construction:

P.S. 1, Tottenville	1878
P.S. 26, Linoleumville (now Travis)	1880
P.S. 18, West New Brighton	1890
P.S. 20, Port Richmond*	1891
P.S. 3, Pleasant Plains	1894
P.S. 10, Egbertville	1894
P.S. 12, Concord	1894
P.S. 4, Kreischerville (now Charleston)	1896
P.S. 13, Rosebank	1896

P.S. 16, New Brighton (now Tompkinsville)	1896
P.S. 15, Tompkinsville	1897
P.S. 17, New Brighton	1898

Some of the buildings listed above have had additions, or new buildings constructed on an adjacent site.

Shortly after consolidation, the parents living in the community now known as Westerleigh felt the need for a public school, and P.S. 30, R. was organized in the Villa Hotel. Large quarters were needed soon and a new building was erected in 1904 on land given by the National Prohibition Society. Gradually as the population increased in other sections of the Island, new schools were erected.

Through the years, shifts in population have resulted in the closing of some school buildings. A few of these schoolhouses are used now for other purposes. The former P.S. 6, Rossville at 971 Rossville Avenue (then New York Avenue) was erected in 1901 and was closed in 1945. The building is used by the Marimac Novelty Company as a factory. The former P.S. 9 on Eighth Street, near Beach Avenue, New Dorp was erected in 1894 and was closed in 1932. This building was occupied by the 122nd Police Precinct until 1963. P.S. 23 on Mersereau Avenue, Mariners Harbor, which was built in 1895 and enlarged in 1905, has been used by the Bethlehem Steel Company since 1942. Old P.S. 29 which later became old P.S. 35, at 498 Manor Road, Castleton Corners, was erected in 1889 and is now the Elim Gospel Tabernacle. P.S. 31 at 650 Bloomingdale Road, Pleasant Plains, built in 1903, and P.S. 32 on Osgood Avenue near Targee Street, Stapleton, erected in 1901, are both factories. P.S. 33, on Midland Avenue, Grant City, built in 1901, has been used by St. Christopher's Parochial School since 1957.

School buildings that have been demolished include P.S. 2, Richmond Valley; P.S. 7, Greenridge; P.S. 24, Summerville; P.S. 25, Bloomfield; P.S. 27, New Springville; P.S. 34, Fort Wadsworth; P.S. 43, Brighton Heights; and P.S. 47, Prince's Bay.

NEW ELEMENTARY AND JUNIOR HIGH SCHOOLS

Since World War II there have been several new elementary and junior high schools constructed on Staten Island to meet the needs of a growing population. These include a new P.S. 3, named the Pleasant Plains; P.S. 14, Stapleton (Vanderbilt School); P.S. 35, Sunnyside (Clove Valley); P.S. 38, Midland Beach (George Cromwell); P.S. 50, Oakwood (Frank Hankinson); J.H.S. 51, Graniteville (Edwin Markham); J.H.S. 49, Stapleton (Berta A. Dreyfus). The last two are the first junior high schools on Staten Island.

Each of the public elementary and junior high schools is designated by name, as well as by number. About half of them are named for localities and others after community leaders. A complete listing is given in the *Official Directory of the Board of Education of the City of New York* (the Red Book), which is available in the office of each school.

Many schools have been enlarged and modernized. In October 1962 there were 34 elementary school buildings (including two annexes), two junior high schools, and five public high schools. Schools under construction as of that date were:

J.H.S. 27, West New Brighton	– named for Anning S. Prall (29)
J.H.S. 2, Midland Beach	– named for George Egbert (former member of Local School Board) (47)
P.S. 18, West New Brighton	– to replace 1890 building

SITES

Sites have been acquired for several new schools on Staten Island. P.S. 31, New Brighton, to be named William T. Davis, will replace P.S. 17 and P.S. 23, to be named Richmondtown, will replace P.S. 28. P.S. 55, Eltingville, to be named Henry M. Boehm, will serve an area which has seen rapid growth. J.H.S. 7, Huguenot, to be named Elias Bernstein (47), will provide a junior high school program for the South Shore area. Other school buildings have been recommended in sections of the Island where many new homes are planned or are under construction. At present plans are being formulated for a new P.S. 9, Tompkinsville to replace P.S. 15 and P.S. 16. This new building will be named in memory of John J. Driscoll, who was principal of P.S. 16 from 1891 until 1930.

HIGH SCHOOLS

Before consolidation high school departments had been established in public elementary schools in Port Richmond, in Tottenville, and in Stapleton, all offering two-year courses. In 1898 a four-year course was organized in Stapleton's Union Free School No. 2. The Tottenville high school department was transferred to Stapleton in 1902 and then to Curtis High School when that building was opened in 1904. The high school department from Port Richmond was transferred also to Curtis. Later Tottenville was re-established in P.S. 1 as a high school with a four-year course. There was a Curtis Annex in P.S. 20 until the Port Richmond High School was constructed in 1927.

In 1935 the Staten Island Vocational High School was opened at its present location. The following year it was renamed McKee Vocational High School after the late Ralph R. McKee who had been Richmond Borough Commissioner of Education and also a vice-president of the Board of Education of the City (47). Previous vocational training had been offered at P.S. 20 and at Elm Park. In 1936, both New Dorp and Tottenville High Schools were opened. A full description of public secondary education on Staten Island has been published in issues of the *Staten Island Historian* (33).

SERVICES

As part of the educational system of the City of New York, Staten Island has most of the services offered in the other four boroughs. In 1898 there were only four kindergartens on the Island. Now every school has such a class. There are also "special service" schools, "600" schools, CRMD classes, classes for the gifted and for the handicapped, after-school playgrounds and community center programs.

SCHOOL ENROLLMENT

About ten thousand children were enrolled in Staten Island schools in 1898. In October 1962 there were 20,755 pupils in the public elementary schools; 3,392 in the junior high schools; and 9,927 in the senior high schools. At the same time, the Catholic parochial schools on Staten Island had an enrollment of 15,838. In addition, children were also attending other parochial schools and private academies.

PAROCHIAL SCHOOLS

Church-supported schools have grown in number on Staten Island, as they have in many parts of the country. Now nearly every one of the 34 Roman Catholic parishes has its own elementary school. Three Lutheran churches maintain parish schools. The Jewish Foundation School of Clifton graduated its first class in 1962. Ascension Day School (Episcopal) closed in 1958 after 25 years of operation.

St. Peter's Academy dates back to 1862, St. Peter's Parochial School to 1890, St. Peter's High School (Boy's Department) on Richmond Terrace to 1915. This last-named building is used now as the Girls' High School. The new Boys' High School was opened in 1935 at Clinton and Henderson Avenues on the estate of the late Nicholas Muller (44, 48).* In the following year a Junior College was erected on the property under the direction of Manhattan College. This has been the Senior Boys' High School since 1941.

The Monsignor Farrell High School opened in September 1962 on Amboy Road, Oakwood Heights, with a group of 350 boys in the first two years. Staffed by Christian Brothers, this school will have a capacity for 1,000 boys. The modern building has a campus of 12 acres. Monsignor Joseph A. Farrell served as pastor of St. Peter's Church from 1930 until his death in 1960.

Construction was started on the Countess Moore High School for girls in 1962. Staffed by the Presentation Sisters, this school, which will accommodate 500 girls, is located on Richmond Avenue, Graniteville on property adjacent to Our Lady of Pity R.C. Church. Classes were organized in the old school building of St. Sylvester's R.C. Church in Concord in September 1962. In the preceding year classes had been organized there for the Monsignor Farrell High School.

Another Catholic high school for girls, St. Joseph's-by-the-Sea, is scheduled to open in September 1963 on the grounds of the Convent by the same name on Hylan Boulevard. It will be staffed by the Sisters of Charity of St. Vincent de Paul, the order founded by Mother Seton in 1809 (as previously reported in connection with St. Vincent's Hospital).

PRIVATE ACADEMIES
The cornerstone of St. Louis Academy on Drumgoole Boulevard and Bloomingdale Road was laid in 1929. This is a day school and a boarding

school operated by the Sisters Marianites of the Holy Cross, a French order that had conducted a school on Main Street, Tottenville for many years. Other Catholic academies are St. Dorothy's at 1200 Hylan Boulevard, Old Town, on property once owned by the Italian banker, Tocci, and the wine manufacturer, Pio Goggi; St. Joseph's Hill Academy at 850 Hylan Boulevard, Arrochar, which opened originally in the old mansion known as Clar Manor that had been built about 1850; and St. John's Villa Academy on Cleveland Place, Arrochar, an elementary school for both boys and girls and a high school for girls.

Notre Dame Academy, a girls' private academy, was founded in 1903 by the Sisters of Montreal's Congregation de Notre Dame with an initial enrollment of twelve students. The original building was on the property at the corner of Howard Avenue and Louis Street, Grymes Hill. Three years later the John Scott estate at 76 Howard Avenue was purchased. This house is now the administration building, chapel, and dining room. In 1921 the adjoining Heyn property was acquired. This mansion became known as the Villa and is the present Convent for the Junior Sisters. The Dreyfus estate, purchased in 1925, became the high school. A new high school, erected in 1959, is known as the Dreyfus High School. In 1946 the academy became the motherhouse for the U.S. Province of the teaching order that had been founded in Canada in the 17th century by Blessed Marguerite de Bourgeoys.

The Augustinian Academy* for boys was founded in 1899 at Our Lady of Good Counsel Church on Austin Place. In 1926 the academy was moved to 144 Campus Road, Grymes Hill. There it functions as a boys' high school and a seminary. The building, Italianate in architecture, was awarded a prize in 1926 for the best architectural style of the year.

Staten Island Academy,* which was founded in 1884 in Stapleton, as reported in another section, has continued its educational program from kindergarten through high school, administered by a headmaster. In September 1962 the enrollment was 260. Dongan Hall on Todt Hill was purchased by the Academy as its Lower School. This building was erected in 1910 by Edward R. Stettinius who later became Secretary of State during the Truman administration. The Upper School remains on Stuyvesant Place, St. George.

COLLEGES

Wagner College

Wagner Memorial Lutheran College, founded in Rochester in 1883, moved to the Island in 1918 with 16 students. At that time its prime purpose was to train young men for the ministry. Reverend Dr. Frederic Sutter, present pastor of Trinity Lutheran Church in Stapleton, a Staten Islander, and a graduate of Wagner, was instrumental in having the college locate on Staten Island. Cornelius G. Kolff, then president of the Chamber of Commerce, had suggested the location to Dr. Sutter, who recommended the site to the college board of trustees. The Cunard property atop Grymes Hill was acquired and later the adjacent property belonging to Captain Jacob Vanderbilt,* previously mentioned. Cunard Hall* was built in 1851 by Sir Edward Cunard (29). The old mansion now houses various offices of the college.

Wagner College also purchased the estate of General William Greene Ward* who had lived on Grymes Hill with his family after the Civil War. His home "Oneata" (circa 1860), now part of the West Campus is the Music Building of the college.

Wagner gradually broadened its curriculum so that by 1928 it received approval by the State Board of Regents with power to confer Bachelor of Arts and Bachelor of Science degrees. Two years later the Administration Building was erected in Tudor Gothic style. In 1933 the school became coeducational. A school of nursing, affiliated with Staten Island Hospital, was founded in 1943. Now this non-sectarian liberal arts college prepares students for nursing, teaching, and business careers. Masters degrees are offered in Education and in Business Administration. In the fall of 1962 there were about 1,300 day students and over 400 evening students. The $1 million Horrmann Library, dedicated in September 1961, perpetuates the family name associated with Staten Island since the early 1900s.

Wagner College* offers cultural events for members of the community and displays a vital interest in community planning (31). A magnificent view of the waters of New York Harbor, of Sandy Hook, of the Brooklyn shore, and of the Manhattan skyline is visible from the campus which is 370 feet above sea level.

Notre Dame College

Mother St. Egbert joined the faculty of Notre Dame Academy in 1921.

Ten years later she organized college classes under the supervision of Fordham University and became dean of the Notre Dame College (47). In 1933 the College received its own charter and Mother St. Egbert continued as dean until 1954 when she became its first president, a position that she still holds. In 1934 the Gans Mansion, built in Georgian style, was purchased. Located on Grymes Hill, not far from Wagner College, this is the Administration Building of Notre Dame. Several new buildings have been erected since 1938 (9).

Notre Dame,* as a liberal arts college for women, confers the degrees of Bachelor of Arts, Bachelor of Science, and Bachelor of Science in Elementary Education. Its student body numbers about 400 women.

Staten Island Community College

Staten Island Community College* opened in temporary quarters at 50 Bay Street, St. George in September 1956, as a branch of the State University of New York. It became accredited as a unit of the City University of New York in 1962. As a two-year coeducational institution it offers the degree of Associate in Arts in two-year transfer curricula in liberal arts, science, pre-engineering, and industrial laboratory technology and the degree of Associate in Applied Sciences in two-year terminal courses in business technology and in electrical and mechanical technology. The student body has grown from an original register of 112 students to about 600 day students and 775 evening students in October 1962. In 1960 the college acquired the first floor of a former bank building at 30 Bay Street. This is the present library. In October 1962 negotiations were started to lease space in the new Richmond Building at 350 St. Mark's Place to relieve the overcrowding in the Bay Street buildings. A 40-acre tract of land near Ocean Terrace and the Clove Lakes Expressway has been selected as the site for the new Community College. It is hoped that the first three buildings on the new campus will be completed by the fall of 1964.

ST. FRANCIS SEMINARY*

St. Francis Seminary on Todt Hill opened in 1928 as a preparatory school for the Franciscan Fathers (46). There the young men complete four years of high school and are then transferred to a novitiate at Middleburg, New York. The seminary is located near the highest point on the seacoast between Maine and Florida. From the 86-foot tower atop the natural elevation of 408 feet, one can see for miles in all directions. At one time the City of New York maintained a robot radio transmitter on the tower for police and fire department communications.

NURSERY SCHOOLS
Wagner College Nursery School, located in the South Beach Houses, is a privately operated nursery school used as a laboratory school for Wagner students who are majoring in early childhood education. Other nursery schools were listed under day nurseries in the section on institutions.

TRANSPORTATION
Transportation facilities on Staten Island began to improve after consolidation. However the problem of adequate transportation remains, and will become greater as the population of the Island increases within the next few years. A series of articles in the *Staten Island Advance* presented various aspects of this continuing problem (85).

AUTOMOBILES AND ROADS
Automobiles gradually replaced the horse and carriage. An interesting article in the *Staten Island Historian* tells of the early automobiles on the Island (42). It is reported that a Mr. Duffei of Oakwood Heights and Dr. George Jessup of New Dorp were the first residents to own their own cars. The latter was the first physician in the country to use a car in his profession (42). The early cars were steamers which were replaced within a few years by the gasoline automobiles. Frequently some of these antique cars appear in parades on the Island or are displayed on special occasions.

Roads
With the advent of the automobile came a demand for better roads. A few streets had been improved with stone and water-bound macadam. Gradually these were replaced by concrete or asphalt macadam until by 1913 about two-thirds of the streets had been paved (53). Some roads such as Richmond Road and Forest Avenue were widened. Sections of Hylan Boulevard were opened between 1924 and 1927, incorporating the old Southfield Boulevard that had been completed about 1900 between Parkinson Avenue

and Guyon Avenue. Drumgoole Boulevard (originally called Ramona Boulevard) opened in 1939 to accommodate bridge traffic from the Outerbridge Crossing. Seaside Boulevard, paralleling South and Midland Beaches is a fine divided highway, completed in 1962, which will become a part of the proposed South Shore Drive.

Progress has already been made on the network of parkways and expressways planned for Staten Island to accommodate traffic using the Verrazzano-Narrows Bridge. These include:

Clove Lakes Expressway – extending 8.3 miles from the Goethals Bridge to the Verrazzano-Narrows Bridge, with a spur connecting with Bayonne Bridge, completion scheduled for 1964

Willowbrook Parkway – extending 6 miles from the Bayonne Bridge to Great Kills Park

West Shore Expressway – extending 8.7 miles along the west shore of the Island linking the Outerbridge Crossing with the Clove Lakes Expressway, with an interchange at Tottenville to connect with the Richmond Parkway and the South Shore Drive

Richmond Parkway – extending 12 miles from Outerbridge Crossing to the Clove Lakes Expressway

FERRIES*

In earlier sections of this report, the growth of ferry service between Staten Island and the mainland has been traced.

Staten Island to Manhattan Ferry

In 1905 the City of New York (Department of Docks and Ferries) began operating the ferries between St. George and South Ferry, Manhattan. The last side-wheelers, the *Castleton* (originally called the *Erastus Wiman*) and the *Stapleton* (formerly known as the *Robert Garrett*), both operated by the Baltimore and Ohio Railroad, were replaced by five new screw-propelled, steel-hulled, double-enders, each named for one of the boroughs of the City. After many years of service these ferries were superseded by more modern vessels (7). Following is a list of the ferries on the St. George-Manhattan run and the dates when they were placed in service:

Mayor Gaynor	1921	Gold Star Mother	1937
President Roosevelt	1921	Mary Murray	1937
American Legion	1926	Miss New York	1937
Dongan Hills	1929	Private Joseph F. Merrell	1951
Tompkinsville	1930	Cornelius G. Kolff	1951
Knickerbocker	1931	Verrazzano	1951

All of these ferries, except the first three on the list, are still in operation. Of the remaining nine, six are kept in service at all times, one is docked at the Marine and Aviation Department's repair facility at Pier 7, Tompkinsville, ready for emergency use and the others are in dry dock for annual overhauling.

The three ferries launched in 1951 were built at the Staten Island yard of Bethlehem Steel Company. Seats are provided for 1,800 passengers on the three decks, although often another thousand crowd a ferry during the commuter rush-hour. Three vehicular lanes on the lowest deck accommodate 45 vehicles. The older ferries have a seat capacity of 1,350 and carry only 25 vehicles.

The *Knickerbocker* was named for Diedrich Knickerbocker, the legendary author of Washington Irving's *History of New York*. The *Mary Murray* honors Mrs. Mary Lindley Murray, a Revolutionary War heroine who entertained General Howe and other British officers in 1776, thereby enabling George Washington and his army to retreat. A painting of Mary Murray is on the second deck of the ferry which bears her name.* The *Verrazzano* gives recognition to the discoverer of New York Bay and of Staten Island. The *Private Joseph F. Merrell* plays tribute to a Staten Island World War II hero who received the Congressional Medal of Honor posthumously. A bronze plaque in the cabin of the ferry describes the heroic deed. The *Cornelius G. Kolff* is named for a well-known Staten Island real estate developer and leader. A bas-relief has been placed on the ferry bearing Kolff's name.

The Department of Marine and Aviation of the City of New York, formerly called the Department of Plant and Structures, operates these ferries on a 15-minute schedule. During the rush hours, however, ferries run every 10 minutes and in the early morning hours after midnight, every half-hour. The vessels are equipped with radar for use during the heavy fogs which sometimes blanket Upper New York Bay. The 1961 report of the Department of Marine and Aviation indicated a daily average of 70,397 passengers (77), a daily increase of 2,276 over 1960. During a two-hour period in the morning and in the evening when commuter traffic is heaviest, about 20,000 Staten Islanders board the ferries (85).

Harbor Sights

The five-cent, five-mile, 25-minute excursion across Upper New York Bay affords the tourist, as well as the daily commuter, fascinating sights (18, 38). In addition to the ocean liners, freighters, and tugboats, there are many other kinds of harbor craft. One of the most unusual is the *Drift-master*, operated by the U.S. Army Corps of Engineers. Since 1915 the Army has been clearing the waters of New York Harbor of the driftwood which is continuously collecting. Huge steel nets scoop up the debris which is then dumped on incinerator barges that are seen burning in the bay. Small craft, called junk boats, often salvage scrap metal from the barges (38, 39).

Several islands in Upper New York Bay add interest to the excursion from South Ferry to St. George. Historic Governors Island,* now Fort Jay and headquarters of the First U.S. Army, was the country residence for English colonial governors of New York. The circular red brick Castle Williams was erected in 1807-1811 by Colonel Jonathan Williams, nephew of Benjamin Franklin. Today the building is used as a military stockade.

Liberty Island was known as Bedloe's Island until 1956. It was named after its first owner, the Walloon, Isaac Bedloe. The Statue of Liberty,* created by the French sculptor, Frederic Auguste Bartholdi, was presented to the United States by the people of France to commemorate the 100th anniversary of American independence. American school children contributed the money for the pedestal. The Statue, dedicated in 1886 by President Grover Cleveland, is now a national monument under the jurisdiction of the National Park Service. In October 1962 the cornerstone of the new American Museum of Immigration was laid. This building, to be erected at the foot of the Statue, is scheduled to be opened in the near future.

Ellis Island, which formerly housed the immigration station, has not been used since 1954. Many proposals have been made for the use of the red brick buildings which still stand on the island that was owned in the 18th century by a Manhattan butcher named Samuel Ellis.

Another landmark in Upper New York Bay is Robbins Reef Lighthouse* which was put in service in 1839 and rebuilt in 1883. Originally a hand-mechanism operated the rotating lens and bell (71). The Dutch called the ledge of rocks "Robyn's Rift," meaning "seal's reef."

Stapleton Landing

Early ferries had made scheduled stops at Stapleton which was known as Second Landing. When the ferry terminal was built at the foot of Wall Street, St. George in 1886, service to Stapleton was discontinued. However, the teamsters had trouble ascending the steep grade from the St. George ferry landing and agitated for a stop at Stapleton. Finally in 1909 the City began operation of a ferry from that village to Manhattan. This was chiefly a "team ferry" to accommodate the breweries of that area. Service was extremely poor and schedules uncertain. Passengers and most vehicles preferred the St. George ferry, and the Stapleton ferry was abandoned in 1913 (72).

Ferry Terminals

A new ferry terminal was built at St. George in 1905 to provide better facilities for the patrons. A wooden viaduct was constructed for the use of trolleys until a more substantial structure was erected in 1911. This one was doubled in width in the 1930s and the pedestrian sidewalk was covered. A spectacular fire in 1946 destroyed the St. George Ferry Terminal which was replaced in 1951 by the present fire-proof structure. Fine new approaches were constructed also. A visit to the modern terminal* will reveal the many facilities for vehicular, bus, rail, and pedestrian traffic. A three-acre parking lot accommodates the commuters who leave their cars at St. George.

A new ferry terminal at South Ferry, Manhattan opened in 1956. The moving escalator from street level to boarding level was a welcome innovation. Many stores were provided for the convenience of passengers.

Tottenville-Perth Amboy Ferry

In the early 1900s the Staten Island Rapid Transit took over the Tottenville-Perth Amboy ferry which had been operated by the Staten Island Railroad Company since 1867. The Rapid Transit's operation ceased in October 1948. The last trip was made by the double-ended sidewheeler, the *Charles W. Galloway*, that had been built in 1922 (74). The line was later taken over by the Sunrise Ferry Corporation which operated a diesel-powered screw propeller ferry, the *Piermont*, accommodating nine cars. At the present time Captain Elmer Johnson of Meiers Corners operates the line, but financial difficulties threaten to terminate the service. The Outerbridge Crossing carries most of the traffic from the southern end of Staten Island to New Jersey.

Port Richmond-Bayonne Ferry

Ferry service between Port Richmond and Bergen Point, Bayonne, New Jersey dates back to the sailing vessels of the 18th century. Steam ferries, which operated under various ownerships from 1849, were replaced in 1945 by diesel-propelled ferries. A new ferryhouse was erected at the foot of Richmond Avenue, Port Richmond in 1879 to replace the old ferry landing which had been at the foot of Ferry St. The diesel ferries were operated by different owners throughout the year (69). The last, Captain Elmer Johnson, leased the *Taurus* from the Sunrise Ferry Company in September 1961. Service was terminated three months later. The terminal remains, now owned by Rando Dock, Inc.

Travis-Carteret Ferry

The launch service between Linoleumville (now Travis) and Carteret, New Jersey that had been established for the employees of the American Linoleumville Company filled a need for other passengers. In 1916 the Cartaret Ferry Company, a subsidiary of the Brooklyn and Richmond Ferry Company, started service with an iron-hulled sidewheeler, the *Cartaret*, which had been built in 1885. In 1920 the company purchased a wooden-hulled sidewheeler that had been a navy gunboat during the Civil War, renaming it the *Clinton* (68). Patronage fell off after the opening of the Goethals Bridge in 1928 and service was discontinued in 1929. Launch service was resumed until December 24, 1960 when all ferry service at this point was discontinued.

Holland Hook-Elizabethport Ferry
Sailing vessels had operated between Holland Hook and Elizabethport, New Jersey prior to the American Revolution. Later steam ferries were used, such as the double-ended sidewheeler, *Uncas*, until they were replaced in 1932 by diesel-propelled ferries. Harbor Ferries, Inc. operated this line from 1954 until February 1961 when it was abandoned because of lack of patronage. The Goethals Bridge accommodates traffic at this point.

St. George-Brooklyn Ferry
Ferry service between Staten Island and Brooklyn has existed since early days. Until a few years ago two ferry lines operated from St. George, one terminating at 39th Street and the other at 69th Street. The 39th Street line was discontinued in 1946 (7).

Service was irregular between Brooklyn and 69th Street (Bay Ridge) until 1913 when the Brooklyn and Richmond Ferry Corporation, Inc. purchased the line. It used old sidewheelers, such as the *Albany* and the *Secaucus*. In 1954 the City of New York acquired all the ferries and terminal facilities which it leased to the 69th Street Brooklyn Ferry Corporation. The seven diesel-electric steel ferryboats, city-owned but privately operated, make the one and three-quarter mile run in about twelve minutes. The names of these ferries and dates of launching are:

Hamilton	1940	St. George	1942
Diffenbach	1940	The Narrows	1946
Hudson	1941	The Tides	1947
The Gotham	1941		

Most of the traffic to Brooklyn is vehicular. Each ferry can accommodate 42 vehicles.

RAILROAD

The early history of the railroad on Staten Island was traced in the preceding section. In 1899 the railroad and ferry to Manhattan were purchased by the Baltimore and Ohio Railroad for $2 million. The company operated the ferries until the City gained control in 1925. Today the railroad is operated by the Staten Island Rapid Transit Railway Company, a subsidiary of the Baltimore and Ohio. The passenger trains were electrified in 1925 with new steel cars placed on the 14.3 mile run between Tottenville and St. George. At that time a subway connection between Staten Island and the Brooklyn 4th Avenue Subway was proposed. It never materialized.

In the early 1940s diesel engines replaced the coal-burning locomotives which had continued to pull the freight cars. At the railroad shop in Clifton these 8 diesel engines and the 48 passenger cars are maintained (11).

Service to South Beach and along the North Shore to Arlington was abandoned in 1953 because passengers found bus transportation adequate from St. George to those points.

Under New York State law, all grade crossings in the State must be eliminated. The project on Staten Island, which started in 1936, was halted during World War II. Crossings were being eliminated in the Oakwood Heights-Bay Terrace section in 1963. The grade crossing elimination program on the Island will be completed when this improvement is made in the area between Jefferson Avenue and Tysens Lane.

Freight

A freight terminal was established at St. George in 1889, remaining there until its removal to Jersey City in 1934. The Baltimore and Ohio Railroad maintains two freight yards in Staten Island – one at Arlington and the other at St. George. The cars are assembled and delivered there, and necessary repairs made. The freight trains are carried across the Arthur Kill on the world's longest vertical lift railroad bridge. This $11 million structure which opened in August 1959 replaced the bridge that had been constructed in 1889. Freight cars are interchanged with the Central Railroad of New Jersey at Cranford Junction, New Jersey, with the Lehigh Valley Railroad at Cranford, and with the Pennsylvania Railroad at Linden, New Jersey.

A marine terminal at St. George maintains the diesel tugboats, the steel barges and the carfloats used in the freight operations from Jersey City to Staten Island and other piers in the metropolitan area (11).

TROLLEYS*

Ownership of various trolley lines on Staten Island continued to change after consolidation as it had since the first horse railroad company was organized in 1867. The routes of the different lines have been recorded previously. In 1902 the Richmond Light and Railroad Company purchased the Staten Island Electric Railroad Company. The power plant was in Livingston* and the repair shop at Brook Street, Tompkinsville (now the garage of the Department of Sanitation).* Between 1927 and 1934 these trolleys were operated by the Richmond Railways Inc. (73).

The Midland Company, referred to in another section, was reorganized in 1907 as the Staten Island Midland Railway with a power plant overlooking Brady's Pond in Grasmere. This plant was dismantled in 1917 (73). Carbarns at the intersection of Clove and Richmond Roads, later used by the Department of Sanitation, have been demolished to make way for the Clove Lakes Expressway. This line met several reverses and finally the City Department of Plant and Structures took over the Midland Railway in 1920. The cars, painted red, were nicknamed "Red Mikes" by Staten Islanders. These trolleys continued to operate until bus franchises were awarded to the Tompkins Bus Company in 1927 for the eighteen routes of the Midland system (73).

The City of New York also operated trackless trolleys on the Island between 1920 and 1927. Power for the overhead wires was generated at Sea View Hospital. The routes of these trolleys were from Richmond to Tottenville, from Meiers Corners to Linoleumville (Travis), and from Meiers Corners to Sea View Hospital, later extended to Egbertville.

BUSES

In 1934 buses replaced all the remaining trolley lines. Several private owners such as the Tompkins Bus Company, the Staten Island Coach Company, and the Isle Transportation Company operated the buses until the City took over the entire system in 1947. The Board of Transportation continued operation of the buses until the first New York City Transit Authority was organized in 1953. Now 22 different bus routes provide service to all sections of the Island. A Staten Island Transit Guide, indicating these routes, is printed in the Staten Island Telephone Directory and is reproduced on page 240.

There are also two New Jersey buses that operate out of the Port Authority Bus Terminal in Manhattan, use the Lincoln Tunnel, Hudson Boulevard, and then cross the Bayonne Bridge to Port Richmond. This trip takes about one hour and fifteen minutes. The terminus of the Boulevard Transit Company bus is the old ferry terminal in Port Richmond. The bus then retraces its route. The "Red and Tan" bus, operated by the Hudson Bus Transportation Company follows Richmond Avenue in a southerly direction to Amboy Road Eltingville, continuing in a westerly direction to Pleasant Plains where it uses the Outerbridge Crossing to Perth Amboy. At that point some buses terminate, while others continue to Keansburg, New Jersey.

PROPOSED TUNNEL

As early as 1919 civic leaders urged construction of a tunnel under the Narrows between Staten Island and Brooklyn. The request for a subway was submitted to the Board of Estimate and by 1921 two alternate routes were recommended. One of these was from Hyatt Street, St. George and the other was from Maryland Avenue, Rosebank, each to be connected with the 4th Avenue Subway in Brooklyn. The St. George site was decided upon and ground was broken for a shaft in July 1923, the Brooklyn shaft having been sunk three months earlier (44). Originally the plan called for both freight and passenger service, but Staten Islanders were interested only in the rapid transfer line, excluding provision for freight. The project was held up and finally abandoned. In 1930 interest was aroused again in a tunnel to connect with the 8th Avenue Subway in Brooklyn (48). Nothing came of this or of further proposals fifteen years later. When the new viaduct was constructed at St. George in 1950, the shaft that had been sunk in 1923 was filled in.

BRIDGES

Staten Island had been linked to New Jersey by a railroad bridge in 1889, but the need for a vehicular bridge became apparent after World War I as the population expanded and the number of motor vehicles increased. In 1921 the Port of New York Authority,* a public corporation, was established by the States of New York and New Jersey to develop and operate transportation and terminal facilities in the Port District of the two states.

Part of the program has been the construction of three bridges connecting Staten Island and New Jersey. Goethals Bridge spans the Arthur Kill between Holland Hook and Elizabeth. This cantilever type bridge, opened in 1928, bears the name of General George W. Goethals who built the Panama Canal and was the first consulting engineer for the Port of New York Authority.

Outerbridge Crossing, a cantilever bridge, spanning the Arthur Kill between Pleasant Plains and Perth Amboy, also was opened in 1928. This structure was named in honor of Eugenius H. Outerbridge who was the first Chairman of the Port Authority.

Bayonne Bridge, opened in 1931, spans the Kill Van Kull, connecting Port Richmond and Bayonne. This is the world's longest steel arch bridge – a beautiful sight from the hills of the Island or the Manhattan ferry.

Plans call for the completion of the $325 million Verrazzano-Narrows Bridge,* between Fort Wadsworth and Fort Hamilton, Brooklyn in 1964. This will be the longest suspension bridge in the world, with a center span of 4,260 feet. The channel clearance will be 228 feet to allow passage of the largest ocean liners. In the fall of 1962 the giant steel towers of the bridge, rising 690 feet above the water, were a spectacular sight from the Manhattan ferry and from the Belt Parkway in Brooklyn. To the Staten Islander they were a symbol of the unprecedented growth that is inevitable in the next decade. The towers, like giant sentinels, suddenly loomed ahead as the driver reached a hilltop, drove through Clove Valley, or rounded a curve in the road.

The bridge across the Narrows has a long history. As far back as 1930 forward-looking citizens were advocating such a span (48). Periodically since then various groups have urged construction. The Army and Navy refused to approve the structure, contending that the entrance to New York Harbor would be blocked were the bridge to be destroyed in the event of attack. Finally plans were approved and ground was broken in August 1959. The construction and maintenance of the span is under the jurisdiction of the Triborough Bridge and Tunnel Authority. The bridge will provide Staten Islanders with a new access to the other four boroughs and will also be "a by-pass route" for traffic which does not need to go through Lower Manhattan.

AIRPORT

A commercial airport was founded by George Schaaf, a Staten Islander, in 1926 near Richmond Avenue, New Springville. This is reputed to have been the first commercial airport within the City of New York. The City has taken over this property as part of the Fresh Kills Reclamation Project. Staten Island Airport, originally established in 1939 by Edward J. McCormick, is on the opposite side of Richmond Avenue, near the Farmers' Market (Greenridge Auction Market). This 165-acre tract of land has been sold for a shopping center. Newark Airport is accessible to Staten Island, but La Guardia and International Airports are at a considerable distance. Eventually helicopter service probably will connect the Island with the three major city airports.

PARKING LOTS

Public parking facilities have been provided by five off-street parking lots on Staten Island. These are located in St. George, Port Richmond, Stapleton, and West New Brighton. Others are in the planning stage. Parking meters in business areas accommodate shoppers (4).

PROMINENT CITIZENS‡
WRITERS

As indicated in other sections of this report, Staten Island has inspired the creative artist and writer since it was described by Verrazzano. Many writers of note have lived and worked on the Island during the twentieth century. Only a few will be mentioned (1, 55).

The world renowned poet, Edwin Markham (1852-1940), moved to Staten Island from California in 1902. His first residence was at the corner of Livermore and Waters Avenue, Westerleigh. Later the poet lived with his family at 92 Waters Avenue until his death in 1940. He is best known for his poem, *The Man with the Hoe* (29). Markham was a familiar figure to Staten Islanders as an active participant at community functions,

‡It is difficult to determine the composition of a list of prominent citizens within any community. For the purposes of this report, those mentioned either have become known nationally or have been recognized officially in some way. The newspapers and current bulletins of the Staten Island Institute of Arts and Sciences and the Historical Society offer an opportunity to become aware of the current work of authors, artists, musicians, and civic leaders (1, 37, 55, 78, 83). In 1961 a list of prominent Staten Islanders was prepared for the Tercentenary Commission (79).

often reading his poems from public platforms. The poet's son, Virgil, teaches at Wagner College, where the library houses a collection of about 15,000 volumes willed to the College by the poet. J.H.S. 51, Graniteville is named the Edwin Markham School. His name has been given to the Edwin Markham Child Care Center, formerly at the Edwin Markham Houses, but now at the Stapleton Houses. Several streets also perpetuate the name in Markham Court, Drive, Lane, Road, and Walk within the boundaries of the housing project. There is also a Markham Place in Westerleigh.

Another Westerleigh author was Florence Morse Kingsley who wrote more than 30 books during her residence on Staten Island from 1894 until her death in 1937. She has been mentioned previously.

There are several authors of children's books living on Staten Island today. Among them is Olive Earle (Mrs. Harry Daugherty) who went to the Island in 1934 to paint background murals for exhibits at the Staten Island Zoo. The natural beauty of Staten Island appealed to her and she remained to become an enthusiast, writing and illustrating several children's books that deal specifically with the Island's natural history (20). Many of her books appear on the Board of Education list, *Library Books for Elementary and Junior High Schools*. Recently Miss Earle illustrated *The Staten Island Walk Book* (92).

Phyllis Whitney has written many mystery stories which are listed on the Board of Education Library List. She is also the author of several historical novels. Of particular interest to Staten Islanders is her *Step to the Music*, a story of the Island during Civil War Days.

Frances Tysen Nutt used local background for her historical novel, *Three Fields to Cross*, which take the reader to many of the landmarks mentioned in this report. Mrs. Nutt is a descendant of Thys Barentsen, one of the original settlers of the Island and a daughter of David J. Tysen who has been mentioned.

Another Staten Island writer of national reputation is Amy Vanderbilt, author of books on etiquette. She was born at 161 Maine Avenue, Westerleigh, and attended P.S. 30 in that locality.

ARTISTS

It would be impossible to list the names of all the local artists of the twentieth century who have received recognition for their work. Reference can be made to two surveys listed in the bibliography (78, 93).

MUSICIANS

There have been many fine musicians on the Island during the Cosmopolitan Period. Two of national reputation will be mentioned. The late Maude Morgan, famous harpist, was attracted to the rural atmosphere of Staten Island. She held private concerts in her lakeside home on Drumgoole Boulevard (opposite St. Louis Academy). The studio in which she lived was a remodeled icehouse on a pond that was once part of the Max Maretzek estate.

Eileen Farrell (Mrs. Robert Reagan), Metropolitan opera star, moved to Staten Island from Connecticut in 1944. She lives with her family on Grymes Hill. Mr. Reagan founded the Community Concert Association on Staten Island in 1951 and has been president of the organization since that time (21).

ARCHITECTS

Ernest Flagg (1857-1947) was considered one of the world's leading architects of his time (29). He moved to Staten Island in 1897, living there until his death at the age of ninety. He owned vast acreages of land in the Todt Hill-Country Club Grounds area. Flagg designed the Singer Building and St. Luke's Hospital in New York, the Corcoran Gallery of Art in Washington, D.C., the United States Naval Academy at Annapolis, the Huguenot Memorial Church on Staten Island, and Flagg Court in Bay Ridge, Brooklyn, which was considered one of the largest apartment houses in the country in 1947. Flagg was noted for his original designs. He used serpentine rock which he quarried from Todt Hill. Remains of a quarry may be seen from Todt Hill Road at the edge of the Richmond County Country Club golf course. Many homes along Todt Hill Road, Flagg Place, and Richmond Road are constructed of this quarried serpentine. The Flagg Mansion is now occupied by St. Charles Seminary.* The Old Water Tower on his property has been remodeled as a private home.

PHOTOGRAPHERS

Alice E. Austen (1865-1952) is considered one of the earliest woman photographers of note. Unfortunately such recognition came only a few years before her death. Miss Austen lived with her family at "Clear Comfort" overlooking the Narrows (now known as the Austen House).* She recorded the fashionable social life of Staten Island during the latter part of the 19th century for her own personal enjoyment and that of her friends. The stock market crash of 1929 wiped out her financial resources. Eventually she lost her home. Crippled by arthritis and without funds, Alice Austen was admitted to the Farm Colony. When she had to vacate her apartment in 1945 she left her collection of photographs and negatives, numbering about 8,000, in the custody of the Staten Island Historical Society. It was not until 1950 that the Museum realized their value. Experts throughout the country became interested. Publications such as *Holiday* and *Life* reproduced some pictures and printed stories on this remarkable woman. October 7, 1951 was declared Alice Austen Day at the Staten Island Historical Museum. There, in her wheelchair, Alice Austen received long-delayed recognition. Money was raised by the Historical Society from the sale of her pictures and she was placed in a private nursing home (3, 62, 67). Many of her photographs are displayed at the Museum.*

There are many skillful photographers on the Island today. Their work is frequently exhibited at the Museum of the Staten Island Institute of Arts and Sciences.*

MUSEUM WORKERS

Many people who have been affiliated with the Museum of the Staten Island Institute of Arts and Sciences have become nationally known. Of these Ned J. Burns (1899-1953), who devoted 35 years to museum work throughout the country, was outstanding. The Burns family moved to Staten Island in 1911 and young Ned went to public elementary schools and to Curtis High School. Burns was one of William T. Davis' boys who went on field trips around the Island and mastered the art of collecting, mounting, and identifying insects. He was employed at the Staten Island Historical Museum for five years and at the American Museum of Natural History as a preparator for six years. He then became chief preparator at the Museum of the City of New York when it was first organized in the Gracie Mansion. Burns is best known for his dioramas. Among his earliest was one portraying the Peace Conference at the Billopp House. This is still on display there.* At the Museum of the City of New York, he constructed many dioramas and also a scale model of New York City as it was in the 17th century. After six and a half years at this Museum, Burns joined the National Park Service which was establishing museums at many of its historical parks. Eventually Burns became Chief of the Museum Division of the National Park Service. One of his last projects was the John Peter Zenger Memorial Room in the Federal Memorial Building (Subtreasury Building) at Wall and Nassau Streets (49).

Another one of William T. Davis' boys was the late Carol Stryker who was the first director of the Staten Island Zoo. His wife, Miriam C. Stryker, who still lives on the Island, a zoologist and naturalist, is an instructor at the American Museum of Natural History. She organized the Queens Children's Museum in Forest Hills in 1950 and has been its director since that time.

Others who have been associated with the Museum program have been mentioned in another section dealing with William T. Davis.

PHILANTHROPIST AND CIVIC LEADERS

Many philanthropists and civic leaders have contributed to the growth of Staten Island during the twentieth century. The few who are noted here have already received public recognition. Those who are carrying on such work today will be acclaimed by future generations.

Dr. Louis A. Dreyfus (1867-1920)* and his wife, the former Berta Schreiber (1857-1943), contributed to many philanthropic organizations. Among them are the Richmond Memorial Hospital (now called the Dreyfus Foundation), the Staten Island Hospital, Wagner College, Trinity Lutheran Church, and the Staten Island Council of Boy Scouts. Their gift of Hero Park, adjacent to their home on Grymes Hill, has been mentioned. After her husband's death, Mrs. Dreyfus continued her work as a civic leader. When she died, Mayor Fiorello La Guardia ordered the flags on public buildings flown at half-staff. Junior High School 49 is named the Berta A. Dreyfus school. Dr. Dreyfus, inventor and manufacturer, went to Staten Island in 1902 as a chemist with the Muralo Company in New Brighton. He patented a device for making a cold water paint and also invented artificial chicle. The firm that he founded has been noted

(40, 46). The couple lived in a Bavarian style cottage which they called *Quatre Vents,* meaning the "Four Winds," from 1937 until their deaths. This is now the home of the Rev. Carl J. Sutter.

David J. Tysen, 2nd (1841-1928) was a real estate developer and philanthropist. He developed areas in the New Dorp section of the Island (46). Tysen owned a large farm around the present Tysens Lane area and had a tomato cannery near the site of New Dorp High School. David Tysen built his home at the highest point on the Island at Todt Hill Road and Ocean Terrace. The house, remodeled, is still standing. Mr. Tysen's gift to the Staten Island Hospital made possible the Tysen Residence for Nurses. The Lake-Tysen* House which was moved from Tysens Lane to Richmondtown in July 1962 had been in the Tysen family for years.

William G. Willcox (1859-1923) and his wife, Mary Otis Willcox (1862-1933) were leading philanthropists and civic workers. They endowed institutions such as the Staten Island Hospital, Staten Island Museum of Arts and Sciences, and Staten Island Academy. They were also active in the Richmond Society for the Prevention of Cruelty to Children. Mr. Willcox was the first Staten Islander to become President of the Board of Education of the City of New York. P.S. 48 in Concord has been named the William G. Willcox School, and the name has fittingly been placed on the Cerebral Palsy Unit of that school. Mrs. Willcox organized the Red Cross on Staten Island during World War I and was president of the organization for sixteen years (47).

No account of prominent citizens would be complete without the name of Cornelius G. Kolff (1860-1950), well-known real estate developer and civic leader. He was a familiar figure on the Island with his well-kept beard, silk hat, and red necktie, remaining active until his death at the age of eighty-nine. Mr. Kolff settled on Staten Island in 1893, having boyhood memories of his grandfather's home on Richmond Terrace. Cornelius Kolff,* after whom one of the ferries is named, designated himself as "Staten Island's most obedient servant" and was responsible for increased interest in both past history and future development of the borough. At his own expense, he wrote and printed many pamphlets, some factual, some imaginative. Among them were *A Short History of Staten Island, A Staten Island Boy in Holland, The Riviera of New York Harbor, The Haven of Wooden Shoes,* and *Staten Island Fairies*. Mr. Kolff interested himself in all kinds of civic programs. One of the founders of the Staten Island Chamber of Commerce, organized in 1895, he served as its first secretary. He campaigned for the Staten Island Free Port after studying free ports in Europe (17, 47). Louis W. Kaufmann became Kolff's real estate partner in 1906. The business, founded in 1893, incorporated in 1923, is still operated as Kolff and Kaufmann, Inc. Kolff was active in the Staten Island Historical Society and worked for the acquisition and restoration of the Conference House in Tottenville. There is a memorial to him in this landmark.* This Staten Island booster lived on Harbor View Place in Shore Acres, a section he developed after the death of J. Harry Alexandre who had a large estate there. Kolff's daughter, Emily, who is active in many organizations and charities on Staten Island, lives in the beautiful home facing the Narrows.

PATTERNS OF GROWTH

The isolation of Staten Island from the other four boroughs has affected the lives of the people who reside there. Developments through the years have been characterized by a slow, easy, steady pattern of change while needs and interests have been met without dramatic or spectacular action.

The building of the Verrazzano-Narrows Bridge is a wonderful example of man's efforts to change his physical environment to suit his purposes. With the completion of this astonishing engineering feat, the Borough of Richmond really will become an integral part of the great metropolis – The City of New York. Many advantages will be enjoyed by its citizens who will find a richer, fuller life emerging with the continued but more rapid growth of Staten Island.

BIBLIOGRAPHY

1. ABBOTT, MABEL. "Staten Island Literary Associations." *The Staten Island Historian*, I: 19, 22, July 1938.
2. ALDRICH, AMEY. "Looking Back: An Island Farm Gave Succor to Ailing Boys." *Staten Island Advance*,* December 18, 1961.
3. "Alice Austen Day." *The Staten Island Historian*, XII: 26-27. October-December 1951.
4. BARNES, HENRY A. "Space Increased for Parked Cars." *Staten Island Advance*,* 77:A12, April 28, 1962.
5. BENLINE, ARTHUR J. "Citizens' Help Needed to Battle Air Pollution." *Staten Island Advance*, 77:C4, April 28, 1962.
6. BERMAN, HAROLD, M.D. "Over 6,000 in Willowbrook." *Staten Island Advance*,* 77:A15, April 28, 1962.

7. BETANCOURT, B. C., Jr. "The Staten Island Steam Ferries." *The Staten Island Historian*, XVI: 17-19, July-September 1955.

8. BIERBOWER, HAROLD J. "New Ship Docks at Port Ivory." *Staten Island Advance*,* 77:B9, April 28, 1962.

9. BOWER, ROSEMARY. "Mother Saint Egbert, Leading Symbol of Notre Dame College's Development." *Staten Island Advance*,* November 8, 1962.

10. BRITTAIN, PHILIP J. "Shore Recreation Area Demolished." *Staten Island Advance*,* May 10, 1962.

11. CANNON, RAY J. "S.I.R.T. Set for Growth." *Staten Island Advance*,* 77:A6, April 28, 1962.

12. CASSIDY, HAROLD H. "Grand and Petit Jury Panels Picked for Supreme Court." *Staten Island Advance*,* August 18, 1962.

13. ———. "New Names, New Functions on Tap for Island Courts." *Staten Island Advance*,* May 4, 1962.

14. "City O.K.'s Funds to Link Islands off South Beach." *Staten Island Advance*,* May 25, 1962.

15. COHALAN, REV. FLORENCE D. "A History of St. Patrick's Parish." *The Staten Island Historian*, XXIII: 10-13, April-June 1962. XXIII: 20-22, July-September 1962.

16. Community Council of Greater New York. Bureau of Community Statistical Services Research Department, *Staten Island Communities: Population Characteristics and Neighborhood Social Resources*. New York: The Council, 1960. P. 119. (Mimeographed)

17. "Cornelius G. Kolff, Long Civic Leader, Succumbs at 89." *Staten Island Advance*,* February 27, 1950.

18. CUNNINGHAM, JOHN T. and JOHNSTON, JAY. "Staten Island Ferry, New York's Seagoing Bus." *National Geographic*, CXV: 832-943, June 1959.

19. DAVIS, WILLIAM T. *History of the Staten Island Historical Society*. Staten Island, N.Y.: Staten Island Historical Society, 1936. P. 15.

20. EARLE, OLIVE L. *Plants and Animals of Staten Island*. Staten Island, N.Y.: Staten Island Institute of Arts and Sciences, 1953. P. 24.

21. ELLIS, EDWARD. "Opera Star Eileen Farrell Loves Staten Island the Most." *New York World-Telegram and Sun*, March 8, 1962.

22. EMELIN, ARTHUR C. "400 Employees at Wallerstein Work in a Beehive of Activity." *Staten Island Advance*,* 77:A15, April 28, 1962.

23. ENDRESS, ERWIN. "Court Reorganization Won't End Existing Congestion, Says Judge." *Staten Island Advance*, August 15, 1962.

24. ———. "Lawman Covers a Watery Beat." *Staten Island Advance*,* August 15, 1962.

25. ———. "Piel's to Close Plant, Drop Nearly 300 Jobs." *Staten Island Advance*,* November 6, 1962.

26. FEGEL, ARTHUR. "Nassau History Started with a Little Junk Shop." *Staten Island Advance*,* 75:B12, March 25, 1961.

27. GASTEYER, CARLIN. "Highlights of the Institute's History." *The New Bulletin*. Staten Island Institute of Arts and Sciences, II: 56-58, January 1962.

28. HAMPTON, VERNON B. *Fifty Years of Schooling in Richmond Borough*. (Prepared at the request of Dr. William Jansen, Superintendent of Schools), 1948. P. 6. (Typewritten)

29. ———. *Staten Island's Claim to Fame*. Staten Island, N.Y.: Richmond Boro Publishing and Printing Co., 1925. P. 55-57, 78-81, 89-90, 134-136, 147-149, 168-169.

30. HARKINS, WALTER. "Police Ready for Growth." *Staten Island Advance*,* 77:B17, April 28, 1962.

31. HARTER, D. LINCOLN. "Wagner Helps Staten Island." *Staten Island Advance*,* 77:A6, April 28, 1962.

---

*Back issues of *The Staten Island Advance* are on microfilm at the St. George Public Library, Staten Island.

32. HINE, CHARLES GILBERT ED. *History and Legend of Howard Avenue and Serpentine Road, Grymes Hill, Staten Island.* Staten Island, N.Y.: Hine Brothers Printery, 1914. P. 80.

33. HOGBEN, MAURICE DENZIL. "Public Secondary Education in U.S.: A Perspective." *The Staten Island Historian,* XXI: 1-12, January-March 1960. XXI: 15-19, April-June 1960. XXI: 21-28, July-September 1960. XXI: 34-36, October-December 1960.

34. HOLLE, DR. HENRY A. "Rosebank Focal Point in Quarantine Activities." *Staten Island Advance,** 77:B6, April 28, 1962.

35. HOSTRUP, B. M. "Brief History of Gypsum Manufacturing on Staten Island." *The Staten Island Historian,* XVIII: 6, January-March 1957.

36. ——. "Gypsum Plant Rose After Fire," *Staten Island Advance,** 75:E2, March 25, 1961.

37. "Island's Leaders of Last 50 Years on 'First 10' List." *Staten Island Advance,** April 29, 1950.

38. JONES, STUART. "Here's New York Harbor." *National Geographic,* CVI: 773-813, December 1954.

39. KELLER, ALLAN. "Sea-Going Rake Cleans the Harbor." *New York World-Telegram and Sun,* October 31, 1961.

40. KOPPENHAVEN, CARL. "Mayor Orders Flags at Half-Staff for Mrs. Dreyfus." *Staten Island Advance,** August 18, 1943.

41. KRIST, ROBERT. "Fort Wadsworth." *The Staten Island Historian,* XVIII: 20-22, July-September 1957. XVIII: 25-28, October-December 1957.

42. LAWRENCE, ALICE. "Staten Island's Early Automobiles." *The Staten Island Historian,* XIII: 9-12, April-June 1952.

43. League of Women Voters of New York. *New York City: Big City, Big Government; What It Is, How It Works.* The League. 1961. (25¢ a copy)

44. LENG, CHARLES W. and DAVIS, WILLIAM T. *Staten Island and Its People.* Vol. I. New York: Lewis Historical Publishing Co., Inc., 1930. P. 337, 353-413, 420-426, 505-508, 520, 522-529.

45. ——. *Staten Island and Its People.* Vol. II. New York: Lewis Historical Publishing Co., Inc., 1930. P. 548, 560, 578-585, 591-607, 637-641, 702-703, 718-721, 748-752, 761-768, 778-780.

46. ——. *Staten Island and Its People.* Vol. III. New York: Lewis Historical Publishing Co., Inc., 1930. P. 4-7, 13-14, 18-20, 33-42, 127-128, 137, 147, 161-162, 271-272, 287-289, 311-312.

47. ——. *Staten Island and Its People.* Vol. IV. New York: Lewis Historical Publishing Co., Inc., 1930. P. 323, 326-327, 365-366, 389-390, 403-405, 429-430, 435-436, 468-475, 477-484, 489-491, 554-558, 563-564.

48. ——. *Staten Island and Its People.* Vol. V. New York: Lewis Historical Publishing Co., Inc., 1933. P. 36-52, 86-91, 128-129, 231-232, 239, 245-246, 266-268, 282-283, 315, 331-334, 336.

49. LEWIS, RALPH H. "Ned J. Burns, Educator, Naturalist, and Museum Expert." *Proceedings of the Staten Island Institute of Arts and Sciences,* XVI: 61-74, Fall 1954.

50. LOERY, GORDON. "A History of the William T. Davis Wildlife Refuge." *Proceedings of the Staten Island Institute of Arts and Sciences,* XIX: 26-34, Fall 1956.

51. LUDINGTON, MARIAN. "50 Years Marked by Scouts." *Staten Island Advance,** 77:A18, April 28, 1962.

52. McMILLEN, LORING. "Borough Historian Traces Island's Growth in Last 75 Years." *Staten Island Advance,** 75:B2, March 25, 1961.

53. ——. *Staten Island, The Cosmopolitan Era.* Staten Island, N.Y.: Staten Island Historical Society, 1952. P. 18.

54. McSHEEHY, S. S. "Lake Look Won't Change." *Staten Island Advance,** July 2, 1962.

55. MARKHAM, VIRGIL. "Literary Traditions on Staten Island." *The Staten Island Historian,* XVII: 33-36, October-December 1956, XVII: 1-5, January-March 1957. XVIII: 13-16, April-June 1957.

56. MORRIS, CHARLES W. "Athletes and Athletics. "Staten Island's Claim to Fame." *Tercentenary Booklet.* Staten Island, N.Y.: Staten Island Tercentenary Commission, 1961. P. 42-46.

244

57. MORRIS, IRA K. *Memorial History of Staten Island.* Vol. II, New York: New York: Memorial Publishing Co., 1898. P. 175, 482-487, 488-494, 526.
58. New York City, Housing Authority. *Project Statistics.* New York: The Authority, June 30, 1961.
59. New York City, Department of Parks. *Commissioner's Report to the Mayor. 28 Years of Progress (1934-1962).* New York: The Department, 1962, P. 80.
60. ———. *Recreational Facilities for New Yorkers.* New York: The Department, 1961. P. 39.
61. New York State Education Department, Division of Secondary Education. *New York State and Local Government.* Albany: The Department, 1959. P. 239.
62. "Newly Discovered Picture World of Alice Austen." *Life,* 31: 137-144, September 24, 1956.
63. NICHOLS, CAPTAIN FRED F. "A-Use Planned by Coast Guard." *Staten Island Advance,** 77:B6, April 28, 1962.
64. ———. "The U.S. Coast Guard Base." *Tercentenary Booklet.* Staten Island, N.Y.: Staten Island Tercentenary Commission, 1961. P. 29.
65. PHILLIPS, DREW. "Missing Links Being Built." *New York World-Telegram and Sun,* August 17, 1962.
66. POPP, ROBERT J. "Fancied View from Bridge: A Peek at Ft. Wadsworth's History." *Staten Island Advance,** June 27, 1962.
67. REDDY, GEORGE O. "Fame Came Late: Death Ends Alice Austen Saga." *Staten Island Advance,** June 10, 1952.
68. REED, HERBERT B. "The Blazing Star Ferry." *The Staten Island Historian,* XXIII: 7-8, January-March 1962.
69. ———. "The Port Richmond-Bergen Point Ferry." *The Staten Island Historian,* XX: 23-24, July-September 1959.
70. ———. "Richmond Beach." *The Staten Island Historian,* XX: 7-8, January-March 1959.
71. ———. "Robbins Reef Lighthouse and Kate Walker." *The Staten Island Historian,* XXIII: 13-14, April-June 1962.
72. ———. "The Stapleton Ferry." *The Staten Island Historian,* XXI: 19-20, April-June 1960.
73. ———. "Staten Island's Trolley Railways." *The Staten Island Historian,* XV: 25-28, October-December 1954. XVI: 5-7, January-March 1955.
74. ———. "The Tottenville-Perth Amboy Ferry." *The Staten Island Historian,* XXI: 34, October-December 1960.
75. RIDER, FRED. "Gas Co. Spends $13 Million." *Staten Island Advance,** 77:C10, April 28, 1962.
76. ROWAN, COL. E. M. "History of Ft. Wadsworth." *Tercentenary Booklet.* Staten Island, N.Y.: Staten Island Tercentenary Commission, 1961. P. 50.
77. "70,397 Ride Manhattan Ferries Daily." *Staten Island Advance,** Jan. 31, 1962.
78. SMITH, DOROTHY. "Staten Island Artists." *The Staten Island Historian,* II: 17-19, 24, July 1939.
79. "Staten Island's Hall of Fame." *Tercentenary Booklet.* Staten Island, N.Y.: Staten Island Tercentenary Commission, 1961, n.p.
80. STEINMEYER, HENRY G. "The Comedy Opera Club." *The Staten Island Historian,* XXII: 31, October-December 1961.
81. ———. "Sock and Buskin on Brook Street." *The Staten Island Historian,* XVII: 38-40, October-December 1956.
82. ———. "South Beach: The Resort Area." *The Staten Island Historian,* XIX: 20-22, July-September 1958.
83. STOCK, MARION L. "Islanders Hungered for Books." *Staten Island Advance,** 75:D17, March 25, 1961.
84. TERKELSEN, STANLEY. "City Charts $30 Million Pep-Up for Piers." *Staten Island Advance,** November 4, 1961.

85. ———. "Transit: Going Where?" (series), *Staten Island Advance*,* June 18, June 19, June 20, June 21, June 22, 1962.

86. ———. "Miller Field Survives Changes, Rumors." *Staten Island Advance*,* November 16, 1961.

87. ———. "Remember Days When Island Boasted 24 Postmasters." *Staten Island Advance*,* September 2, 1954.

88. THOMPSON, EDWARD. "Fires Bigger Problem." *Staten Island Advance*,* 77:A14, April 28, 1962.

89. TRAUTMAN, LES. "Remember the Crowds, Fun, Bands, Hotels When Midland Beach Was in the Heyday? *Staten Island Advance*,* June 27, 1950.

90. TWIGG, WILLIAM C. "Big Farm at Harbor in 1886." *Staten Island Advance*,* 75:E14, March 25, 1961.

91. VAN NAME, CALVIN D. *Staten Island. A Report by the President of the Borough of Richmond to the Mayor.* 1921.

92. WEINGARTNER, MATHILDE P. *Staten Island Walk Book.* Staten Island, N.Y.: Staten Island Institute of Arts and Sciences, 1962. P. 24.

93. WHITEHEAD, JAMES L. "The Island and the Bay: Staten Island in Art from 1776 to the Present." *Proceedings of the Staten Island Institute of Arts and Sciences*, XIX: 3-25, Fall 1956.

94. WIDDECOMB, LAWRENCE W. "The Practice of Law on Staten Island During the Past Seven Decades." *The Staten Island Historian*, XX: 30-32, October-December 1959.

95. WITTEK, RAYMOND A. "Con Edison, 2nd Area Substation Takes Form." *Staten Island Advance*,* August 29, 1962.

96. ———. "Enterprising Dad, 3 Sons Build Flourishing Ship Supply Service." *Staten Island Advance*,* January 11, 1962.

97. ———. "Ivory Soap Still Floating Along with Leaders after 83 Years." *Staten Island Advance*,* June 6, 1962.

98. ———. "P and G Industrial Products Form Large Part of Sales." *Staten Island Advance*,* October 25, 1961.

99. ———. "Over the Fence is Over the Border in Stapleton." *Staten Island Advance*,* June 20, 1961.

100. ———. 'Silence', 'Think,' Form Prescription for Laymen While on Retreat." *Staten Island Advance*,* October 24, 1961.

---

*Back issues of *Staten Island Advance* are on microfilm at the St. George Public Library, Staten Island

Chapter IX

A LOOK INTO THE FUTURE

WITH THE COMPLETION of the Verrazano-Narrows Bridge, a new era will open for Staten Island and its residents. Greater accessibility to the heart of New York City will be assured and the extensive development of the Island itself will be a reality.

The Regional Plan Association, a private planning group, has predicted that a population of 250,000 by 1965 will be doubled by 1985 (2). This rapid growth will tend to make the Borough of Richmond one Island-wide community with the present rural-suburban life gradually disappearing as the population increases and the undeveloped land is utilized.

Intelligent, sound planning will be needed to protect the area from haphazard growth and to preserve some of the natural woodlands and marshlands (3). The Park Land Acquisition Act, approved by the voters in 1960, provides for the acquisition and development of several parklands. Furthermore, the "City Planning Commission has taken, and is taking, a number of steps to insure the healthy and desirable development of Richmond." Under the Mayor's Land Bank Program, the City is retaining title to many potential sites for schools, libraries, firehouses, and other public buildings.

*Richmond
Borough Hall*

HOUSING

At the present time, about four-fifths of the Island's residential areas are zoned for one and two-family homes, row houses, or garden-type apartments, while the other fifth has been zoned for larger apartments in harmony with the surrounding neighboring. It is hoped that the new zoning code which became effective December 15, 1961 will protect the Island against too many tall apartment houses and against the building of business centers in residential areas.

It may be noticed as one crosses on the ferry between Manhattan and St. George, that a few high-rise apartments are changing the skyline of the Island. Plans for additional buildings of this type have been announced for property now occupied by the American Dock Terminal in the Tompkinsville-St. George area. Previously undeveloped areas, particularly on the South Shore, are being developed rapidly as residential communities.

Future housing in outlying sections of the Island depends upon construction and maintenance of adequate storm and sanitary sewers. Under the revised City Charter, effective January 1, 1963, the Department of Public Works is charged with this responsibility. Mr. Meyer Wiles, Deputy Commissioner in the Department, has reported that lack of storm and sanitary drains "in large areas of the Borough of Richmond will continue to pose fiscal problems but with the cooperation of the City Planning Commission, the Board of Estimate, and the developers of industrial and residential districts, these problems are certain to be satisfactorily resolved."

MODEL COMMUNITY

The City Planning Commission has recommended an urban-renewal project in the Annadale-Huguenot* section of the Island. This undeveloped area offers an opportunity to plan a "model community." The streets, to be redesigned in curves, will follow the natural contour of the land. Specific areas for schools, churches, shopping centers, recreational facilities, and other community needs will be designated (7, 13).

RECREATION

The City Planning Commission and the Parks Department have set aside vast acreages on Staten Island for future recreational purposes. A number of small areas for neighborhood parks have been included in the general plan.

PROJECTED PLANS FOR PARK AREAS

Some present park areas will be increased. The Conference House Park will be extended along the beachfront from Tottenville to Mount Loretto, making this the largest historical park in the City of New York. Great Kills Park will be enlarged with the acquisition of all beachfront property between Miller Field and the present boundaries of the park. This includes Cedar Grove Beach which has been a private beach colony for over fifty years. Wolfe's Pond Park in Prince's Bay also will be extended. A new park area will be known as Lemon Creek Park,* Prince's Bay. Provisions will be made there for a boat basin, a marina for small boats, and a bathing beach (6).

Plans have been projected for a large 400-acre park area in the Charleston-Rossville-Huguenot section of the Island between the Richmond Parkway and the West Shore Expressway. At Fresh Kills, along Richmond Avenue, a huge landfill project is now under way. It is estimated that 3,300 acres of land eventually will be reclaimed for park and highway purposes and for industrial development. Some of this reclamation is in connection with the Richmondtown Restoration which will be described. According to a newspaper reporter about one-third of the refuse from the City finds its way to this Fresh Kills project (6).

ATHLETIC STADIUM AND SKATING RINK

An athletic stadium and outdoor skating rink have been planned by the Staten Island War Memorial Association and the City Parks Department. Great Kills Park has been suggested for the location of the stadium and Clove Lakes Park for the ice skating rink. These facilities will be constructed with funds collected from Staten Island citizens for a Staten Island war memorial plus additional monies from the City. The Parks Department will provide maintenance of both projects.

INDUSTRY

Undoubtedly the bridge across the Narrows will encourage new industries to utilize the many advantages offered by Staten Island. These include an excellent labor supply and accessibility to the world's largest market. Mr. Richard B. Irwin, executive vice president of the Staten Island Chamber of Commerce, reports that "since construction began on the bridge, representatives of several industries have been taking a close look" at the area. "The B.F. Goodrich Company, manufacturer of rubber and chemical products, has already announced plans to build its eastern warehouse in Mariners Harbor and the Crown Zellerbach Company has acquired a 100-acre site along Arthur Kill Road, Charleston, for a large manufacturing operation" of paper products.

INDUSTRIAL PARK

The City Planning Commission has proposed a 747-acre "industrial park" on the northwestern shore of the Island adjacent to Gulfport, bounded by Clove Lakes Expressway, West Shore Expressway, Victory Boulevard and the Arthur Kill. "The buildings will be one- and two-story split level structures, on landscaped plots providing adequate loading and parking space. The remaining area will be devoted to parks, streets, recreational facilities, railroad lead lines, drainage easements, and a sewage treatment plant" (2).

SHOPPING CENTERS

To meet the needs of a growing population, regional shopping centers will be established in convenient areas. In 1962 two large tracts of land were acquired for such future development. One is located on Hylan Boulevard, near Tysens Lane, New Dorp and the other is the present Staten Island Airport property at New Springville (4). During 1961 and 1962 many large supermarkets and small businesses were erected along Hylan Boulevard between Grasmere and New Dorp, and the Island's first discount department store opened in December of the latter year on Forest Avenue, Mariners Harbor. Inevitably, large Eastern department stores will establish branches on the Island as they have done in other growing communities.

PIER REDEVELOPMENT

In February 1962 the Department of Marine and Aviation announced the results of an intensive survey of the Staten Island piers as part of the waterfront redevelopment program for the entire New York City area. Recommendations were made for rehabilitation of Piers 6, 7, 12 and 13, demolition of Piers 8, 9, 10 and 11, and reconstruction of the Foreign Trade Zone. Although these improvements were not included in the 1963 budget, it is inevitable that this east shore waterfront will be rehabilitated after the bridge is completed. Then Staten Island will become the natural area for cargo movements because of its direct accessibility to the other boroughs of the City and to New Jersey by means of the new expressways and the present turnpikes. The development of terminal facilities will be an integral part of the future industrial growth of the Island. Increased truck traffic in areas between Clifton and St. George will necessitate road improvements which will also revitalize the entire east shore of the borough.

UTILITIES

Consolidated Edison, Brooklyn Union Gas Company, and the New York Telephone Company give assurance that their facilities will be able to meet the needs of the anticipated population growth. A new aqueduct beneath the Narrows under construction in 1962 and slated for completion in 1965, will provide an adequate supply of water directly from the Catskill System to underground storage tanks that will be constructed along the Victory Boulevard side of Silver Lake (9).

INSTITUTIONS

Plans have been announced for the establishment of several new institutions on the Island within the next few years. These should offer employment opportunities to residents. A $50 million state mental hospital under the jurisdiction of the New York State Department of Mental Hygiene has been planned for an area in the Ocean Breeze section of Dongan Hills. The State has already acquired a large acreage bounded by Seaview, Oceanside, Cromwell, and Quincy Avenues. This marshland will be reclaimed by hydraulic fill pumped from the Lower Bay.

The Department of Mental Hygiene has reported plans for a new research institution for mental retardation to be constructed on property adjoining Willowbrook State School. This will be the first facility of its kind in the world (11).

It has also been announced that a short term training and rehabilitation center with a capacity for twenty adolescent girls will be established on Forest Hill Road opposite the State School. The building will be named the Adele Levy Center in memory of a member of the State Youth

Commission and president of the Citizens' Committee for Children. The girls, from ages 15 to 18, will be referred by the courts and will engage in a supervised work program at Willowbrook State School during the day.

The unused buildings of the former Sea View Hospital are the subject of much speculation. The Department of Hospitals has proposed renovation of the pavilions for a public nursing home for aged persons of the City (8). This would provide geriatric care for chronically ill patients.

EDUCATION
PUBLIC SCHOOLS

The cooperation of the Local School Board, the P.T.A.s, the Office of the Borough President, the Homebuilders' Association, the Staten Island Real Estate Board, and civic leaders, working with the Board of Education and the City Planning Commission assure the Borough of Richmond that future school needs will be met. A new senior high school and several elementary and junior high schools are in the planning stage. Sites are now being acquired for future needs.

PRIVATE SCHOOLS

Plans for two Catholic girls' high schools were reported in the preceding section. Probably additional elementary parochial schools will be established within a few years.

COLLEGES

Construction on the $9.5 million Staten Island Community College* is scheduled to start in 1963. Occupancy is anticipated in September 1964. The 40-acre campus is near the Clove Lakes Expressway in Sunnyside. In November 1962 the Board of Higher Education announced that this two-year institution may become a four-year college.

Wagner College* is also planning new buildings in its twenty-year development program that started with the Horrmann Library which was dedicated in September 1961.

Notre Dame College for Women* is also engaged in a building program for the 1960s. These three college campuses within New York City, with ample space for expansion, will continue to conserve the natural beauty of Staten Island.

TRANSPORTATION

Leo Brown, Commissioner of the Department of Marine and Aviation, has expressed the following opinion: "The future of Staten Island is indelibly linked with the growth of our so-called megalopolis tri-state area. It will be a focal point for the handling of consumer goods and services, aided immeasurably by the completion of the Verrazzano-Narrows Bridge and the connecting feeder-throughways. It cannot help but become a radius of transportation facilities." New England, Long Island, and New Jersey traffic will use the bridge and the network of cross-Island expressways to by-pass the congestion of Manhattan.

The routes of the parkways that were under construction in 1962 have been described previously. Another proposed roadway is the Shore Front Drive which will be constructed under the Federal-State Highway program to protect the shorefront communities against erosion by high tides and storms. This scenic highway, 13.5 miles in length, will parallel the beaches from the Verrazzano-Narrows Bridge to the West Shore Expressway interchange at the Outerbridge Crossing. The present 2.3 mile section of Seaside Boulevard from Fort Wadsworth to Miller Field will become part of this Shore Front Drive.

Increased local traffic will necessitate road improvements throughout the Island. Undoubtedly the volume of traffic on the new expressways will make it necessary to plan new approaches for the three existing bridges to New Jersey which are operated by the Port of New York Authority.

BUSES

Bus transportation on Staten Island is adequate for the areas it serves. However, additional bus routes will be required by a growing population. Mr. Daniel T. Scannell, member of the New York City Transit Authority, reports that "prior to the opening of the Verrazzano-Narrows Bridge, it is the Authority's intention to make a careful study of the effect that this bridge will have upon transit operations, and to make whatever changes are indicated which will be to the maximum benefit of the Authority and the citizens of the borough."

FERRIES

Most of the commuters between St. George and Manhattan will continue to travel by ferry unless express buses across the Bridge become a reality. Therefore more adequate ferry service and additional parking facilities at the Ferry Terminal will be demanded. Approval for construction of three new ferries has been given by the Board of Estimate. Each of these 294-foot diesel-electric ferryboats will accommodate 260 more passengers than the ferries that were commissioned in 1951 but will carry about the same number of vehicles. These will be the first new vessels placed in service since 1951. Commuters will welcome the elimination of smoke nuisance and air pollution caused by the old oil-fired steam boilers (1).

RAILROADS

Paul K. Partee, retired General Manager of the Baltimore and Ohio Railroad, stated in a recent speech that "under agreement with the City of New York, the Staten Island Rapid Transit guarantees to provide passenger service with no reduction in the number of trains operated, until 1969." The communities along the South Shore of the Island are therefore assured of rail transportation for several years to come. Efforts to remove the tracks on the abandoned North Shore line have been defeated, so it is possible that service may be restored. Freight service can be handled with present facilities.

RICHMONDTOWN RESTORATION

The rich historical heritage of Staten Island will be preserved for posterity in the proposed Richmondtown Restoration. This project will be a living museum, tracing the development and culture of Staten Island and its people through three centuries. It is estimated that the Restoration will cost $4 million, to be shared equally by the City of New York and by the Richmondtown Restoration. A scale model of the project is displayed in the Staten Island Historical Museum.*

A nucleus of buildings has remained in Richmondtown throughout the centuries. Included are the original schoolhouse, erected in 1696 (previously described); the old County Clerk's and Surrogate's Office which is the present Museum building; the Third County Courthouse in Greek Revival style which also contains exhibits; St. Andrew's Church, originally erected between 1709 and 1712; the Parsonage of the Reformed Dutch Church,* built in 1855; the Treasure House,* constructed by

254

Samuel Grosset, a tanner, in 1700; the Simon Swaim House, to be restored as a farmhouse; the Bennett House,* to be restored as a town house of the 1930s; and the Stephens House,* to be restored as a general store. Adjacent to the Third County Courthouse is the homestead graveyard of the Rezeau-Van Pelt* family (5, 14, 15).

A few buildings elsewhere on Staten Island will be relocated in Richmondtown to complete the village. The Lake-Tysen House,* an excellent example of Dutch Colonial architecture, erected about 1740, was moved to its site in the Restoration in July 1962. Others to be moved are the Britton Cottage,* typical home of a prosperous farmer; the Finley House,* or cooper's shop; the Morgan House,* or basketmaker's shop; and the Boehm House,* which will be restored as the home of Dr. Thomas Frost who was sheriff as well as physician.

The Restoration also will include a district school, a blacksmith shop, a tannery, a grist mill, a saw mill, a law office, and a carriage factory. The Reformed Dutch Church, originally erected in 1789, will be reproduced.

It is expected that this unique restoration of typical village life showing crafts and industries, as well as architectural development, will attract people from all over the nation. The Verrazzano-Narrows Bridge will bring the restored village within easy reach of anyone living or visiting within the metropolitan area.

ENVISIONING THE FUTURE

Albert V. Maniscalco, President of the Borough of Richmond, envisions a bright future for the estimated 500,000 residents of Staten Island. He notes: "The opening of the Verrazzano-Narrows Bridge and its coordinated network of arterial expressways will open the Island's overabundant, and as yet undeveloped recreational, educational, cultural and economic facilities to the inhabitants of the Metropolitan New York area. Despite this change of pace, Staten Island will maintain and even improve its natural and community facilities.

"Every effort is being made to zone for the future so that all of the land area of Staten Island will serve a useful purpose. The establishment of sound zoning principles will enable the Island to grow without congestion, to strengthen its economy and commercial importance and to provide homes with light, air and open space that will spell the difference between continued suburban living and big city strangulation. We will expand without sacrificing our wonderful greenness and natural beauty.

"We will have an area in which to work and to play and to live. It will be without parallel. Our South Shore beaches will rival those of Long Island. Our parks, already ranked with the best, will be expanded and improved.

"Expanded educational facilities will be provided throughout the Island at all levels. We will see Staten Island Community College located on its own campus, as fine as any college in the state.

"The coming of the bridge will bring the future more swiftly upon us, but we will meet it with determination and a civic pride which will continue to make Staten Island *the* ideal place to live within the limits of New York City."

The building of communities is an essential part of the great story of freedom, which is the history of our country. Staten Island is now making history and Staten Islanders, like all typical Americans, imbued with pride in the home town, are carefully assessing changes and developments initiated by the bridge construction.

It is this "pride in the home town" which history will reveal as the cohesive force that held together the framework of relationships needed to assure Staten Islanders a community in which people could work, play, hope, dream, love and be loved.

Every community has a history that is potentially interesting to its residents. Staten Island is no exception. Since the nature of a community reflects the dreams, aspirations, and daily works of man, individually and collectively, the future of Staten Island will reflect the needs, desires and sacrifices of its residents. Time alone will reveal the effect of the Verrazzano-Narrows Bridge on the growth of the borough of Richmond.

BIBLIOGRAPHY

1. BURNS, ROBERT S. "For Staten Island: Three New Ferries." *New York Herald-Tribune*, August 25, 1962. P. 22.
2. ELLIS, EDWARD. "Staten Island: Goodbye to a Way of Life." *New York World-Telegram and Sun*, March 6, 1962. P. 21.
3. FELT, JAMES. "Sensible Zoning Protects Borough from Haphazard Growth." *Staten Island Advance,** April 28, 1962. P. 20.
4. "50-Acre New Dorp Tract Sold for Shopping Center," *Staten Island Advance,** October 23, 1962. P. I, II.

5. HOFFMAN, ROBERT. "Richmondtown," *Staten Islander Magazine*, I: 24-27, 34-37, 47, October 1958.

6. McSHEEHY, S. S. "City Speeds Lemon Creek Development." *Staten Island Advance*,* May 25, 1962.

7. ——. "Islanders Assured of Voice in South Shore Renewal." *Staten Island Advance*,* August 17, 1962.

8. ——. "Nursing Homes Lash Plans for Aged at Sea View." *Staten Island Advance*,* May 17, 1962.

9. ——. "Tunnel Under Bay to Assure Island of Plenty of Water." *Staten Island Advance*, April 28, 1962. P. B2.

10. MOSES, ROBERT. "Island to Set Pace for Whole City, Moses Predicts." *Staten Island Advance*,* April 28, 1962. P. 1.

11. "New Research Institute Slated for Willowbrook." *Staten Island Advance*,* March 15, 1962.

12. New York City, Department of City Planning. "New Homes for Urban Industry." *Newsletter*, September 1962.

13. ——. "1962-1963 Urban Renewal Study Program." *Newsletter*, May-June, 1962.

14. "Richmond Restoration." *The Staten Island Historian*, XVII: 11-24, April-June 1956.

15. *Tercentenary Booklet*. Staten Island, N.Y.: Staten Island Tercentenary Commission, 1961. P. 48-49.

16. TERKELSEN, STANLEY. "Park May Not Rise on Fresh Kills Landfill before 1980." *Staten Island Advance*,* October 24, 1961. P. 13.

---

* Back issues of the *Staten Island Advance* are on microfilm at the St. George Public Library, Staten Island.

APPENDIX

THE VERRAZZANO-NARROWS BRIDGE

A new era of living will, indeed, be written as the Verrazzano-Narrows Bridge is completed and opened for use in 1965.

It seems appropriate, therefore, to reproduce the following excerpt from "Seven Wonders of the World," an article by Don Wharton which appeared in the October 1962 issue of the *Rotarian.†*

"The bridge now being thrown across the Narrows at the entrance to New York Harbor will have the world's longest main suspension span – 4,260 feet from tower to tower. That's more than four-fifths of a mile of steel hanging in the sky 228 feet above the ship channel between Brooklyn and Staten Island. The central span, with 12 traffic lanes, will be the heaviest ever built. And when completed in 1965, the bridge will be the world's most costly – 320 million dollars, which is more than the combined costs of what are now the world's three longest main-span suspension bridges: the Golden Gate at San Francisco, the Straits of Mackinac Bridge in Michigan, and the George Washington Bridge over the Hudson. Actually, the Narrows is one of the most expensive single one-place structures of any kind, costing four times as much as the Pentagon Building in Washington, D.C. Each of the two bridge towers, 690 feet high with foundations reaching down 105 feet on one, 170 feet on the other, has two legs, and each leg is immense enough to squeeze in the Washington Monument with room left over for most of the Statue of Liberty.

"The *Engineering News-Record* has observed that 'everything about the Narrows Bridge is big, bigger, or biggest.' For example, the contract for supplying and erecting the four steel cables and the suspending ropes alone came to $56,900,000 – more than the total cost of the Golden Gate Bridge in San Francisco. The four steel cables, passing over the bridge towers must hold up a suspended dead weight of 84,000 tons plus their own weight of 39,000 tons plus a potential live weight, from traffic, of 10,000 more tons. This means huge anchorages at the two ends, in a way the most fabulous part of the Narrows Bridge. When I first visited the anchorage at the Brooklyn end, it was a tremendous hole in the ground, 344 feet long, 230 feet wide, some 50 feet deep. You could have dropped a whole football field into the hole and still had room around the edges for thousands of spectators. Week by week this space was built up and up and up into what in effect is one huge solid monolith of concrete and imbedded steel, faced with granite above water, as high as an 18-story building, shaped and weighted so that the dead weight of the bridge will not tip it over or pull it bodily into the water. This one block weighs 410,000 tons – more than the weight of the whole Empire State Building in New York City.

"Because of size and location, this bridge is destined to become one of the world's most spectacular landmarks. A ship's captain informed me that when one of the towers had been built up to only half its full height, he had sighted it from 20 miles at sea. Everyone coming to New York by ocean liner will pass under this bridge, plane passengers will spot it easily, many motorists will drive out of their way just to cross it. Appropriately, the bridge's designer is a man who in his youth came through these very Narrows to America, seeking experience as a bridge builder. That was in 1904; Othmar Hermann Ammann was 25, an aspiring civil engineer fresh from working on his first bridge – a little 30-foot stone arch for a mountain railroad in Switzerland. Today Ammann is 83, a trim, straight-standing scholarly looking man who commutes daily to the offices of his engineering firm in New York. He came to America without a job, found one on his first call, stayed on, and became the world's foremost designer of suspension bridges. He designed the George Washington Bridge and designed or acted as consultant for the Triborough Bridge, the Throg's Neck Bridge, and the Bayonne Bridge. The Narrows Bridge is the climax of his career. The details were worked out by his staff, but the basic concepts are his. One startling aspect of its immensity: designs had to take into account the curvature of the earth! Because of that the towers, though perfectly perpendicular to the earth's surface, are $1^5/8$ inches farther apart at their summits than at their bases."

---

† Reprinted with permission from *The Rotarian* and *The Reader's Digest*. Copyright 1962 by the Reader's Digest Association, Inc.

INDEX AND SKETCHES

Throughout this section, (E.H.) signifies amendments Edna Holden made to her original 1964 material in her 1974 planned revision. (R.D.) stands for additions made by Richard Dickenson. **Boldface** *signifies a new index entry or additional information about a previous entry.)*

A

Abbott, Mabel, 148

Abraham J. Wood House

This New York City Landmark stands at 5910 Amboy Road, and is also known as the 5910 Amboy Road House. The farmer and oysterman Abraham J. Wood purchased this property in 1840 and erected the house shortly thereafter. The main section of Wood's Greek Revival house may have been an addition to an earlier building (now part of the west wing). The house, which has many features typical of vernacular Greek Revival design on Staten Island, is notable for its entranceway. (Dolkart, 293.)

Abraham Manee House, 36

This building is also known as the Manee-Seguine Homestead, and the Abraham Mannaat House. It stands at 509 Seguine Avenue in Prince's Bay (Block 6666/1). This house has a complex building history that may extend back to the construction of a one-room dwelling by a Paulus Regrenier in the late seventeenth century.

Abraham Manee constructed a major rubble-stone addition early in the eighteenth century. The Seguine family acquired the property in the 1780s and made further additions early in the nineteenth century. The house is privately owned. (Dolkart, 293.)

Actors Home, 108, 172

Adams and Wells Expresses, 72

Adams, John, 41

Adolph Rodewald House, *see* Nicholas Muller House

Aero Defense Station, 167

African Americans, 58, 67, 88, 119; *see also* Evelyn King, *Black Man on Staten Island*; Churches, African American; Black; and Historically Black

Afro-Americans, *see* African Americans

Air Pollution Control, Department of, 163

Albany (Fort Orange), 11–12, 102

Aldrich, Thomas Bailey, 146

Alexander, Junius Brutus, 64, 106, 116; *see also* Richmond County Country Club

Algonkian, Algonquin, 3

Alice Austen House, 25, 44, 115, 238

New York City Landmark/ SR/NR/NHL. 2 Hylan Boulevard, Rosebank, Block 2830/49. Erected 1690s; remodeled 1846, ca. 1852, and 1860–1878.

Note original stone cottage, later additions. Observe Gothic gingerbread features added about 1850. Used as British headquarters during American Revolution. Early home of N. Y. Yacht Club may be seen nearby. Excellent view of the Narrows and Verazzano-Narrows Bridge. (E.H.)

This was the home of Alice Austen (1866–1952), one of America's outstanding early photographers. The original one-room Dutch Colonial house was gradually enlarged. The house was restored by New York City and is now a museum commemorating Alice Austen's artistry. (Dolkart, 279.)

The original house, among the city's older homes, dates to the 1690s. It was once part of a farm near the scenic Narrows. Alice's grandfather, John H. Austen, bought in 1844. He expanded the small one-and-one-half-story farmhouse, named it "Clear Comfort" and give it a romantic Gothic Revival facelift that included steeply peaked dormer windows and flourishes of gingerbread wood trim. The parlor is restored to look as it did in the 1890s with an arrangement of

ornate period furniture, rugs, Delft fireplace tiles and Oriental vases. (*Historic Houses, 30.*)

Allen House (ca. 1850), 63

Allison Pond, 174

Almstaedt, Isaac, 126

Amboy Road, 20, 24, 34, 45, 57, 101, 103, 104, 177, 221, 234

Observe old houses, all privately owned, between Prince's Bay and Tottenville. Many are over a century old; some were built by oystermen. Examples: house number 5475 was built ca. 1830, and 6475 ca. 1820. (E.H.)

5910 Amboy Road House, *see* Abraham J. Wood House

America, Americans, 12, 41, 43–44, 53

American

colonies, 21

delegates, 41

docks, 115, 123, 196, 250

Linoleum Manufacturing Company, 120, 127, 143, 200

Museum of Natural History, 148, 239–240

Revolution, 39, 42, 46, 88, 227

rural communities, 53

soldiers, 41

Amundsen, Captain Roald (Norwegian Explorer)

Memorial tablet in Amundsen Plaza, at Amboy Road and Clarke Avenue, Oakwood. (E.H.)

Annable, Courtland V.

In 1868 Henry Caesar, a Manhattan banker, purchased an undeveloped woodland site at the southeast corner of Henderson and Clinton Avenues and then erected a home. In 1904 Caesar sold his home to Courtland V. Annable, who razed the house and erected a new structure on it, set back 100 feet from Clinton Avenue. Annable, when he first came to Staten Island, was a member of the firm of Lindsay, Annable and Nicoll, among Manhattan's wealthier law firms.

The most modern conveniences of the time went into the structure, built by Henry Spruck, a Stapleton contractor. Large French plate glass windows gave the owner a commanding view of his terraced lawns and gardens. Most of the interior trim was of expensive mahogany and the flooring was composed of the best oak that could be purchased. Annable died in 1927 and a year later his estate sold his home to Supreme Court Justice Frank S. Gannon of the 2nd Judicial District, which included all of Long Island and Staten Island.

Judge Gannon died in 1933 and a year later the Emigrant Industrial Savings Bank foreclosed on the home. The house stood unoccupied for a year. In 1935, it was leased to the Arden School, a private school for boys that formerly occupied the old Rodewald/Muller building across the street from the Annable home. (The Rodewalk/Muller building later became the administration building of the Staten Island Division of Manhattan College. It is now Saint Peter's High School for Boys.)

In 1938, the Arden School merged with Dongan Hall, a finishing school for girls on Todt Hill Road, Dongan Hills (Dongan Hall later merged with Staten Island Academy), and the Annable home was once more unoccupied. Emigrant Industrial Savings Bank, which foreclosed the mortgage on the property in 1934, decided to raze the palatial Annable home "to save taxes." (*Staten Island Advance*, August 21, 1939.)

Cotta Company just across the Arthur Kill, Atlantic opened its factory on East Broadway, Tottenville, in 1898. In 1907 the Tottenville works combined with the huge Perth Amboy plant and the smaller Excelsior Company of Rocky Hill, New Jersey, to form the expanded incorporated Atlantic Terra Cotta Company. (80, Sachs, 1988)

Augustinian Academy/Prep School, 83, 170, 222

144 Campus Road at Clove and Serpentine Roads on Grymes Hill (Block 629/25.) Note the Northern Italian style architecture, beautifully landscaped grounds, sundial, and the view of Clove Valley and the Staten Island Expressway. (E.H.)

The Augustinian Society was incorporated under a special Act (Chapter 22) of the New York State Legislature on April 15, 1870, and was the owner of the Augustinian Prep School. The original corporation members were Thomas Galberry, Michael J. Collins, Edward A. Dailey, George A. Meagher, John J. Feddigan, James McMahon and Henry Cox. The object and purpose of the Augustinian Society is the Christian education of young men and their training and preparation for the priesthood in the Order of Saint Augustine of the Roman Catholic Church. The

order has its main U.S. headquarters in Villanova, Pennsylvania. Its principal institution in New York City is Saint Nicholas of Tolentine parish on Fordham Road and Andrew Avenue in the Bronx. The Augustinians own other property at Parsons Boulevard and Union Turnpike in Queens.

On June 15, 1922, the Reverend Edward J. Dohan, O.S.A., acting for the corporation, purchased the Staten Island property from Erickson Norman Nicholas, et al., for $21,000. The property was improved with a seminary and school building costing $350,000. The school was not endowed, but sustained by earnings of missionaries attached to the Augustinian Society. Additions to the property were made in 1951, 1955 and 1957.

A 1934 report listed the Reverend Henry A. Caffrey, O.S.A., as rector of the school. But it was a former assistant principal and teacher at the Augustinian Academy who wrote of the class of 1969 witnessing the final commencement. (Sunday *Staten Island Advance*, June 25, 1969.) The following year, the school was converted to a retreat house.

However, it was not until 1985 that the Augustinian fathers sold the property to developers. By 1992, the NYC Building Department was starting procedures to either have the buildings torn down or sealed up as a safety measure. At the same time, the NYC Finance Department was poised to seize the 18-acre site for back taxes and penalties of nearly $800,000. The owner at that time was Villanova Realty. It had plans to convert the old academy building into 30 condominium apartments and build another 300 townhouses on the remaining vacant land. (*Staten Island Advance*, May 5, 1992.)

The Federal Deposit Insurance Corporation (FDIC) planned an auction of the property for December 21, 1993. FDIC became the receiver of the Howard Savings Bank after October 2, 1992. Howard held the mortgage on the Academy property. (*Staten Island Advance*, November 23, 1993.) Wagner College recently purchased the property.

B

He was a pioneer in the life insurance industry. Born in Philadelphia, to which the Bard family had fled during the British occupation of New York City, he was a great grandson of Dr. John, a grandson of Dr. Samuel and son of Dr. John Bard and Mary (Bard, a cousin) Bard. The first Dr. John (1716–1799) was the son of Peter Bard a Huguenot refugee from the Revocation of the Edict of Nantes. While in Philadelphia, Dr. John became a friend of Benjamin Franklin. Dr. John purchased a farm in Hyde Park, New York, and in 1788 he was chosen as the first president of the Medical Society of the State of New York. Bard College takes its name from him.

Dr. Samuel (1742–1821) was the second Bard in line as a physician. He founded the New York Hospital in 1791 and when the American Government was established in New York City, George Washington selected Dr. Samuel as his personal doctor. He was elected president of the original College of Physicians and Surgeons in 1811.

William graduated from Columbia College in 1797. In October 1802, he married the daughter of Nicholas Cruezer or Cruger. His bride's name was Catherine, and she was born in Santa Cruz, Virgin Islands. During his lifetime, the completion of the Erie Canal advanced New York City's claim as the United States' premier shipping port, and created needs both for large amounts of capital to invest in big projects and for protection for those projects. In 1830, Bard involved himself in both these emerging sectors by securing a charter for the New York Life Insurance and Trust Company. The company's sales force, placed throughout New York State, sold insurance policies, and the proceeds were invested in real estate, creating a large pool of capital for further investment. Bard's company later merged with the Bank of New York.

Eliza (born Hyde Park ca. 1808), one of the three daughters of William and Catherine, married Rufus King Delafield (1802–1874), a manufacturer of Rosendale cement (used in fortifications and public works). She became the mother of Eliza, Edward A. (1837–1884), William Bertram (1839), Rufus (1840),

Henry P. (1842–1904), Catherine (1846) and Richard (1853–1930). (*Dictionary of American Biography*, 597–600; 1850 U.S. Census of Richmond County.) Rufus King Delafield's brother Richard (1798–1873) was a military engineer who likely visited his former home when stationed in New York. William Bertram was a participant in the removal of a seeming Confederate fabric from the Gardiner-Tyler House during the Civil War.

William purchased the property through which Bard Avenue was cut. (R.D.)

Barentsen, Thys, 17–18, 237

Barker Street, 120

Barlow, (Major General) Francis Channing, 89

Barlow Avenue, 89

Barnes, Stephen D. House

New York City Landmark at 2876 Richmond Terrace, Mariner's Harbor (Block 1211/87). Built ca. 1853, this is a Captain's Row home with an eclectic combination of Italianate and Gothic Revivals, and unusual bull's-eye windows in the attic below the deep cornice. Note the trompe l'oeil ground-floor window detail and that of the main entrance door. It camouflages the barricades installed to ward off vandals. (Willensky, 821.)

Barrett, (Major) Clarence T., 68–69, 90, 190

There is a statue in Major Barrett's honor in a triangular park adjacent to Borough Hall in Saint George. Unveiled in 1915, a life-sized heroic figure of "Victory;" a Greek soldier maimed after battle holds a spear with a shield behind his shoulder. Read inscription on the memorial. (E.H.)

The bronze statue to Major Clarence T. Barrett was first unveiled on Nov. 11, 1915 as a legacy of his daughter, Mrs. Edward Hardin. It was cast by Sherry Edmundson Fry (1879–1966), a well known artist of the period. Affixed to the Tennessee marble pedestal are the words "Loyal, honest, brave and true." Originally the statue was located a few blocks from its current location. It also included a drinking fountain and display fountain. (*Staten Island Advance,* April 18, 1988, p. 2.)

Major Barrett, a nephew of Nathan Barrett and a landscape architect received his rank as a result of gallant and meritorious services during the successful campaign against Mobile, Alabama culminating in April 1865. Among numerous other positions, he was a trustee in the family-related Old Staten Island Dyeing and Printing Establishment in West Brighton, adjacent to the Staten Island Cemetery where his Uncle, Nathan Barrett, is buried.

Major Barrett's former estate comprises the lands of the Staten Island Zoo, also known as Barrett Park. (R.D.)

Barrett, (Colonel) Nathan, 68

Barrett Nephews Company, 68, 90, 119, 200, 205
Now the site of Corporal Lawrence Thompson Park, in West Brighton, but formerly the factory of a dry cleaning firm organized in March 1851 by Colonel Nathan Barrett (d. Oct. 25, 1865), President. Nephews Nathan M. Heal (the first Vice President) Joseph H. Heal (d. Feb. 26, 1895) and Edwin Baldwin Heal (d. March 25, 1853) were also part of the original co-partnership titled "Barrett, Nephews & Co.'s Fancy Dyeing Establish-ment." Abraham C. Wood was Secretary and Treasurer. (Clute, 325–326.)

Barrett Park, 90, 190; *see* Staten Island Zoo

Barry, Commodore John (1745–1803) American Naval officer, born in County Wexford, Ireland. He settled in Philadelphia in 1760 and entered the infant U.S. Navy during the American Revolution performing brilliant exploits. He was recalled to service as a senior captain in 1794. Perhaps to honor him as an example of the U.S. Irish-American population, or perhaps because he participated in the beginning of the U.S.

Bermuda; *see also* Walker family

Spaniard Juan de Bermudez is credited with the island's discovery; he stumbled upon it in 1503 while returning from the Caribbean to Europe. For the next century or so Bermuda's only visitors were shipwrecked sailors. Those who lived to tell the world about their find painted a picture of an island beset by devils and treacherous waters. While these tales were to have inspired Shakespeare to set *The Tempest* in Bermuda, they did little to encourage permanent settlement.

In 1609, a British ship en route to Jamestown ran aground off what is now Saint George's Island. The captain, Admiral Sir George Somers, and his crew built two new ships from the wreckage and continued their journey. Three years later a group of British settlers led by Governor Richard Moore landed here to establish a settlement on Saint George's. (Birnbaum, 35.) Moore named the island Somers Island.

The first person from the infant United States to visit Bermuda in search of health did so in 1799, starting a long relationship between the neighboring countries. During the Civil War, Bermuda was an ideal Southern entrepôt. John Tory Bourne, a Bermudian and commission merchant, became the Commercial Agent for the Confederacy at Bermuda. The real importance of the islands was recognized when a future Staten Islander, Major Norman S. Walker of the Confederate Army, was sent to England with two million dollars in bonds and instructed to return to Bermuda as resident Disbursing Agent. Walker's object, as General Josiah Gorgas (1818–1883), Chief of the Confederate Ordnance Bureau, pointed out, was for light swift steamers to run cargoes from Bermuda through the Union blockade to Confederate ports.

Major Walker was a diplomat as well as a fiscal agent and was ably seconded by his clever wife — perhaps some day her lively diary will be published. The Walker family resided in the building now called the Glove Hotel. There they received southern diplomats and agents. (14, 1968 Quarterly)

C. M. Allen, U. S. Consul in Bermuda, noted in a dispatch of March 23, 1863, that Walker claimed to be an agent of the Confederate States of America and is said to hold a commission from Jefferson Davis. (13–14, Walker). (R.D.)

Bernstein, Elias, 219

Berry Apartments, 62, 176, 186

Bethel Methodist Episcopal Church

and Cemetery, 57, 88, 101, 164

Amboy Road, Tottenville, near Page Avenue. A church was first erected on this site in 1841; this church dates from ca. 1886. Note the Civil War monument to the right of the front walk and the monument to Joseph S. Decker, Spanish-American War veteran. (E.H.) The Joseph S. Decker Camp of the United War Veterans erected "The Hiker" monument that stands in Tompkins Park at the intersection of Bay Street and Victory Boulevard. (R.D.)

Bethlehem Children's Home, 215

Bethlehem Steel Company, 164, 196, 214, 218, 227

Bible, 56

bicycling, 117, 140

Biddle Mansion, 62

This New York City Landmark is also known as the Henry Hogg Biddle House. It stands at 70 Satterlee Street in Tottenville (Block 7966/75). It dates from the late 1840s.

"The Biddle House, overlooking the Arthur Kill, exemplifies an unusual aspect of vernacular design on Staten Island – the combining of Dutch Colonial-style spring eaves with Greek Revival columned porticoes. This structure is the only extant local house with two-story porticoes and spring eaves on both the front and rear elevations. These elements add a sense of grandeur to the relatively small waterfront dwelling." (Dolkart, 296.)

Billiou, Pierre, 17, 21, 60, 170

Billiou-Stillwell-Perine House, 25, 27, 44–45, 148, 188, 191

This building is on New York City, New York State and national landmark registers. It is also known as the Billiou-Stillwell-Perine House. Its earliest portions date from the 1660s; additions were made from ca. 1680 to ca. 1830. It has been given the address of 1476 Richmond Road in Dongan Hills (Block 3299/10).

"The original stone section of this house was erected by Pierre Billiou in the 1660s, shortly after the first permanent settlement was founded in the region known as Olde Dorp. Constructed according to medieval building traditions, the house is the oldest surviving building on Staten Island. Billiou's daughter married Thomas Stillwell and they built the first of several additions to the house. For 150 years, beginning in 1764, members of the Perine family owned the house. In 1919 this became the first site on Staten Island to be acquired by a historical society for use as a house museum." (Dolkart, 290.)

Billopp

Avenue, 42

Christopher, 21–22, 26, 28, 33, 39, 41, 44

the Borough President on all official proclamations. However, this practice has fallen into disuse partly because the New York City Council, the authorizing body, never officially adopted the borough seal and flag. (E.H.)

Borough Hall, 42–43, 46, 51, 91, 147, 160, 162–163

This building is also known as Staten Island and/or Richmond Borough Hall. It stands at 2–10 Richmond Terrace in Saint George (Block 7/1). It was erected in 1904–1906 by Carrere & Hastings, and is now on the landmark registers of New York City, New York State, and the federal government.

Borough Hall is the most prominent feature of Staten Island's governmental center and one of the great early twentieth-century civic monuments of New York City. Carrere & Hastings designed Borough Hall in a style reminiscent of the brick-and-stone chateaux erected in France during the early seventeenth century. This is especially evident on the east elevation, facing New York Harbor, where the façade consists of a central pavilion flanked by projecting wings, all crowned by a mansard roof. The massing creates a courtyard reached by a long flight of stairs. A tall clock tower, visible from the harbor, rises from the center of the west elevation. (Dolkart, 275.)

Title to the vacant land previously owned by S. I. Rapid Transit Railway Co. and Jacob R. Telfair, was vested to City of New York on October 12, 1903.

In 1903, the Borough of Staten Island commissioned the architectural firm, Carrere & Hastings (the former a Staten Island resident) to design a new borough hall as a symbol of the island's importance in the recently consolidated Greater New York. An early French Renaissance style was chosen for the five-story building which was dramatically sited on a hill above the St. George Ferry Terminal. The brick and limestone building has a massive central pavilion crowned by a mansard roof with projecting wings that form an open court at the front elevation. The overall composition is surmounted by a tall brick clocktower that forms the focal point of the Staten Island Civic Center. (*A Report on the Public Landmark Buildings*, 56.)

Borough Historian, 25, 113, 157, 188

Borough Presidents, 106, 151, 158–159, 183, 188, 255

(Unless otherwise noted, the text was extracted primarily from *The Illustrated History of Staten Island* [Staten Island: Slenar and McAloon, ca. 1953] and *Staten Island Advance*, December 26,

1999.)

Staten Island's first borough president was George Cromwell, who served from 1898 to 1913. Mr. Cromwell was a descendant of the Cromwell family famous in English history. He died at his estate "Far View" at Todt Hill and Four Corners roads, on Monday, September 17, 1934. His death, at age 74, was a result of an apoplectic stroke, that put him in a coma, from which he never recovered. He was survived only by his wife, Hermine De Rouville of Montreal, whom he married 15 years before, shortly after his retirement from the public arena where he had been Republican assemblyman, borough president four times, state senator and a member of the Charter Revision Committee. His defeat in 1913, by Democrat Charles McCormick, has been attributed to the far reaching plans he had Louis C. Tribus, the borough consulting engineer and acting Commissioner of Public Works, draw up. Opponents accused him of "Manhattan-izing" Staten Island and demanded an investigation.

The 1912 investigation by Raymond B. Fosdick, the Commissioner of Accounts was given to then Mayor William J. Gaynor (1909–1913) who wrote Mr. Cromwell that he was completely exonerated of any "wrongdoing,

illegality or negligence in the government of the borough." (*See* obituaries in *Staten Island Advance* September 14, 1934, and *New York Times*, September 18, 1934.)

His accomplishments include establishing Saint George as the borough's civic center and the building of the first Staten Island Ferry Terminal, the Courthouse on Stuyvesant Place, the Saint George Library and the walls along Richmond Terrace and Bay Street.

Charles J. McCormack succeeded George Cromwell in the office of borough president in the November 1913 election, and was inaugurated in 1914. He was the popular candidate of the Democratic Party. In the short time he was to remain in office, he got free Manhattan transfers for ferry riders, forced island industries to cut down on harmful air pollution and oversaw key sewer and road projects. After several periods of ill health, McCormack died on July 11, 1915, in the second year of his term in office. (*Staten Island Advance*, December 26, 1999.)

The third borough president, Calvin Decker Van Name, was born in Mariners Harbor on January 3, 1857. He was the descendent of two of Staten Island's older Dutch families. He was appointed to office on the death of McCormack and subsequently elected borough president in 1915.

Under Van Name's sponsorship, the great municipal piers at Stapleton and Tompkinsville were built, a proposal to build a garbage plant at the site of the Fresh Kills landfill was defeated, water first arrived from the Catskills to the newly built Silver Lake reservoir, and the city's first concrete roads were introduced, to accommodate heavy truck traffic. Van Name is buried in the Decker family plot, Lake Cemetery, West New Brighton.

Matthew Cahill, the fourth borough president, was born on Lafayette Avenue and what is now Cassidy Place, New Brighton, in 1871. By 1906 Matthew Cahill had become county coroner, and, by 1915, tax appraiser. In 1921 he secured the Democratic nomination for borough president, defeating Van Name. Cahill, the Democratic leader, did not long enjoy the presidency he entered on January 1. On July 14, 1922, he died suddenly of "acute indigestion" (some say he was poisoned). Mayor John F. Hylan ordered all Borough, County and City building flags at half-mast. His body lay in state in the Borough Hall "War Service Room" and funeral services were officiated by Monsignor Cassidy at St. Peter's Church, New Brighton.

John A. Lynch was appointed Cahill's successor. Lynch was born October 11, 1882, on Caroline Street, West Brighton, in the parish of Saint Rose of Lima (now Sacred Heart), son of the late Michael and Ellen Lynch. He lived in that community all of his life.

A graduate of P.S. 18, "Jack" Lynch first went to work with his father, a builder. But, shortly afterwards he became a partner in an insurance business. When he was 21, he bought out his partner to become sole owner. Jack Lynch served for a time as commissioner of deeds in 1913, and in 1914 he was first vice president of the old West Brighton Board of Trade. About the same time he was a volunteer fireman with the Castleton Fire Patrol Company.

He first entered politics in 1916 by organizing the Richmond County Shawnee Club, a Democratic group, and served as president. Two years later he was elected to the State Senate, but was defeated for reelection. Borough President Matthew Cahill died in July 13, 1922. On July 17, three aldermen — Edward T. Atwell, Walter T. Warren and David S. Rendt — elected Lynch to fill the unexpired term. In the fall of 1922, Mr. Lynch won the borough presidency election and was reelected in 1925 and again in 1929.

Under his watch, Hylan Boulevard and Forest Avenue were completed from shore to shore. He witnessed the twinned opening of the Outerbridge Crossing and the Goethals Bridge by the Port Authority — ideas he had proposed as a state senator more than a decade earlier. (*Staten Island Advance*, December 26, 1999.)

In 1933, while running under the banner of the Richmond County Democrats, he was defeated for reelection by Joseph A. Palma. He ran for the borough presidency once more, in 1945, but was defeated by his lifelong friend and political colleague, Cornelius Hall.

Jack Lynch died at his 411 Oakland Avenue home on Tuesday, March 9, 1954, at the age of 71. His burial was in Moravian Cemetery from Casey Funeral Home, then on Victory Boulevard. (*Staten Island Advance*, March 19, 1954.)

The sixth borough president, Joseph Palma, was born June 5, 1889, in Rosebank. Mr. Palma was a graduate of P.S. 14, Stapleton, and attended Business College on the Island. In 1909 he became a member of the New York State detective force, and six years later was named a special operative in the Secret Service. He headed the Secret Service's Michigan and New York units and later was principal agent of the Treasury Department's famed detective unit.

In 1927, while serving a six-year stint in Detroit, Mr. Palma met industrialist Henry Ford, gave him some public relations assistance and they became fast friends. Two years later Mr. Palma retired from the Secret Service and opened an exclusive Ford franchise agency, which he and his sons operated until about 1958.

He was elected borough president on the Republican-Fusion ticket in November 1933 by a slim vote margin of 541. While in office he oversaw the building of the Franklin Delano Roosevelt Boardwalk in South Beach, the transformation of Pier 6 into the Cromwell Center in Tompkinsville, and the establishment, in Stapleton, of the nation's first foreign trade zone. During the waning years of the Great Depression and World War II, Palma earmarked millions for new schools, roads and drainage facilities, and left numerous projects on the drawing board.

Joseph A. Palma died in his home at 700 Victory Boulevard, Silver Lake, on the 18th of October 1969. He was 80 years old, twice a widower, and survived by seven sons, two daughters, two sisters, 28 grandchildren and 19 great-grandchildren. His funeral was held at the Martin Hughes Funeral Home, 998 Bay Street, Rosebank, with a mass in Our Lady of Good Counsel, Roman Catholic Church, Tompkinsville. He was buried in Saint Peter's Cemetery. (*Staten Island Advance*, October 19, 1969, 1.)

Staten Island's eighth borough president was Cornelius A. Hall. The "Hall of Borough Hall" was born in West Brighton in 1888 and grew up in this community. In 1924 he went into the construction and real estate business with his brother Edward. In 1930, under "Jack" Lynch, he became assistant commissioner of public works. In 1945 Hall assumed the office of borough president, winning the election on the Republican, Fusion and American Labor party tickets. During his term of office he made improvements in the bus and ferry transportation, including the construction of the second Saint George Ferry Terminal, further elimination of grade crossings, the shifting of Staten Island's poorly run private bus services to the city and the prevention of suspension of passenger service on three Staten Island Rapid Transit Lines. He is also credited with improved zoning, the development of Great Kills Park and restoration of Old Richmondtown. However, Cornelius Hall was also deemed "Ultimately responsible for the Fresh Kills landfill." He "claimed the project would prove of great value to the Island through reclamation of valuable land from now worthless marshlands…." Also, the first steps towards the planning and construction of the Verazzano Bridge by Robert Moses and the Port Authority occurred under Hall's administration.

Although his term of office was due to expire at the end of 1953, the 27-year veteran public official filed for retirement on January 12, 1953, for an April 15th effective resignation date. He gave "Nervous Collapse" as the reason for his resignation. However, he died suddenly on March 5th, more than a month prior to his proposed resignation and three months prior to his 65th birthday in June.

His remains laid at the Casey Funeral Home on Victory Boulevard, and his burial was at St. Peter's Cemetery. A furor erupted when Mayor Vincent Impellitieri ordered all flags lowered on public buildings of the City of New York in honor of Cornelius Hall. Joseph Stalin (1879-1953), the Soviet Union leader for 29 years, was more widely known than Cornelius Hall. His headlined death was coincidentally on March 5, 1953, the same day as that of Borough President Hall. For those who did not know of the death of President Hall, the lowered flags were mistakenly construed to be in honor of Stalin, the veritable symbol of Communism and the Cold War!

Judge Edward G. Baker was chosen to replace Hall by the Democratic county organization, headed by Jeremiah A. Sullivan (father of retired judge Thomas Sullivan), and was appointed to the post by Mayor Impellitieri, and Borough Works Commisioner Thomas F. Reilly Jr., then acting borough president. Staten Island's ninth borough president was born on Manhattan but moved to Staten Island with his parents at age 5. He attended P.S. 30 in Westerleigh, Curtis High School and the University of South Carolina. He received his legal training at Fordham Law School.

Baker, a Democrat, agreed to complete Hall's term and was elected that November with an overwhelming 67 percent of the vote, carrying every one of the 115 election districts in the borough. But like his predecessor, transportation issues too, soon dogged him. As the Board of Transportation threatened to cut bus service on the South Shore, Staten Island Rapid Transit shut down the North and East Shore passenger lines stranding 1,300 train-riding

commuters. The Transit Authority replaced the Board of Transportation during Baker's term.

A New York Supreme Court bench opening enticed Baker to a judgeship, and he immediately jumped ship after having served just one year as the borough's top politician. He occasionally served on the Appellate Term of the Supreme Court; and despite failing health missed few of the sessions of the state Constitutional Convention in 1967. There he chaired the Committee on Local Government and Home Rule.

Baker was married to the former Miss Jessie Payne of Westerleigh in October 1931. She survived him, as did two daughters, Mrs. Clark Dewaters of Wayne, New Jersey, and Mrs. Jane Wolfe of Pequannock, New Jersey, and siblings Harold of Whitney Avenue, Grasmere, Mrs. Theodore Theban of Foster Road, Princes Bay, and Mrs. Gladys Belser of Columbia, South Carolina

From 1955 to 1965, Albert V. Maniscalco served as tenth borough president.

It was an era of explosive growth. The Verazzano-Narrows Bridge, a cause Maniscalco once championed in the state assembly, opened under his watch and thousands migrated here, lured by easy access to greener pastures. A popular Democrat affectionately called "Uncle Al," Maniscalco played a key role in the creation of the Greenbelt and the establishment of Staten Island Community College and Richmond College, which were later consolidated into the College of Staten Island. Also, 24 new public schools were erected during his tenure, giving him the title of "Education Borough President." He died at the age of 90 in 1999.

Robert T. Connor, a Republican, was the eleventh borough president, holding the office from 1966 to 1977. He made a moratorium on city land auctions a top priority. He also petitioned the city to take over the failing Staten Island Rapid Transit and mounted losing efforts to restore the defunct North and East Shore passenger lines, which had been shut down in March 1953 during the Baker years. He also pushed for free Manhattan transfers for ferry riders. An ardent opponent of secession, Connor ordered a secession study because, he said, residents demanded it. He also strongly opposed the South Richmond Plan to develop the South Shore, considering the ultimate defeat of the plan his greatest legacy. However, after he was hanged in effigy by an angry mob for supporting a plan to build a theme park on the West Shore, Connor, who became a Democrat for his second term,

resigned to take a civilian naval position under President Jimmy Carter.

Upon Connor's resignation, Anthony R. Gaeta, also a Democrat, promptly quit his City Council job to take over as the twelfth Borough President, and served from 1977 to 1984. Gaeta won an easy victory in his first general election later that year. During his tenure, Gaeta worked unsuccessfully to have Shooter's Island removed to improve maritime traffic, to bulldoze Capodanno Boulevard through Miller Field, to limit the expansion of the Fresh Kills landfill and to cut the clothing sales tax. He also battled developers who had their eye on Sea View Hospital. He oversaw the closing of the nationally infamous Willowbrook State School, warning Islanders they would have to tolerate neighborhood group homes and halfway houses to conform with new state laws. Plans for the Teleport and the Stapleton homeport were initiated under Gaeta, who resigned the office after growing weary of constant battles with then Mayor Ed Koch over the Fresh Kill landfill. His death occurred in 1988.

Ralph J. Lamberti became the thirteenth borough president upon Gaeta's resignation, and held the office from 1984 to 1989. Lamberti, a Democrat and the first borough president to have never held a prior political office, was consumed by land-use issues during his five-year stint. He pushed to halt city land auctions, helped save South Shore Little League fields from developers, and fought for affordable housing for seniors. Lamberti also battled Brooklyn by fighting to keep that borough's landfill open and promoting the idea of a one-way toll on the Verazzano-Narrows Bridge. Lamberti, who adopted the mantra "equal treatment or we secede," was a vigorous opponent of changing the city charter to eliminate the Board of Estimate, which all but killed Staten Island representation in city government. His support of a proposal to build a city jail in Rossville may have cost him re-election.

Guy V. Molinari took office as the fifteenth borough president in 1990. Molinari, a Republican with a long history in Island politics, continued in Borough Hall many of the battles he first began in the state Assembly and the U.S. Congress. He successfully fought attempts to build a city jail in Rossville, a power plant in Travis and a coal port along the North Shore, and has pressed hard for the closure of the Fresh Kills landfill. Molinari brought the former U.S. Navy homeport to Stapleton and one-way tolls to the Verazzano-

Narrows. An early opponent of secession, Molinari later supported the 1993 referendum. His tight alignment with Mayor Rudolph Giuliani has paid off in new schools, park and beach renovations, and the elimination of the ferry fare and free public transit transfers in Manhattan. Molinari has played a key role in the anticipated transformation of Saint George Station, to include a renovated ferry terminal, a lighthouse museum and a minor-league baseball stadium. (*Staten Island Advance*, December 26, 1999.)

Boston, 68, 82

Bowling Green Park, 72

Bowne Mansion (1840), 144
Drumgoole Boulevard and Richmond Avenue, Greenridge. Note old English architecture. Built by Obadiah Bowne. Purchased in 1853 by Edward Banker, ship chandler, and descendant of Dutch family of Bancker that lived in New Amsterdam in 1686. Building now owned by Staten Island Lodge of Elks, No. 841. (E.H.)

Boyd's City Dispatch Post, 72

Brady, Matthew B., 91

Breweries, 14, 70, 116, 122–123

Brewer Drydock Co., 164, 195

Bridges
"Declared as 'The most beautiful structure of Steel of 1931' by the American Institute of Steel Construction, the Bayonne Bridge is

now a National Historic Civil Engineering Landmark." The world's longest steel arch is just 25 inches longer than the Sydney Harbor Bridge in Australia, which was built about the same time and which the Bayonne Bridge resembles. The Bayonne Bridge, though, links Bayonne, New Jersey, with Port Richmond on Staten Island. The great bridge builder, Othmar H. Ammann, designed it. Ground for it was broken September 18, 1928, and it was opened to traffic November 15, 1931, three years, one month, 28 days and $13 million later. (Mysak, 1997, 54–59)

The Goethals Bridge is named in honor of George W. Goethals (1858–1928), major general, President Theodore Roosevelt's appointee as chief engineer and builder of the Panama Canal, Canal Zone Governor, and the first consulting engineer of the New York-New Jersey Port Authority. The bridge connects Elizabeth, New Jersey, with Howland Hook, Staten Island. Bridge construction began July 1926. The Goethals Bridge was dedicated the same day as the Outerbridge Crossing, June 20, 1928, and opened to traffic on June 29 the same year. (Mysak, 1977, 48.)

The Outerbridge Crossing, designed by John Alexander Waddell, connects Perth Amboy, New Jersey and Tottenville, Staten Island, and is almost a twin to the shorter Goethals Bridge. Eugenius H. Outerbridge, first chairman of the Port Authority (1921–1924), and a Staten Island resident, was an honored guest at the dedication of "his" bridge on June 20, 1928. The Outerbridge Crossing opened to traffic 9 days later. (Mysak, 1977, 36, 42, 44.)

The Verrazzano-Narrows Bridge, opened November 21, 1964, connects Bay Ridge, Brooklyn, and Grasmere on Staten Island, New York. Othmar Ammann, the Swiss born designer of the bridge, died in 1965 at the age of 86, a year after the opening of his final triumph, the Verazzano Narrows Bridge, then the world's longest suspension bridge. (Mysak, 1997, 67.)

The first step toward this immense project was made in 1948. The Department of the Army, after careful consideration as to the effect on navigation by the possible hazards of war, granted permission for the building of the bridge in 1949. The Port of New York Authority and the Triborough Bridge and Tunnel Authority in 1954 joined to study the new needs of arterial facilities within the New York Metropolitan Area.

Construction of the formidable Narrows Bridge by the Triborough Bridge and Tunnel Authority [TBTA] was then delayed, according to Robert Moses, by the following:

1. Time-consuming approvals of the Federal and State Governments and the City of New York,
2. Negotiations for financing the $315 million cost of the project,
3. The time needed to gain acquisition of right-of-way, and
4. The necessary more complete design studies, cost estimates and subsurface investigations.

The TBTA retained Ammann & Whitney, Consulting Engineers, to prepare the plans and supervise the construction of the bridge and its immediate approaches.

The financing of the unprecedented sum of $325 million for a bridge project and the general responsibility for its success rest with the Triborough Bridge and Tunnel Authority under the leadership of its chairman, Robert Moses, and his fellow Commissioners, George V. McLauglin and William J. Tracy.

In 1954, Robert Moses announced the decision to build the bridge: "This span will be the most important single piece of arterial construction in the world. It will be the biggest bridge, the highest (243') bridge, the most expensive ($379 million) bridge.... To avoid uprooting families from their homes, we propose to use as much land as we can in Fort Hamilton, which is a military reservation, and Fort Wadsworth across the Narrows on Staten Island. The TBTA is the only one with the right to build this bridge. The Port Authority, a bi-state agency, can build it for us. An elaborate arrangement has been worked out under which the PA will build for the TBTA and the latter will collect the tolls." (*Staten Island Advance*, December 11, 1954, 1.)

After careful preparation and study of New York's earliest history by Carlo de Ferrariis Salzano, then Consul General of Italy in New York, a suggestion was made to the State of New York for the naming of the bridge. The Italian communities of New York, the Italian Historical Society of America, headed by the indefatigable John La Corte, were enthusiastic about supporting these and other efforts. This led the New York State Legislature, in 1960, to pass a law naming the new span the Verrazzano Bridge, after Giovanni da Verrazzano, the Florentine explorer who discovered New York harbor on April 17, 1524. (Lipinsky, 1958/1964, 22–23.)

282

Editor of *New York Express*, Richmond County representative in the New York State Legislature. The site of his estate is at Forest Avenue and Clove Lakes Park. Observe the trees and the pond. (E.H.)

4746 Amboy Road, Eltingville

This house, built in 1690, stands at 137 Giffords Lane at Dewey Street in Great Kills.

This business, no longer in existence, stood at 2110 Richmond Road in Grant City.

This house, built in 1800, stands at 501 Todt Hill Road in Dongan Hills. It on what was once part of the Governor Dongan Tract. Abraham Burbank (ca. 1944–1822) was from 1794 to 1798 supervisor of the town of Castleton. Note Daughters of the American Revolution plaque. (E.H.)

C

This church, built in 1894, stands at Bement and Castleton Avenues in West New Brighton. Note the stained glass windows from the former Randall Memorial Church at Sailors' Snug Harbor. (E.H.)

The low land near the Saint George waterfront was once nearly level with Richmond Terrace. Prior to the Civil War, this area was known as Camp Washington. Newspaper stories recount a game the Quickstep Baseball Club played at Camp Washington on Thanksgiving Day, 1859. Sixteen regiments trained for service in the Civil War at Camp Washington, beginning with Wilson's Zouaves in May 1861 and ending with the First National Regiment in September 1862. Camp Washington then returned to recreational use and in 1873 the Staten Island Cricket and Baseball Club was organized there. (Hine and Davis, 1925, 7.)

These two-story wood-frame houses with the tall front columns were built by oystermen between 1840 and 1850. They stand on Richmond Terrace between Mariners Harbor and Port Richmond.

John Murphy, Cardinal Farley, was associated with Saint Peter's Church in New Brighton during his early ministry. The future cardinal was on Staten Island from 1870 to 1872. In 1902, he was appointed the fourth archbishop of New York and in 1922 he was elevated to cardinal by the reigning pontiff, Pope Pius X. Father Cassidy of Saint Peter's Church was present at the archbishop's elevation to cardinal. The imposing tower of Saint Peter's Church is known as the Cardinal's Tower, Cardinal Farley being present at the dedication. (Judson, 1925, 134–135)

Carriage Museum, 139; see Historic Richmond Town

Carteret Ferry, 33, 43, 79, 230
This was the name of the ferry that ran from New Blazing Star (Travis), Staten Island, to Carteret, New Jersey. It was named for Sir George Carteret (1610–1680). In 1664, Carteret became co-proprietor of New Jersey. James, Duke of York, later King James II, named New Jersey in honor of Carteret's birthplace, the island of Jersey in the Channel Islands.

Carteret, New Jersey, 33, 79, 143, 230

Caruso, Enrico, 149

Cary Avenue, 57, 77, 122

Castle Garden, 65

Castle Williams, 51, 228

Castleton, 28, 53,62, 75–76, 94, 97, 134

Castleton, 226,

Castleton Avenue, 28, 58, 92, 101, 105, 108, 124, 131–132, 136, 141, 150, 170, 176, 211

Castleton Corners, 28, 66, 76, 139, 176, 218

Castleton Division (of Staten Island), 94

Castleton Park Apartments, 113

Catholic churches, 59, 92, 103, 138, 169–170

Cebra Avenue, 57, 60

Cedars of Lebanon, 82

Cemeteries
(Old) **African Methodist Episcopal Church Cemetery**, .25 acres, established in Rossville ca. 1850. It is on the west side of Bloomingdale Road, north of Woodrow Road, and is currently neglected. Rossville AME Zion Church is at 584 Bloomingdale Road.

Androvette Family Burying Ground, size unknown, was on the south side of Sharrotts Road, near the Arthur Kill in Charleston. It has been obliterated. Its current ownership is unknown.

Asbury Methodist Church Cemetery is on the west side of Richmond Avenue and the south side of Amsterdam Place in New Springville. It is owned by the Asbury Cemetery Association, 63 Erastina Place, Staten Island, New York, 10303. Currently, the cemetery is 625 feet along Richmond Avenue, and from 280 to 300 feet deep; its rear border is at Freedom Avenue. It was originally two cemeteries: the churchyard of Asbury Methodist Church, and the New Springville Cemetery to its south. In 1896, a Mrs. Mersereau owned the New Springville Cemetery; on July 5 of that year, the president of the church's board of trustees called the board together after the church services were over to announce she had transferred the deed to her cemetery to the church. At that point, the cemetery was renamed the Asbury New Springville Cemetery. In 1955, when the Cemetery Committee was formed, it became the Asbury Methodist Cemetery. The cemetery contains several gravesites of interest. Colonel Ichabod B. Crane of the U.S. Army, born in Elizabeth Town, New Jersey, July 18, 1787, died Staten Island, October 5, 1857. Colonel Crane's wife Charlotte, born May 25, 1798, died September 25, 1874. William M. (the Crane's son?), died December 26, 1880, aged 46. Juan, an Indian boy from the Umpqua tribe in Oregon, who died on Staten Island on Christmas Day 1856. James A. McKimm, September 25, 1971.

Baron Hirsch Cemetery opened in Graniteville about 1900. It consists of 88 acres on the west side of Richmond Avenue. The cemetery office is at 1126 Richmond Avenue, Staten Island, New York 10314. The telephone number is (718) 698–0612.

Bethel Methodist Episcopal Church Cemetery opened in Tottenville at an unknown date. The cemetery is on the Amboy Road and Bethel Avenue. The church, called Bethel United Methodist Church, is at 7620 Amboy Road.

Cemetery of the Resurrection opened in Pleasant Plains in 1980. It is on Hylan Boulevard between Bedell Street and Sharrott Avenue, and is about 124 acres. The cemetery's history begins with the trustees of Saint Patrick's Cathedral in the City of New York, incorporated April 14, 1807, by an act of the legislature of the State of New York. On September 14, 1978, Saint Patrick's trustees purchased Block 7664/360 (103.2632 acres) and Block 6775, Lot 1 (23.3060 acres) from the Mission of the Immaculate Virgin for the Protection of Homeless and Destitute Children, also known as Mount Loretto. The price was four million dollars. Block 7664 contained a cemetery and a small house at 108 Bedell Street. Saint Joseph's Union of Staten Island leased and occupied the house. This cemetery is notable for Guardian Angel's Plot, for fetuses and infants lost to miscarriage, stillbirth and abortion. The plot features a statue sculpted by Otello Guarducci of Great Barrington, Massachusetts, which was dedicated on Memorial Day 2000. (*Staten Island Advance*, June 13, 2000, C3.) The cemetery is maintained by the cemetery office at 361 Sharrott Avenue.

Christ Church Columbarium opened in the church chapel in New Brighton in 1985. The address is Christ Church, 76 Franklin Avenue, Staten Island, New York 10301.

Clove Baptist Church Cemetery opened in Concord at an unknown date. The cemetery occupied the northwest corner of Clove Road and Richmond Road, at Emerson Hill, and was .25 acres in size. It is also known as the Old Clove Baptist Churchyard and as the First Baptist Church Cemetery. Its history began when some members of the First Baptist church in Concord relocated to Richmond Avenue in Graniteville, opened the North Baptist Church, and started a cemetery in Hillside; for more information on that cemetery, see below. Later in the nineteenth century, some members of the North Baptist Church split off into the Graniteville (or First) Baptist Church on Willowbrook Road. They, too, opened a small cemetery, which informally grew into Lake Cemetery, also known as First Baptist Church Cemetery. As the cemetery is now abandoned, the best records are maintained at the New York City Real Estate Division, 2 Lafayette Street, New York, New York 10007.

Church of the Ascension Columbarium is located at 1 Kingsley Avenue in West New Brighton. A November 7, 1930, exemption report by Deputy Tax Commissioner Frank J. Schwartz indicated that religious services were held in this building for the first time on Sunday, October 26, 1930. At that time, the religious corporation still had a parish house and a church on Richmond Terrace in West Brighton.

Farm Colony Cemetery, or Potters Field, opened at Seaview circa 1830. The land lies on the west side of Manor Road and the north side of County House Road. The cemetery is neglected and has no tombstones. The New York City Economic Development Corporation currently maintains control of it.

Fairview Cemetery opened at Castleton Corners in 1876. It is on the south side of Victory Boulevard, west of Manor Road, and occupied 13 1/2 acres. It is maintained by the North Shore Cemetery Association, 1852 Victory Boulevard, Staten Island, New York, 10314.

Frederick Douglass Memorial Park opened in Oakwood in 1934. It is on the northwest corner of Amboy Road and Montreal Avenue, and occupies 14 acres. It is maintained by Frederick Douglass Memorial Park, 3201 Amboy Road.

Fountain Cemetery opened in West New Brighton in 1860. It is at the south end of Van Street and Tompkins Court on Richmond Terrace. It is maintained by the Staten Island Cemetery Association, at 140 Tysen Street, Staten Island, New York, 10301.

Hillside Cemetery opened in Graniteville circa 1898. It is on the west side of Richmond Avenue, south of Forest Avenue and Monsey Place, and occupies 1.6 acres. It is maintained by the Willowbrook Park Baptist Church, 1780 Richmond Avenue, Staten Island. Its history is entwined with that of the aforementioned Clove Baptist Church Cemetery.

Huguenot Dutch Reformed Cemetery opened in Huguenot at an unknown date. It is on Amboy Road and Huguenot Avenue. It is maintained by the Huguenot Dutch Reformed Church, 5475 Amboy Road, Staten Island, New York.

Journeay Family Burying Ground opened in Annadale at an unknown date. It is on the northwest corner of Carlton Boulevard and Halpin Avenue on the crest of the hill above the creek. The New York City Department of Parks maintains the Journeay Family Burying Ground records at its Staten Island headquarters.

Lake-Silvie Cemetery opened in Graniteville at an unknown date. It is on the west side of Willowbrook Road and the south side of Forest Avenue, where it occupies 1.8 acres. It is maintained by Meislohn-Silvie Funeral Home, 1289 Forest Avenue, Staten Island, New York.

Marine/Old Quarantine Cemetery opened at Silver Lake in 1850. It is on the north side of Victory Boulevard near the eighteenth hole of the Silver Lake Golf Course. It is maintained by the New York City Department of Parks.

Marine Society of New York Cemetery opened at Edgewater in 1830. As of 1913, it was located on Vanderbilt Avenue, west of Center Street, and occupied 18.25 acres. The written history of this cemetery goes back to November 1918, when William Anderson, Chairman of the Retreat Committee of the Marine Society of the State of New York, prepared an application for tax exemption for a Tompkins Avenue cemetery in Block 556 Lot 88. In the application, Mr. Anderson indicated that the Marine Society, a charitable corporation, took title to the 4.5 acre cemetery for seamen about 1882. Many interments were made from the hospital on grounds at the time that the hospital was owned by the state. On December

9, 1918, a deputy tax commissioner reported that there were no burial slabs visible at that time on that plot. However, he was "reliably informed" that there were a large number of burials from the Marine Hospital in former years "and the bodies are there now," but the neighbors removed the slabs for sidewalks and other purposes. On January 20, 1919, Mr. Anderson states that fully half the area was covered with burials of those who died at the adjacent state hospital, but none of the burials had taken place in the past fifteen years. The cemetery has since been obliterated. Information on it is available via the U.S. Public Health Service, Washington, D.C.

Merrell Family Burying Ground opened in Graniteville in 1699. It is on the north side of Merrill Avenue, west of Richmond Avenue, and occupies .5 acres. Information regarding it is available at the New York City Division of Real Estate, 2 Lafayette Street, New York, New York 10007.

Moravian Cemetery opened at New Dorp in 1763. It is on the corner of Richmond Road and Todt Hill Road, and occupies 100 acres. Is it maintained by Moravian Cemetery, 2205 Richmond Road, Staten Island, New York. Further information on it is available on p. 24 of the original Resource Manual.

Mount Loretto Cemetery opened in the Princes Bay/Pleasant Plains area at an unknown date. It is on the grounds of Mount Loretto Home on Hylan Avenue near Sharrott Avenue. It is maintained by the Mission of the Immaculate Virgin, 6581 Hylan Boulevard, Staten Island, New York.

Mount Richmond Cemetery opened in Richmond in 1909. It is on the west side of Clarke Avenue near Arthur Kill Road, on a lot 165 feet by 400 feet. It is maintained by Mount Richmond Cemetery, 420 Clarke Avenue, Staten Island, New York 10306–6139. The phone number is (718) 667–0915. Eastern European Jews from the Lower East Side of Manhattan formed the Hebrew Free Burial Association (HFBA) in 1888. The group bought Mount Richmond in 1909, and began burials there. In 1911, the fire at the Triangle Shirtwaist Company on Washington Place killed 146 young women, many of whom were Jewish immigrants. Many are buried at Mount Richmond with the words "Died at the Fire" etched on their headstones. Among the graves are indigent Jews, sometimes buried without markers, Holocaust survivors who died penniless and, more recently, arrivals from the Ukraine's Chernobyl disaster who came to the United States for treatment. Further information is available at the HFBA, 363 Seventh Avenue, New York, New York. The HFBA's telephone number is (212) 239–1662. Further information is also available at www.jewishgen.org/cemetery and at the entry for Silver Lake Cemetery.

New Springville Cemetery opened in that town at an unknown date. It is on the west side of Richmond Avenue, adjoining Asbury Cemetery. It is maintained by the Asbury Cemetery Association, 63 Erastina Place, Staten Island, New York 10303.

New York Nursery and Child Hospital Cemetery opened at Castleton Corners at an unknown date. It was off Manor Road, where it occupied .33 acres. It has been obliterated. Further information on it is available at the office of the Borough Historian, Borough Hall, Staten Island, New York 10301. The telephone number is (718) 816–2137.

Ocean View Cemetery is the "mother cemetery" for United Hebrew, Saint Agnes, and Frederick Douglass Memorial Park cemeteries.

The Seguine, also known as

the Sleight or Blazing Star Family Burying Ground opened in Rossville in 1750. It is on Arthur Kill Road between Huguenot Avenue and Rossville Avenue, and occupies .6 acres. It became a New York City landmark in 1968, and is the subject of the book *Blazing Star Burying Ground* published by the Staten Island Institute of Arts and Sciences in 1997. Further information is available at the New York City Division of Real Estate, 2 Lafayette Street, New York, New York 10007.

Sailors' Snug Harbor Cemetery opened at Randall Manor in 1834. It is on Prospect Avenue at Devon Place, east of Allison Pond Park, off Brentwood Avenue, and occupies 2.9 acres in two sections. It is maintained by Sailors' Snug Harbor, P.O. Box 150, Sea Level, North Carolina 28577.

Saint Agnes Cemetery opened at an unknown date. It is north of Amboy Road, and occupies 106 acres. It is now part of Ocean View Cemetery, q.v.

Saint Andrew's Church Cemetery opened in Richmond at an unknown date. It is on the corner of Old Mill Road and Richmond Hill Road, and occupies 1.25 acres. It is maintained by Saint Andrews Episcopal Church, 40 Old Mill Road, Staten Island, New York.

Saint John's Church Columbarium opened in Clifton at an unknown date. It is maintained by Saint John's Episcopal Church, 1331 Bay Street, Staten Island, New York.

Saint John's Evangelical Lutheran Church Cemetery opened in Port Richmond in 1850. It is West of Jewett Avenue at Catherine Court, and occupies .4 acres. It is maintained by Saint John's Lutheran Church, 9 Catherine Court, Staten Island, New York.

Saint Joseph's Cemetery opened in Rossville at an unknown date. It is on Barry Street, west of Rossville Avenue, and occupies 1.3 acres. It is maintained by Saint Joseph-Saint Thomas Church, 6135 Amboy Road, Staten Island, New York.

Saint Luke's Cemetery, which includes the Woglum Family Burying Ground, opened in Rossville at an unknown date. It is near Arthur Kill Road, across from Zebra Lane. It is maintained by All Saints Episcopal Church, 2329 Victory Boulevard, Staten Island, New York.

Saint Mary's Cemetery opened in Grasmere at an unknown date. It is on the corner of Parkinson Avenue and Kramer Street, and the corner of Parkinson Avenue and Reid Avenue, and occupies .9 acres. It is main-

tained by Saint Mary's Cemetery, 115 Parkinson Avenue, Staten Island, New York 10305.

Saint Mary's (Protestant Episcopal) Church Memorial Garden opened in Castleton, West Brighton, at an unknown date. It is on Davis Avenue at the corner of Castleton Avenue. It is maintained by Saint Mary's Church, 347 Davis Avenue, Staten Island, New York 10310.

Saint Mary of the Assumption Church Cemetery opened in Elm Park at an unknown date. It is near the southwest corner of Walker Street and Trantor Place. It is maintained by Saint Mary of the Assumption Church, 2230 Richmond Terrace 10302.

Saint Michael's Home Cemetery opened in Annadale at an unknown date. It is maintained by the Presentation Sisters of Staten Island, 419 Woodrow Road, Staten Island, New York.

Saint Peter's Cemetery opened in West Brighton in 1848. It is in two sections on either side of the intersection of Bement Avenue and Clove Road, and occupies 9.8 acres. It is maintained by Saint Peter's Cemetery, 52 Tyler Street, Staten Island New York, or 53 Saint Mark's Place, Staten Island, New York.

Sandy Ground Cemetery opened in Rossville at an unknown date. It is on the south side of Crabtree Avenue, west of Bloomingdale Road. This New York City Landmark is maintained by Rossville African Methodist Episcopal Church, 584 Bloomingdale Road, Staten Island, New York.

Second Asbury African Methodist Episcopal Church Cemetery, formerly the Cherry Lane or the Old Slaves Burying Ground, opened in Westerleigh in 1880. It was on the south side of Forest Avenue, near North Avenue, and occupies .5 acres. On May 26, 1915, Charles A. Mulligan, Deputy Tax Commissioner for the First District, filed a report. "I have examined the premises and find no outward evidence of there being a cemetery; no mounds or headstones, and the plot not fenced; have interviewed 10 persons, 4 of whom reside in the vicinity, and they inform me that it is about 20 years since the last interment; a Mr. Davis residing a short distance from this property for the past 40 years [possibly Joseph Davis, 60, a laborer residing at 94 Elizabeth St. — R.D.] states that he dug one of the last graves at least 20 years ago. It was also stated that the plot is entirely filled with bodies, graves having been open promiscuously without regard to space." Nevertheless, an apparently incomplete listing of burials

(on p. 28, Vol. 1, "Gravestone Inscriptions") dates from 1880 to 1903, making the last burial some 12 years from the date of the tax commissioner's review of the site. (R.D.) The cemetery has been obliterated. The site is now occupied by the Angiulli Plaza Shopping Center. A plaque about the cemetery, once inside the bank on the site, is now missing. Further information is at the office of the Borough Historian, Staten Island Borough Hall, Staten Island, New York 10301. The telephone is (718) 816–2137.

Silver Lake Cemetery opened in Sunnyside in 1887. The cemetery is along Victory Boulevard, Block 594/100, south of Silver Mount Cemetery, and occupies 4.5 acres. Its story begins with the incorporation of the Hebrew Free Burial Association, also known as Chedra Aguda Achim Chesed Shel Emeth or Brotherhood Society of True Charity, on January 24, 1889. The first corporate board consisted of president Barnet Friedman, vice-president Louis Michilitsky, secretary Selig Berman, treasurer Mark Silva, and trustees Max Cohen, Abraham L. Stone, Abraham Greenberg, Levy Minsky and Gabriel Cohen. According to a 1951 application for tax exemption, the HFBA's purpose was "Burial of the dead of the Jewish faith where insufficient funds are available for decent burial in accordance with religious tenets." On September 2, 1892, the society purchased land from Fredericka Thauner, widow of John G. Thauner, for $4,000. However, the March 7, 1951 tax exemption indicates Lot 100 was previously part of Lot 1 of Silver Mount Cemetery. This may explain why burial records begin in 1887; the cemetery ceased new burials in the 1960s. Further information is available at www.jewishgen.org/cemetery, or at HFBA, 363 Seventh Avenue, New York, New York. The telephone number is (212) 239–1662. *See also* Mount Richmond Cemetery.

Silver Mount, originally Coopers, Cemetery, opened at Silver Lake in 1866. It is across from the Silver Lake Park and Golf Course, and occupies 17 acres. It is maintained by the Silver Mount Cemetery Association, 918 Victory Boulevard, Staten Island, New York 10301.

Simonson/Hillyer Family Burying Ground opened in Port Richmond in 1855. It is at Catherine Court and Simonson Street. It is currently abandoned and its owners are unknown.

Staten Island Cemetery opened in West Brighton in 1840.

It is at 1642 Richmond Terrace, between Tompkins Courts and Alaska Street, and occupies 1.6 acres. It is maintained by the Staten Island Cemetery Association, at 16 Eldridge Avenue, Staten Island, New York. Historians Leng and Davis mention "a Negro who died about 1845 who once owned the Staten Island Cemetery." In his early life Joseph Ryerss was a slave in the family of Judge Gozen Ryerss. Judge Ryerss's will freed him in 1802, but not until April 24, 1811, were certificates of manumission issued to Joseph Ryerss and his son. In 1812, Joseph Ryerss bought the West Brighton property, adjacent to the Trinity Chapel of Saint Andrews, where he was the sexton. He lived and farmed there until his death in 1842. His burial there, together with those of other family members, some as early as 1829, constituted a family burying ground. John J. Clute and Jacob Bodine witnessed Ryerss's 1842 will. (*Staten Island Advance*, June 13, 1988.)

Sylvan (Grove) Cemetery, also known as Ye Olde Burial Hill, opened in Travis at an unknown date. It is on the west side of Victory Boulevard, north of Glen Street, and occupies 2.75 acres. It is abandoned, and further information is available at the New York City Real Estate Division, 2 Lafayette Street, New York, New York, 10007.

Trinity Chapel Cemetery operated in West Brighton between 1802 and 1860. It is at 58 Van Street, adjacent to Staten Island Cemetery. It is abandoned, and information on it is available at the New York City Real Estate Division, 2 Lafayette Street, New York, New York, 10007.

United Hebrew Cemetery opened in Richmond in 1906. It is on the south side of Arthur Kill Road, near Clarke Avenue, and occupies 100 acres. It is maintained by United Hebrew Cemetery, 122 Arthur Kill Road, Staten Island, New York 10306.

Vanderbilt Family Grounds opened in New Dorp at an unknown date. The entrance gate to it is at the northwest boundary of Moravian Cemetery. Further information on it is maintained at the Bank of New York, (212) 464-2783.

Vaughn Cemetery opened in Rossville at an unknown date. It is on the north side of Arthur Kill Road near Zebra Lane, adjoining Saint Luke's Cemetery. Its owner is unknown.

West Baptist Church Cemetery opened in Charleston at an unknown date. It is on the west side of Arthur Kill Road, north of Sharrotts Road. Further informa-

tion is available at the New York City Real Estate Division, 2 Lafayette Street, New York, New York, 10007.

Woodland Cemetery opened in Sunnyside at an unknown date. It is on the east side of Victory Boulevard on the corner with Highland Avenue, and occupies 12 acres. It is maintained by the Woodland Cemetery Association, 982 Victory Boulevard, Staten Island, New York 10301.

Woodrow Methodist Episcopal Church Cemetery opened in Woodrow at an unknown date. It is on Woodrow Road west of Huguenot Avenue, and occupies 1.25 acres. It is maintained by Woodrow United Methodist Church, 1075 Woodrow Road, Staten Island, New York.

1888 on Arthur Kill Road have been landmarked. (E.H.)

The four identical houses at 71–73, 75–77, 81–83 and 85–86 Kreischer Street are rare surviving examples of their type. Built in 1890 by prominent local landowner Peter Androvette as housing for workers in the adjacent Kreischerville Brick Works, they, along with the nearby Kreischer House, reflect the evolution of a Richmond County hamlet into a company town. Although the homes are clad in wood shingles, the sidewalks are paved in Kreischer brick. (Dolkart 195). The Androvetteville cemetery off Sharotts Road has been obliterated, but the Saint Luke's and the West Baptist cemeteries remain. (R.D.)

This house was erected in 177 and was originally at 819 Willowbrook Road, New Springville. It was the headquarters for the American Committee of Safety during the American Revolution. The house was built of fieldstone, with 22-inch-thick walls. Dismantled in 1969, the house's stone and timber were moved to Historic Richmond Town, *q.v.* (E.H.)

The early history of the Church of Saint Andrew is closely connected with that of the Society for the Propagation of the Gospel in Foreign Parts, chartered June 16, 1701, and its missionary on Staten Island, the Reverend Aeneas Mackenzie. He named the Church of Saint Andrew in 1708 and procured the building of the church and rectory in 1709. On August 6, 1711, William Tiller and his wife donated the land on which the church was erected. (Church of Saint Andrew, 1925, 15–25.)

What follows is new information on Staten Island's African American, black, or historically black churches. The source for this information is Richard Dickenson, "A Pictorial Directory of Churches of Color on Staten Island" (unpublished manuscript, 1994). According to legend, **Bethel Community Church**

(Block 248/27) was founded in 1896 at the home of Mr. James and Mrs. Victoria Newcombe, 111 Targee Street, Stapleton. The incorporation of Bethel African Methodist Episcopal Church came in 1909. Bethel African Methodist Episcopal Church of Tompkinsville was incorporated July 13, 1917, at which point it occupied property at 110 Van Duzer Street. Fourteen people were present at the incorporation. Those elected as trustees for three years included: George W. Hall, 5 Van Duzer Street, Pastor and Presiding Officer; James Wilson, 107 Marion Avenue, Stapleton; and Phoenix B. Armstrong, 280 Gordon Street, Stapleton. Elected trustees for two years were N. V. Harrison and French Jones. One-year trustees were Jacob Anderson and Percy B. Owens. Joseph V. Hamson, Ernest V. Moore and Frank DeCordenes were trustees without listed responsibilities.

In 1919, Mary K. Burkhardt conveyed the property to George H. Hall. In 1925 Leah S. Flake conveyed part of the property to the church trustee. In 1940 C. Asapansa-Johnson, Pastor and Chairman of the Trustees had the old 22'x 60' single-story frame building demolished to erect a new building. The replacement building has a cornerstone

inscribed "Bethel AME Church and Community Center, October 26, 1941."

An item in the Saturday, June 10, 2000, *Staten Island Advance* stated "The present property at 51–53 Van Duzer St. was purchased in 1921 and the first church was located in a former blacksmith shop. A fund-raising effort aided by prominent Islanders allowed the congregation to raze the building and erect a new church." Also, "In the 1940s the church left its denomination to become an independent congregation after the African Methodist Episcopal called for the removal of the pastor, the Rev. Comna Asapansa-Johnson." A Clergy Exemption application of March 15, 1944 indicates that Rev. C. and Mamie Lee Asapansa-Johnson resided at 29 Livingston St., in a house they purchased on October 1, 1943.

By 1977, the Most Reverend Francis E. Harris was Pastor and Chairman of the Trustee Board. Edward Craig was the treasurer; Nadine Roland, the secretary; and Carl Meyers, the financial secretary. The other trustees were Mrs. Eulalie Joe, Robert Jackson, Eva Lake, William Bayson and George Gibson.

The story of the buildings of the **Faith Christian Center** begins with the Staten Island Board of

Jewish Education. The SIBJE was incorporated March 15, 1954. On April 6, 1958, Abe Solar Associations, Inc., donated 37,000 square feet of property at 547 Targee Street Stapleton "for a school building and other activities." At that point, the SIBJE had space at 300 Vanderbilt Avenue, and the following officers: president Max Levy; vice-president Jacob Cooperstein; treasurer Louis R. Miller; and secretary Rueben E. Gross. It was these people who erected the building that the Faith Christian Center, incorporated July 17, 1984, occupies.

The buildings of the **Fellowship Baptist Church** go back to the Reformed Church of Mariners Harbor. The Reformed Church was incorporated January 22, 1907. Its minister at the time was the Reverend DeWitt G. Rockefeller. The signers of the incorporation papers included three elders, James E. Merrill, Cornelius Simonson and Edward M. Eadie, and three deacons, Henry S. Shea, Henry P. Appleton, and Charles E. Barckmann. The group purchased a parsonage the next year. The Fellowship Baptist Church was incorporated June 17, 1966. Signers of its incorporation papers included the pastor, the Reverend Arthur D. Phillips; Chairman of the Board of Trustees Mr. Stanley Brown, and Financial Secretary Mrs. James Williams. On May 12, 1975, Fellowship Baptist purchased the church and parsonage from Reformed Church. The property is at 3036 Richmond Terrace (Block 1236/43).

First Central Baptist Church acquired its land from the Jewish Congregation Tiferetz Israel, which had purchased land at 117 Wright Street (Block 521/79) in October 1926, and had started building a temple there in November that same year. First Central Baptist was organized about 1978. In 1985 its then pastor, The Reverend Calvin Rice, started renovations. He received support from more than 500 adults and children. Renovations included installing a baptismal pool, improving the façade, adding air conditioning, constructing classrooms, and remodeling the lower level for the pastor's study, the trustees' room and a reception room.

The First Church of God in Christ was organized in 1929, and incorporated in 1949. On January 8 of that year, the congregation held a meeting for the purposes of incorporation at 265 Broadway. It elected officers: the Reverend Frank Cook became the president, Jerome Chadwick the secretary, Ruth Chadwick the financial secretary, and Frank Harris the treasurer. The congregation also elected trustees: Clarence Sexton, Jerome Chadwick, Frank Harris, John Thompson, John Connelly, William Marten, William Glover and Martha Lamb. Incorporation became official February 21, 1949. On August 23, 1954, after occupying space in Mariners Harbor and at a West Brighton storefront, the congregation acquired the property at 181 Clove Road, West Brighton, from the Salem Evangelical Free Church, which was in the process of moving to its present home at 634 Clove Road. At that point, the church consisted of a single-story frame building dating from 1908. As of 2001, the congregation was in the process of restoring the building, including the finishing of the lower church hall.

Full Gospel Tabernacle Church, United Holy Church of America (U.H.C.A.) was incorporated February 15, 1973. Its property is at 1070–74 Castleton Avenue, West Brighton, Staten Island, 10310 (Block 207/39). Its pastor is the Reverend Mary E. Frazer.

The Glorious Church of God in Christ Jesus uses space originally occupied by the First Baptist Church of New Brighton. First Baptist was organized in 1884. It conducted its early services in Lyceum Hall, Union

Sunday School rooms on Cleveland Street, and under tents. They also used a building belonging to the Church of the Redeemer on Clinton Avenue and Fillmore Street. That building, which was the Church of the Redeemer's second home, had been damaged in the Blizzard of 1888, and that accident, plus a decline in church activities, led the Church of the Redeemer to construct a new house of worship. The Church of the Redeemer moved into its new home in 1895, leaving their old one for the Baptists to use. In 1897, the Baptists moved into their new home, complete with hardwood floors and a twelve-room rectory, at 238 Hamilton Avenue in New Brighton. They left the Church of the Redeemer's old building to others. (It is currently the Unitarian Church.) First Baptist incorporated in 1898, and remained at Hamilton Avenue for the next sixty-three years.

Meanwhile, the Glorious Church of God in Christ Jesus was incorporated in Kings County, Brooklyn, May 3, 1956. Its first meeting elected a full slate of trustees, but staggered their terms to create three three-year terms of office. At that first election, Willie Durant, Arthur Wilson and Damond Presman for elected for a one-year term; Raymond Johnson,

Bessie Smith, and Mary Lindsey for a two-year term; and Bishop Perry Lindsey (the presiding officer), Walter Wilson and Otto Pye for a three-year term.

First Baptist left Hamilton Avenue in 1961. In 1966, it merged with Mariners Harbor Baptist Church to create Willowbrook Park Baptist Church. That left Hamilton Avenue vacant. The City of New York purchased it at public auction September 14, 1976. The Glories Church of God in Christ Jesus purchased it from the City of New York January 11, 1977.

Greater New Hope Baptist Church traces its origins to its organization by the Reverend David W. Moss in 1951. It was incorporated as "New Hope Baptist Church" April 11, 1956. At that point, the Reverend Moss was the presiding officer, Lilliam Fletcher Chadwick and Essie Bellamy were subscribers, and Cora Watkins and Sarah Mason were subscribers and inspectors of election, that is, responsible for overseeing the election of the trustees required under the laws of the State of New York.

When the Reverend Robert Howell became pastor, he purchased a storefront church at 601 Cary Avenue in West Brighton (Block 211/73). The congregation purchased the storefront

from the pastor December 30, 1963. The congregation then renovated the storefront for Sunday School, Vacation Bible School, tutoring for elementary and junior high school students, remedial reading, arts and crafts, choir rehearsals, and junior recreation.

On April 8, 1966, Howell resigned his position to become pastor of New Saint Paul's Baptist Church in Newark, New Jersey. Title to the property went to Ethel Douglas (later Ethel Carruthers), a member of the board of trustees, then residing at 82 Alaska Street, Staten Island. The congregation was reincorporated February 11, 1971, at which point the word "Greater" was added to the name. The new incorporation meant only a small change in leadership. The pastor at this point was the Reverend A.L. Moody. Hilton Holcomb and Robert Carruthers were elected to one-year terms as trustees. Turner Bellamy and Hugh Bennet were elected to two-year terms. Cora Watkins and Sarah Mason returned as inspectors of election. During the mid-1970s, when the Reverend Robert Moody was pastor, Mr. Charles Landrum chaired the board of trustees; in recent years he has taken the title of deacon. On June 13, 1993, the congregation recorded its history by placing this plaque on the Cary Avenue side of its church: "Greater New Hope Baptist Church 1951–1978. Founded by Rev. Moss, Established and Incorporated by Rev. A.L. Moody."

In 1956, a little storefront at 201 Jersey Street in New Brighton was the birthplace of **Hall's Temple Reformed Church of God in Christ**. The congregation later moved to 483 Jersey Street. Then, with the support of the trustees, the Reverend A.F. Hall, Sr., bought, in 1972, the ca. 1900 brick-built former Saint Paul's Lutheran Church on Cary Avenue. The year before, Saint Paul had merged with Saint Luke's Lutheran on Decker Avenue.

Mount Calvary Holy Church was incorporated February 20, 1958 as Mount Calvary Church of God in America, Inc., 798 Richmond Terrace. The first trustees were the Reverend Archie M. Johnson of 798 Richmond Terrace; George Briggs of 72 Cassidy Place (chair); Dennis F. Grady of 77 Fillmore Street; Eugene Latta of 170 Broadway; Thomas G. Green of 99 Mooney Lane; Fleming Bass of 183 York Avenue; and Hettie Kirby of 25 Mooney Lane. Mount Calvary's present home, 9 DuBois Avenue in West Brighton (Block 215/200), was conveyed to it by

El Bethel Assembly of God, which, prior to changing its name October 28, 1944, was the Staten Island Scandinavian Assembly.

Bishop Thomas E. Brown (died 1987) and his son, the Reverend Victor A. Brown, co-founded **Mount Sinai United Christian Church of Evangelism** (nondenominational) in the basement of their home in 1981. The congregation eventually moved to 76 Victory Boulevard, and to its present quarters, 199 Victory Boulevard (Block 33/1), July 24, 1994. Their current place of worship is in the 1898 building constructed by Congregation B'nai Jeshurun. The oldest of the Hebrew places of worship on Staten Island, it was incorporated May 10, 1888 as "The Congregational Benevolent Society B'nai Jeshurun of Richmond County." The president of the organization was Moses Aaron Jacobs.

New Direction Baptist Church also traces its building back to a Jewish congregation. Congregation Aguadath Achim Anshee Chessed, nicknamed Triple AC, Triple A, and the Jersey Street schul, was founded in 1911 by thirteen men who had all come to the United States from Europe. One of them was Lewis Levy, who purchased clothes on the Lower East Side and brought them back to Staten Island to sell. Levy later entered the real estate business, and built a house for his family on Winter Avenue in New Brighton. Levy and the other founders began holding services in a Taft Avenue store belonging to Abraham Singer, another founder. The names of the other eleven were: Morris Siegler, Jacob Cohen, Mordecai Blumberg, Chaim Blumberg, Abram Cooperstein, Hirsch Kaplan, Morris Levinson, Abraham Lipshitz, Meyer Pave, Israel Sabin and Abraham Shedrowitz. These men constructed a brick synagogue at 386 Jersey Street sometime before 1914.

New Directions Baptist Church was founded in 1968. It was incorporated at the New Brighton Church of God in Christ of Staten Island on October 1, 1970. Its incorporators were: The Reverend Frederick Douglas Cook, John H. Holmes, Ronaldo Jefferies, Merrill E. Richardson, Alva Franks, Jerilden Formes and Effie Linwood. On Jun 29, 1971, New Brighton Church of God in Christ purchased the synagogue of Congregation Aguadath Achim Anshee Chessed, and installed on its façade a stone inscription: "The Founder of This Church is Jesus Christ, 1968, Elder Frederick Douglas Cook, Pastor." Congregation Aguadath Achim Anshee Chessed moved to 641 Delafield Avenue, formerly the home of Yeshiva Tifereth Torah, a school for boys. (*Staten Island Advance*, November 3, 2000, A35.)

Rossville A.M.E.Z. Church, 584 Bloomingdale Road, Staten Island, New York 10309 (Block 7267/101), was organized December 5, 1850, at the home of William H. Pitts, age 40, formerly of Virginia, in Rossville. The first members of the church were: Caeser Jackson, 48, of New York; Francis Williams, 45, of New York; William Webb; William H. Stevens; John J. Henry, 35, of New York; Moses K. Harris, 30, of Orange, New York; Israel Pitts, 45, of Virginia; Isaac Purnell; Ishmael Robbins, 35, of Virginia; Henry Jackson, 33, of Staten Island; Elizabeth Titus; Sarah J. Landin, wife of Robert; Esther V.S. Purnell (a noted teacher), 36, of Maryland; Ann M. Bishop, 20 of Virginia; Grace Williams; and Louisa Harris, 19, of Virginia, wife of Moses. Jackson, Williams, Webb, Stevens and Henry were chosen trustees; the Reverend William H. Pitts was appointed pastor. The first church was erected 1854, a plain wooden structure seating about 150 persons. Occupied until 1897, the congregation moved to the new church on Bloomingdale Road on December 19 of that year.

The congregation of **Stapleton United Union American**

Methodist Episcopal may have existed as early as 1798. A March 16, 1991, *Staten Island Advance* article entitled "Staple Church Marks 190 Years," noted that "The Stapleton church began after the Revolutionary War as a small mission with a handful of members." In 1801, it appears on records as Stapleton Methodist Church. In 1813, the congregation became a member of the Union Church of Africans Conference, later known as the U.A.M.E. Church.

On December 20, 1848, the incorporation record for the African Union Church lists as incorporators: Peter Spicer, age 23, of New York; Henry Johnson, 24, of Pennsylvania, Joseph Dillon, 38, of New York, Isaac Barney, 30, of Connecticut, and William Corissey, 37, of New York. Isaac Barney, who was an elder or governing officer and then pastor of the church, is buried on Stapleton U.A.M.E.'s grounds. When the congregation was incorporated as the Union American Church of Stapleton, Methodist Episcopal Church, Village of Edgewater, there were five trustees. Henry Jones served as congregational president, Charles Robinson, age 28, as secretary, and James Spicer, 37, John Thomas and George Watson as trustees.

The congregation has owned the same lot so long that both streets near it changed their names. The property faced Riker Street, now incorporated into Tompkins Avenue, at the intersection with McKeon Avenue, now Tompkins Street. (Its current address is 49 Tompkins Avenue.)

The congregation erected a single-story frame building of 20' x 30' on its 51' x 100' lot in 1881. In 1899, when Staten Island commenced its annual recording of tax-exempt property, the congregation's real estate was wholly tax exempt. In 1915, the Reverend George Mathis, pastor of Stapleton U.A.M.E., successfully applied for church tax exemption. The congregation has built three churches in succession on the same lot. Its most recent building went up in 1922, but that building has been renovated a great deal; there is a marked change in photographs taken in 1940 and 1999.

Saint Paul's Apostolic Faith Church of Giving Grace, Inc. was incorporated June 20, 1966 by the congregation's secretary, Christine Gorman, its minister, Miss Pearlie Hedgepeth, its assistant secretary, Mr. Edward Gorham, Messrs. Willis Tailor, Willinen Ellibee and Joseph Banbo of Staten Island, and trustees from Mount Vernon in the Bronx, Amityville, Long Island, and Stamford, Connecticut.

The 25' x 100' frame brick veneer building Saint Paul's occupies is estimated to date from 1920. It belonged to the Italian Christian Church of Staten Island, which was organized about 1919. The ICCSI purchased the 11 Pike Street property in 1934 from E.M. Carolan. On June 10, 1947, the ICCSI incorporated. Its pastor at the time was Andrew Rodolico. Its presiding officer was Joseph Demola, Sr., and other trustees were Luca Cerbone, Frank Carlo, Ettore Pirano, Fiorina Signorello, Dominick Tomasella, John Barone and Joseph Casella. By October 29, 1958, the ICCSI had changed its name to The Christian Pentecostal Church of Staten Island, and started a building fund for a new church. In 1964, the congregation engaged an architect and purchased property at 900 Richmond Road in Concord at auction from the City of New York. The congregation erected a two-story brick building with a basement on their new property. It sold the old property to Saint Paul's in 1967.

Saint Philip's Baptist Church, incorporated February 10, 1891, is located at 77 Bennett Street in Port Richmond, Staten Island 10302 (Block 1007/1). A church historian, Charles West, cited the following as those who "joined together to organize their own house of worship about 1870": John Taylor, age 25, born in Virginia, Leroy Dungey, 22, Virginia, William Beverly, 26, Virginia, William Reynolds, James Poole, 21, Staten Island, and John Cannon.

After the initial organization, Saint Philip's became a colored people's mission of the Reform Church of Port Richmond and on February 3, 1871 a Sunday School was formed by the group. On either April 21, 1874, or February 8, 1879, the group became a Baptist mission. (A memorial stone in the church lists 1879–1966.) By April 1880 the mission was using Park Baptist Church in Port Richmond for services in the chapel. The first church site at 134 Faber (now Elm) Street, Port Richmond, was purchased in 1884 in the name of Thomas Dungey, 25, a Virginia native and his wife Margaritta. There was a neighborhood protest against the purchase of church property by blacks, but prominent members of the Park Baptist Church notably Messrs. Alfred DeGroate and Mr. Moore, assisted with the legal work and organization of the church. The cornerstone laying came in 1887, with construction costs carried to completion at a total cost of $3,030.30. On Easter Sunday,

April 21, 1889, the church was dedicated under the Reverend Granville Hunt, the first pastor of Saint Philip's. Trustees at the time of incorporation were: Thomas S. Dungey, William H. Moore, John A. Connor, William C. Hunter and James Poole.

The current 1926 Gothic-style brick edifice was acquired February 14, 1966 from the Zion Lutheran Church of Staten Island, now located at their third edifice, 505 Watchogue Road, Staten Island. The Bennett Street building was Zion Lutheran's second church, having moved into it from the building at Avenue in Port Richmond. At that time there were over 220 members of Saint Philip's and the officers were the Reverend William A. Epps, pastor; Harry A. Chambers, Treasurer; Helen Chambers, church clerk; and Charles K. Smith, chairman of the board of trustees.

The **Silver Lake Temple, Inc.** (incorporated March 12, 1968) — a holding corporation for the charitable fraternal activities of the Silver Queen chapter of Eastern Star and the Silver Lake Lodge of Masons — acquired the Elm Street church building on July 6, 1973, and held it for a number of years. The Mar Thomas Church of Staten Island, a congregation of Christians largely from Kerela, India, now inhabits the building. The name refers to Saint (Doubting) Thomas who was said to have been executed near that part of India, in Madras.

Shiloh African Methodist Episcopal Church is located at 779 Henderson Avenue, Staten Island, New York, 10301 (Block 186/113). It was incorporated December 29, 1915. Its incorporators were John H. Lewis, then age 50, William A. Morris, 37, and George W. White, 30. Serving as the first trustees were John C. Robinson, George E. Prime, and John H. Faulks. Later trustees included William H. Pedro, Peter Perkins and Watson Truax, who were in turn followed by Dennis Reddick, William A. Morris and Johnson Jones.

Vanderbilt Avenue Moravian Church, 329 Vanderbilt Avenue (Block 556/19), was incorporated October 18, 1889, as the First Moravian Church of Edgewater. It changed its name November 30, 1946. Clarence Leeker, President, and Marion Schmitt, Secretary, of the Board of Trustees, First Moravian Church of Edgewater, filed the certificate of change of name.

NAME	Pop.	Key Notable Interest	TOWN
Annadale	150	Hamlet, on railroad (RR)	Westfield
Bloomfield	100	Farming	Northfield
Bulls Head	200	Farming	Northfield
Castleton Corners	300	Farming	Castleton
Chelsea	100	Hamlet	Northfield
Clifton	5,066	Manufacturing, on RR	Southfield
Concord	500	Hamlet	Southfield
Dongan Hills	200	Florists	Southfield
Edgewater	16,000	Village	Staten Island
Egbertville (ND)	100	Hamlet	Northfield
Elm Park (PR)	500	Residential, on RR	Northfield
Eltingville (Seaside)	200	Hamlet, on RR	Westfield
Erastina (MH)	...	Locality, on RR	Northfield
Factoryville (WNB)	...	Locality, on RR	Castleton
Ft. Wadsworth	...	Fort on RR	Middletown
Four Corners (CC)	300	Farming	Castleton
Fresh Kill	150	Farming	Westfield
Garretson (DH)	200	Summer resort, on RR	Southfield
Gifford (GK)	400	Fishing	Southfield
Graniteville (PR)	200	Hamlet	Northfield
Grant City	150	Summer resort	Southfield
Grasmere	...	Locality, on RR	Southfield
Great Kills (Gifford)	400	Fishing, on RR	Southfield
Green Ridge	300	Hamlet	Staten Island
Holland Hook	...	Locality	Northfield
Huguenot	150	Hamlet, on RR	Westfield
Kreischerville	1,000	Brick	Westfield
Linden Park (DH)	175	Summer resort	Southfield
Linoleumville	700	Manufacturing	Northfield
Livingston (WNB)	...	Locality, on RR	Castleton
Mariner Harbor	2,400	Oysters, on RR	Northfield
New Brighton	17,000	Resort, on RR	Castleton
New Dorp	800	Summer resort, on RR	Southfield
New Springville	400	Farming	Northfield
Oak Wood (Gifford)	200	Summer resort	Southfield
Pleasant Plains	300	Residential, on RR	Westfield
Port Richmond	7,000	Manufacturing	Northfield
Prince's Bay	200	Oysters, on RR	Westfield
Richmond	500	Court House	Southfield
Richmond Valley	200	Hamlet, on RR	Westfield
Rosebank (Egwtr.)	5,066	Manufacturing, on RR	Southfield
Rossville	600	Farming	Westfield
Sailors' Snug Harbor	...	Asylum	Castleton
St. George (N.B.)	...	Locality	Castleton
Tompkinsville	8,000	Residential, on RR	Mid. & C.
Tottenville	2,500	Oysters, on RR	Westfield
Travisville	150	Hamlet	Northfield
W. New Brighton	3,000	Manufacturing	Castleton
Woodrow	150	Farming	Westfield
Woods of Arden	...	Summer resort	Southfield

Abbreviations: CC = Castleton Corners, DH = Dongan Hills, Egwtr. = Edgewater, GK = Great Kills, MR = Mariner(s) Harbor, ND = New Dorp, PR = Port Richmond, RR = railroad, W = West, WNB = West New Brighton. Adapted from Gazetteer of Suburban New York, The Brooklyn Daily Eagle Almanac (1897), 72–76. R.D.)

The building was erected in 1700 by Governor Day. During the American Civil War (1861–1865), the building housed the offices of Confederate agent and future Staten Islander Major Norman S. Walker. The present Confederate Museum reveals Bermuda's not-quite neutral role in that harsh but strangely glamorous war. Its holdings include portraits of Major Walker and his wife, Georgiana. The Bermuda National Trust owns the building, and the Bermuda Department of Tourism on the East End of Bermuda has current information on it.

Also known as Bentley Manor and the Christopher Billopp House, 7455 Hylan Boulevard, Tottenville (Block 7826/300). The house was built circa 1675. It is historically significant as the site of a September 11, 1776, conference involving the British Admiral of the Fleet in America, Richard Lord Howe, and three delegates of the Continental Congress, Benjamin Franklin of Pennsylvania, John Adams of Massachusetts and Edward Rutledge of South Carolina. The conference proved an unsuccessful alternative to prevent the Revolutionary War. (Dolkart, 297.)

The Conference House stands in the 226-acre Conference House Park, across the Raritan Bay from Perth Amboy and at the southernmost tip of both Staten Island and the State of New York. It includes a large basement kitchen with glazed brick floors and a vaulted root cellar. On the main floor, original hand-hewn beams span the Conference Room ceiling. The second floor has three rooms. There is also a sizable attic. Today, the only remaining object that belonged to the Billopp family is a 17th-century sea chest. Other notable furniture includes a double-backed Queen Anne settee. Exhibitions demonstrate life in colonial times, while rose and herb gardens perfume the air of the park and provide the materials for lectures and classes on herbs. (*Historic Houses*, 1992, p. 33.)

Con-Ed had offices at 60 Bay Street and at Richmond Terrace in Livingston, successively. The Livingston office is now closed, and the company has been reorganized into four smaller companies. (R.D.)

The one-hundredth anniversary of the consolidation of the boroughs of New York City was acknowledged and celebrated during 1998.

The question of creating one large city by combining New York with Brooklyn and several smaller contiguous cities and towns first took tangible shape when the New York State Legislature, by Chapter 311, Laws of 1890, created the Commission of Municipal Consolidation Inquiry. The commission officers were: President Andrew H. Green; vice president J.S.T. Stranahan; Secretary Albert E. Henschel; and State Engineer and Surveyor Campbell W. Adams. New York (Manhattan) members were Frederick W. Devoe, John L. Hamilton, and J. Seaver Page. Edward F. Linton and William D. Veeder represented Brooklyn. John Brinckerhoff represented Queens County; George G. Greenfield, Richmond County (Staten Island); and Charles P. McClelland, Westchester County.

This commission presented a bill to the legislature in 1893 submitting the question of consolidation to a vote of the people of the districts affected. It failed to come to a vote before the legislature adjourned. The same bill was reintroduced in 1894, passed, and was signed by the governor.

The vote was cast at the November 6, 1894, election, and all the districts voted in favor of consolidation except the city of Mount Vernon, the town of Westchester and the township of Flushing. (*Brooklyn Daily Eagle Almanac*, 1898, 135.)

The 1894 Act had provided for some members of a commission to draw up a charter for the consolidated city. On June 9, 1896, Levi Parsons Morton (1824–1920), former U.S. vice president and from 1895 to 1897 governor, appointed additional members. The officers of the commission were President Andrew H. Green; Mayor William L. Strong of New York; Mayor Frederick W. Wurster of Brooklyn; Mayor Patrick Jerome Gleason of Long Island City; State Engineer and Surveyor Campbell W. Adams; Attorney-General Theodore E. Hancock; and members chosen from the areas affected. Benjamin F. Tracy, Seth Low, John F. Dillon and Ashbel P. Fitch were chosen to represent New York; Mr. Fitch did not qualify, and Thomas F. Gilroy was appointed in his stead. Stewart L. Woodford, Silas B. Dutcher, and William C. DeWitt represented Brooklyn. Garret J. Garretson of Jamaica, represented Queens County. George M. Pinney, Jr. (born March 8, 1856; died

July 8, 1921), represented Staten Island.

On February 19, 1896, the charter drafted by this commission was presented to the state legislature. It was passed, and Governor Morton signed it into law May 4, 1897. The first elections for the consolidated city took place November 2, 1897. Those elected took their offices January 1, 1898. (John Foord, *Public Services of Andrew Haswell Green*, 1913, 194–195.)

This house is also known as the Kreuzer-Pelton House. It stands at 1262 Richmond Terrace (Block 149/1) in West Brighton. It was built in 1722, with additions made in 1770 and 1836. It is privately owned.

Cornelius Van Santvoord, a native of Leyden, Holland and a minister of the Dutch Reformed Church in Port Richmond erected the original one-room house in the Dutch Colonial tradition. Cornelius Cruser added the steep-roofed central wing. Daniel Pelton added the two-story Federal-style brick end section. (Dolkart, 271.) The two additions were respectful of, but distinguished from, the original one-room cottage. The varying dimensions of the rooms and the width of the central hall reflect the affluence of those who added to the structure. The different textures of the materials used in construction blend together and also create an attractive contrast.

During the Revolutionary War, Mrs. Kreuzer occupied the house. General Courtlandt Skinner of Perth Amboy, commander of the American Loyalists, maintained the residence as his headquarters during this time. Various traditions regarding the house date from this time. It is believed that Prince William Henry, who later became King William IV, Queen Victoria's immediate predecessor, was occasionally the guest of General Skinner, and that Major John Andre, the spy, was billeted in the house during the Revolution. Another tradition has it that a small party of New Jersey patriots attempted a night landing in the small cove on the shore of the Kills, immediately west of the house. However, a party of British met them, and a skirmish ensued in which General Skinner was mortally wounded. (J.J. Clute, *Annals of Staten Island*, 1877, 110.)

D

this building, which was erected in 1931 and which stands at 100 Richmond Terrace in Saint George. A flight of steps leads to an arched entrance set into the high basement of this two-story courthouse. The central entrance projects one full bay. It is set apart by four double-height fluted ionic columns supporting a triangular pediment. The windows have triangular pediments and the formal classicism continues with rusticated quoins. There is a total floor area of 13,400-sq. ft. The lobby has wood paneling, terrazzo flooring and a marble staircase. The second floor courtrooms have carved wood paneling, molded door and window enframements, and an ornamental cornice frieze. The Family Court is part of the imposing Civic Center in Saint George. The formal classical style freestanding building, surrounded by a lawn, echoes in particular the Richmond County Courthouse. (*The Architecture of Public Justice*, 1993, 135.)

Dongan, (Governor) Thomas, 20, 28, 62, 150

Dongan (1634-December 14, 1715) is best known as a soldier and colonial governor of New York. He was born at Castletown, in the county of Kildare, Ireland, being a younger son of Sir John Dongan, Baronet. He adopted the profession of arms and when Charles I was beheaded spent some years in France in the service of Louis XIV (the Sun King) in a regiment composed of Irishmen. Commissioned colonel in 1674, he was recalled about 1677 and shortly thereafter received from Charles II an appointment as Lieutenant governor of Tangier. Tangier was then under the English flag as a wedding gift from Catherine of Braganza, Portugal, to her husband, Charles II. Dongan remained at this post until 1680. His friendship with the royal Stuart family brought him additional preferment, and by a commission dated Sept. 30, 1682, he was appointed "Governor and Admiral of the Province of New York" by its Roman Catholic proprietor, James, Duke of York. Debarking at Nantucket, Mass, Aug. 10, 1683 he proceeded overland to New York. On Aug. 25, 1683, he arrived at his new post and organized the administration on the 27th of August.

The territory under his jurisdiction for the Duke of York included not only New York itself but also the dependencies of Pemaquid, Martha's Vineyard and Nantucket. During the five years following his arrival, he governed the province with such ability and energy that he has been referred to by competent authority as "one of the very best of all the colonial governors." (Osgood, *American Colonies in the Seventeenth Century*, II, 131.)

The Duke's instructions provided for the calling of an assembly of representative freeholders, and one of the new governor's first acts was to issue writs of election. The body thus chosen met for the first time on October 17, 1683, and its first statute defined more fully the organization and powers of the assembly and came to be known as the "Charter of Liberties." After James's accession to the throne, however, the measure was disallowed by both the Privy Council and James himself, and New York, which had now become a royal province, was again without a representative assembly. Another early undertaking provided for the erection of the twelve original counties. Staten Island was designated Richmond County for the Duke of Richmond, Yorkshire, natural son of King Charles II. The Island's sections, known as North, South and West Divisions, and Castleton, later became Northfield, Southfield, Westfield and Castleton.

On April 16, 1687, Governor Dongan took over about 5,100 acres along the Kill Van Kull from John Palmer (*q.v.*), calling it the "Lordshippe or Manner (Manor)

of Cassiltowne" (the origin of the name Castleton Corners and Castleton Avenue). In the following year, 1688, Dongan erected his Manor House — sometime referred to as a hunting lodge — the date of its erection "having been marked upon one of the timbers with white paint." The house stood in the middle of the square bounded by the Shore Road (now Richmond Terrace) on the north, Cedar Street on the south, Dongan Street on the east, and Bodine Street on the west, at West New Brighton. This may have later led to the Manor Road name. Other names we know today were encouraged by Walter Dongan (one of his three nephews) and his descendants to keep the name alive on the island for two centuries. They are Dongan Hills, Dongan Hall of the Staten Island Academy, and Dongan Street in West New Brighton, near the site of the family home demolished in 1878.

Dongan devoted himself most energetically to the development of the colony. He strengthened the defenses and took steps to determine more definitely the boundaries of the province. He even dreamed of establishing a postal system, to extend from Nova Scotia to the Carolinas, which might serve as a bond of union between the English colonies in America. Though he was himself a Roman Catholic, his administration was marked by a broad tolerance in religious matters. In 1687 he submitted to the home government a report on the state of the province which contains a remarkable description of New York at that time. His greatest service, however, consisted in his early recognition of the growing power of the French to the northward and in his insistence that the home government aid him in checking it. French Jesuits were active among the Iroquois and were using their influence for political ends, while efforts were being made from Quebec to establish something in the nature of a protectorate over those tribes. Dongan protested vigorously to De la Barre, the governor of Canada, and to his successor, the Marquis de Denonville. As early as 1684 he had caused the arms of the Duke of York to be erected in the Iroquois villages, a step which he regarded as equivalent to the establishment of a protectorate. In 1713, twenty-nine years after he had erected the arms of the Duke of York in the Iroquois villages, the French by the treaty of Utrecht formally recognized the English protectorate over the Iroquois Indians.

By the winter of 1687–1688 an open conflict seemed immi-

nent, and Dongan raised a force for the defense of Albany, superintending the arrangements in person. His vigorous policy, which was undertaken almost solely upon his own responsibility, at length bore fruit when James II rather tardily gave it the sanction of his approval.

In 1686 England established the Dominion of New England and two years later included New York and New Jersey in it. Then in August 1688 Sir Edmund Andros superseded Dongan. But instead of returning at once to England, he decided to remain in New York where, following the overthrow of James II in the Revolution of 1689, he was unfortunate enough to fall a victim to the fanatical anti-Catholic crusade in the colonies. He fled to New London, Connecticut, then returned to Hempstead; finally in 1690, he again fled, and after hiding in New Jersey made his way to Boston where he returned to England in 1691. Once there he was unable to recover his ancestral lands from anti-Catholic confiscation. Upon the death of an elder brother in 1698 he became second Earl of Limerick, a title which he retained until his impoverished death. As Dongan was not married, his estates in America passed to three nephews, one of whom, Water Dongan, left descendants. A

Landmark July 30, 1968, and is on the state and national registers of historic places. It stands at 111 Canal Street in Tappen Park, Stapleton (Block 523/1). It was designed by Paul Kuhne and erected in 1889, the same year as the incorporation of Edgewater. It was originally intended to house Edgewater's civic activities.

The building is of Romanesque Revival design, built of red bricks with stone trim. The building itself is T-shaped. The window openings have keystone arches and unusual transoms composed of one full circle and two half-circles. The dormer windows pierce the eaves. The building is dominated by a central square tower with a hipped roof. (Dolkart, 276; Department of General Services, 1992, 57; Department of General Services, 1993, 119.

Egbert-Finley House, 27

The house was erected in 1790 as the home of Abraham Egbert, after whom the community of Egbertville was named. Originally, it was a one-and-one-half story clapboard cottage. About 1800, an extension was added. The addition on the building's left was erected later as a cooper's workshop. Note the large door for removing finished barrels and the unusual outside oven. The building originally stood at 3274 Richmond Road in Egbertville; it has

been moved to Historic Richmond Town. (E.H.) *See* Historic Richmond Town.

Egbert Square

The square is on the corner of Richmond and Forest Avenues in Port Richmond. Read the memorial plaque honoring Stanley Egbert and other World War I heroes of the area. (E.H.)

Egbertville, 62, 64, 137

Eger Lutheran Home, 107, 216

This long-term care facility is at 120 Meisner Avenue in Egbertville. The Keppler House, erected circa 1890, is still standing. The new nursing home facility opened in 1971. (E.H.)

electricity, 127

electric railroad, 140

electric trolley, 140

Elim Gospel Tabernacle, 76, 218

Elks Club, 177

Elm Park, 79, 125, 140, 142, 144, 220

Elizabeth (New Jersey), 129, 143, 235

Elizabeth Ferry, 140–142, 196, 231

Elizabeth Street, 57, 77

Elizabethtown Point (New Jersey), 33, 41, 44, 142

Elizabethport, 141, 231

Elliott, Samuel McKenzie, 58, 63, 80

Born in Inverness, in the Scottish Highlands, his father was an officer in the British Army. He was said to have graduated with an M.D. from the Royal College of Surgeons in Glasgow in 1828. He determined to make the treatment of diseases of the eye a specialty. In 1833 he sailed for America in the British ship *Theresa Anderson*, as surgeon in charge.

Upon arrival he went to Cincinnati and became a student under the celebrated Alban Goldsmith, for whom he named one of his sons. After some intervening time he opened an office on William Street in New York City, affixing a sign with the word "Oculist." This was apparently the first time the title was used by a physician in America. In 1851, he was said to obtain a diploma from the New York Medical College. (*New York Times*, Sunday, May 1, 1875 [obituary].)

As a sideline to his successful practice, he decided to invest in real estate and became a developer of some 30 homes over about 28 years, purchasing his first parcel of Staten Island property from William Bard in the fall of 1839. Subsequent purchases were also made from Thomas E. Davis, George J. Codmus and John Y. Cebra, over the next 30-odd years. He constructed homes on them until a couple of years before his death, and called the development Bay City.

Elliott had a reputation for eccentricity that can be recovered only by careful study of the census. The 1850 Census of Richmond County (Staten Island), New York, shows him as a 44-year-old oculist with his 48-year-old wife, Latitia, who was born in Ireland. Their five children are also enumerated: Samuel L. (age 14), Alban Vaughn (12), twins William St. George and Elizabeth Pearson (10) and Catherine (8). Elliott was also enumerated in the 1850 Manhattan Census with his wife Diana at 109 11th St., and at his office at 535 Broadway. In the 1859–60 City Directory, he was reported to have lived in Connecticut while practicing at 7 Astor Place, New York City.

His stellar medical reputation brought him such distinguished patients as General Winfield Scott, John J. Audubon, Henry W. Longfellow, William H. Prescott, Charlotte Cushman, N. P. Willis, George P. Morris, Edward L. Youmans and Mrs. Sarah Shaw. She persuaded her husband, Francis George Shaw, the banker, philanthropist and abolitionist, to move to Staten Island, with their four girls and one son. In later years her daughters would marry distinguished men such as George William Curtis, Robert Bowne Minturn [the younger], Charles Russell Lowell, and Francis C. Barlow. The Shaw family lost their only son in the Civil War. Colonel Robert Gould Shaw died in a hopeless charge at

Fort Wagner, South Carolina in 1863. The unit he commanded was the first Northern Black Regiment, the 54th Massachusetts.

As a Lieutenant Colonel, Elliott organized the 79th New York (Highland Guard) Brigade, mustered in on April 27–29, 1861. After passing through Baltimore and arriving at Washington, D.C., he asked for the appointment of a Colonel for the regiment. James Cameron, brother of Simon Cameron, Secretary of War (1861–1862), was appointed but killed by a cannon shot in the first Battle of Bull Run. Lieutenant Colonel Elliott's horse was shot out from under him and rolled over on him, injuring his spine. He convalesced at the Willard Hotel in Washington, but never fully recovered from that injury.

Two of his three sons, all physicians, were in the regiment. Samuel L. was 2nd Lieutenant in Company K. William St. George Elliott was 1st Lieutenant in Company I, and was wounded at Chantilly, Virginia, on September 1, 1862. His daughter Elizabeth served as enrolling officer. At the end of the war, Elliott received a brevet commission as a brigadier general.

There was a narrow strip of land on which the doctor erected a church so small it was like a toy, but though small it was very complete with a barrel organ fitted with the entire music for the Episcopal service. This church was called Saint Mary's, and when it became too small, a new Saint Mary's at Castleton and Davis Avenues was built on land donated by William Bard in March 1853.

The *New York Tribune* of May 7, 1875 spoke of him as "emphatically one of the men who impart the element of the picturesque to common affairs, a person of very strong, original, eccentric character. A man of positive genius in his profession." He was buried at Silver Mount Cemetery, where on Saturday, April 9, 1988, his birth was commemorated, and his gravesite and headstone were cleaned and rededicated. The restoration was done under the guidance of the cemetery staff and Artists Memorial. Members of the North Shore Veterans of Foreign Wars, and an honor guard from Fort Hamilton took part in the ceremony planned by Friends of Abandoned Cemeteries, with an invocation by the Reverend William English, Rector of Saint Mary's, which Elliott had founded. Dr. Albert B. Siewers, Jr., who lives on a former Elliott property, made a generous contribution that allowed work to begin on this restoration project. (*Staten Island Advance*, April 13, 1988, C9.)

Elliott House, 58, 63, 80

This house is also known as Samuel McKenzie Elliott House and 69 Delafield Place House, Livingston. It is at 69 Delafield Place (Block 137/51). It was possibly designed by Calvin Pollard, and erected circa 1850. It is a New York City Landmark and on the state and national registers of historic places. Currently, it is privately owned by the Walsh family.

Samuel McKenzie Elliott, a prominent oculist and eye surgeon and a vocal abolitionist, built this beautifully proportioned stone house as a real-estate investment. Elliott, who began purchasing property in northern Staten Island in 1839, built so many suburban houses in the vicinity that the area became known as Elliottville. The Scottish-born doctor/developer is known to have commissioned several designs from the prestigious New York City architect Calvin Pollard, and this Gothic Revival house may be one of them. (E.H.; Dolkart, 271.)

Ellis Island, 229

Emerson Hill, 106, 134, 173, 175

Emerson, Ralph Waldo, 75, 80

The author (1803–1882) visited his brother, Judge William Emerson, who lived on the hill that now bears his name. P.S. 12 was named The Ralph W. Emerson.

Note the beauty of the wooded areas on Emerson Hill, the lovely homes and the spectacular views. (E.H.)

Erastina, 127, 144

On June 25, 1886, 20,000 Staten Islanders attended the opening of Buffalo Bill's Wild West Show at Mariner's Harbor, in Erastina. That show was an exciting spectacle, with lots of horses and cowboys. (*Staten Island Advance*, June 23, 2000, A34; R.D.)

F

Faber, John Eberhard, (Faber Family, p. 155), 150

Faber Pool, 150, 183

Faber Street, 150

Fach, Albert C., 176

factories, 68–69, 119–123

Factoryville, 53, 68, 70, 79, 87, 92, 95, 137, 149

Factoryville School, 94

Fairmount Park (Pennsylvania), 82

Fall of Babylon, 144

Family Court, 160

Fardon, Thomas, 75

Far East, 11, 12, 197

Farm Colony-Seaview Hospital Historic District, 201, 213, 239

This New York City Landmark is located on Rockland and Brielle Avenues in Seaview (Block 534/1).

This historic district, consisting of the buildings and grounds of two municipal institutions, illustrates the commitment made by New York City at the turn of the twentieth century to improve social and health-care services for the needy. "Prior to the establishment of a county poor-house, the destitute poor were provided for by being boarded in private families, and sometimes under circumstances such as now would not be tolerated, as when children were paid for taking care of their helpless parents, of which there were several circumstances." (Bayles, 1886, 649.) In 1829 the Richmond County Supervisors purchased the farm of Stephen Martineau, located in the town of Northfield and containing about one hundred acres, the basis for the aforementioned county poorhouse.

The New York City Farm Colony was established in 1902 by the New York City Department of Public Charities. Able-bodied paupers were sent to the facility to learn discipline and self-sufficiency, raising vegetables for themselves and for other public institutions. Construction began at the Farm Colony (once known as the Richmond County Poor House) in 1904. The builders erected a series of striking Colonial Revival dormitories and other structures of local rubble stone. These buildings, designed by William W. Renwick, James L. Aspinwall and Mr.

Owen, set the style for buildings by other architects erected during the following ten years. Between 1930 and 1934, the capacity of the farm colony was doubled with the construction of a series of Colonial Revival brick structures designed by Charles B. Meyers. Fields that were farmed by the colony's residents border the entire complex.

Separated from the farm colony by Brielle Avenue, Seaview Hospital was founded in 1905 for the treatment of tuberculosis. The architect Raymond F. Almirall conceived the plan for the hospital and designed the original facility. Later additions include Renwick, Aspinwall and Tucker's two groups of small open-air pavilions designed in 1917 for ambulatory patients. The hospital buildings were all set within a therapeutic environment that provided abundant fresh air and landscaped vistas. Most of the buildings are no longer in use. (Dolkart, 284–286.) *See also* Seaview Hospital.

This area, which is a New York City Landmark and also on the state and national registers of historic places, includes Fort Richmond, now Battery Weed, Fort Wadsworth (Block 3128/1), and Fort Tompkins on Hudson Road.

The fort is named for James Samuel Wadsworth (1807–1864), who died in an enemy field hospital of a head wound obtained on the second day of the Wilderness campaign. In 1862, Horatio Seymour had politically defeated Wadsworth's Republican quest for the office of New York State Governor.

Until recently, Fort Wadsworth, at the foot of Bay Street, was the nation's oldest continually manned military installation. A Dutch blockhouse was established in 1663. It was the site of settlement of the third patroon, Cornelius Melyn, in 1642. Known as Signal Hill during the American Revolution. Fortifications were strengthened during the War of 1812, and succeeding wars. Observe Battery Weed at the water's edge, a City Landmark. Note the Quadrangle at Fort Tompkins used as Parade grounds and in the late 1800s for tennis courts. Excellent vantage point to observe the Verazzano-Narrows Bridge, the New York City skyline and harbor. A military museum once in old Fort Tompkins was constructed between 1847 and 1861. The contents have since been moved to Fort Hamilton.

Built at a crucial site on the edge of the Narrows at the entrance to New York Harbor, Fort Richmond was designed in 1845 by the army's chief engineer, Joseph Totten, but construction did not begin until two years later. Due to inadequate funding, work dragged on until 1861. The trapezoidal granite building, named for General Stephen Weed after his death at Gettysburg in 1863, is a magnificent example of military architecture. Fort Tompkins, a pentagonal granite structure, is set on a hill above Fort Richmond. The fort contained gun emplacements that were burrowed into the hill. (Dolkart, 280.)

Frederick Law Olmsted House, 65, 82, 145

This house stands at 4515 Hylan Boulevard in Eltingville (Block 5378/30). It is a New York City Landmark.

The high stone base of the present house was probably erected in the early eighteenth century as the foundation for a barn. The building appears to have been converted into a residence by the addition of the framed upper stories in the 1830s. Samuel Akerly, a renowned agricultural reformer, purchased the house and land in 1839. Nine years later, the young Frederick Law Olmstead (1822–1903) bought the property, relandscaped the site, and undertook a variety of agricultural experiments there. In 1853, Olmstead moved to Manhattan, where he embarked on a career as America's first landscape architect. (Dolkart 291.)

Free Magyar Reformed Church, *see* Saint Peter's German Evangelical Reformed Church.

Fremont, (Major General) John Charles, 90

Fremont Avenue, 90

French Church, 22

See the state historic marker on this site, on Arthur Kill Road north of Richmond Avenue in Greenridge. (E.H.)

Fresh Kills, 4, 28, 34, 36, 41, 78, 140, 200, 207, 249

Fresh Kills Landfill

The area under discussion here is Tax Blocks 5900, Lots 275, 285, 300, 350 and 400. The City of New York vested the lots off the Great Fresh Kills on February 27, 1947, for use as a Marine Unloading Plan (Mss. Exemption Files).

"State Department of Environmental Conservation Commissioner John P. Cahill and New York City Department of Sanitation Commissioner Kevin Farrell signed a consent order on May 15 that will close the 3,000-acre site by January 1, 2002."

"The freshly inked consent order represents a modification of an existing order under which the landfill has operated since 1990...."

"The rush to close Fresh Kills has resulted in the city's newly updated Solid Waste Management Plan, which stresses borough self-sufficiency for their trash disposal. Rather than construct new facilities in areas like Red Hook, Brooklyn or Hunts Point in the Bronx, the plan is to retrofit, or convert existing waste transfer stations across the city. In so doing, Staten Island's burden will be Islanders' trash only. According to the city's new waste plan, over half of the city's waste, or 6,400 tons a day, will travel by barge to Linden, New Jersey, where a new, 20-acre $50 million barge-unloading facility is proposed." (*Star Reporter*, June 2000, 2, 4.)

Fresh Kills Road, 35, 76, 77

Fresh Kills School, 76, 94

Frost, George (M.D.), 131, 211

Frost, Thomas (M.D.), 49, 52, 255

Fulton, Robert, 78

Funk, Isaac, 111

Funk & Wagnalls, 111

G

Gage, James Pike, 69

Gans Mansion, 224

Gaoler's House, 74

garden clubs, 176, 191–192

Gardiner-Tyler House, 92

This building is a New York City Landmark and is on the state and national historic registers. It stands at 27 Tyler Street in West Brighton (Block 305/76).

A Greek Revival mansion with a portico supported by four Corinthian columns. Also known as Castleton Hill, and the Julia Gardiner House. Originally the 11-acre Eliza Racey (d. 1849) estate, purchased in 1852 from William Henry Racey (a son of Eliza) by widowed Juliana (b. February 8, 1799, daughter of Michael McLachlan of New York, October 4, 1864) Gardiner. She resided there with her son, David Lyon Gardiner (b. May 23, 1816, d. May 9, 1892), a Northfield Supervisor (1864 Richmond County Board of Supervisors), his wife Sarah Thompson Gardiner, and three children.

In 1862, six of Julia Gardiner Tyler's seven children, were sent for safekeeping from the Civil War from their Virginia home of Sherwood Forest to this mansion. About Thanksgiving Day, 1863, they were joined by their mother, former First Lady Julia Gardiner-Tyler (b. July 23, 1820, d. July 10, 1889), daughter of Juliana, sister of David Lyon Gardiner, and widow of tenth president John Tyler (b. 1790, d. January 17, 1862). She had recently been in Bermuda with her fast friends, the Confederate Norman Walker family who later moved to Staten Island. In 1868 the house was sold to William Maxwell Evarts (1818–1901), a family friend. Evarts was also Chief Counsel for President Johnson in the impeachment proceedings of 1868; Attorney General in the cabinets of Presidents Johnson and Grant (1868–1869); Secretary of State in the cabinets of Presidents Hayes and Garfield (1877–1881); and Senator from New York (1885–1891); (Dolkart, 283, Seagar.)

Garibaldi and Meucci Memorial Museum, 69, 128, 201

This house, located at 420 Tompkins Avenue in Rosebank (Block 2966/32) was erected circa 1845.

It is a New York City Landmark and is on the state and national historic registers.

The Sons of Italy preserve this small house as a memorial to two great Italians. Giuseppe Garibaldi, the liberator of Italy, lived in the house in 1851–53 while in exile in the United States. Garibaldi was a guest of Antonio Meucci, one of the early developers of the telephone. (Dolkart, 278.)

On August 23, 1962, the Sons of Italy Foundation (Inc. 1905) acquired this 200' x 133' property from the Supreme Lodge, Order of Sons of Italy in America, both with their headquarters in Philadelphia Pennsylvania. The property had been previously acquired, on July 24, 1928, from the Italian-American Historical and Patriot Society, Inc. Prior to that, the property had been again owned by the Supreme Lodge of the Order of Sons of Italy in America, Inc., by deed, dated 13 January, 1915.

The two-story frame building was then approximately 200 years old, and contained the Garibaldi bedroom on the second floor. (Mss. NYCDF 1967; R.D.)

Garner House, 138, 150, 212

This building stands at Bard Avenue and Castleton Avenue in West New Brighton. It was built in Victorian French Renaissance style by Charles Taber, who called the estate Martinsdale. It was used as Saint Austin's School for Boys from 1883 to about 1898, when the school moved to Connecticut. It is now a convent for Saint Vincent's Medical Center. (E.H.)

This huge Victorian mansion proclaims by size, if not by beauty, the prodigious wealth garnered by nineteenth-century entrepreneurs. It is connected to wholesaler F. F. McCurdy, "cotton king" Henry M. Taber, and cotton mill owner William T. Garner. Ulysses S. Grant considered retiring here, but Mrs. Grant happened to visit the house on a warm, damp day, and was plagued by mosquitoes, which led to a reconsideration of plans. (Willensky, 1988, 817.)

This privately owned home is at 955 Richmond Road at Spring Street in Concord. It was erected circa 1770. The old stone section of the house is near the road. Note the fireplace. The mansard, or French, roof is of a later period. It is also known as the Clinch House after its owner Charles P. Clinch, sometime Collector of Customs of the Port of New York. (E.H.)

Geschwind Foam Rubber Company, 205

Gettysburg (Pennsylvania), 89, 108, 167

Giffords Lane, 35, 56, 60

Giffords Lane School, 94

Gilman, Arthur, 102

Goethals Bridge, 201, 226, 231, 235

Goggi Villa, 172, 222
1200 Hylan Boulevard in Old Town.

golf, 107, 178–179, 182

Goodhue House, 64, 183
This building stands at 304 Prospect Avenue in New Brighton. It is designed in square Italian villa style architecture. It is now known as Goodhue Home, operated by the Children's Aid Society as a recreational center. (E.H.)
"'Woodbrook,' (B. Haynard and James Patterson) circa 1845 residence of commission merchant Jonathan Goodhue (1793–1848), shows its age. But it still conveys some of the elegance it must have possessed when it was a villa commanding the vast acreage of the Goodhue estate, still largely intact." (Willensky,

1988, 812.)
Like many of Staten Island's first suburbanites, Jonathan Goodhue was an important figure in the life of the Port of New York. Originally from Salem, Massachusetts, by 1809 he had established Goodhue and Co. in New York City, a commission firm that acted on behalf of shipping interests throughout the world.

When this house (called "Woodbrook" on early maps) was built on 73 acres in 1841, Clinton Avenue was opened up as Goodhue's private drive to provide access to the property from Richmond Terrace. An imposing structure in the Renaissance Revival style (unusual for Staten Island), it is the third oldest suburban residence (after the Pavilion on the Terrace and the Judge Jacob Tysen House) still standing in New Brighton. The house is basically a three story cube atop a full basement. Prominent and characteristic features include the projecting cornice supported by brackets, and the center emphasis achieved by the projecting bay with angle quoining and entrance portico; quoins mark the corners of the house as well. The setting of this house is particularly beautiful. Set at the brow of the incline rising above Prospect Avenue, the house is bathed in light and air and establishes a dramatic presence in the surrounding landscape. The house remained in the possession of the Goodhue family until it was donated to the Children's Aid Society in 1912. (*Staten Island Walking Tours*, 1986, 14.)

Gothic Cottage, 63

Gothic Style, 58, 63, 102–103, 105, 170

Governor's Island, 51, 228

Gozen Ryerss, 66

Grace Methodist Episcopal Church, 101

Founded in 1897, this church merged with the Kingsley and Trinity Methodist congregations in 1996 to form Faith United Methodist Church. Note the terra cotta trim on the original Gothic style edifice. (E.H.)

Graniteville, 59, 60, 66, 69, 77, 118, 135, 162, 219, 221, 237

Graniteville Baptist Church, 59

Grant, General Ulysses Simson, 90, 150

Grant City, 90, 110, 126, 140, 149, 161, 174, 177, 204, 206, 207, 218

Grant Street, 65, 125, 132, 138

Grasmere Lake, 108

Gravesend (Long Island), 27

Great Kills, 36, 49, 53, 60, 77, 98, 104, 124, 130, 136, 145, 157, 170, 173, 179, 184, 226

Great Kills Harbor

Walk along Mansion Avenue and along the beachfront. Observe all kinds of pleasure craft, yacht

clubs, yacht basin. In July 1971 Great Kills Park was designated as part of the planned Gateway National Recreation Area. (E.H.)

Greek Revival, 53, 54, 56, 62, 92

columns, 254

homes, 53

Greeley, Horace, 88

Green, Andrew H., 151

Green, John Cleve

Green was born in New Jersey in 1797. His brother, Henry Woodhull (1804–1876) was sometime Chancellor of New Jersey, and a sister married Theodore Frelinghusen (1787–1862), sometime U.S. Senator from the State of New Jersey. John Green began his working life at the firm of Nathaniel L. & George Griswold, located on South Street in Manhattan. Nathaniel (ca. 1773–1847) and George (1778–1859) were shippers, and Green worked as a supercargo, an agent on board ship in charge of the sale and purchase of cargo. Accompanying ships on their voyages, he spent his spare time in study and made himself into a man of culture and education. He left the Griswolds for the employ of Samuel Russell of Russell & Co. in Canton, China in 1833.

In 1839, Green, now a wealthy and respected merchant in his own right, settled in New York. He married Sarah Griswold, daughter of his former employer George Griswold; his connection with Staten Island comes from the summer place he owned in New Brighton. He continued to be active in the business community, as a merchant in the China trade, a director of the Bank of Commerce and a member of the Chamber of Commerce. He involved himself in local charities and churches. His interest in education stretched beyond the boundaries of Staten Island: he served a term as president of New York University and made generous contributions to Princeton University.

Green also entered local public life, and played an important role in settling problems that had arisen at the Quarantine Station, which state authorities kept trying to place on Staten Island, against much opposition from local residents. Previous Commissioners of Quarantine had selected Seguine's Point as the site for quarantine facilities and had erected facilities there. However, in their eleventh annual report, published in 1857, the Commissioners of Immigration, who were responsible for tending to the immigrants who were potential candidates for quarantine, charged that the buildings were inadequate for the yellow fever patients they were required to house. Richard Thompson, who

was the health officer and the physician-in-chief of the Marine Hospital, Dr. Rockwell, the resident physician, Dr. Miller, the Commissioner of Health, and J.N. Phillips, the President of the Board of Health, concurred with the Commission-ers of Immigration's findings regarding the Quarantine Hospital. Consequently, the buildings could not be used for quarantining sick people entering New York Harbor. Then, arson destroyed the buildings. On January 19, 1859, the state selected three new commissioners of quarantine, George W. Patterson, former governor Horatio Seymour, and Green, to straighten out the situation. Green was credited with developing practical quarantine procedures. He was also active in Staten Island public service during the Civil War.

Green died April 29, 1875. Sarah Griswold Green died in 1893. In 1902, the City of New York purchased the site for Curtis High School, Hamilton Avenue and Saint Mark's Place, from Mrs. Green's estate. For further information, *see* obituaries in the *New York Times*, April 30, 1875, and the *Staten Island Gazette* for May 1875, and William K. Selden, *The Legacy of John C. Green* (1988), a copy of which is in the Special Collections of Milbank Memorial

Library, Teachers College, Columbia University. (R.D.)

Greenridge, 3, 22, 23, 61, 76, 78, 90, 123, 133, 139, 145, 149, 184, 215, 218, 236

Griffin Street, 55, 71, 75

Grimshaw Confectionery Co., 125

Grosset, Samuel, 29, 255

Ground Briefs, 17

Grymes, (Madame) Suzette, 64, 80

Grymes Hill, 1, 40, 89, 106, 109, 115, 120, 128, 144, 150, 172, 173, 175, 223, 224, 240

Called Signal Hill during the American Revolution. Observe view of New York Harbor from Howard Avenue. Note lovely old homes; educational institutions; old standpipe formerly used for emergency water supply for the area. *See also* entries for Augustinian Academy, Cunard House, Notre Dame, College of St. John's University, and Wagner College. (E.H.)

Major George Howard bought the hill in 1830 and in 1836 it became the home of Madame Suzette Grymes, the widow of the first governor of Louisiana. Jacob Hand Vanderbilt, brother of "The Commodore" also lived in the area during the nineteenth century. The largest of the estates, Horrmann Castle, was built about this time and was a local landmark until the 1970s. (Jackson, 1995, 517.)

Gulf Oil Company, 202

Gun Factory Road, 68

Gustave A. Mayer House

This building stands at 2475 Richmond Road in New Dorp (Block 942/37). It is a New York City landmark. It was built for David R. Ryerss in 1855–1856. With its boxy massive, arcaded porch, deep, bracketed eaves, round-arched openings and square cupola, this house epitomizes the Italian villa form that became popular in the United States in the 1850s. In 1889, Gustave A. Mayer, the confectioner who invented the Nabisco sugar wafer, purchased the property. Mayer used the basement of the villa as a workshop to experiment with novelties for his business. Members of the Mayer family occupied the house for one hundred years. It is currently privately owned. (Dolkart, 289.)

Guyon, Jacques, 20, 36, 146

Guyon Avenue, 20, 226

H

Hagadorn, Francis, 71

Hagadorn, William, 71

Half Moon (ship), 11

Hall, Joseph, 68

Halloran, (Colonel) Paul Stacey, 165

Halloran General Hospital, 165, 215

Hamilton, Alexander, 73

Hamilton Park Cottage, 110

This building is located at 105 Franklin Avenue in New Brighton (Block 58/27). Erected circa 1855, it is a New York City Landmark and on the state and national registers of historic sites.

The cottage is an example of modified Greek Revival architecture with an Italianate influence. Note the interior brick walls and the "eyebrow" windows on the third floor. (E.H.)

Hamilton Park (originally known as Brighton Park) was one of Staten Island's early suburban residential parks and among the early self-contained, limited access suburban subdivisions in the United States. Laid out around 1850–1852 by Charles Hamilton, Hamilton Park had dwelling sites set on curving drives amid a naturalistic landscape. Development proceeded slowly; only three or four houses were erected in the 1850s, but in the 1860s the German-born architect Carl Pfeiffer designed twelve additional residences. The Hamilton Park cottages were among Pfeiffer's first American commissions. Somewhat simpler and less picturesque than the earlier Harvard Avenue House, this Italian style brick building has a magnificent arcaded loggia. (Dolkart, 273.)

Hankinson, Frank, 77, 217, 219

Hampton, Vernon B., M.D. 77, 93, 133

Hannah Street, 53, 64, 74, 131, 208

Happy Land, 180

Harbor Hills Golf Links, 178

Harbor Road, 57

Harden, Colonel, 91

66 Harvard Avenue House, *see* Pritchard House

Hawkins, (Professor) John M., 138

Haughwout, 36

Heberton Avenue, 101

Henderson Avenue, 80–81, 113, 130, 174, 221

Hendrickson, William, 14

Henry McFarlane House

This building stands at 30 Hylan Boulevard in Rosebank (Block 2830/49). It is a New York City Landmark, and is on the state and national historic registers. The site adjoins the Alice Austen House's property, and enjoys commanding views across New York Harbor. The house has had many owners and has been substantially enlarged since the original cottage was constructed, circa 1841–1845, apparently by the merchant Henry McFarlane. Circa 1860, dry goods merchant Henry Dibblee made the earliest addition, doubling the size of the dwelling, copying the original detail so that the house appeared to be a single structure. Between 1868 and 1871, the house served as the New York Yacht Club headquarters, during which time the yacht club first successfully defended the America's Cup. The house is owned by the New York City Parks Department and is being occupied by residential tenants until it can be restored. Its telephone number is (718) 390–8035. (Dolkart, 278.)

Hero Park, 164, 182, 240

The central feature of this park, located at Victory Boulevard and Louis Street on Grymes Hill, is a sixteen-foot-high boulder of hornblende gnessoid granite, detached from the Highland Belt of Byram geneiss (which lies under northern New Jersey and southern New York) by glaciers during the Ice Age. This rock has had several names; first, Sugar Loaf Rock, then Druid's Rock. Legend has it that Indian tribes met there. There is greater documentation concerning the field around the boulder as a popular place for children to play.

Dr. and Mrs. Louis Dreyfus donated the property for the park. Max Schling landscaped the property, and the Forman Company prepared a number of bronze tablets for the site. The park was dedicated May 31, 1920. Among the speakers were Fiorello H. LaGuardia, there in his capacity as President of the Board of Aldermen, the predecessor agency of the City Council; former Staten Island Congressman Montague Lessler; Borough President Calvin D. Van Name; Parks Commissioner Francis D. Gallatin; the Reverend E.A. Dodd of Saint John's Church in Clifton; Rabbi J. Bienenfeld; and William G. Willcox, a resident of Livingston, president of the Board of Education, and chairman of the Board of Trustees of Tuskegee Institute, founded by the late Booker T. Washington. (R.D.)

At that point, the rock had three bronze tablets. One of them, depicting an eagle holding two American flags, was inscribed: "This HERO PARK AND MEMORIAL is Lovingly Dedicated to the Memory of the Splendid Sons of Staten Island Who So Nobly Gave Their Lives in the World War 1917–1918." A second tablet read: "This Granite Bolder Left Here During the Glacial Period Has Been Known for Generations as SUGAR LOAF ROCK and Marks the Boyhood Playground of Many of the Men Whose Gallant Deeds It now Commemorates." A third tablet bore four columns listing the 144 Staten Island men who died in the war. There were four additional bronze tablets at the four entrances to the park, each reading: "This Park is a PUBLIC SANCTUARY Entrusted to the Guardianship of the People." The deceased were further commemorated by the landscaping. The south, or upper, side of the park was planted with 144 Koster blue spruce trees. At the foot of each tree was a small bronze tablet embedded in concrete giving the name, military rank, place of death and age of one of the 144 Staten Island men who died in the war. White birches, weeping birches, weeping willows, arbor vitae, oak, copper beech trees, Japanese maples, other sorts of maples and a mulberry tree completed the landscaping. Concrete benches stood among the trees.

Although the American Scenic and Preservation Society praised the new park with the words "everything about this memorial is complete and permanent," the bronze tablets have been missing since the 1970s. For further information on the park, see *Twenty-fifth annual Report of the American Scenic and Preservation Society*, 1920, 160–162, and *Staten Island Advance* July 18, 1999.

Hessians, 39, 41, 43, 46

Het Kloven, 1

High Rock Park Conservation Center, 186

The Staten Island Institute of Arts and Sciences administers this site, which is on Nevada Avenue in Egbertville. (E.H.)

Hiker Monument, 163

A fourteen-foot-high heroic bronze figure by Allen G. Newman (1875–1940) given to the City in 1916 by the Joseph Decker Camp of the United Spanish

War Veterans. Originally next to Borough Hall it was moved to Tompkinsville Park in 1925. Feist and Sons donated their labor and granite materials to the erection of this monument. The tablets at the base of the monument are dedicated to veterans of all wars, particularly the Joseph S. Decker Camp of the United War Veterans Spanish-American War of 1898, the Robert Gould Shaw Post No. 12 of the Grand Army of the Republic, World War I veterans and veterans of the American Revolution.

Colonel Robert Gould Shaw (1837– 1863) for whom G.A.R. Post No. 12 was named, was the scion of a prominent abolitionist family resident in Livingston. Not quite 27 years old, he led his Fifty-fourth Massachusetts Regiment in an ill-fated assault on Fort Wagner in Charleston Harbor, South Carolina, on July 18, 1863. The Fifty-fourth was the first black unit of troops recruited in the North. Shaw was buried with his men at the battle site, but his fame spread throughout the country, so much so that his family commissioned the noted sculptor, Augustus St. Gaudens to create a statue of Colonel Shaw with his men. That statue now stands across from the State House and on the border of the Boston Commons. The 1989 movie *Glory* is based on the story of Colonel Shaw and the Fifty-fourth.

Section 148 of the laws relating to local historians, as amended by chapter 820 of the New York State Laws of 1947, reads: "Section 148. A local historian shall be appointed, as provided in this section, for each city, town or village, except that in a city of over one million inhabitants a local historian shall be appointed for each borough therein instead of for the city at large; and a county historian may be appointed for each county. Such historian shall be appointed as follows: For a city, by the mayor; for a borough, by the borough president; for a town by the supervisor; for a village by the mayor; for a county, by the board of supervisors. Such historian shall serve without compensation, unless the governing board of the city, town, village or county for or in which he or she was appointed shall otherwise provide. In a city having a board of estimate, a resolution or ordinance establishing compensation or salary for such historian shall not take effect without the con-

currence of such board."

Section 149 covers the duties of the local historian. "It shall be the duty of each local historian, appointed as provided in the last section, in cooperation with the state historian, to collect and preserve material relating to the history of the political subdivision for which he or she is appointed and to file such material in fireproof safes or vaults in the county, city, town or village offices. Such historian shall look into the condition, classification and safety from fire of the public offices of such county, city, town or village and shall call to the attention of the local authorities and the state historian any material of local historic value which should be acquired for preservation."

An alphabetical roster of borough historians begins with the current one, Richard Dickenson. Mr. Dickenson was born in Greenville, New Jersey, June 26, 1929. Borough President Guy V. Molinari appointed him Borough Historian in October 1991. He was a Centennial Historian, responsible for historical materials during the hundredth anniversary of the unification of New York in 1989. He is the compiler of *Census Occupations of Afro-American Families on Staten Island* (1981) and *Afro-American Vital Records and Twentieth-century*

Abstracts (1985).

Marjorie Decker Johnson was also a Centennial Historian.

Evelyn King was a Centennial Historian and the author of "Black Man on Staten Island," Chapter XXVIII of *Black Man in American History*, published by the Board of Education in 1970.

Cornelius Kolff was "Staten Island's most obedient servant." He was in almost every civic movement in the Island's first fifty years as the Borough of Richmond. As a realtor Mr. Kolff was responsible for negotiating many important land purchases, among them the East Shore city piers and World War I Fox Hills Base Hospital. In 1895 Mr. Kolff had played an important part in forming the Staten Island Chamber of Commerce. For a quarter of a century he served as its secretary and held the presidency for three years. As chairman of the Chamber's Free Port committee he had a vital part in bringing the foreign trade zone to the Island. (Smith, 1970, 193.)

Charles W. Leng was born in Factoryville in West Brighton in 1852 and died on Staten Island January 23, 1941, at the age of 81. An entomologist, he had what was once rated as one of the best beetle collections in the country. He served, in 1881, as secretary of the Natural Science Association and later as director of the Staten Island Institute of Arts and Sciences. In 1890 he was appointed curator of the Brooklyn Entomological Association; in 1921 he was appointed as the first official local historian for the Borough of Richmond (Staten Island) by Borough President Calvin D. Van Name. He held the office for more than 10 years, and is said to have recommended Loring McMillen as his successor. He is best known for coauthoring, with William T. Davis, the five-volume *Staten Island and Its People*. (*New York Times*, January 25, 1941.)

Loring McMillen was born on Staten Island March 10, 1906, and died there March 19, 1991. Borough President Lynch appointed him borough historian in 1932, and he served until his death 59 years later. In 1965, he became Staten Island's first representative on the original New York City Landmarks Commission. Among his accomplishments were the founding of Richmondtown Restoration in 1967–1978. Beginning in 1985, he wrote the *Chronicles of Staten Island* and transcribed court records going back to the 1700s. (*Staten Island Advance*, March 11, 1986, and March 20, 1991; *New York Times*, March 21, 1991; *Staten Island Historian* IX:1 (Summer/Fall 1991).)

Ira K. Morris was born in Monmouth County, New Jersey, and died April 4, 1921, at age 74. He was known as Staten Island's historian at the turn of the century. He served with the cavalry during the Civil War, receiving a wound that ultimately contributed to his death. For sixteen years, he edited the *Richmond County Standard*, and for several years was also editor of the *Richmond County Sentinel*. He was best known as the author of the *Memorial History of Staten Island* (1900). (*Staten Island Advance*, April 5, 1921; *New York Times*, April 5, 1921.)

Ann Novotny was the author of *Alice's World, The Life and Times of an American Original: Alice Austen, 1866–1952* (New York: Chatham Press, 1976)

Charles L. Sachs was a centennial historian, formerly the chief curator of the Staten Island Historical Society, and the author of *Made in Staten Island* (New York: Staten Island Historical Society, 1988).

Theodore Scull was the author of *The Staten Island Ferry*, published in New York in 1982.

Barnett Shepherd was a Centennial Historian, formerly the executive director of the Staten Island Historical Society, and the author of *Sailors Snug Harbor,*

1801–1976, published in 1979.

Dorothy Valentine Smith (1905– 1984) was the author of *This Was Staten Island* and *Staten Island: Gateway to New York*, the latter published in 1970. Her former home and property, at Clove Road and Victory Boulevard, has been designated a New York City Landmark.

Raymond Tysen, the son of Judge Jacob Tysen, was born in the Neville-Tysen Home on Richmond Terrace near Tysen Street, now a city landmark, and later lived in the Judge Tysen Home on Fillmore Street, near the entrance to Sailors' Snug Harbor. He was an outstanding lawyer who was reputed to have written an early history of Staten Island. (No copies can be found.) Tysen died in Savannah, Georgia at age 31, and is buried in Staten Island Cemetery.

Royden Woodward Vosburgh was a genealogist and historian born in Buffalo, New York, February 5, 1875. Beginning in 1913, Mr. Vosburgh, as archivist and historian of the New York Genealogical and Biographical Society, devoted himself to the copying of New York State church records, completing 92 such records. His connection with the Staten Island Institute of Arts and Sciences began in 1922, and resulted in the publication of nine volumes, comprising 1,643 pages of Staten Island church records and gravestone inscriptions. In this work William T. Davis and Charles W. Leng assisted him. About 10,000 gravestone inscriptions were copied and Mr. Vosburgh typed six copies. One was deposited at the Staten Island Institute of Arts and Sciences; the others distributed to libraries in Washington, Albany, New York and Brooklyn. He was also coauthor of *The Church of St. Andrew*, published under the auspices of the Staten Island Historical Society in 1925. He died May 18, 1931, age 57. His home was at 13 Lenox Place, New Brighton.

John B. Woodall received his Ph.D. from Columbia University. He was formerly the editor of *Staten Island Historian*, and the author of *History of Christ Church, New Brighton*.

Shirley Zavin was the author of *Staten Island: An Architectural History* (Staten Island: Staten Island Institute of Arts and Sciences, 1979.)

Historic Richmond Town, 1, 24, 28, 29, 35–36, 41, 43, 46, 49, 62–63, 66–67, 74, 92, 98–99, 115, 131, 135, 139, 160, 100, 192, 203, 241, 254

This site is off Richmond Road at Court Street and Center Street (Block 3298/1). It is a New York City Landmark and also on the state and national historic registers.

Observe site of British redoubts overlooking Fresh Kills. Note arched stonework of town bridge over Richmond Creek. Visit Saint Andrew's Church, Voorlezer's House, Third County Courthouse, Staten Island Historical Museum, and Carriage House Museum. Observe Rezeau-Van Pelt homestead graveyard, foundation of old Gaol on northeast corner of Arthur Kill Road and Center Street, parsonage of Reformed Dutch Church, Lake-Tysen House, Britton Cottage, and other restored buildings. P.S. 23 is named The Richmondtown. (E.H.)

The Staten Island Historical Society was originally incorporated on August 15, 1856. The incorporators were Nathan Barrett, John T. Harrison, Amos Pearce, John Barker, John B. Staples, Richard P. Smyth, William A. Ross, John Eadie, Benjamin F. Cook, Abraham Jones, Bruce A. Chilton, Calvin Barker, P. A. Guy and Joseph Park. "The business and objects of said Society shall be to collect and preserve whatever may relate to the History of Staten Island and to establish a Library and Reading Room, and in connection therewith to promote Scientific and other Knowledge by means of Lectures upon Scientific and Literary Subjects." The first year trustees were Israel D. Johnson, Lot C. Clark, John B. Staples, William Farley Gray and Benjamin F. Cook, "all of Richmond County, Staten Island."

On October 1, 1900, the following incorporators executed another certificate of incorporation: David J. Tysen, Ernest Flagg, Henry P. Morrison, George Cromwell, Charles H. Blair, Calvin D. Van Name, Wilbur Fiske Wood, Justus J. Smith, E. C. Bridgeman, Theodore S. Oxholm, L. W. Freeman, William J. Steele, Nathaniel J. Wyeth, David H. Cortelyou and Ira K. Morris. Their purposes were more diverse than those of the 1856 incorporators. They included: "preserve historical data and historical localities and landmarks relating to Staten Island and Richmond County, to collect relics, to promote interest in and further study of the same, and to purchase, receive and maintain such real estate on said island as will adequately preserve its records and provide for its places of meeting, and to hold in trust such properties, real or personal or mixed, as may be transferred by gift, purchase devise or bequest."

By order of the Supreme Court of the State of New York, dated August 7, 1922, the Staten Island Historical Society, Inc., and the Staten Island Antiquarian Society Inc., were consolidated. The new corporation was decreed to be known as the Staten Island Historical Society, Inc. (R.D.)

Due to its central location, the town of Richmond became the seat of county government on Staten Island in 1729. Richmondtown's importance declined after Staten Island joined New York City in 1898, although its courthouse remained in use until the Richmond County Courthouse opened. In 1939 the Staten Island Historical Society inaugurated the preservation of Richmondtown, including the restoration of historic village buildings and the relocation of endangered buildings from other Staten Island sites. The museum village, which is owned by New York City and operated by the historical society, recalls three centuries of life on Staten Island. The names and dates given below are those used by the "Richmondtown Restoration historic village and museum complex."

Basketmaker's House, built circa 1810–1820 and originally located in New Springville, this modest clapboard Dutch Colonial cottage was erected for the basketmaker John Morgan.

Bennett House, built circa

1839, with an addition circa 1854, this clapboard house with Greek Revival elements is located on its original site. Built as a residence with a cellar bakery, the house belonged to the shipping merchant John Bennett and his family from the late 1840s through the early twentieth century.

Boehm House, built 1740 and added to in 1840, an extremely simple pre-Revolutionary War clapboard house, was the home of the teacher Henry M. Boehm from 1855 to 1862. It was moved to this site from Greenridge.

Britton Cottage, built circa 1670, with additions circa 1755, circa 1765 and 1800, this wood and stone farmhouse was moved from New Dorp Beach in 1967. The central stone section, which was probably built around 1670, may have served as Staten Island's first government building. The Britton family owned the house from 1695 to 1704 and again from 1895 to 1915.

Christopher House, erected circa 1720 with an addition in 1730, was originally a one-room-and-attic vernacular stone house on the Dongan estate (see Peter Housman House). It was the home of the patriot Joseph Christopher during the Revolutionary War and is said to have

been the meeting place of the American Committee of Safety. It was moved to Richmondtown in 1969.

Eltingville Store, a modest board-and-batten commercial building erected circa 1860 was originally a one-room grocery store in the village of Eltingville.

Guyon-Lake-Tysen House, built circa 1740 with additions circa 1820 and circa 1840, was a superb Dutch Colonial-style house erected in the New Dorp-Oakwood area by the Huguenot settler Joseph Guyon and moved to Richmondtown in 1962. The gambrel roof, spring eaves and front porch are especially notable. The kitchen wing was added around 1820 and the dormer windows twenty years later.

Historical Museum, erected 1848, with additions circa 1918, was originally the Richmond County Clerk's and Surrogate's Office. This simple brick building constructed in the tradition of the Federal style, served the county government until around 1920, when civic functions moved to Saint George. The building was converted into a museum in the 1930s.

Kruser-Finley House, erected circa 1790 with additions circa 1820 and circa 1850–1860 is a modest clapboard building moved from Egbertville in 1965, when it was endangered by the construction of the Willowbrook Parkway. Originally a one-room house, the structure was extended around 1820 and again around 1850–60, when a shop, thought to have been used by a cooper, was added.

Parsonage, erected circa 1855 is located on its original site. This vernacular Gothic Revival clapboard building with gingerbread detail was originally the parsonage of the Reformed Dutch Church in Richmondtown.

Rezeau-Van Pelt Cemetery, used from 1780s to the 1860s, is a rare surviving eighteenth-century private graveyard, used by two families who occupied the Voorlezer's House in the eighteenth and nineteenth centuries, after the house ceased to be used as a school.

Stephens-Black House was erected circa 1838–1840. Stephen D. Stephens erected this simplified Greek Revival house, and his family lived here until 1870, operating the one-story general store (reconstructed in 1964) that was added to the rear at some point after the main house was completed.

Third County Courthouse, now the Visitors Center, also known as the Clarke Avenue Court and the Old County Court, was erected in 1837. Richmondtown was the county seat from 1729 until the 1898 consolidation into Greater New York/New York City. The county court officials moved to Saint George in 1920 when the Richmond County Courthouse opened.

This spectacular Greek Revival style building has a pedimented portico with four Doric columns. The cupola contains the courthouse bell. In plan, the building is composed of a central block with flanking wings. The front is of local traprock; the sides and rear are brick. The main courtroom is now an auditorium (Department of General Services, 1993, 137). With its Doric portico and square cupola, this Greek Revival courthouse was the centerpiece of Richmondtown during its period as a governmental center. The courthouse remained in use until 1919.

In 1844 one of the most important cases in the United States was tried in this courthouse. Polly Bodine was accused of setting fire to a house where she was babysitting for young cousins, who died in the fire. Everybody was related to the defendant and it was impossible to select an impartial jury, so the trial was moved. This established the principle of change of venue. Polly was acquitted.

Treasure House, erected circa 1700 with additions circa

1740, circa 1790 and circa 1860, still stands on its original site. This modest clapboard building was the house and workshop of Samuel Grosset, a tanner and leatherworker. The Treasure House derives its name from the local legend that a $7,000 cache of British coins was found hidden in its walls around 1860.

Voorlezer's House, erected circa 1695, is the oldest surviving building from the settlement of Richmond. This two-story clapboard structure was built by the Reformed Dutch Church as a school, church, and home for the "voorlezer," or lay reader and teacher. Its restoration in 1939–1942 was Richmondtown Restora-tion's first. (Dolkart, 287–289.)

The Historical Society also owns the Decker Farm, located at 135 Richmond Hill Road (Block 2390/194), and the Billiou Perine House, 1476 Richmond Road (Block 3299/10).

New York City's only historic village was first opened to the public by the Staten Island Historical Society in 1935, when it opened the County Clerk's office and established the Historical Museum. In 1939, it acquired and restored the Voorlezer's House, the oldest surviving elementary school in the country. (*Historic Houses*, 1992, 34.)

Historical Museum, 26, 35, 41, 46, 49–50, 115, 125, 139, 188
Historical Society, 188
History of Richmond County, 47
Hoffman and Swinburne Islands, 71, 100, 169, 208

These two islands were used to quarantine sick travelers coming into New York Harbor, and later for a merchant marine training school (E.H.)

In 1916, Deputy Tax Commissioner Henry J. Kathmann stated that the State of New York owned Hoffman Island, and that the island contained eleven and one- eighth acres and twelve buildings of various dimensions, used as hospitals for persons with contagious diseases. A more detailed breakdown was included with the statement. A similar list was made for Swinburne Island, which had on it a morgue, crematorium and vault. These listings were made in conjunction and "apparent intention" to transfer local quarantine functions from the State of New York to the federal government. (R.D.)

Holland, *see* Netherlands
Holland Hook, 36, 41, 140–141, 143, 196, 231, 235
Hollick Arthur, 147
Holmes-Cole House, 21, 27

This home is located on Hylan Boulevard near Bay Terrace, at the foot of Justin Avenue in Great Kills. It was built by the

Holmes family, descendants of Obadiah Holmes, who built Britton Cottage. Later it was the home of the Cole family. It is the birthplace of Ann Holmes Perine, Revolutionary War belle, owner and occupant of Billiou-Stillwell-Perine House. Restored in 1940 by the Reverend Lefferd M. A. Haughwout. It has a cellar kitchen, central entry with a room on either side. A fireplace and some original floorboards remain. Rectangular blocks of brown sandstone are painted white. Note the gambrel roof. (E.H.) The home was razed to make room for a subdivision. (Willensky, 1988, 893.)

Horrmann Castle, 172

This home was located at 189 Howard Avenue (Block 614/14). It was the home of William Horrmann, modeled after a castle on the Rhine, and was demolished in 1968. (E.H.) The building was described as "Bavarian, French Renaissance, Flemish, Spanish and English Queen Anne all heaped together and topped by a crow's nest with an onion-shaped cupola." (Willensky, 1988, 893.) On March 27, 1945 the Presentation Sisters of Staten Island applied for tax exemption for the place. Their application described it as a 3-1/2 story brick mansion with seventeen rooms,

four baths, and storage in the basement, attic and in a tower, attached to which were a two-story, three-car garage and a greenhouse. The sisters received their exemption and vested title in the building June 5, 1945. On June 25, 1945, the sisters incorporated. Signing the incorporation papers were the Most Reverend Francis Joseph Spellman of 452 Madison Avenue in New York, and Helen Lyons, Agnes Murphy, Helen Ward, Mary Hayde and Margaret Gilsenan, all of Green Ridge, Staten Island. The incorporation enabled the sisters to "enlist the services of young women for work in religion and to prepare them for such life and to carry on philanthropic and religious work by personal service and other practical means; and to propagate and spread the doctrine and practices of the Roman Catholic Church." On May 22, 1954, the sisters purchased a second building, at 225 Howard Avenue (Block 614/10). In March of 1955, they converted this building to a convent, with seven bedrooms and three baths on a 200' x 200' lot. (R.D.)

Hotel Castleton, 51, 113, 152, 177

This site, on Saint Mark's Place opposite Curtis High School, housed the Castleton Hotel and

This museum is located at 336–340 Lighthouse Avenue in Richmond (Block 2275/1 and 4).

Based on property acquired by Jacques Marchais Klauber on May 16, 1945, the Center was incorporated by the University of the State of New York on December 29, 1945. The directors, until the first annual meeting were: Jacques Marchais, Harry Klauber, Edna May Montgomery (all of 340 Lighthouse Ave.), Howard P. Michener (of 298 Lighthouse Ave.) and Helen A. Watkins.

In a filing of March 10, 1952, Helen A. Watkins, Executive Secretary, described the property as 120' x 113' irregular, containing a museum, and library, each one story high in a building 27' x 66'. At that time, the only other officer was Ethel DeMary, Recording Secretary. The directors were Watkins, Howard P. Michener, Thomas Schleier, Lee Landes and James Whitehead.

The corporation held title to the real estate by virtue of the provisions contained in the last will and testament of Harry Klauber, who died on Staten Island, December 29, 1948. He bequeathed his chemical corporation and other businesses to his sister, "Tessie" Horowitz. Helen A. Watkins was a witness to his will.

Mr. Klauber's wife, Jacques

Marchais Klauber had recorded the property in her name on July 6, 1945. In her will of January 28, 1948, Jacques Marchais Klauber bequeathed $100 to each of her three children – Brookings Montgomery Jr., Jane Check and Edna May Montgomery. Her husband, Harry Klauber, was both the Executor for and recipient of all the rest of her estate. Helen A. Watkins, a neighbor on London Road, Staten Island was one of the two witnesses, Therese Horowitz, her sister-in-law, was the other.

The corporate purposes were to:

(a) "Foster, promote and encourage interest, study and research in the culture, Literature and art of Tibet [there were 2,000 unique and historical works of art already there];

(b) Gather and disseminate information concerning the history of Tibetan Art;

(c) Gather and preserve books, manuscripts, papers, relics, objects of art and other such as may relate to Tibetan art [over 1,000 books and 500 photographs were available for member use];

(d) Acquire by purchase, gift, devise, lease or otherwise, the title to, or the custody and control of property to be used in furtherance of the aforementioned purposes."

Harry Klauber, in his last will and testament, provided that all of the property at 336 and 340 Lighthouse Ave "be made and preserved into a Memorial for my late beloved wife Jacques Marchais Klauber." He set aside $25,000 of his estate for the perpetual care of this Memorial — the Jacques Marchais Center of Tibetan Arts. Due to pending litigation, it was not opened to the public until February 1952.

In a New York Times article of September 10, 1968, on Tibetan art, Helen Anglade Watkins was identified as the 86-year-old caretaker. She told how Miss Marchais (Jacques was also her father's name), an actress who became an Oriental art dealer, built the temple as a center for a study group in Tibetan art and religion. She remembered the October 1948 night when Miss Marchais presided over the dedication of the altar. Within a few months she was dead, and her husband died a few months later.

Miss Watkins published the *Story of the Jacques Marchais Center of Tibetan Arts*. In it she mentions meeting the Klauber couple in 1926–1927 when Mrs. Klauber had built a small house at 340 Seaview Avenue on Lighthouse Hill, which she had purchased in 1921. Later, the street name was changed to Lighthouse Avenue. Mrs. Klauber's professional name was Madame Jacques Marchais, composed of a family name, Marchais, and the pet name for her, Jacques. Her father, she said, had hoped for a son!

Mr. and Mrs. Klauber had met and married in 1918 in New York City. She had, at that time three teenage children by her first marriage. They then resided with their paternal grandparents in Evanston, Illinois. They later came to live with their mother at Lighthouse Avenue, and she brought them up. In the meantime, Mr. Klauber purchased more land for her, which she proceeded to improve.

The provisions of Mr. Klauber's Will were litigated in the courts for five years. By that time, the expenses of the litigation exhausted the funds left for its maintenance "and it was impossible to arrange a proper staff of competent persons to carry out the provisions of the will." For further information on the Jacques Marchais Center, *see* the manuscripts in the New York City Department of Finance.

This building, erected in 1929, stands at 475 Victory Boulevard in Tompkinsville.

Jewett/Taintor House

This house, since demolished, stood at 2105 Richmond Terrace.

There is an intriguing passage in the 1900 *Memorial History of Staten Island* by historian Ira Morris. It occurs in the chapter entitled "In Old Slavery Days" and has to do with Benjamin Perine, the last Staten Island slave, who died in 1900. The passage states that Benjamin was born December 2, 1796, at a place called Merserau's Ferry, at Dr. Van Pelt's house on Richmond Terrace, "where Mrs. Tainter's residence is now located." Various aspects about this statement are explored in "Epilogue II" of Afro-American Vital Records and 20th Century Abstracts published in 1985 by the Sandy Ground Historical Society. But the one not delved into is "Mrs. Tainter's residence."

Where is, or where was her residence? Ira Morris infers that Mrs. Tainter's house was built after 1796, and this is highly likely given the source and origin of the family that lived in it. The fact that her house was in Port Richmond, where David Merserau's ferry was, is further corroborated in a sentence in the Port Richmond section of a May 9,

1908, article, "A Glimpse Up Shore" in *The Staten Islander* newspaper. The sentence states, "Mrs. Tainter's charming residence and grounds have been placed in condition for summer occupancy." A 1916 topographic map shows the house on the site, with a view of the waterfront. However, 1919 department records indicate that Standard Oil of New York had a certificate of occupancy for one of the buildings, possibly the stable. Mrs. Tainter herself died in 1924, and at that point her property housed an automobile repair-and-parts shop. A Works Progress Administration photographer took a photograph of it for tax assessment during the late Great Depression; it is the only currently known photograph. Mrs. Tainter's "charming residence" is no longer on the face of this earth.

The Jewett/Tainter House was significant not only because it was on the site of the birthplace of the last slave born on Staten Island, but also because of its connections with the Jewett family. The story begins in the early nineteenth century with John Jewett. John had three sons and a daughter: George, John, Jr., Charles H. and Elizabeth. In 1842, John, George, John Jr. and Charles took over a site left from an 1838 corporation called the

Staten Island Whaling Company, and turned it into the John Jewett and Sons Company. At least two of the brothers married. John Jewett, Jr., married Mary Bunce Jewett; he died in June of 1856 and she died in January of 1887.

George W. Jewett moved to Brooklyn and married Gertrude Duryee. He became a wealthy man, both from his family firm and from a linseed oil manufacturing company, located near the site of the present-day Bayonne Bridge, in which he invested in 1869. George W. and Gertrude D. Jewett had three children. Their daughter Mary was born July 11, 1842. The 1850 census shows that twin sons, George W. and Cornelius D. Jewett, were born in 1845. Cemetery records show little George W. was buried on December 23, 1858, and that Cornelius joined him in the family plot April 4, 1866. George W. Jewett, Sr., died April 5, 1877, in tragic circumstances, at the age of 61. His will indicated that he was involved in many community charities. He left legacies to: The Five Points of Industry (Manhattan); Home of Aged and Indigent Females, Brooklyn; New York City Hospital; Staten Island Half Orphan Asylum (a.k.a. Society for the Relief of Destitute Children of Seamen, organized in 1840 and now the Society for

Children and Families); The (Unitarian) Church of the Redeemer on Staten Island (organized in 1851); and The Samuel R. Smith Infirmary (opened 1861 and now the Staten Island University Hospital).

George Jewett also left bequests to his wife Gertrude, his brother Charles H., 57-year-old Margaret Connors, his boys' Irish nurse; and to his daughter. At that point, Mary was married to Charles Taintor, who had been born March 12, 1840, in Windham, Connecticut. Charles and Mary had started their family, which grew to six children: George J., Mary, Henry S., Cornelius D., Charles W., and Philip. Charles Taintor died April 21, 1887, on Staten Island. Mrs. Tainter used the money inherited from her father to support her children and her mother. Gertrude D. Jewett died in the Jewett/Taintor Mansion July 3, 1901, at age 87 years and 11 months. The estate her husband left her then went to Mary, who was both her daughter and her co-executor.

Mary continued to use her family funds for her own and her children's support. The 1920 census placed her at 2105 Richmond Terrace with her two unmarried sons, Cornelius and Philip, both of whom seemed to be living off family income. Mary died December

10, 1924, in a boarding house on East Putnam Avenue, Greenwich, Connecticut, called "The Elms."

By then, the male line of the Jewett family had died out. In 1882, John Jewett and Sons Company became the Jewett White Lead Company and finally the National Lead Company. The Taintor family may have also died out. The last document describing Charles and Mary Tainter's children was generated in 1936, and listed the children as follows: Mrs. William Hamilton (May) Burke of Greenwich, Connecticut, died June 1931; Harry Sherman Taintor of Aiken, South Carolina, died December 10, 1924; Philip N. Taintor of Riverside, Connecticut; Charles West Taintor, died November 20, 1911; George J. Taintor, died March 5, 1893; and Cornelius D. Taintor, of Stamford, Connecticut, died May 17, 1922.

The 34-room mansion, which in its heyday overlooked Kill Van Kull in a neighborhood full of other mansions, such as that of the Faber family, is also gone. The neighborhood later became known for its many shops dealing with automobiles. According to a member of the family currently living near its location at 2105 Richmond Terrace, the building was demolished in the 1950s. (R.D., March 8, 2000.)

Jewett White Lead Works, 68, 119

Joline, 36

John Frederick Smith House

This house, also known as the Dorothy Valentine Smith House, stands at 1213 Clove Road in Sunnyside (Block 247/38). It is a New York City Landmark.

The prominent local banker and insurance dealer John F. Smith erected this house between 1893 and 1895 in a restrained version of the Queen Anne style. The house was the lifelong home of Smith's daughter Dorothy, the author of several books and articles on Staten Island's history and a founder of Richmondtown Restoration. (Dolkart, 283.)

John King Vanderbilt House, 53

The house stands on 1197 Clove Road (Block 246/56) in Sunnyside. Built by John King Vanderbilt in 1836, it is representative of a Staten Island farmhouse of the 1830s, and reminiscent of a Vermont farmhouse. Clapboard exterior, brick interior walls. Dorothy Valentine Smith, who lived next door and who was John King Vanderbilt's great-great-granddaughter, purchased the home in 1955 and subsequently restored it. (E.H.) For further information, *see* Dolkart, 183.

JohnsonAvenue, 121

Johnson, Elmer, 230

Johnson family, 146

Johnston Brothers, 121

Joseph H. Seguine House,

This house, erected in 1837, stands at 440 Seguine Avenue in Prince's Bay (Block 6694/173). It is a New York City Land-mark and on state and national historic registers. Its telephone number is (718) 390–8035.

Note the Greek Revival style of architecture, with six large columns. Semi-circular window opens into attic story. Sandstone foundation blocks brought from Connecticut. Pins in beams and rafters made of locust wood. (E.H.)

This sophisticated Greek Revival country house is located at the highest point on the Seguine family's ancestral farm. The farmer, shipping merchant, and industrialist Joseph Seguine, born in the nearby Abraham Manee House, belonged to the fifth generation of his family to live on Staten Island. (Dolkart, 293.)

In Lemon Creek Park, along the southern shore of Staten Island, the Seguine House, a stately Greek Revival structure, faces Prince's Bay. The Seguine House is notable for its large portico with paneled piers surmounted by a classical pediment. Formerly sheathed with clapboard, the elegant two-and-a-half-story house is insulated with brick and mortar. (*Historic Houses*, 1992, 36.)

Kreischer Street in Charleston (Block 7950/131, 134, 136, 137 and 138). They are rare surviving examples of their type. Prominent local landowner Peter Androvette built them as housing for workers in the adjacent Kreischer Brick Works. They, along with the nearby Kreischer House, reflect the evolution of a Richmond County hamlet into a company town. The houses are clad in wood shingles, and the sidewalks are paved in Kreischer brick. (Dolkart, 295.)

Kreuzer-Pelton House, see Cornelius Cruser House, 25, 44

Kroesen, Hendrick, The Voorlezer, 23

L

Ladies' Auxiliary, 75

Ladies' Relief Society of New Springville, 94–95

Lafayette, Marquis de, 51, 107

Lafayette Avenue, 59, 68, 98, 147, 183

Laforge, 56

Lake, John E., 125

Lakeman-Cortelyou House, 27

Lake-Tysen House, 26, 241, 255

This house was built by Joseph Guyon circa 1740. A kitchen was added in 1800. In 1812, ownership passed to Daniel W. Lake, and in 1839, the house went to Lake's son-in-law, David J. Tysen. In July 1962, the house was relocated from its original site on Tysen's Lane, New Dorp, to Rich-

mondtown. The architectural features of this Dutch Colonial home include a gambrel roof with dormers, a spring eave over the front piazza, a divided door, interior paneling, and a fireplace with Dutch tiles. See also Richmond Town Historic. (E.H.)

Land grants, 20

Landmarks, 35

Lane Theater

This theater is located at 168 New Dorp Lane in New Dorp (Block 4210/36). Its interior is a New York City landmark. John Eberson, one of the preeminent theater architects of the twentieth century, designed this theater in 1937–1938. The Art Moderne foyer, lounge corridor, and auditorium of the Lane Theater make up one of the last surviving historic theater interiors on Staten Island. (Dolkart, 289.)

Lamoka culture, 3

Lapide, Jean, 21

Larsen, Peter, 174

Latourette, 36, 172, 179, 182, 195

Latourette Golf Course, 107, 172

Latourette House, 107, 172

This building is on Richmond Hill Road in New Springville (Block 2350/1). It is a New York City Landmark, and on the state and national historic registers. Erected circa 1836 as the home of David Latourette, this large Greek Revival style structure commands an excellent view of the Historic Richmond Town complex. (E.H.)

The house is one of the few early nineteenth-century brick country houses on this scale to survive in New York City. In 1928, the Latourette farm was sold to the city for use as a park and golf course. Circa 1936, the Parks Department undertook a series of alterations that included the removal of dormer windows, the reconstruction of the four tall chimneys, the replacement or reconstruction of the floor, cornice and railings on the original front porch and the extension of the porch along the south elevation. The building is currently used as the Latourette Golf Course Field House. Its telephone number is (718) 390–8035. (Dolkart, 286.)

This is a picturesque setting in Prince's Bay, where many pleasure craft sail. Its unusual rolling drawbridge is no longer in use. A large city park is planned for this area. (E.H.)

This hill overlooks Historic Richmond Town. At the corner of Lighthouse Avenue and Edinboro Road one can observe an octagonal lighthouse with a limestone base. Called Richmond Light when it was erected as a range light about 1912, it is now called Staten Island Light and is a New York City Landmark. Further down on Meisner Avenue are Wyeth House and Keppler House. (E.H.)

This neighborhood was formerly known as Elliottville. It took the name Livingston from the former Staten Island Rapid Transit Station that was demolished in 1938. The station was located at Kill

Van Kull near Bard Avenue, in the former residence of Anson Livingston. Anson, whom records describe as a "gentleman," was born May 1, 1807, in New York, the son of Judge Brockholst Livingston and his second wife, the former Anna N. Ludlow of New York. (*Staten Island Advance*, September 11, 1989, B1.)

In December 1829, Anson Livingston married Ann Livingston, the daughter of Henry Walter Livingston and the former Mary Allou. Anson and Ann Livingston had three children: Mary, who married a Captain Harrison, Ann, and Ludlow, who married a Mary Keif and who died in 1873. Ludlow and Mary Keif Livingston had a daughter, Anna, who died in 1892. (R.D.)

Livingston power plant, 127, 206, 233

local government and services, 97

Lockman Avenue, 133, 176, 216

Longfellow, Henry Wadsworth, 81, 146

Long Island, 3, 11, 18, 27, 33, 67, 118, 122, 199, 215, 253, 256

Long Neck, 20, 25, 33, 53, 57, 79, 120, 135

Long Neck Chapel, 57, 135

Long Neck School, 94, 135

Louis Street, 64, 164, 222

Louis De Jong and Company, 68, 119, 198

The building stands at 330 Tompkins Avenue in Rosebank. It is located near the Garibaldi and Meucci Memorial Museum and near 441 Tompkins Avenue, the site of the former Bachmann's Brewery, currently the Sun Chemical Corporation, maker of color pigments. This area was the center of several industries. (E.H.)

Louis Ettlinger and Sons, 119

Louisiana, 64

Low, Daniel, 107, 109, 134

The Staten Island Museum owns a bust of this well-known Staten Islander, who lived from 1792 to 1874, created by the American sculptor Hiram Powers.

Lowell, James Russell, 81

Lowell, Josephine Shaw (Mrs. Charles Russell), 81, 131

Founded the Charity Organization Society. Visit the Lowell Fountain at Avenue of the Americas side of Bryant Park, Manhattan. It is a memorial to Mrs. Lowell. (EH)

Born in Boston December 16, 1843, she came to Staten Island as a small child, the daughter of Francis George and Sarah Sturgis Shaw. She was the sister of Anna Shaw Curtis and Colonel Robert Gould Shaw. Widowed during the Civil War, she wrote a report on the Staten Island poorhouse, which led to her appointment in 1876 as the first woman commissioner of the State Board of Charities. That board, in 1882, formed the Char-

Field Historic District. The General Services Administration declared it excess property in 1970. (E.H.)

mills and millstones, 20–21, 109

These were at various places on Staten Island. For example, Britton's Mill was in the Clove Lakes area. Millstones may be seen at the Billiou-Stillwell-Perine House, the Staten Island Historical Museum, and at Voorlezer's House. A millpond and sawmill are at Historic Richmond Town, and there are plans to reproduce at least two mills at this reconstruction: Crocheron's Tide Grist Mill and Dunn's Sawmill. (E.H.)

Minthorne Street, 53, 140

Mission of Immaculate Virgin for the Protection of Homeless and Destitute Children, 42, 51, 132, 140, 215

This institution, known colloquially as Mount Loretto, is located on a tract in Pleasant Plains between Amboy Road, Hylan Boulevard, Sharrott Avenue, and Lower New York Bay (Block 7664/1). In 1964, it contained at least 645 acres.

This tract first entered U.S. history during the American Revolution, when it was a redoubt. During the War of 1812, it was the site of Fort Smith. In 1868, a lighthouse was erected on the tract. Currently, the property consists of large, modern dormitories, cottages, a gymnasium, schools, a statue of the founder of the institution, and the historic lighthouse. (E.H.)

The Mission of the Immaculate Virgin was incorporated May 23, 1877, by Mathew Leavy, Bernard Reilly, James E. Dougherty, William D. Reilly, James O'Neill, Hugh O'Donnell and John C. Drumgoole. It began acquiring property at this Staten Island site the day after Christmas, 1882, and added parcels in 1885 and 1906.

The Mission maintained and conducted a large institution for boys and girls at Mount Loretto, caring at one time for approximately 855 children. Among the various parcels were located dormitories, a trade school, classrooms, three gymnasiums, laundries, an infirmary and administrative buildings. In 1964, the tax-exempt institution was supported by the City of New York, Nassau County, Suffolk County, Westchester County, Catholic Committee for Refugees, the Catholic Welfare Bureau, and private charges.

In 1995, Mount Loretto relocated its population of orphans, troubled youth and developmentally disabled clients. It leased its former elementary school, Saint Aloysius, to the Board of Education to hold third graders from

Estate, also known as Fox Hill Villa. The Sanborn map listed the site as "Mount Manresa House of Retreat (R.C.)" According to its incorporation papers, Mount Manresa was formed:

1. "For the moral and mental improvement of men, and for missionary purposes, and to carry out by concerted action and by corporate organization, a system of spiritual retreats for laymen; and

2 To establish a centre of spiritual discipline, with a view of grounding the layman in the fundamental principles of moral and religious life, and to hold up to his striving the motives and ideals which make for the upbuilding and sustaining of manly character; and

3. To further the study of Social Studies, with a view of training competent speakers and writers on the great social problems of the day; and

4. To provide a suitable place or places for the carrying on the work of the corporation." (R.D.)

Muller House, see Nicholas Muller House

Municipal and Magistrate's courthouses, 99, 159

These courthouses were erected in 1929–1930. The former is at 71 Targee Street in Stapleton, and is now the Criminal Court. The latter is at 2927 Castleton Avenue in West New Brighton, and is now the Civil Court. The architecture of both is Georgian in style. (E.H.)

Murals

There are historical murals and paintings in various bank buildings. *See also* Borough Hall. (E.H.)

Murray, Mary Lindley, 227

Museum of the City of New York, 36, 239

museums, *see* Jacques Marchais Center of Tibetan Art; Staten Island Historical Museum; Staten Island Museum. (E.H.)

music and art, 186–187, 237–238

Music Building of Wagner College, 65

Music Hall, 73

N

Narrows, 1, 11, 33, 40, 46, 50–51, 89, 100, 102, 163, 166, 173, 203, 207, 234–235, 239, 242, 251, 253, 259–260

The Narrows, particularly the Verazzano-Narrows Bridge and the Manhattan skyline, may be observed from the foot of Hylan Boulevard, from Fort Wadsworth, and from Von Briesen Park. (E.H.)

Nassau Smelting and Refining Company, 165, 201

National Park Service, 228, 239

Natural History Notes, 147

natural resources, 69

Nautilus (steamboat), 78

Nautilus Hall, 51

Nautilus Street, 100

Negroes, *see* African Americans

Neville House, *see* Tysen House

Netherlands, 11–16, 27

New Amsterdam, 13, 18, 22

Newark Bay, 1

New Blazing Star, *see* Travis

New Blazing Star Ferry, 33, 79

New Brighton, 13, 44, 53, 58–61, 65, 68, 70, 73, 77, 79, 90, 92, 98, 110, 112–115, 123–124, 127–129, 133, 137–138, 142, 146–148, 157, 160, 170–171, 175, 177–178, 183, 199, 203, 210, 218–219, 240

New Brighton Village Hall

This building is at 66 Lafayette Avenue in New Brighton (Block 71/117). It was designated a New York City Landmark October 14, 1965, and was listed on state and national historic registers in 1978. Its history is tied to that of New Brighton, which, in the 1860s, was becoming a site for suburban homes of prominent Manhattanites. In 1871, New Brighton erected a Village Hall to take care of its growing administrative needs. The architect was James Whitford, who had arrived in Staten Island from England in 1852 and did much work locally.

Whitford designed a well-constructed building in the French Empire style then in vogue. The building is three stories high, of red brick, with a stone foundation, a flight of steps leading to a large arched entrance, and a tall mansard roof. The ground floor has arched windows, there is a projecting center bay, the second floor windows are flat-arched, and the third floor dormer windows have gabled roofs.

In 1898, Staten Island became one of New York City's five boroughs. Thereafter, the Village Hall functioned as a courthouse, a Selective Service Office, and a medical center for the Health Insurance Plan (HIP) of New York. Its last tenant left in 1968. In 1971, the Martin Luther King, Jr., Heritage House purchased the building, intending to turn it into a community center. However, the plan failed, and in 1977 the building reverted to the City of New York due to nonpayment of taxes. It remained in the hands of the Division of Real Property until 1981, when the Division sold it to a private individual. The sales agreement stipulated that the building be repaired within three years of the date of sale, but that did not happen. For more on this building, consult Dolkart, 271, and Department of General Services, 1992, 63, and 1993, 121.

New Brunswick, 79

New Dorp, 19, 20, 24, 28, 36, 40, 53, 60, 66, 87, 104, 114, 117, 118, 128, 129, 135, 139, 157, 161, 167, 173, 174, 175, 184, 188, 206, 218, 220, 225, 241, 250

New Dorp is among Staten

restored the building in 1991–1993. For further information, *see* County Clerk Map #634 and Dolkart, 296.

New York State Armory, 166

This building is at 321 Manor Road near Martling Avenue in West New Brighton (Block 332/4). Morton W. Smith, son of Colonel Richard Penn Smith, owned a farm on this site prior to its becoming an armory. It houses a display of firearms, tanks, guidons, and a forge and anvil used by a cavalry unit. (E.H.)

New York State Assembly, 52, 91

New York State Freedom Train, 52

New York State Legislature, 93, 151

New York State Senator, 91

New York State Telephone Company, 129, 209

New York Yacht Club, 115

Nicholas Muller House, 138, 221

This building is now Saint Peter's Boys High School (Block 92/1).

The building was originally known as the Adolph Rodewald House, because it was constructed ca. 1857 for German-born merchant and broker Adolph Rodewald. In 1886, this house was sold to Nicholas Muller. Although basically similar to the Goodhue House, *q.v.*, the ornamentation here is much more elaborate. Twin pediments mark the lateral sections of the façade; elaborate, almost Baroque-inspired frames encircle the oculus window in

each. Window surrounds are of interest; the keystone emphasizes their slight point. Dentils, scrollwork and ornamental brackets appear at several locations. The columns of the façade-wide porch are unusual in that they employ what is known as entasis, a convex bulge midway up the column, an architectural subtlety introduced originally by the ancient Greeks. This and the other ornamentation suggest that a sophisticated architect designed this structure. (Preservation League of Staten Island, 1986, 13.) Neat and crisp in dark red with white trim, this house is the most distinguished building on the small St. Peter's campus. (Willensky, 813.)

Nicholas Muller was born in the Grand Duchy of Luxembourg, November 15, 1836. He immigrated to the United States with his parents, who settled in New York. Employed as a railroad ticket agent for over twenty years, he became one of the promoters and original directors of the Germania Bank, New York City. A Democrat, he served in the State Assembly in 1875–1876. He then served two consecutive terms as a member of the House of Representatives: March 4, 1877 to March 3, 1881, and March 4, 1883 to March 3, 1887. Back in New York, he was appointed president of the city police board in 1888, president of the excise board and quarantine commissioner. Reelected to Congress, he served from March 4, 1899 until his resignation December 1, 1902. His last appointment, as tax commissioner, came in 1904. Died in New Brighton, December 12, 1917, and is interred in Greenwood Cemetery, Brooklyn, New York. (*Biographical Directory of the American Congress*, 1971, 1549.)

This building is at 160 Heberton Avenue (Block 1020/1). It was designated a New York City Landmark March 22, 1988.

School District No. 6, Port Richmond, purchased land from Charles Cartlige, John Bogert and John Decter to build this school in 1889. The school underwent an addition in 1905. The 1910 directory placed the school on Heberton Avenue, named the principal as Eugene G. Putnam, counted 27 classrooms for grades

K to 8B and identified an annex of three classrooms on Richmond Avenue. The school was designated the Port Richmond on March 22, 1916. The 1920 directory identified the principal as Lewis H. Denton, and counted 33 classrooms for grades K to 6B. The 1930 directory also named Lewis H. Denton as principal, and counted 39 classrooms for grades K to 8B.

One of Staten Island's few remaining nineteenth-century public school buildings, this Romanesque Revival building reflects the diversity of design that characterized this period when independent school boards designed and constructed the schools within their districts. This system was eliminated when New York City was consolidated in 1898 and standardized designs were required throughout the City. The dominant feature of the 1891 part of the school is its four-story square clock bell tower, crowned by a tall pyramidal roof, which sits upon a round-arched arcade. The tower and the style of the building were intended to express civic pride. James Warriner Mounton designed an addition to accommodate the expanding enrollment of the area. Erected in 1897–1898, it was designed to harmonize with the original school. It too is Romanesque in style, with gabled pyramidal roofs, ornamental cornices and moldings, and was designed to give an appearance of strength and massiveness.

At some point in its career as a school, the building's name was changed to Public School 20 Annex. In 1993–1994 the architectural firm, Diffendale & Kubec, converted the vacant building to Parkside Senior Housing low-income units, fulfilling a dream by the former executive director and board of the Northfield Local Development Corporation, who moved their offices into the building. For further information, *see* Dolkart, 282, and Department of General Services, 1992, 59.

North River, 79

North Shore, 3, 20, 23, 79, 87, 117, 119, 127, 140, 143, 232, 254

North Shore Advocate, 149

North Shore Ferry, 79, 142

North Shore Railroad, 114, 140, 144

North Shore Route, 140, 143

Notre Dame College of Saint John's University, 110, 222–224, 252

This institution is at 300 Howard Avenue on Grymes Hill (Block 589/65). On May 18, 1933, the Board of Regents, acting on behalf of the Education Department of the State of New York, granted Notre Dame College a provisional charter for a college of instruction of women studying

for the degrees of Bachelor of Arts and Bachelor of Science in Education.

In 1934, Joseph C. Schlachter applied to the Commissioners of Taxes and Assessments on behalf of Sister Saint Catherine of the Angels, President and Treasurer of the Academy of Our Lady of the Blessed Sacrament, probably for tax-exempt status. Her application stated: "There is one building on said lot, dimensions approximately 60' x 90', two stories in height, in which there is maintained a high school containing eight classrooms." An appended report indicated there was one building of twelve bedrooms, four baths and four classrooms, used primarily as a dormitory, and a second building, a garage converted to a dormitory, containing seven rooms and three baths. (R.D.)

Notre Dame became affiliated with Saint John's in 1971, at which point it had a beautiful 22-acre campus. (E.H.)

Nova Scotia, 46, 121, 199

Nursery and Child's Hospital

This organization was more formally known as the Country Branch of the New York Nursery and Child's Hospital (incorporated 1854), founded by Staten Islander Mrs. Cornelius (Mary A.) DuBois. The hospital was part of an earlier merger with the old Marion Street Hospital (organized 1823) and the New York Infant Asylum (incorporated 1865). The County Branch opened in 1870. It acquired some 47 acres on Manor Road in Castleton Corners, which it named Chestnut Hill. By 1899, 2,155 women and children were patients.

A stunning feature of the hospital was that it promoted the recognition of female physicians. Between 1872 and 1886, the hospital doctors were among the first women doctors on Staten Island.

Nursery and Child's Hospital closed in 1905, when modern medical treatments began to replace the older reliance on lengthy institutional stays.

O

This site, on South Beach, is the location of the first permanent European settlement on Staten Island. (E.H.)

This church occupies 20–42 Austin Place on Grymes Hill (Block 580/34). The building was originally erected as a convent; note the cloistered walks. It became a church for a Roman Catholic congregation in 1899. The congregation erected a new edifice on Victory Boulevard in 1968. The former church became the gymnasium for an expanded parochial school.

This site is located at 36 Amity Street between Saint Mary's Avenue and Virginia Avenue in the Rosebank area. Many Italians live in the neighborhood, and it is from them that membership in the Our Lady of Mount Carmel Society came. The society was what was called a mutual benefit society, because one of its functions was to provide for the welfare of group members in the days before life and medical insurance. The society also brought together people from the same part of Italy to preserve their local customs. Finally, the society fostered its members' spiritual lives, and it was to this end that the grotto was built. Members of the Mount Carmel Society designed the grotto, and began donating their labor toward its construction 1937. The shrine continues to be used as a place of prayer. On November 2, 2002, the National Register of Historic Places listed the Mount Carmel grotto as traditional cultural property, the first such site in New York State.

Outpatient Clinic, 73

Outerbridge, Eugenius, 114, 116

Born on March 8, 1860, Eugenius Outerbridge was a merchant. He helped to create the New York Port Authority, ancestor of the Port Authority of New York and New Jersey, and served as its first chairman. The Outerbridge Crossing between Tottenville, Staten Island, and Perth Amboy, New Jersey, is named for him. He died November 10, 1932. (R.D.)

Outerbridge, Mary Ewing, 114

Mary Ewing Outerbridge was credited with bringing the first tennis set to the United States, and playing the first tennis game in the country. She died May 3, 1886, at New Brighton, Staten Island.

Outerbridge, Crossing, 226, 230, 235, 253

oystering, 5, 9, 58, 75, 93, 98, 101–102, 164; *see also* Amboy Road, Captain's Row, Staten Island Historical Museum

P

Pacific Ocean, 11

Pacific Squadron, 90

Page, William, 81

The Staten Island Museum owns some of his paintings. (E.H.)

Page Avenue, 69, 71

Paleo-Indian, 3

Palmer, John, 20

John Palmer came from Barbados to New York, and by 1683 had a home on Staten Island. That year, the English government established separate governments for Staten Island and the towns on Long Island. Governor Thomas Dongan ap-pointed Palmer, who was a lawyer by profession, as one of the first two judges of the New York Court of

Oyer and Terminer. Palmer was also a member of the Governor's Council, and generally active in provincial affairs.

Palmer is also noteworthy as sale of land to him provided an opportunity for Dongan to enrich himself. On March 31, 1687, Dongan executed a patent, known as the Palmer Patent or, alternatively, the Dongan Patent, part of Palmer's effort to purchase land. The tract's northwest boundary was a small brook that emptied into Mill Pond; it later separated the towns of Castleton and Northfield, and was known as Palmer's Run. The northeast boundary may have been in the vicinity of the Cornelius Cruser House, *q.v.* However, on April 16, 1687, John Palmer and his wife Sarah conveyed the territory described in the patent to Thomas Dongan in exchange "for a competent summe of lawfull money." Legally unable to convey this property to himself, Dongan still managed to acquire possession of it. For further information, *see* Clute, 1877, 56–60.

Palmer's Run, 20

It is a natural boundary between Port Richmond and West New Brighton. Once used for mills. Near Post Avenue, it is joined by Clove Brook, which drains Clove Valley. For further information, *see* Clove Lakes. (E.H.)

Paramount Theatre, 83, 187; *see also* Vanderbilt House
Park Avenue, 103
Park Baptist Church, 59, 103
Park Hotel, 111
Park System of New York, 169
parks, 1, 117, 182, 191
Parks Department, 107–108, 117, 150, 181, 183, 188, 191, 208, 249
Parker, Ely S., 90
parking lots, 198
Parkinson House, 64

This house is on 2475 Richmond Road in New Dorp. It was built in 1854, and stands on the site of the Rose and Crown Tavern. Currently, it is privately owned. (E.H.)

Parkman, Francis, 80
Patriots, 39, 41, 45
Patroon, 12–15, 17
Patten House, 66
Patti, Adelina, 65
Pauw, Michael, 13
Pavilion Hill, 1, 41, 123

Overlooking harbor at Tompkinsville.

Pavilion Hotel, 65, 87, 90, 112, 138
Pavonia, 13
Peace Conference, 21, 41–42, 240
peace treaty (for Spanish-American War), 163
Peach War, (of 1655), 8, 15
Pelton Avenue, 148
Pendleton House, 122

This house is at 22 Pendleton Place (Block 64/155). It is a New York City Landmark.

A picturesque shingle house in Victorian Gothic Romantic style. (E.H.)

This house's features include a tower, oriel, varied windows, steeply pitched gables, and a location on a high elevation above the Kill Van Kull. It was built circa 1855, one of many suburban dwellings in New Brighton built as rental units by William S. Pendleton. The English-born architect Charles Duggin designed several of Pendleton's houses, including, probably, this one, although there is no specific documentation attesting to the architect. (Dolkart, 273.)

Pendleton William, 122

Pennsylvania, 79

Pentecostal Group, 59, 169

people of color, see African Americans

People's Ferry, 79

periaguas, 32, 78

Perine Family, 36, 44

Pershing Square, 130

Perth Amboy (New Jersey), 72, 79, 142, 230, 234–235

Peruvian Petroleum Company, 150

Peteler's Hotel, 117

Peter Housman House, 25, 45

This building stands at 308 Saint John Avenue (block 439/45) at the corner of Watchogue Road in Westerleigh. It is a New York City Landmark, and on the state and national registers of historic sites. Watchogue Road was on the stagecoach route, so it was a natural site for a house. The first part of the building, a one-room stone vernacular house, was erected circa 1730 on the Dongan estate. Peter Housman, a prosperous millwright, erected a large clapboard extension circa 1760, which put the original fireplace in the dining room. With its steep roof and unusually deep overhang, the addition matches the architectural form of the original building (Dolkart, 283.)

Garret Housman owned the house during the American Revolution. This Housman was a Loyalist, and New Jersey "cowboys" burned his feet in the fireplace because he refused to reveal the hiding places of his money and silver. (E.H.)

Philadelphia (Pennsylvania), 33, 66–67, 78–79, 82, 121

Phillips, Wendell, 81, 88

photography, 125–126, 189, 238–239

Picture Cover Binding Inc., 203

Piel Bros. Brewery, 122, 204

Pier 18, 79, 168

Pig War, 8, 14

Plank Road Company, 78

Planter's Hotel, 58, 65, 87, 125

This hotel stood at 368 Bay Street, at Grant Street in Tompkinsville. Erected in the 1820s, it was a two-story post colonial brick building with a parapet gable and dormers with curved windows. Wealthy southerners patronized the hotel. The building later became a pho-

Presbyterian Church, 24, 61, 105

Presbyterian Meeting House, 61

Presentation Sisters, 133, 221

Prince of Orange, 36

Prince's Bay, 20, 36, 41, 51, 53, 62, 71, 109, 118, 121, 128, 132, 180, 194–195, 199, 212, 218, 249

It was named for the Dutch-born Protestant Prince of Orange and Duke of Nassau (1650–1702) who, in the Revolution of 1689, became King William III (with his wife Queen Mary, daughter of James II, as joint sovereign), and banished his Catholic father-in-law at the Battle of the Boyne in 1690. (R.D.)

Princeton (New Jersey), 79

Pritchard House

This house stands at 66 Harvard Avenue in New Brighton in the Hamilton Park area. (Block 58/77). It is a New York City Landmark, and on the state and national historic registers.

Erected circa 1845, the house was designed in the Greek Revival style, with a wing that in 1853 was remodeled in the Italianate manner. Many original features, including carved marble fireplaces and French doors, remained intact. (E.H.)

The house is the only intact survivor of Hamilton Park's original suburban residences, predating the houses that Carl Pfeiffer designed in the 1860s. It is a yellow stucco house with gray stone trim. Features include a notable wooden porch, a balcony, a projecting window hood, and a front entrance placed to command the downhill view to the west. The house has been modified to turn it around, so the former front entrance now opens to a large backyard. The yard hides the house behind a privet hedge, birch trees, and wisteria.

David Seeley, the current owner, suggests that Pritchard House is misnamed. Pritchard, the former owner, opposed the landmarking of his property at the time. (R.D.) For further information, see Willensky, 1988, 810, and Dolkart, 273.

Private Schools, 137–138, 221–222

Francis School, for grades 6–12, at 4240 Amboy Road (Block 5226/192), opened 1970.

Richmondtown Preparatory School at 910 Richmond Road (Block 3168/39).

Staten Island Academy, 715 Todt Hill Road on Todt Hill (Block 872/27). Staten Island Academy traces its roots to the (Anton) Methfessel Institute, founded on Harrison Street in Stapleton in 1862. It began as a boarding school for boys but later added girls. When enrollment outgrew the original building the Institute (later renamed Edgewater Institute) moved to new quarters at 44 Van Duzer Street. By

September 5, 1884, The Staten Island Academy and Latin school had opened officially at the Van Duzer Street facility, with Mr. Frederick Partington as the first Headmaster. In 1891 the trustees bought a tract of land at the corner of Wall St. and Stuyvesant Place in Saint George, and the cornerstone was laid in 1895. That building was razed in 1974. In 1923, the Delafield family gave the school a 230,000 square-foot section of what is now Walker Park (but then called Delafield Square) in Livingston. The Academy sold it to the City of New York on June 19, 1931. The school now occupies a campus on a site that was originally the home of the American financier and industrialist Edward Reilly Stettinius, Sr. (1865–1925), also known as Dongan Hall. The Head of Staten Island Academy's Junior School for 2001 was Ms. Christine Boutross. The Head of the Upper Preparatory Division was Mr. Frank Crane. For further information, see Willensky, 843, and *Staten Island Advance*, "The County Legacy," 1962, no page.

Procter and Gamble Manufacturing, 200

Procter and Gamble was founded in 1837 in Cincinnati as a partnership between William Procter, a candle maker, and James Gamble, a soap maker. The company started out making its famous Ivory soap along with cooking fats and cottonseed oil. The Staten Island plant opened in 1907.

The 124-acre former Procter and Gamble plant in a section of Mariner's Harbor was known for decades as Port Ivory. (E.H.) It was a place where 1,900 Staten Islanders once worked, helping to fuel the powerhouse household product company that brought consumers Ivory soap, Pampers, Tide detergent, Mr. Clean and Duncan Hines cake mix. Declining sales and a downsizing of manufacturing locations led to the closure of the Port Ivory plant in November 1991.

On December 28, 2001, the Port Authority closed a $46.8 million deal to buy the property, which it will use to expand neighboring Howland Hook Container Terminal. That expansion could create another 1,900 jobs on the waterfront. (*Staten Island Advance*, January 12, 2001, B1.)

Prohibition Park, 105, 111–112, 141; *see also* Westerleigh Park

In 1899, the Honorable Bird Coler, Comptroller of the City of New York, approved a lease requested by the Commissioners of the Sinking Fund. The two-year lease was for "The Villa" (a building about 28' x 63') at Prohibition Park owned by National Prohibition Park Company.

There would be an annual rental of $800 for the first year, and $250 for the second, with the privilege of renewal at the $250 rate. (Board of Education Minutes, February 3, 1899, 71.)

This building occupies lots at 98 Grant Street and 149 Saint Paul's Avenue in Tompkinsville (Block 506/81). It is a New York City Landmark.

Middletown Township School District commissioned Edward A. Sargent to design this building in 1897–1898. The school district intended to name the building the Daniel D. Tompkins School, but Staten Island became part of New York City just as the building was completed, so it was renamed P.S. 15. The picturesque building, with its

Public School 1, Summit Street and Yetman Avenue, Tottenville, circa 1930. Source: New York City Board of Education Archives, Teachers College, Columbia University.

Public School 2, Wiener Street, Richmond Valley, March 9, 1934. Source: New York City Board of Education Archives, Teachers College, Columbia University.

chamfered pavilions, Queen Anne detail, and tall clock was designed by Staten Island's most talented late nineteenth-century architect, many of whose residential works are in the Saint George-New Brighton Historic District. (Dolkart, 276.)

The 1910 directory named the principal as Pauline Goerlich and counted thirteen classrooms for grades K to 6B. The school was designated the Daniel D. Tompkins, March 22, 1916. The 1920 directory provided the same information, except that it named Mary M. Conway as principal. The 1930 directory placed the school at the same address, named

as assistant to the principal in charge Margaret E. Hyde, and counted 13 classrooms but for grades 1A to 6B. The 1940 directory identified the school as the Daniel D. Thompkins (the h is a mistake), named the principal teacher in charge as May E.L. Van Dam, and counted 10 classrooms for grades K to 6B.

Public School 20, 101; *see* Northfield Township District School

Public School Society, 76

public schools, elementary (grades K-5)

Tottenville School, 58 Summit Street, Tottenville, Staten Island, New York 10307 (Block 7898/1). According to a 1993 *Staten Island*

Advance article, this is Staten Island's oldest continuously used public school. It is a New York City Landmark. It began as Tottenville Academy in 1878, and was later enlarged for the new P.S. 1, erected in 1882 and modified in 1905 and 1907 by School District No. 5 of the Town of Westfield. The 1910 Board of Education directory placed it at Bentley Manor on Academy Place, gave the principal's name as Nathan J. Lowe, and counted 27 classrooms for grades K-8B. The school became known as the Tottenville on March 22, 1916. The 1920 directory gave the same address and principal, and counted 24 classrooms for grades K-10B. The 1930 directory gave the same address and principal, but counted 42 classrooms for grades K-8B. The 1940 directory gave the address as Summit Avenue and the assistant to the principal in charge as Ellen K. Carlsen, and counted 32 classrooms for grades K-8B. The principal in 2001 was Mr. William Glawon.

P.S. 1 Annex stands at 6581 Hylan Boulevard, Staten Island, New York 10309 (Block 7664/1). Under a 10-year lease, the former Saint Aloysius dormitory-style school of Mount Loretto has been renovated into a 450-seat school combining the third grades of P.S. 1 Tottenville and P.S. 3, Pleasant Plains. The unusual arrangement of a public school in a religious facility came about when Mount Loretto lost funding from the Child Welfare Administration, sending the youth population into the State's jurisdiction. (*Staten Island Advance*, September 6, 1995.)

Richmond Valley stood at Weiner Street in Richmond Valley (Block 7565/1). School District No. 1 for the Town of Westfield erected the building on the southwest corner of Weiner and Butler Streets in Richmond Valley, near Tottenville, between 1896 and 1904. The 1910 directory, and all subsequent directories, placed the school on Weiner Street. The 1910 directory gave the name of the principal and senior teacher as Mrs. Elizabeth T. Medell, and counted two classrooms for grades 1A to 5A. The school was designated the Richmond Valley on March 22, 1916. The 1920 directory gave the principal and senior teacher as Ava A. Butler, and counted two classrooms for grades 1A to 4B. The 1930 directory gave the assistant to the principal in charge as Ava A. Butler, and counted two classrooms for grades 1A to 4B. The 1940 directory listed Ava A. Butler as the teacher in charge, and counted two classrooms for grades 1A to 3B. On September 23, 1954, the building and site were surrendered to the Board of Estimate. The building has since been demolished.

Old P.S. 3, Church Street near Sharrott Avenue in Prince's Bay (Block 5221/350). School District No. 6 of the Town of Westfield purchased the plot from Abraham Latourette and began occupying it in 1894. The school was built between 1894 and 1906. The 1910 directory placed the school on School Street in Prince's Bay, named the teacher in charge as Gould J. Jennings, and counted 13 classrooms for grades K to 8B. The school was designated The Pleasant Plains on March 22, 1916. The 1920 directory placed the school on Latourette Street in Pleasant Plains, named the teacher in charge as Eloise Kinne, and counted 13 classrooms for grades K to 8B. The 1930 directory had the same address, named the assistant to the principal in charge as Margaret L. Lynd, and counted 12 classrooms for grades K to 8B. The 1940 directory had the same address and same assistant, but counted 15 classrooms for grades K to 8B.

New P.S. 3, 80 South Goff Avenue, Pleasant Plains, Staten Island, New York, 10309 (Block 6796/43). This school was renamed for Margaret Gioiosa, who died in 1990. She was a member of the Staten Island District School Board and was named an *Advance* Woman of Achievement in 1984. The school was erected subsequent to title vesting on October 24, 1956. The principal for 2001 is Mr. Dennis Sarlo.

P. S. 3 Annex, *see* P.S. 1 Annex

Old P.S. 4, Shore (Arthur Kill) Road. This school erected as Westfield Township School No. 7 (*q.v.*) between 1896 and 1906, and is a New York City Landmark. The 1910 directory placed it on Fresh Kill (Arthur Kill) Road in Kreischerville, named the principal as Henry F. Albro, and counted 12 classrooms for grades K to 8B. The school was designated The Kreischer on March 22, 1916. The 1920 directory placed it on Arthur Kill Road, gave the same man as principal, and counted nine classrooms for grades K to 8B. The 1930 directory placed it on Arthur Kill Road in Charleston, named the teacher in charge as William O. Van Velsen, and counted 12 classrooms for grades K to 8B. The 1940 directory gave the same address, named the teacher in charge as Augusta C. Marcus, and counted 12 classrooms for grades 1A to 8B.

New P.S. 4, 200 Nedra Lane and Arden Avenue, Eltingville/Arden Heights, Staten Island, New York 10312 (Block

6025/30). This was built as the Maurice Wollin School in 1983–1984. It was named for the district superintendent of Staten Island schools from 1965 to 1976, who died in 1981. He was assistant superintendent when the "Resource Manual" was published in 1964. The principal in 2001 was Marc Harris.

Old P.S. 5, Amboy Road near Huguenot Avenue, Huguenot, Staten Island, New York. School District No. 2, Bloomingview, Town of West-field, purchased land from Ben-

jamin J. Prall in 1895 to erect this school. The 1910 directory placed it on Amboy road, listed the principal and senior teacher as Annie E. Cole, and counted four classrooms for grades 1A to 7B. The school was designated The Huguenot on March 22, 1916. The 1920 directory placed it at the same address, named Annie E. Cole as senior teacher only (not principal) and counted the same number of classrooms for the same number of grades. The 1930 directory reported the same information, except that

Public School 5, Amboy Road, Huguenot Park, February 5, 1931. Source: New York City Board of Education Archives, Teachers College, Columbia University.

Annie E. Cole was designated the teacher in charge. On February 10, 1937, this building and site were surrendered to Commissioners of the Sinking Fund.

New P.S. 5, Kingdom Avenue and Deisius Street, Eltingville, Staten Island, New York, 10312 (Block 6566/1). This building replaced the aforementioned Old P.S. 5. The 1940 directory placed the new building between Eylandt Street, Stecher Street, Deisius Street and Kingdom Avenue in Huguenot, named the teacher in charge as Benjamin B. Chappell, and

counted 11 classrooms for grades K to 8B. Minutes of the Board of Education for June 14, 1964, p. 864, gave the grades taught as K-6. The principal in 2001 was Catherine Corso.

Old P.S. 6 has a history complicated by the tendency to refer to schools as new or old. The Board of Education Archives indicate that a P.S. 6, erected in 1894, was surrendered to the Commissioners of the Sinking Fund on July 7, 1902, and was demolished in 1932. The building usually called Old P.S. 6 was on a lot at Grove Street between

Public School 6, Grove Street between Rossville Avenue and Totten Street, Tottenville, undated. Source: Staten Island Historical Society.

Rossville Avenue and Totten Street in Rossville. The site was vested February 8, 1900, and the City of New York erected the building in 1901. The 1910 directory placed the building on Rossville Avenue, named the principal and senior teacher as John J. Richards, and counted four classrooms for grades 1A to 8B. The school was designated the Betsey Ross on March 22, 1916. However, no documented link has been found between Betsey Ross (Elizabeth Griscom Ross, 1752–1836) and Colonel William E. Ross, for whom

Rossville was named about 1837. Colonel Ross built a replica of Windsor Castle for his home, which became known as Ross Castle. He sold Ross Castle to Caleb Lyon, moved to New York City and then to Albany, where he died on January 31, 1866. The 1920 directory placed the Betsy Ross (note spelling change) on Rossville Avenue, listed Benjamin B. Chappell as senior teacher but not principal, and counted the same number of classrooms for the same number of grades. The 1930 directory placed the school at 1016

Public School 7, Arthur Kill Road between Muldoon Avenue and Saint Michael's Home, April 9, 1934. Source: New York City Board of Education Archives, Teachers College, Columbia University.

Rossville Avenue, with Benjamin B. Chappell as teacher in charge, the same number of classrooms and the same grades. The 1940 directory dropped the street number, listed the teacher in charge as Grace H. Kelly, and counted seven classrooms for grades 1A-8B. The Board of Education Minutes for on December 5, 1945, p. 2287, noted that use of the building for an elementary school was discontinued on December 5, 1945. Marimac Novelty Company used it as a factory thereafter. (Holden, 202.) The *Staten Island Advance* for April 25, 1999 noted a new P.S. 6 was being built at Page Avenue, Academy Avenue and Bartow Avenue in Richmond Valley on the South shore. The 900-seat school opened in September 2000. The principal for 2001 was Ms. Carol Ildebrando.

P.S. 7, Fresh Kill (Arthur Kill) Road, east of Washington Avenue in Green Ridge. School District No. 3, Town of Westfield, erected the building in 1868, and the New York City Board of Education made an addition in 1905. It was first occupied on September 10, 1906. The 1910 directory placed the school on Fresh Kill Road, listed the principal and senior teacher as Laura K. Cropsey, and counted two classrooms for grades 1A to 5B. The

school was designated "The Green Ridge" on March 22, 1916. The 1920 directory repeated the information in the 1910 directory. The 1930 directory placed the school on Arthur Kill Road in Prince's Bay (not Green Ridge), named the teacher in charge as Alice R. McArdell, and counted the same number of classrooms and grades. The school discontinued June 30, 1932. The site and building were surrendered to the Board of Estimate on August 25, 1939.

Old P.S. 8, School Street and Linden-wood Road in Great Kills. School District No. 8 of the Towns of Southfield and Westfield purchased the lot for this school from Eleanor A. Wiman. The building was erected in 1892 and additions were made in 1902–1904. The 1910 directory placed the building on Linden-wood Avenue (note change in street designation) in Great Kills, named the teacher in charge as Else F. Randolph, and counted eight classrooms for grades K to 8B. The school was designated the Great Kills on March 22, 1916; however, soon thereafter, it was replaced by a new building.

New P.S. 8, Lindenwood Road (note, not Avenue) and Park Terrace, Staten Island, New York 10308 (Block 5221/1). This building was occupied on February 26,

1917. The 1920 directory placed it on Lindenwood Avenue in Great Kills, named the principal as Frank G. Ingalls, and counted 11 classrooms for grades K to 8B. The 1930 directory listed the assistant to the principal in charge as Addie E. Deveson and counted 16 classrooms for grades K to 8B. The 1940 directory listed the assistant to the principal in charge as Edith C. Seguine and counted 27 classrooms for grades K to 8B. Additions to the school were made circa 1955. The school was renamed the Shirlee Solomon in honor of the longtime educational activist who was instrumental in the construction of seventeen elementary, intermediate and high schools across Staten Island, plus two special education schools. In 2001, the principal was Robert Sheldon.

Old P.S. 9. Beach Avenue and 8th Street in New Dorp. Union Free School District No. 3, Town of Southfield, purchased land for this school from David J. Tysen and his wife Frances W. Tysen. The school was erected in 1894. The 1910 directory placed the school on Knight Avenue, named the principal as Frank Hankinson, and counted four classrooms for grades 1A to 6B. The school was designated the De Vries on March 22, 1916. The 1920 directory gave the school the same address, classroom count and grades, but named the teacher in charge as J. Herbert

Public School 9, Beach Street and 8th Street, New Dorp, May 19, 1938. Source: New York City Board of Education Archives, Teachers College, Columbia University.

Hoyt. The 1930 directory placed the school on Beach and 8th Streets (note, not Beach Avenue), named the teacher in charge as M. Louise Tompkins, and counted five classrooms for grades 1A to 3A. The building was withdrawn for school purposes on April 18, 1932. Beginning on May 25, 1932, it was used as a furniture storehouse. The 1940 directory indicates the 122nd Precinct occupied the building. According to Holden (p. 201), the police remained there until 1963. However, the building was surrendered to the Board of Estimate on October 4, 1951.

New P.S. 9, Lindenwood Road and School Street, (Block 18/15). Title vested on April 3, 1963. The principal for the school for 2001 was Mr. Robert J. Sheldon.

Old P.S. 10, stood at the foot of Egbert Avenue in New Dorp. School District No. 4, Town of Middletown, erected it in 1894. The 1910 directory placed it at Richmond Road in New Dorp, named Frank Hankinson as principal, and counted two classrooms for grades 1A to 4B. The school was designated the Egbert on March 22, 1916. The 1920 directory gave the same information, except that the senior teacher (not principal) was Anna T. Dermody. The 1930 directory gave

the same information as the 1930 directory, except that Anna T. Dermody was the teacher in charge. The 1940 directory gave the same information, except that the teacher in charge was Lillian Boeddinghaus.

Old P.S. 11 was on Jefferson Avenue between Garretson Avenue and Cromwell Avenue. School District No. 3, Southfield and Middletown, erected the building in 1888 and added to it in 1906. The 1910 directory placed the school on Jefferson Street (note change), named the principal as Frank Hankinson, and counted six classrooms for grades K to 7B. The school was designated the Thomas Dongan on March 22, 1916. C.B.J. Snyder's design received preliminary approval on June 14, 1918, and a new building was erected at 50 Jefferson Street, Dongan Hills, Staten Island, New York, 10312, in 1918. The 1920 directory placed the school on Jefferson Avenue, named the teacher in charge was Alfred DeB. Mason, and counted five classrooms for grades K to 6B. The 1930 directory placed the school at 50 Jefferson Street, named the principal as Pauline Goerlich, counted twelve classrooms for grades K to 8-B, and added two annexes, P.S. 33 and P.S. 38. The 1940 directory had the same address, named

Public School 12, 109 Rhine Avenue and Steuben Street, Stapleton, May 23, 1938. Source: New York City Board of Education Archives, Teachers College, Columbia University.

the assistant to the principal in charge as Mrs. Jane Cerreta, and counted 22 classrooms for grades K to 8B, plus the same two annexes. The principal in 2001 was Henry W. Murphy.

Old P.S. 12, Rhine Avenue, Danube Avenue and Steuben Street in Concord. School District No. 2, Towns of Southfield and Middletown, erected this in 1894. Board of Education Minutes for February 3, 1899, p. 71, indicate City Comptroller Bird S. Coler approved a request for an annex, consisting of a two-year lease for the upper floor of a two-

story brick building on Steuben Street in Concord, 30′ x 85′, on a fenced-in plot 75′ x 100′, owned by Robert Solomon, who charged $480/year and allowed the school to renew the lease. Instead, the school made additions to its own buildings between 1900 and 1904. The 1910 directory placed the school on Steuben Street, Concord, named the principal as Thomas C. Harty, and counted 18 classrooms for grades K to 8B. The school was designated the Ralph Waldo Emerson on March 22, 1916. The 1920 directory gave the same street name but identified the neighborhood as Stapleton (not Concord), listed the same principal and counted the same classrooms and grades. The 1930 directory placed the school at 109 Rhine Avenue in Stapleton, named the assistant to the principal in charge as Elizabeth Chapman, and counted 19 classrooms for grades K to 8B. The 1940 directory placed the school on Rhine Avenue and Steuben Street in Stapleton, named the assistant to the principal in charge as Mrs. Nora O'Donahue, and counted 14 classrooms. According to a June 10, 1994, *Staten Island Advance*

article, P.S. 13 closed in 1977 and the building became part of Concord High School.

Old P.S. 13, Clifton Avenue, Pennsylvania Avenue and Anderson Street. School District No. 1, Town of Southfield, built the school in 1888 and added to it in 1908. The 1910 directory placed it on Pennsylvania Avenue in Rosebank, named the principal as Sheldon J. Pardee, and counted 34 classrooms for grades K to 8B. The school was designated the Rosebank on March 22, 1916. The 1920 directory placed the school at Pennsylvania Avenue and Anderson

Public School 13, 191 Vermont Avenue, Rosebank, sometime between 1905 and 1915. Photograph by W.J. Grimshaw. Source: Staten Island Historical Society.

Place (not Street), named the principal as Else F. Randolph, and counted 33 classrooms for the same grades. The 1930 directory placed the school at 161 Hylan Boulevard, with the same principal, and 35 classrooms for the same grades. The 1940 directory placed the school at the same address, named Herbert S. Walsh as principal, and counted 36 classrooms for the same grades.

New P.S. 13, 191 Vermont Avenue, Rosebank, Staten Island, New York 10305 (Block 2852/1). Ground was broken for the school in November 1979, and the school opened in December 1981. The Community Board named it for Margaret Lindermeyer, a community activist and a *Staten Island Advance* Woman of Achievement

in 1962, who had died in 1969. The principal for 2001 was Ms. Dorren Dillon.

Old P.S. 14, northwest corner of Broad Street and Brook Street in Stapleton. School District No. 1 and Union Free School District No. 2, Towns of Middletown and Southfield, erected the building in 1895 and made additions in 1906–1908. The 1910 directory placed the school on Broad Street and Brook Street, named as principal A. Hall Burdick, and counted 35 classrooms for grades K to 8B. The school was designated the Vanderbilt on March 22, 1916. The 1920 directory placed the school at Broad Street and Wright Street, named the principal as Frank Hankinson, and

Public School 14, corner of Broad Street and Brook Street, Stapleton, circa 1908. Source: New York City Board of Education Archives, Teachers College, Columbia University.

(Top) Public School 15, Grant Street and Saint Paul's Avenue, Tompkinsville, July 29, 1934. Source: New York City Board of Education Archives, Teachers College, Columbia University. (Middle) Public School 16, Daniel Low Terrace and Madison Avenue, Tompkinsville, no date. Source: Staten Island Historical Society. (Bottom) Public School 17, Prospect Avenue and Fairview Avenue, New Brighton, July 29, 1934. Source: New York City Board of Education Archives, Teachers College, Columbia Uni-

counted 34 classrooms for the same number of grades. The 1930 directory placed the school at 75 Broad Street, named the principal as William W. Rogers, and counted 36 classrooms for the same grades. The 1940 directory placed the school at the same address, named the principal as I. Victor Burger, and counted 35 classrooms for the same grades.

New P.S. 14, 100 Tompkins Avenue, Stapleton, Staten Island, New York, 10304 (Block 545/110). The Cornelius ("Commodore") Vanderbilt school was named for the famous Stapleton resident, who built a ferry business and then a railroad fortune. The principal for 2001 was Mr. Frank Carpenito.

P.S. 15, *see* P.S. 15 in the general index.

Old P.S. 16, Madison Avenue (now Daniel Low Terrace) and Monroe Avenue, Tompkinsville. School District No. 4, Town of Castleton, purchased land from James Hayes and Jacob Lafarge in 1871 to build this school, and enlarged it in 1896 and 1905. The 1910 directory placed the school on Madison Avenue, named the principal as John J. Driscoll, and counted 23 classrooms for grades K to 8B. The school was designated the Henry W. Slocum on March 22, 1916. The 1920 directory placed the school on Monroe Avenue, named the same principal, counted 22 classrooms for the same grades, and added an annex at Brighton Heights, Shelter of Richmond County Society for the Prevention of Cruelty to Children, Castleton Avenue, New Brighton. The school was enlarged again in 1924. Albert Melniker, dean of Staten Island architects, provides a memoir of those days: "The original school with a clock tower was designed by Edward Sargent. It was a Kindergarten through 8th grade school. In 1924 during our graduation ceremonies, the new school building was under construction." (Albert Melniker to

Richard B. Dickenson, April 10, 1996.) The 1930 directory placed the school on Daniel Low Terrace but otherwise contained the same information. The 1940 directory placed the school at the same address, named the principal as J. Herbert Hoyt, and counted 36 classrooms for the same grades.

New P.S. 16, 80 Monroe Avenue, Staten Island, New York, 10301. The current building is known as the John J. Driscoll School, for the principal there from 1891 until his death in 1930. He attended P.S. 16 when it was called Castleton School 4. He was a teacher there in 1875, and was principal when it was renamed Henry Warner Slocum

Public School 19, 32 Greeleaf Avenue near Post Avenue, West New Brighton, circa 1908.
Source: New York City Board of Education Archives, Teachers College, Columbia University.

(1827–1894) for the Civil War general and Brooklyn Congressman. He was also the principal there on June 15, 1904, when the *General Slocum*, an excursion vessel, burned. It was the worst single disaster in the history of New York City and among the more deadly accidents in all maritime history, with at least 1,021 people dead. The funerals from the East Village lasted more than a week. (Jackson, 1995, 457.) The John J. Driscoll School currently houses grades K through 5. Its principal for 2001 was Mr. Leonard Mandelbaum.

P.S. 17, Linden Street between 10th Street and Prospect Avenue in New Brighton. School District No. 3, Town of Castleton, purchased land from the family of Smith Ely, a mayor of preconsolidation New York, to build this school in 1871. The school underwent additions in 1898, 1904 and 1908. The 1910 directory placed the school on Prospect Avenue, named the principal as Samuel McK. Smith, and counted 31 classrooms for grades K to 8B. The 1920 directory repeated the information, but counted only 29 classrooms. The 1930 directory repeated the information, except that the principal was Frank G. Ingalls. The 1940 directory repeated the information, except that the school

was back up to 31 classrooms and it had an annex of two ungraded classrooms in P.S. 43. During its later career, P.S. 17 served as an Occupational Training Center. Fire destroyed the building in December 1977. The William T. Davis School, P.S. 31 of New Brighton, replaced it. In 1989, the New York City Department of Housing, Preservation and Development agreed to use the land from P.S. 17 to create a 2.8-acre city park.

Old P.S. 18, Market Street, Broadway and Winegar Place (now Campbell Avenue) in West New Brighton. School District No. 2, Town of Castleton, purchased land from Jacob Winegar and Cornelius I. Price to erect this school in 1890, and enlarged it in 1905. The 1910 directory placed the school on Broadway in West New Brighton, named Timothy F. Donovan as principal, and counted 32 classrooms for grades K to 8B. The school was designated the John Greenleaf Whittier on March 22, 1916. The 1920 directory repeated the information of 1910. The 1930 directory named the principal as Herbert J. McCreary, and counted 33 classrooms. The 1940 directory had the same information as 1930, except for counting 36 classrooms.

New P.S. 18, 220 Broadway, West New Brighton, Staten

Island, New York 10310 (Block 176/10). The school, erected in 1963, is named for John Greenleaf Whittier (1807–1892), the Quaker poet and abolitionist. The principal in 2001 was Mr. Ralph Bronzo.

Old P.S. 19, 32 Greenleaf Avenue near Post Avenue, West New Brighton. School District No. 9 of the Town of Castleton purchased land from Barrett Nephews Company and erected the school in 1889. A May 21, 1989, *Staten Island Advance* article gives the founding history as follows: "A generous strip of the Old DuBois property was purchased as a site. Edward Mersereau, a contractor, built the school. M.J. Simon was the first principal, with a staff of only 2 teachers." The 1910 directory named the principal as G. Alvin Grover and counted 15 classrooms for grades K to 8B. The school was designated the Curtis on March 22, 1916. The 1920 directory repeated the 1910 information, but counted 15 classrooms. The 1930 directory was more specific about the address, 33 Greenleaf Avenue, did not name a principal, counted fourteen classrooms for grades K to 7A, described the school as an annex to P.S. 30, and announced that a new building had been erected.

New P.S. 19, 780 Post Avenue (note address change from above), West New Brighton, Staten Island, New York 10310 (Block 227/24) was the building

387

to which the 1930 directory referred. It was named for George William Curtis, an orator, writer, abolitionist, political figure, humanitarian and longtime resident of West Brighton and Elliottville. The principal in 2001 was Mr. Robert Rando.

P.S. 20, see entry in main index under Northfield District School 6.

New P.S. 20, 161 Park Avenue, Port Richmond, Staten Island, New York, 10302 (Block 1020/1). Ms. Myra Shapiro was the principal in 2001.

P.S. 21 was erected in 1897 on land at Sherman and Prospect Streets, near Sant Street in Port Richmond, purchased from George W. Van Slyck by School District No. 9, Town of Northfield. An addition was made in 1906. The 1910 directory gave the address as Sherman Avenue, Port Richmond, the principal as Samuel Viertel and counted 19 classrooms for grades K to 8B. The school was designated the Elm Park on March 22, 1916. The 1920 directory gave the address as Hooker Place in Port

(Top) Public School 23, between Andros Avenue, Mersereau Avenue and Cedar Street, Mariners Harbor, no date. Source: Staten Island Historical Society.

Richmond, the principal as Lewis H. Denton, and the number of classrooms as 16. The 1930 directory gave the address the school currently uses, 168 Hooker Place (Block 1135/1), Port Richmond. The principal was Mrs. Mary M.C. Shea, and the school was back up to 18 classrooms. In 2001, the school was in Zip Code 10302 and the interim principal was Ms. Dorothy Ambrosino.

P.S. 22 was erected in 1894 on land at Richmond Road near Vedder Avenue in Graniteville, purchased from John L. Richards by School District No. 4, Town of Northfield. An addition was made in 1905. The 1910 gave the address as Richmond Avenue, the principal and senior teacher as Edgar W. Robinson, and counted four classrooms for grades 1A to 5B. In 1912 the City of New York acquired property on the "Southerly Side of Washington St." for the use of the Department of Education. It became the New P.S. 22 at 1860 Forest Ave., Graniteville, 10303 (Block 1706/1). The school was designated the Graniteville on March 22, 1916. The 1920 directory gave the address as Washington and Columbus Avenues in Graniteville, considered the school an

Public School 24, Franklin Avenue and Washington Avenue in Summerville, circa 1908.
Source: New York City Board of Education Archives, Teachers College, Columbia University.

annex to P.S. 21, listed no principal and counted 12 classrooms for grades 1A to 6B. The 1930 directory gave the same address and named the assistant to the principal in charge as Ethel B. Maynard. On October 22, 1930, the building and its site were surrendered to the Commissioners of the Sinking Fund. In 2001, P.S. 22 housed grades 4 and 5, and served as an annex to I.S. 51. Its address was 280 Regis Drive (Block 1653/1) in Graniteville. Its principal was Ms. Karina Costantino.

Old P.S. 23 was located at Andros and Mersereau Avenues and Cedar Street in Mariner's Harbor. Union Free School District No. 5 in Northfield erected it in 1895 on land acquired from Deborah Mersereau. The City of New York built a 1905 addition on five assembled adjacent parcels. The 1910 directory gave the address as Andros Avenue, Mariner's Harbor, named the principal as David J. Keator, and counted 23 classrooms for grades K to 8B. The school was designated the Mariners Harbor on March 22, 1916. The 1920 directory gave the address as Cedar Street between Andros and Mersereau Avenues, named the same principal, and counted 21 classrooms for the same number of grades. The 1930 directory

gave the address as Mersereau Avenue, identified the school as Annex P.S. 24, an annex to P.S. 44, and counted 22 classrooms for grades K to 6B. In 1942, Bethlehem Steel Company began to use the building. (Holden, 202.)

New P.S. 23 was erected in 1963 to replaced P.S. 28 in Richmond Town. Its address is 30 Natick Street, Richmond-town 10306 (Block 4374/1). Its principal in 2001 was Ms. Julie Sherwood.

P.S. 24 was erected in 1895 by School District No. 7 of the Town of Northfield on a 100' x 150' parcel at the southeast corner of Franklin Avenue and Washington Avenue in Summerville, acquired from Jacob V. Decker. The 1920 directory gave the address as Washington Avenue, named the principal and senior teacher as Elsie Gardner, and counted three classrooms for grades 1A to 6B. The school was designated the Summerville on March 22, 1916. The 1920 directory gave the same address, named the principal as Margaret McDonough, and counted three classrooms for grades 1A to 4B. The 1930 directory gave the same address, identified the school as an annex to P.S. 44, and counted three classrooms for grades 1A to 4A. The school was later demolished.

Old P.S. 25 was erected in 1895 by the Town of Northfield on a 100' x 100'; parcel at Chelsea Road (Watchogue Road near River Road in Bloomfield), purchased from Marcellus T. Merrill. An addition was erected in 1905. The 1910 directory placed the school on Chelsea Road in Bloomfield, did not name a principal and counted two classrooms for grades 1A to 3B. The school was designated the Bloomfield School on March 22, 1916. The 1920 directory gave the same address, identified the school as an annex to P.S. 26, and counted two classrooms for grades 1B to 3A. The 1930 directory gave only an address on Bloomfield Road. The building and site were surrendered to the Commissioners of the Sinking Fund on December 14, 1932. The school was later demolished.

New P.S. 25 is located at 6581 Hylan Boulevard near Mount Loretto in Pleasant Plains; telephone (718) 984–1526. It is both the Richmond Career and Vocational School and a District 75 School for Special Education. The principal for 2001 was Stephen DiCarlo.

Annexes B and C are at 669 Castleton Avenue (Block 102/1) on the grounds of Saint Vincent's Campus, Sisters of Charity

Public School 26, 4108 Victory Avenue, Linoleumville, May 23, 1938. Source: New York Board of Education Archives, Teachers College, Columbia University.

Health Care System. The building houses the Treatment Program, Staten Island Children's Community Mental Health Center of the Staten Island Mental Health Society, Inc.

Annex D, or old P.S. 4, is at 4210 Arthur Kill Road (Block 7515/7).

Old P.S. 26 was erected in 1880 by School District No. 3 of Long Neck (Travis) in the Town of Northfield, on land at Richmond Turnpike (now Victory Boulevard), Prospect Avenue and Wild Avenue in Linoleumville, donated by the American Linoleum Manufacturing Company. The second floor was added in 1896, and another addition was made in 1904. The 1910 directory gave the address as Richmond Turnpike in Linoleumville, named the principal as Lewis H. Denton, and counted 17 classrooms for grades K to 8B. The school was designated the Carteret on March 22, 1916, after Sir George Carteret (circa 1610–1680). Sir George succeeded his father as bailiff of his native island of Jersey, and also became lieutenant governor. He sheltered the Stuart princes, the future Charles II and James II, when their father, Charles I, was beheaded. In 1664, the future James II granted him coproprietorship of New Jersey in recognition

Public School 27, Richmond Avenue, New Springville, circa 1908. Source: New York City Board of Education Archives, Teachers College, Columbia University.

of his past services to the crown (R.D.). The 1920 directory gave the address as 4108 Richmond Turnpike and Wild Avenue, identified the teacher in charge as Elsie Gardner, and counted 13 classrooms for grades K to 6B. The 1930 directory gave the same address, with the additional information that the address was also 4108 Victory Boulevard, identified the principal in charge as Else G. Rouse (apparently Miss Gardner married), and counted 14 classrooms for grades K to 8B.

New P.S. 26 is located at 4108 Victory Boulevard, Travis 10314 (Block 2634/1). The principal for 2001 was Ms. Judith Kaye Horowitz.

Old P.S. 27 was erected in 1881 on 45,000 square feet of land purchased by School District No. 2 of Northfield from Hiram J. Corson. On September 25, 1907, title was vested, by condemnation, in a new P.S. 27. The 1910 directory placed the school at Richmond Avenue in New Springville, named the principal and senior teacher as Fred A. Holder Eggert, and counted two classrooms for grades 1A to 5B. The school was designated the Springville on

Old Public School 29, Manor Road, West New Brighton, no date. Source: Staten Island Historical Society.

March 22, 1916. The 1920 directory gave the same address, named the teacher in charge as Lillian Boeddinghaus, and counted two classrooms for grades 1A to 3B. The 1930 directory repeated this information. The 1940 directory repeated the information, but omitted the name of the principal. The next year, the building was surrendered to the Board of Estimate. (Minutes of the Board of Education May 28, 1941.)

P.S. 28 was erected on 50,302 square feet of land purchased in 1906 by the City of New York from Stephen D. Stephens. The building was erected in 1908. It was turned over to the Commissioners of the Sinking Fund on January 27, 1909. The 1910 directory placed the school on Centre Street in Richmond, named the principal as Frank Hankinson, and counted four classrooms for grades 1A to 6B. The school was designated the Richmond on March 22, 1916. The 1920 directory gave the same address, identified the senior teacher as Anna M. Martin, and counted four classrooms for grades 1A to 7B. The 1930 directory provided the same address and named the same principal, but counted four classrooms

Public School 29, Victory Boulevard and Slosson Avenue, Castleton Corners, January 26, 1923. Source: New York City Board of Education Archives, Teachers College, Columbia University.

for grades 1A to 8B. The 1940 directory gave the same address, named the teacher in charge as John Richards, and counted five classrooms for grades 1A to 8B.

Old P.S. 29 was erected on a 38,625 square foot parcel of land purchased by School District No. 1 in Castleton from the estate of Japheth Alston on December 1, 1866. The school was erected in 1889. The 1910 directory placed the school on Manor Road in West New Brighton, named the principal as William B. Rafferty and counted five classrooms for grades K to 6B. The school was designated the Castleton Corners on March 22, 1916. The 1920 directory gave it the same address, identified it as P.S. 30 Annex, did not name a principal, and counted the same numbers of classrooms and grades. In an unusual move, the school was redesignated the Bardwell, after Dr. Darwin Bardwell, the district superintendent of schools from 1902 to 1915, and the person responsible for bringing Staten Island's rural school system into harmony with the rest of New York City's educational system. The 1930 directory placed the school on Victory Boulevard and Slosson Avenue, identified it as P.S. 35 Annex, named the assistant to the principal in charge as Mary M. O'Connell, and counted 13 classrooms

for grades K to 8B. Also working at P.S. 29 in the 1930s was Albert Melnicker, the dean of Staten Island architects and at that time an Architect with the Board of Education Bureau of Construction. The 1940 directory gave the same address, identified the assistant to the principal in charge as Mrs. Else G. Rouse, and counted 11 classrooms for grades K to 8B.

New P.S. 29 is located at 1581 Victory Boulevard, 10314 (Block 331/1). An addition to the school was built in 1950. The principal in 2001 was Ms. Augusta Mitchell.

P.S. 30 was erected in 1899. In 1903 or 1904, the City of New York purchased 27,750 square feet of land from the National Prohibition Park Company and erected an addition in 1904. The 1910 directory placed the school on Fiske Avenue in West New Brighton, named the principal as William B. Rafferty, and counted ten classrooms for grades K to 8B. The school was designated the Westerleigh March 22, 1916. The 1920 directory gave the same address, identified an annex at Sea View Hospital, Manor Road, New Dorp, named the same principal and counted eleven classrooms for the same grades. The 1930 Directory placed the school on Fiske Avenue and Westerleigh Boulevard, named the same prin-

(Top) Public School 32, 14 Osgood Avenue between Targee and Van Duzer Streets, Stapleton, May 23, 1938. Source: New York City Board of Education Archives, Teachers College, Columbia University. (Middle) Public School 33. Richmond Avenue and Midland Avenue, Grant City, January 7, 1933. Source: New York City Board of Education Archives, Teachers College, Columbia University. (Bottom) Public School 35. Manor Road at Sturges Street, West New Brighton, June 6, 1938. Source: New York City Board of Education Archives, Teachers College, Columbia Uni-

cipal and counted 36 classrooms for the same grades. It also identified two annexes: four classrooms for grades K to 8B at Sea View Hospital on Manor Road in

New Dorp and an unknown number of classrooms at P.S. 19. Also working for P.S. 30 in the 1930s was Albert Melnicker, dean of Staten Island architects and then an Architect with the Board of Education Bureau of Construction. The 1940 directory named the principal as Mayhew M. Dodge, counted 37 classrooms for grades K to 8B and identified only one annex, at Sea View Hospital on Manor Road. In 2001, the school's address was 200 Wardell Avenue between Fisk Avenue and Leonard Avenue in the 10314 ZIP code (Block 423/9). The principal was Robert S. Turetsky.

Old P.S. 31 was erected on a 40,000 square foot parcel that the City of New York purchased from Hubbard R. Yetman, executor of the estate of James S. Guyon, who had died on April 21, 1903. The building was erected in 1904. The 1910 directory placed the school on Pleasant Avenue in Bogardus Corners, also known as Little Africa and Harrisville, named the principal as Elizabeth Curtis, and counted two classrooms for grades 1A to 2B. Although Old P.S. 31 was in a historically black community, the school's district included both black and white schoolchildren. The school was designated the Guyon on March 22, 1916. The

1920 directory gave the same address, named the senior teacher as Julia Hurd, and counted two classrooms for grades 1A to 3B. The 1930 directory placed the school on Bloomingdale Road, identified Julia Hurd as the teacher in charge, and counted two classrooms for grades 1A to 3B. The site and building were surrendered to the Board of Estimate on June 28, 1939, but the surrender was withdrawn on August 25, 1939 so that the Board of Education could use the building as a furniture warehouse. The 1940 directory identified the building as such. The Board of Education finally surrendered the building to the Board of Estimate on January 28, 1942 (Board of Education minutes, January 28, 1942). The Sandy Ground Historical District considered establishing a library and museum in the building to preserve the community's history, but the building burned down in 1981 (*Staten Island Advance*, November 5, 1982, A10.)

New P.S. 31, also known as the William T. Davis School, is on 55 Layton Avenue in the 10301 ZIP Code (Block 49/182). The architectural firm of Millนes & Melnicker designed the building to replace P.S. 17 in New Brighton. Architect Albert Melnicker described the work thus:

"This was a difficult site but it turned out to be a functional building." (Albert Melnicker to Richard Dickenson, Staten Island, April 10, 1996, personal communication.) On September 13, 1965, the Art Commission of the City of New York approved a terra cotta mural and relief bust of William Thompson Davis in the center of a 10' x 8' map of Staten Island, for P.S. 31's main entrance. C. Spammpinato of Sea Cliff, Long Island, did the art work. The building honors William Thompson Davis, grandson of P.S. 52.'s John C. Thompson, an entomologist who was also known as coauthor of the Leng and Davis five-volume history of Staten Island, and other literary collaborations. P.S. 31's principal in 2001 was Mr. Arnold Obey.

Old P.S. 32 was erected in 1901 by the City of New York on a parcel of condemned property. In 1907 and 1908 the city acquired surrounding parcels to create a 32,134 square foot tract. Former owners of these lands included George and John Zimmer, George Bechtel and Paul Gorham. The 1920 directory placed the school on Osgood Avenue in Stapleton, named the principal as Thomas C. Harty and counted eight classrooms for grades K to 4B. The school was designated the Grymes on March 22, 1916. The 1920 directory gave the same address, identified the school as an annex to P.S. 15, named no principal and counted the same number of classrooms and grades. The 1930 directory placed the school at 14 Osgood Avenue, named the assistant to the principal in charge as Mary P. Beyer, and counted the same number of classrooms and grades. The 1940 directory gave the same address but said that the school was being used by the Works Progress Administration; it counted nine classrooms.

New P.S. 32 is at 32 Elverton Avenue in the 10308 Zip Code (Block 5444/12). The school is bounded by Barlow Avenue, Stieg Avenue and Leverett Avenue. On February 14, 1966, the Art Commission of New York City gave final approval to the brick and reinforced concrete structure designed by Giorgio Cavaglieri, F.A.I.A., and the wrought iron decorative fence designed by Mary Gallery. On November 9, 1967, the Art Commission approved a sculptured railing at the entrance court. The principal in 2001 was Ms. Irene Sessa.

P.S. 33 was erected between 1901 and 1905 on three parcels totaling 47,376 square feet that the City of New York purchased

from the estates of Elizabeth Thompson, Anna B.C. Vroom and John D. Mulcahy. The 1910 directory placed the school on Washington Avenue in Grant City, named the principal as Frank Hankinson, and counted two classrooms for grades 1A to 6B. The school was designated the Grantland on March 22, 1916. The 1920 directory placed the school on Midland Avenue, identified it as an annex to P.S. 11 and counted two classrooms for grades 1A to 5A. The 1930 directory provided the same address and annex information, but counted three classrooms for the same number of grades. The 1940 directory provided the same address and annex information, but returned the classroom count to two classrooms for the same number of grades. On July 17, 1957, the City of New York sold the property, consisting of a one-story building on a 226' x 175' lot, to Saint Christopher's Roman Catholic Church.

P.S. 34 was erected on a 66,549 square foot plot condemned for purchase by the City of New York in 1902. The building was erected between 1903 and 1904. The 1910 directory placed it on Fingerboard Road in Rosebank, named the principal as Charles W. Sutherland, and counted 9 classrooms for grades K to 6B. The school was designated the Fort Wadsworth on March 22, 1916. The 1920 directory provided the same address, added an annex in Arrochar at Lake View Home, named Charles W. Sutherland as teacher in charge (not principal), and counted eight classrooms for grades K to 5B. The 1930 directory placed the school at Fingerboard Road and Grant Avenue, identified it as an annex to P.S. 39, named no principal and counted eight classrooms for grades K to 7B. The 1940 directory provided the same address, dropped the annex, named the teacher in charge as Helen E. Meade, and counted eight classrooms for grades K to 6B.

Old P.S. 35 had its roots in Old P.S. 29, *q.v.* A plot of 30,600 square feet, between Targee Street, Elm Street and Gordon Street in Stapleton was condemned for P.S. 35 on July 12, 1907. There is no entry for the school in the 1910 or 1920 directory. The 1930 directory placed the school on Manor Road in West New Brighton, identified it as an annex to P.S. 29, and counted four classrooms for grades 4A to 5B. The 1940 directory gave the same address and annex information and counted the same number of classrooms but for grades 3A to 4B.

New P.S. 35 is at 60 Foote Avenue in the 10301 Zip Code (Block 160 and a merged Lot 127). Title was vested August 22, 1951. The New York City Art Commission approved a revised

Public School 38, 421–425 Lincoln Avenue between Poultney Street and Oldfield Street, Midland Beach, May 19, 1938. Source: New York City Board of Education Archives, Teachers College, Columbia University.

design for the school May 12, 1952. The Art Commission approval for a bronze identification tablet and a "C of O" were both issued on September 14, 1953. The principal in 2001 was Mr. Witt Halle.

P.S. 36 was located on property located on the south side of Jefferson Boulevard between Lamont Avenue and Ionia Avenue. Multiple lots were condemned to vest title in the property in the City of New York; vesting took place on September 26, 1921. The 1930 directory placed the school on Lamont Avenue and Jefferson Boulevard in Annadale, named the teacher in charge as Abner Winstein, and counted four classrooms for grades 1A to 6A. The 1940

directory gave the same address, named the teacher in charge as Robert D. Winston, and counted 11 classrooms for grades K to 8B. The school is now P.S. 36 Annex, 194 Jefferson Boulevard in the 10312 Zip Code (Block 6262). P.S. 36 is now the Annadale School at 255 Ionia Avenue in the 10312 Zip Code. The school is named for Father John C. Drumgoole, the Roman Catholic priest who was an advocate for poor children and who founded Mount Loretto in 1883. Father Drumgoole died during the Blizzard of 1888. "The original brick school building stands alongside the sprawling new school that opened in 1974." (*Staten Island Advance*, May 1, 1989, B2.)

P.S. 37 is located at 75 Fair-

Public School 40, Henderson Avenue and Lafayette Avenue, New Brighton, May 5, 1926.
Source: New York City Board of Education Archives, Teachers College, Columbia University.

field Street in Great Kills (Block 5486/1). The 1930 directory placed it at Saint Joseph's by the Sea, Huguenot Park, and identified it as an annex to P.S. 5. There was no principal. The directory counted three classrooms but did not note the grades served. Currently, the school is a District 75 special education school.

P.S. 38 is located at 421–425 Lincoln Avenue in Midland Beach in the 10306 Zip Code (Block 3736/6). The school is named for Staten Island's first borough president. The 1930 and 1940 directories named no principal, identified the school as an annex to P.S. 11, and counted

four classrooms for grades 1A to 5B. Michael L. Radoslovich was the chief architect of the new P.S. 38. In February 2001, P.S. 38's Parent-Teacher Association celebrated the school's forty-fifth anniversary by presenting the principal with a plaque and announcing the winners of the "Who Was George Cromwell?" essay contest. The principal in 2001 was Mr. Wildon Rodriguez.

P.S. 39 is located at 71 Sand Lane and 200 MacFarland Avenue in South Beach in the 10305 Zip Code (Block 3097/14). The Art Commission of New York City approved the design for the red brick exterior with terra cotta trimmings on April 14,

Public School 44, Maple Parkway and Walloon Street, Mariners Harbor, June 6, 1938.
Source: New York City Board of Education Archives, Teachers College, Columbia University.

1924. William H. Gompert was the architect, and also the Superintendent of School Buildings. The 1930 directory named the school the Arrochar, placed it on Sand Lane and MacFarland Avenue, identified its annexes as P.S. 34 and P.S. 46, named I. Victor Burger the principal, and counted 18 classrooms for grades K to 8B. The 1940 directory named Cecilia A. Wolfe assistant to the principal in charge and counted 20 classrooms for grades K to 8B. The school was renamed the Francis J. Murphy School after a school board chairman and lifelong Grasmere resident. The principal in 2001 was Mr. Joseph Santello.

P.S. 40 stands on 80,095 square feet of property purchased on March 16, 1924 from James J. Walsh *et al*. The school was named the Robert Richard Randall School after the founder of Sailors' Snug Harbor, now the Snug Harbor Cultural Center. The 1930 directory placed the school on Henderson Avenue and Lafayette Avenue in New Brighton, named Mary M. O'Brien assistant to the principal in charge and counted 20 classrooms for grades K to 6A. The 1940 directory provided the same address and assistant to the principal in charge, but counted 21 classrooms for grades K to 8B.

P.S. 41 is located at 216 Clawson Street in New Dorp in the 10306 Zip Code (Block 3645/7). Title was vested July 15, 1924. The 1930 directory placed the school at Clawson Street and Locust Avenue, named the assistant to the principal in charge as Miriam F. Selby, and counted 18 classrooms for grades K to 8B. On January 21, 1938, the Bureau of Buildings of the Department of Housing and Buildings gave approval to add three floors and a roof to create a school for 1,600 persons. The 1940 directory provided the same address and assistant to the principal in charge, but counted 29 classrooms for grades K to 8B. In February 2001, P.S. 41 celebrated its seventy-fifth anniversary. Mary Lemongino Lugongo, who attended the school in 1926, also attended the celebration, as did a representative from the office of Councilman James Oddo. Borough President Guy V. Molinari sent a proclamation declaring "P.S. 41 Seventy-fifth Anniversary Day." Governor George Pataki sent congratulations, the Parent-Teacher Association presented the school with a plaque, and Assemblyman Robert Strainere presented the school with a citation from the State Assembly. The principal for P.S. 41 in 2001 was Ms. Mary Muardas.

P.S. 42 began on a 520' x 200' block bounded by Richmond Avenue, Augusta Avenue, Wainwright Avenue and Genessee Avenue (Block 5605/1) in Eltingville, acquired on June 16, 1924. Architect A.G. Paletta designed an addition to the school. The 1930 directory placed the school on Richmond and Augusta Avenues in Eltingville, named Jacob Flatow the principal, and counted 13 classrooms for grades K to 8B. The 1940 directory gave the same address, named William G. Van Velsen as teacher in charge, and counted twelve classrooms for grades 1A to 8B. In 2001, the principal was Mr. Arthur J. Hecht.

P.S. 42 is an annex at 25 August Avenue (Block 5605/1) that houses grades 1 and 2.

P.S. 43 stood on Castleton Avenue. The 1930 directory placed the school in Tompkinsville, named Julia V. O'Connell as the teacher in charge, and counted two classrooms for grades 1A to 3B. The 1940 directory placed the school in Saint George, identified it as an annex to P.S. 17, and counted two classrooms but did not note the grades served.

P.S. 44 began on 80 Maple Parkway in Mariner's Harbor in 1927 as a four-story (with basement) 26-room brick building on a 120,679 square foot site. The

Public School 47, Carleton Boulevard near Rossville Avenue, Huguenot, May, 19, 1938.
Source: New York City Board of Education Archives, Teachers College, Columbia University.

school was named for Judge Thomas Brown, who lived in Port Richmond until his death in 1938. The 1930 directory placed the school from south of Walloon Street to Union Avenue, identified P.S. 23 and P.S. 24 as annexes, named J. Herbert Hoyt as principal, and counted 26 classrooms for grades K to 8B. The 1940 directory gave the same address, named Loretta L. Hanrahan as assistant to the principal in charge, and counted 28 classrooms for the same grades. Albert F. Quinn served as principal from 1976 to 1999 (22 years). In 2001, the principal was Ms. Doreen Gardner.

P.S. 45 was constructed in the late 1920s and was named for the tenth president of the United States, John Tyler, who, with his wife Julia Gardiner Tyler, vacationed from their Virginia plantation at Mrs. Tyler's mother's home, a local landmark in West Brighton. The 1930 directory placed the school on Morrison Avenue from Lawrence Avenue to Davis Avenue in West Brighton, named Alva E. Forssell as principal, and counted 16 classrooms for grades K to 8B. Additions were made in the decade of the 1930s. The 1940 directory gave the same address and principal but counted 36 classrooms for the same grades. In 2001, the school's address was

58 Lawrence Avenue in West Brighton, 10311 (Block 276/7) and the principal was Ms. Joyce Fonollosa.

P.S. 46 is on a site at Parkinson Avenue and Old Town Road acquired by the City of New York on June 26, 1928. The school is named for former Borough President Albert V. Maniscalco, an advocate of school building during whose tenure 24 schools were erected. The 1930 directory placed the school in South Beach, identified it as an annex to P.S. 39, named no principal, and counted 11 classrooms for grades K to 8B. The 1940 directory named Mrs. Anna V. Curren teacher in charge and counted the same classrooms and grades. The principal in 2001 was Mr. Joseph L. Cugini.

P.S. 46 appeared in the 1930 directory with an address of Carleton Boulevard near Rossville Avenue in Huguenot, identified as an annex to P.S. 3. It had no principal, and two classrooms for grades 1A to 4A. The site and the building were surrendered to the Board of Estimate on June 28, 1939. The building has been demolished.

P.S. 47 stands on land on the east side of Targee Street north of Venice Street, acquired April 21, 1930. The school was named for William G. Willcox, a Livingston

404

resident and the first Board of Education president from Staten Island, who died in 1923. His wife, Mary Otis Gay Willcox, was the daughter of Sidney Gay, an antislavery editor and an associate of Horace Greeley. Their home, at 113–115 Davis Avenue, a reputed underground railroad station, was demolished in 2001. The 1930 directory listed the school as under construction at Targee Street, Venice Street and Maple Street. The 1940 directory placed the school in Stapleton, named Mary E. Donovan the teacher in charge, and counted 11 classrooms for grades K to 8B. The principal in 2001 was Mr. Angelo Iacono.

P.S. 50 stands at 200 Adelaide Avenue (formerly Brook Avenue) in Oakwood in the 10306 Zip Code (Block 4664/360). This school was named for a former assistant superintendent of Staten Island schools. Its architect, Albert Melnicker, recalled "P.S. 50 was designed by my office in association with Kenneth Milnes, in the 1950s. The school was built with a budget. The polychrome map of the world in the lobby was an item I designed as an educational feature. This was accomplished after a struggle with the Board of Education as to what constitutes art." (Albert Melnicker to

Richard Dickenson, April 10, 1996, personal communication.) The principal in 2001 was Mr. Joseph Agnese.

P.S. 52 stands at 450 Buel Avenue, Dongan Hills, in the 10305 Zip Code (Block 3706/1), on lot acquired January 2, 1963, as vacant land. It is named for John C. Thompson, born in 1807, who was a community leader and developer of Grant City (named in honor of General Ulysses S. Grant). He was the grandfather of William Thompson Davis, for whom P.S. 31 is named. In 2001, Evelyn Mastroanni was interim acting principal.

P.S. 53 stands at 330 Durant Avenue in Bay Terrace in the 10308 Zip Code (Block 5106/1). The Art Commission of the City of New York approved the design for P.S. 53 on September 14, 1964. It was described as "a new three story building located at the high end of large, steeply sloping site," with an element of "reinforced concrete faced with gray cast-stone panels and cherry red brick." The architects were Belfatto and Pavarini of 235 East 42nd Street in Manhattan. On April 22, 1965, the Art Commission approved a design for a marble bas-relief mosaic mural by the artist Lumen M. Winter titled "The Sun" for the auditorium lobby. The mural included panels representing

Aquehonga Indians; the Billopp House of 1668; Music, Art and Science; the sun; the world; the Verrazano Bridge; and the Dutch and the British. The principal in 2001 was Mr. Louis Anarumo.

P.S. 54 stands on property at 1060 Willowbrook Road in Willowbrook in the 10314 Zip code (Block 1987/104) that the City of New York purchased on December 19, 1968. It was named for Charles W. Leng, a beetle specialist who worked closely with William T. Davis writing various books and articles on Staten Island history, including five volumes of *Staten Island and Its People*. The principal in 2001 was Mr. Paul Choset.

P.S. 55 stands on land at 54 Osborne Street in Eltingville in

the 10312 Zip Code (Block 5336/1) the title for which was vested on December 17, 1962. It is named for Henry Martin Boehm (June 13, 1918-March 26, 1862), son of the Reverend Henry Boehm, and a Staten Island schoolmaster and diarist. Father and son are buried in the cemetery of Old Woodrow Church. The principal of P.S. 54 in 2001 was Ms. Kathleen Schultz.

P.S. 56 stands at 250 Kramer Street. Designed by the firm of Mitchell/Giurgola, Architects, it is named for Louis DeSario, a former Staten Island School Superintendent and representative to the New York City Board of Education, who died in 1995 at the age of 64. Opened on September 9, 1998, it was the first elementary

Curtis High School, 105 Hamilton Avenue at Saint Mark's Place, New Brighton, May 28, 1921. Source: New York City Board of Education Archives, Teachers College, Columbia University.

school erected on Staten Island in thirteen years and soon ran about fifty students over its 900-seat capacity. The School Construction Authority claimed it was finished six months earlier than planned and under the $32.85 million budget set for it. Reportedly, Native American artifacts on the site were turned over to American Indian representatives, some of whom were at the opening ceremony. (*Staten Island Advance*, September 10, 1998.) The first principal was Mrs. Alice Singletary, who retired. In 2001, the principal was Ms. Gloria Ambio.

P.S. 57 stands on 140 Palma Drive in Clifton in the 10304 Zip Code (Block 2888/40). Title was vested on November 26, 1972, and a site addition was made in fiscal year 1974–1975. The school was named for Hubert H. Humphrey, former senator from Minnesota and vice president under President Lyndon B. Johnson. In 2001, the principal was Ms. Emma Della Rocca.

P.S. 60 stands at 55 Merrill Avenue in Graniteville in the 10314 Zip Code (Block 1580/44). Title was vested in the vacant land on December 17, 1969. The school was named for Alice Austen, Staten Island's most famous photographer. The interim acting principal for 2001 was Mr. Richard Torricelli.

P.S. 69 stands at 144 Keating Place in New Springville in the 10314 Zip Code (Block 2366/73). It was built in 1975, and named for a Staten Island landowner (founder of Tompkinsville), former governor of New York and former vice president of the United States. In 2001 the interim acting principal was Ms. Jacqueline Barbagallo.

P.S. 80 stands at 715 Ocean Terrace in the 10301 Zip Code. It is also known as the Petrides Educational Complex. It was named for Michael J. Petrides, an educator and former Staten Island representative to the New York City Board of Education, who died in 1994. In 2001, the principal was Mr. Michael Davino.

P.S. 363 is also known as P.S. 40, the Robert Richard Randall School, *q.v.* Its principal in 1999 was Michael Zangwill.

Public schools, high school (grades 9–12)

Concord, 109 Rhine Avenue, Concord (Block 2885/1). The building was erected in 1894, with additions in 1905. Currently, Concord is an alternative high school. It grew out of a small retrieval program housed in McKee High School that moved into Concord, or old P.S. 12, about 1979. Its mission is to serve Staten Island and Brooklyn high school students unable to function in traditional comprehensive high schools, a kind of last effort at schooling before the students, many of whom have arrest records, difficulties with their parents, or chronic behavior problems that lead to suspensions, drop out of education completely or attempt a G.E.D. program. (*Staten Island Advance*, April 17, 1994, G28, and July 23, 2000, A10.) In 1999, the school graduated forty seniors; that year principal Michael Mirakian left, after sixteen years at the school. (*Staten Island Advance*, June 26, 1999, A9.) The principal in 2001 was Ms. Joan P. Kaufman.

Curtis, 105 Hamilton Avenue (corner with Saint Mark's Place), Saint George 10301 (Block 22/1). The building was designed by Charles B.J.

Snyder. Originally named Richmond Borough High School, the name was changed to Curtis High School on December 23, 1903 (Board of Education Minutes, December 12, 1903, 3440.) Also, originally the building was to go between Stuyvesant Place, Wall Street and Jay Street in Saint George, but the location was changed to Hamilton Avenue and the work started anew. The cornerstone was laid December 4, 1902, and the school first occupied February 11, 1904. It was Staten Island's first secondary school building. (Dolkart, 274). Additions to the school were made twice in the 1920s, in 1922 and 1925. Also during that decade, the school received two lobby murals, titled *The Quest for Knowledge*, painted by Florence

New Dorp High School, Clawson Street between Lindbergh Avenue and 10th Street, New Dorp, 1937. Source: New York City Board of Education Archives, Teachers College, Columbia University.

Lundborg (1871–1949) and presented to the school on its twenty-fifth anniversary, in 1927. In 1929, the alumni association dedicated the murals in honor of students who lost their lives in World War I. A further addition was made to the school in 1937. It is a zoned or neighborhood high school that also accepts nonminorities living elsewhere on Staten Island. (*Staten Island Advance*, April 17, 1994, G28.) In 1998, principal Edward Q. Seto requested the alumni association's help in restoring the murals. The association, under the leadership of Anne V. McAuliffe, agreed. The Board of Education selected Swiss-Italian Luca Bonetti as conservator of the murals. The renovated murals were rededicated Sunday, December 6, 1998. (*Staten Island Advance* December 7, 1998, and brochure entitled *The Quest for Knowledge*.) On June 25, 1999, Curtis graduated 341 seniors at a ceremony at Andy Barberi Memorial Field, during a commencement at which New York City Comptroller Alan G. Hevesi, valedictorian Chin Ho Cheng and salutatorian Sandy Tan spoke. (*Staten Island Advance*, June 26, 1999, A11.) The principal in 2001 was Mr. Edward Q. Seto.

Hungerford, 155 Tompkins Avenue in Clifton, provides workshop and basic job skills for special education students. (*Staten Island Advance*, April 17, 1994, G28.) The principal in 2001 was Dr. Mary McInerney.

McKee Vocational High School, 290 Saint Mark's Place

Port Richmond High School, 85 Saint Joseph Avenue, Port Richmond, May 1, 1931. Source: New York City Board of Education Archives, Teachers College, Columbia University.

(Top) Stapleton High School, 1902. Rear: Mr. Simms. Middle row: students surnamed Baeszler, Molaney and Halterman. Front row: Students surnamed Hartman, Gannon and Simms. Source: Staten Island Historical Society. (Middle) Mount Saint Michael, Greenridge, sometime between 1905 and 1925. Photograph by W.J. Grimshaw. Source: Staten Island Historical Society. (Bottom) Saint Peter's School and Church, 200 Clinton Avenue, New Brighton, no date. Image by W.J. Grimshaw. Source: Staten Island Historical Society.

(corner of Wall Street; Block 19/4) is Staten Island's only vocational high school. Previously the Staten Island Continuation and Vocational School, it is open to qualified students from all of

New York City. (*Staten Island Advance*, April 17, 1994, G28.) It has a selective admission process. The school seats 1,094 and has a current enrollment of 636. The principal in 2001 was Ms. Beverly Garcia-Anderson.

New Dorp received its name on December 11, 1935. (Board of Education minutes, December 11, 1935.) The original building, between Clawson Street, Lindberg Street and 10th Street, opened in September 1936. It had a capacity of 1,608 students and an actual enrollment of 850. In 1982, the school moved to its present building on New Dorp Lane near Miller Field, and its former building became the Staten Island Technical High School. On Thursday, April 25, 1996, Staten Island Borough Historian Richard Dickenson helped the school start its sixtieth anniversary celebration. (*Staten Island Advance*, April 26, 1996, A11.) Com-mencement exercises on June 25, 1999, were held at the Sal Somma Field, with speakers Thomas Lavino, Valedictorian, former principal Elizabeth A. Sciabarra and principal Deirdra DeAngelis. (*Staten Island Advance*, June 26, 1999, A10.) In 2001, Ms. DeAngelis was interim acting principal.

Port Richmond, 85 Saint Joseph Avenue (near Innis

410

Avenue; Block 122/1) opened on September 12, 1927 in a building with a capacity for 1,158 people, students, faculty and administrative staff. (Board of Education Minutes November 9, 1927, 2472.) An addition opened on September 9, 1940, added room for another 876. (Minutes of the Board of Education October 9, 1940, 1593.) Construction on a three-story wing began in July 1991, but was still unfinished in 1992, by which point 2,000 people were crammed into a school meant for 1,750. The 1999 commencement was held at the Spiro Sports Center at Wagner College on Grymes Hill. Speakers included Principal Robert J. Graham, U.S. Senator Charles E. Schumer and Valedictorian Danielle Sessa. (*Staten Island Advance*, June 26, 1999, A10.) The principal for 2001 was Mr. Graham.

Saint George School, 450 Saint Mark's Place (Block 16/7) is part of the Board of Education's auxiliary services for high school, offering adults and teens opportunities to earn high school diplomas or general equivalency degrees.

Staten Island Technical, 485 Clawson Street in the 10306 Zip Code (Block 424/1), is open to qualified New York City residents. It offers a curriculum stressing math, science, and the Russian

(Top) Saint Sylvester parochial school, 884 Targee Street near Clove Road, Concord, sometime between 1905 and 1915. Photograph by W.J. Grimshaw. Source: Staten Island Historical Society. (Middle) Castleton Corners Children's Day Nursery, also known as Kingsland Cottage, no date. Source: Staten Island Historical Society.
(Bottom) Castleton Corners Children's Day Nursery, no date. Source: Staten Island Historical Society.

language. Every student must take four years of Russian, and Staten Island Technical is known for its Russian exchange program. (*Staten Island Advance*, April 17, 1994, G28.) The school held its twelfth commencement on June 25, 1999 at Michael J. Petrides Educational Complex in Sunnyside. The 165 graduates heard Councilman Stephen Fiala, Valedictorian Joseph Marrone, Principal Eleanor K. O'Connor, and Dr. Noel N. Kriftcher, former Brooklyn and Staten Island School (BASIS) Superintendent and director of the David Packard Center at Polytechnic University. (*Staten Island Advance*, June 25, 1999, A8.) Ms. O'Connor was still principal in 2001.

Susan E. Wagner is on 50 Brielle Avenue and 1200 Manor Road (Block 955). The 408 members of the Class of 1999 held their commencement exercises at the Susan Wagner football field. Speakers included Principal Michael Tobin and Valedictorian Jordana Beren. (*Staten Island Advance*, June 25, 1999, A8.)

Tottenville High School opened September 14, 1936, in a building at Yetman Avenue and Academy Place, with a capacity of 1,068. (Minutes of the Board of Education, October 14, 1936, 1876.) Currently, the school is at 100 Luten Avenue (corner of Deisius Street; Block 6613/1) in the 10312 Zip Code. The current

Staten Island Children's Services, Richmond, sewing class, January 11, 1923. Source: New York City Board of Education Archives, Teachers College, Columbia University.

building is a neighborhood school that accepts minorities from all parts of the Island. More than 700 seniors graduated on June 25, 1999, for which the speakers were Principal Michael Marotta, Council-man Stephen J. Fiala and Valedictorian Joanna Paladino. That year, Mr. Marotta retired, after six years at Tottenville High School and 36 years in education. (*Staten Island Advance*, June 26, 1999, A9.) John Tuminaro replaced Mr. Marotta, effective June 16, 2000. (*Staten Island Advance*, July 8, 2000, A4.)

South Richmond High School is located at 6581 Hylan Boulevard (Block 6613/1). Title was vested in the property on January 23, 1967. The principal in 2001 was Mr. Stephen F. DiCarlo.

public schools, intermediate (grades 6–8)

I.S. 2, 333 Midland Avenue between Boundary Avenue and Bedford Avenue (Block 3696/100), was named for George L. Egbert, Tompkinsville business-man, former treasurer of the Chamber of Commerce and member of local School Board No. 53, who died in 1957 at age 95. The principal in 2001 was Mr. Allan Newman.

I.S. 7, Huguenot Avenue 10312 (Block 6544/1) was on May 26, 1960, and again on June 14, 1965, named in honor of Elias Bernstein, Jr., a school board appointee who died in 1950. The interim acting principal in 2001 was Mr. Steve Cuccia.

I.S. 24, 225 Cleveland Avenue (Block 5151/108) in

J.B. King Plaster Mill, later the Windsor Plaster Mills and still later the U.S. Gypsum Company, Richmond Terrace, New Brighton, 1895. Source: Staten Island Historical Society.

Great Kills, was named for Myra S. Barnes, the civic leader and advocate for new and improved schools who died in 1962. Title was vested in the school on May 4, 1965. The principal in 2001 was Mr. Richard M. Spisto.

I.S. 27, 11 Clove Lakes Place (Block 308/1) was, on April 28, 1960, named in honor of Anning S. Prall. Mr. Prall served three terms as president of New York City's Board of Education in 1919, 1920 and 1921, one term as a member of the House of Representatives in 1923 and also as first president of the Federal Communications Commission (FCC).

Title was vested in the property for a playground site on April 5, 1965. The principal in 2001 was Mr. Joseph Martucci.

I.S. 34, 528 Academy Place (Block 7894/1) is named for the Totten family. The principal in 2001 was Mr. Jeffrey Preston.

I.S. 49, 101 Warren Street (Block 556/80) was named for Bertha A. Dreyfus, wife of Dr. Louis Dreyfus. Mrs. Dreyfus died in 1943 at the age of 86. Title for the site was vested on April 14, 1959, on the south side of Hill Street and east side of Warren Street, at which point the site contained nine lots with eight

Planter's Hotel, 368 Bay Street at Grant Street, Tompkinsville, no date. Source: Staten Island Historical Society.

414

frame houses, all of which were demolished. The principal in 2001 was Mr. Marc Scher.

I.S. 51, 20 Houston Street (Block 1478/500) is named for Edwin Markham (1852–1940), who was a California teacher, school principal and school superintendent who moved to New York in 1899, where he received sensational acclaim for his book of social-protest verse, *The Man with a Hoe and Other Poems*. The principal in 2001 was Mr. Arnold Raffone.

I.S. 61, 445 Castleton Avenue (Block 100/100), was named for William Alfred Morris. A black businessman who owned a moving company, Mr. Morris was a community leader who participated in the founding of the Shiloh African Methodist Episcopal Church after World War I and the local chapter of the National Association for the Advancement of Colored People in 1925. One of his daughters, Evelyn Morris King, is a leading black historian of Staten Island. In 1995, the school qualified for poverty funds such as free lunches and Aid to Families with Dependent Children, as 66 percent of the students were considered to be living in poverty. (*Staten Island Advance*, August 3, 1995.) In 2001, the principal was Mr. Richard Gallo.

I.S. 73, 33 Ferndale Avenue (Block 2364/1) is named for Rocco Laurie, a decorated police officer slain in the line of duty. In 2001, the principal was Mr. Peter Macellari.

I.S. 75, 455 Huguenot Avenue (Block 6050/2) is named for Frank D. Paulo, a judge of the surrogate court, who died in 1981. The principal in 2001 was Ms. Julie El Saieh-Wolf.

public stocks, 50

Purdy's Hotel, 27

This building stood at 11 Purdy Place in Prince's Bay.

Q

Quarantine, 55, 71–72, 78, 100, 102, 128, 212

The quarantine was established by the State Legislature in 1799 on 30 acres of land in Tompkinsville, which had been part of the Duxbury Glebe. The Glebe was owned by Saint Andrew's Church due to an "extensive and valuable tract of land" bequeathed by Ellis Duxbury, in 1718, to the Rector of St. Andrew's Church. (E.H.; P. Clute, 1877, 263.)

Quarantine Hospital, 33, 100, 128

This building stands at Bay Street and Nautilus Street in Rosebank, on the site of a colonial ferry that crossed to Long Island. The Quarantine Station was evacuated in 1971, with operations shift-

ed to lower Manhattan. (E.H.)
quartermaster general, 87
Queen Anne, 23
Queen's Rangers, 41

R

railroads, 78–80
Randall, (Captain) Robert Richard, 73, 130
  P.S. 40 was named The Robert Richard Randall. Randall Manor is a real estate development on property that was once part of Sailors' Snug Harbor. *See also* Sailors' Snug Harbor. (E.H.)
Randall, John Sr., 172
Randall Manor, 94, 174
Randall Memorial Church, 106, 130
Rando Dock, Inc., 198, 230
rangers, 44
Ranlett, William H., 63
Raritan Bay, 1, 42, 163, 179, 195, 214
Raritan River, 118
Raritans, 3, 33
Ravenhurst, 101, 173
Rebel Church, 24
Recreation House (Recreation Hall), 73
Red Cross, 166, 244
  This building stands at 190 Van Duzer Street (Block 506/1). On May 29, 1947, the American National Red Cross recorded the purchase of this seven-room-and-bath building from the Staten Island Diet Kitchen Association for $5,000. It was situated on a 25'x100' lot at the southwest corner of Van Duzer and Grant Streets in Tompkinsville. Up until then, the Staten Island Chapter of the Red Cross had been situated at 42 Richmond Terrace. The chapter was incorporated May 2, 1917, as the Richmond County Chapter. The president signing the certificate for the Central Committee was Woodrow Wilson(!).
  The Board Members of the Staten Island Chapter of the American Red Cross as of 1948 were Hon. Edward G. Baker, Mrs. Fred Brenner, Mrs. Malcolm B. Carroll, Mr. Edward Crowe, Mrs. Maxwell Ehrlich, Mr. Arthur Foley, Miss Ethel G. Fowler, Mrs. Adolph Frankel, Mrs. Bertram Garbe, Mrs. Frank Gendreau, Mr. Joseph Holszka, Miss Ellen Horrmann, Miss M. Adelaide Irving, Mr. Carl Isaacs, Mr. Manuel J. Johnson, Mr. Clarence B. Kavanagh, Mrs. Eileen McGowan, Miss Ann McWilliams, Mrs. Paul H. Downing, Mrs. C.J.R. Meinert, Mrs. Rudolph Merrell, Mrs. Eduard C. Meurer, Mr. Ernest Miller, Mrs. Harold J. O'Connell, Mrs. M.I. Pitou, Mrs. William Pott, Mrs. Arnold C. Pouch, Mrs. Herbert G. Randell, Mrs. William Seuberth, Mrs. Alfred Shriver, Miss Dorothy V. Smith, Mrs. Robert C. Stanley, Mrs. Albert J. Stem, Mr. Samuel A. Turvey, Mr. Aquila N. Volkhardt, and Mr. L. W. Widdecombe.
Reed, Mrs., 75

Hylan Boulevard, Grasmere (Blocks 3215/1, 8, 16). This school is under the auspices of the Institute of the Sisters of Saint Dorothy. It was incorporated December 13, 1919 for the education and moral and mental improvement of young boys and girls, and for religious missionary work. Those who signed the incorporation papers were Archbishop (later Cardinal) Patrick Joseph Hayes (1867–1939), Irene B. Cox, Gertrude V. Kelly, Mary J. Hardy, and George J. Gillespie, all of different Manhattan residences. However, the school received substantial support from Staten Island residents as well. On June 30, 1932, the sisters acquired from Eliza V. Goggi Lot 16, a 5-acre parcel, on which to build an elementary school. In his will, the Reverend Joseph A. Catoggio, pastor of the Church of the Assumption on Webster Avenue in New Brighton, bequeathed the sisters three vacant lots on Old Town Road. On February 5, 1951, South Atlantic Realty conveyed a 300' x 744' parcel (Lot 1, Block 3215) to the Sisters of Saint Dorothy. In 1999, the principal of the academy was Sister Sharon McCarthy.

Blessed Sacrament Parochial School stands at 840 Blessed Sacrament Place in West Brighton (Block 234/1). The church was incorporated in 1910, and

acquired its property at about that same time. The principal in 1999 was Sister Ann McLaughlin.

Christian High School of Staten Island stands at 900 Richmond Road in Concord in the 10304 ZIP Code (Block 3168/9). Founded in 1989, the school celebrated its tenth anniversary in 1999 with a graduation class of fourteen seniors. The principal that year was Eugene Rella. (*Staten Island Advance*, June 27, 1999.)

Gateway Academy stands at 200 Boscombe Avenue (Block 7577/3).

Holy Child School of Religion stands at 4747 Amboy Road (Block 6205/90). The school was incorporated May 17, 1966. Those signing the incorporation papers were Francis Cardinal Spellman, Archbishop of New York; John J. Maguire, Vicar General of the Archdiocese of New York; the Reverend Francis M. Brennan, rector of the Church of the Holy Child, then at 3989 Richmond Avenue; lay trustees Joseph M. McAuliffe and Patrick M. Plover. The school opened during the 1970–1971 school year.

Holy Rosary School stands at 180 Jerome Avenue in South Beach (Blocks 3247/1, 3270/1). Holy Rosary Church was incorporated on October 1, 1927; its address is 203 Sand Lane. The

City of New York conveyed this lot, 120'x 558', to Holy Rosary Church on August 8, 1954. The original 8-classroom building was situated on a 200' x 558' irregular shaped lot, which also contained a convent. In 1964, a 2-classroom extension to the 2-story building was being constructed. In 1999, the principal was Diane R. Murphy.

Jewish Foundation School for grades one to eight stands at 400 Caswell Avenue in Westerleigh in the 10314 ZIP Code (Block 1511/200). The corporation also operates the Early Learning Center, 835 Forest Hill Road. The schools were founded by the Staten Island Board of Jewish Education, a voluntary Hebrew Association incorporated on March 12, 1954. The incorporators were Irving Cohen, Sidney Jacobi, Samuel I. Gross, Zalme Luloff, Harold W. Cohen, Max Levy, Samuel Jaeger, Louis R. Miller and Rueben E. Gross. In 1999, the school's principal and dean was Rabbi Dr. Richard Ehrlich.

Monsignor Farrell High School for grades nine through twelve stands at 2900 Amboy Road in Oakwood Heights (Block 1257/1, 12). The school was named for the Right Reverend Monsignor Joseph Farrell, Pastor of St. Peter's Church in Saint George. The building housing

this school has been described as a sophisticated California modern type (Willensky, 849.) The school opened Sunday, June 2, 1963, on which date there was a solemn blessing and dedication. Francis Cardinal Spellman, Archbishop of New York, officiated. Monsignor John J. Considine, Supervising Principal of Farrell High School, gave welcoming remarks. Borough President Albert V. Maniscalco gave greetings. The principal in 1999 was the Reverend Emmet Nevin. Currently, the school enrolls 1,200 boys.

Moore Catholic High for grades nine through twelve stands at 100 Merrill Avenue in Graniteville (Block 2236/1). The Church of Our Lady of Pity, which was incorporated November 22, 1923, acquired the three acres of property from the City of New York on September 11, 1956. The principal in 1999 was Douglas McManus. The school enrolls 800 youth of both sexes.

Mount Loretto stands at 6581 Hylan Boulevard (Block 7664/1, and six other lots); this complex also houses annexes to P. S. 1 and P.S. 3. More formally known as "Mission of the Immaculate Virgin for the Protection of Homeless and Destitute Children," the property sprawls between Amboy Road and Hylan Boulevard and from Sharott

Avenue to Richard Avenue. The original seven trustees at the incorporation, dated May 23, 1877 were: Mathew Leavy, Bernard Reilly, James E. Dougherty, William D. Reilly, James O'Neill, Hugh O'Donnell and John C. Drumgoole. The incorporation was executed in the City and County of New York (*i.e.*, Manhattan) and filed on June 8, 1877. The object of their formation was "To provide for the support and protection of Homeless and Destitute children in the City of New York." A 1964 affidavit by Monsignor Henry J. Vier, Treasurer, was issued from the Mission's principal business office at 381 Lafayette Street in Manhattan. It reported that the property consisted of 645 acres, improved by a Convent and Administration Building; a boys elementary school (erected at a total cost of approximately $483,000) and a vocational school (costing approximately $1,150,000). There had recently been completed an infirmary and three staff buildings for the residence of childcare workers. In addition there were dormitories, classrooms, three gymnasiums, laundries and other structures. The institution was supported by Child Care funds from the City of New York, Nassau County, Suffolk County, Westchester County, Catholic Committee for Refugees,

Catholic Welfare Bureau and private charges. The Mission also participated in the New York State School Lunch Program. In 1964, the President of the corporate Trustees of the Mission was His Eminence, Francis Cardinal Spellman.

New Dorp Christian Academy stands on 259 Rose Avenue (Block 4220/29) in New Dorp. It is affiliated with the New Dorp Baptist Church, incorporated on July 10, 1907. Construction of the church building, at the east corner of Rose Ave. and 10th St., began on May 21, 1928. David J. and Frances Tysen, grantors of the property parcel included a covenant provision that indicated that they were in favor of Prohibition and against pollution. The church's Christian Education Building, constructed in 1965 on a parcel acquired in 1946 from Rosena Thompson of Brooklyn. The principal in 1999 was Rev. Dr. John Gueli.

Notre Dame Academy stands at 134 Howard Avenue, Grymes Hill 10301 (Block 589/63). The Board of Regents granted a Provisional Charter of incorporation to Academy of Our Lady of the Blessed Sacrament of Staten Island, New York on September 28, 1922. The purpose was to conduct a school on the elementary and secondary levels as prescribed by the diocesan and state syllabi, the Board of Regents of the State of New York and the Middle States Association of Colleges and Secondary Schools. An elementary and secondary school was to be located at 76 Howard Avenue with the incorporators serving for its first board of trustees. The incorporators included Josephine C. Schlachter, Margaret Guilfoile, Margaret Mahaney, Maud Barron and Sarah Gillis. The property was acquired on December 7, 1925. An amended charter, granted by the Board of Regents on December 14, 1950, accepted the change of name to Notre Dame Academy of Staten Island, Inc. which had been made on December 10, 1946. On August 26, 1921, Heyn Securities Corporation sold Lot 65 to the Sisters of the Congregation of Notre Dame de Montreal, Saint Joseph's Seminary. On December 27, 1922, the Notre Dame Sisters sold the same lot to the Academy of Our Lady of the Blessed Sacrament of Staten Island. The lot became part of the convent. A 2-1/2 story stucco building and a garage were erected on it. The building was used as a children's dormitory and recreation building. Currently, the school offers classes from prekindergarten through the eighth grade. The principal in 1999 was Sister Rose Mary Galligan.

The Notre Dame College of Staten Island stands at 300 Howard Avenue, Grymes Hill (Block 593/367). The institution was incorporated on May 18, 1933, with a provisional charter for a four-year liberal arts college for women. Incorpora-tors were: Michael J. Lavelle, Catherine Doyle, Sarah Gillis, Helen Flynn, Eleanor Coghlin, Annie Bell and Lawrence W. Widdecombe. By 1934, the college had assembled a number of tax lots. In 1939, when he became archbishop of New York, Francis (later Cardinal) Spellman also became president of Notre Dame College; Sister Egbert served as college dean. On January 19, 1940, an absolute charter was granted.

Our Lady Help of Christians School stands at 23 Summit Street and Yetman Avenue in Tottenville (Block 7896/48). The Rev. John D. Verdon, John P. MacEvoy and William J. Dempsey, trustees, incorporated the Roman Catholic Church of Our Lady Help of Christians in 1898. The parish acquired property for the school over a period stretching between 1090 to 1945. The school erected a 125' x 124' two-story brick parochial school building on the 159' x 150' property on November 12, 1956. The first floor had four classrooms, a kitchen and assembly room; the second floor also had 4 classrooms, with two offices, one for the principal and one for the school nurse. There was also a basement for the boiler room and storage. The principal in 1999 was Nancy Lucas.

Our Lady of Good Counsel School stands at 43 Austin Place in Tompkinsville (Block 580/34). The parish was incorporated in 1898, and the property acquired on June 24, 1899. The parish is staffed by fathers from the Order of Saint Augustine, and originally the fathers operated a college and seminary preparatory school for young men, Augustinian Academy, in conjunction with the parish. The parochial school opened in 1923. It was staffed by Sisters, Servants of the Immaculate Heart of Mary, from its founding until 1927, and by the Sisters of Charity of Saint Vincent de Paul, Halifax from 1927 to 1973. Currently, the school is staffed by laity, and offers grades from kindergarten to the eighth grade. The principal in 1999 was Frances Santangelo.

Our Lady Queen of Peace Church School stands at 21 Steele Avenue in New Dorp (Block 3626/13). The Church of Our Lady Queen of Peace, New Dorp, New York, was incorporat-ed on October 20, 1922. The incorporators were Patrick Joseph (later Cardinal) Hayes, Archbishop of New York; Vicar General Joseph F. Mooney; Queen of Peace rector John J. Hopkins; and lay trustees John T. McGovern and Joseph P. O'Reilly. The church acquired the 22,500-square foot property for the school on July 29, 1955. On it was built a two-story parochial school and hall, consisting of sixteen rooms. The principal in 1999 was Deborah Macula.

Our Lady Star of the Sea School stands on Amboy Road in Huguenot (Block 6332/6). A Certificate of Incorporation for the Church of Our Lady Star of the Sea in Huguenot Park was filed in the office of Livingston Bostwick, Richmond County Clerk, on October 5, 1916. The incorporators were John Murphy (later Cardinal) Farley, Archbishop of New York; Vicar General Joseph H. Mooney; Star of the Sea rector James F. Malloy; and lay trustees James McLaughlin and James White. The principal in 1999 was Irma Cummings.

Rabbi Jacob Joseph School for Boys, also known as Yeshiva Merkaz Hatorah, stands at 3495 Richmond Road, Richmond, 10304 (Block 2279/8). Incorporated in 1903, Rabbi Jacob Joseph School's purpose is to educate students of the Orthodox Jewish faith in religious and secular studies from elementary school and high school through post high school level. The limited charter issued to the school on May 21, 1903 by the University of the State of New York contained the names of the following incorporators: Samuel J. Andron, Jacob L. Andron, Are Simon, Nathan Chasan, Bertsch A. Lesser, Baruch Cohen, Abraham Meyers, Israel Miller, Salmon Tenenbam, Aaron Drusin, Samuel Burris and Jacob M. Leibner. A 200' x 225' property was acquired from Alvaro M. and Dorothy E. Sanchez, on July 8, 1976. The school currently enrolls youngsters from the nursery years through the eighth grade. Its principal dean in 1999 was Rabbi Nochem Kaplan.

Rabbi Jacob Joseph School for Girls also known as Yeshiva Merkaz Hatorah, stands at 400 Caswell Avenue in Westerleigh. It, too, serves youngsters from the nursery years through the eighth grade. Its principal/director in 1999 was Shulamith Klagsbrun.

Saint Adalbert's Parish Center stands at 337 Morningstar Road in Elm Park (Block 1136/63). Before the turn of the twentieth century, Polish laborers and their families who lived on Staten Island would travel to Manhattan each Sunday to worship in their native language at the Church of Saint Stanislaus. In 1897, Islander Stanislaus Jakubowski suggested creating a Polish parish on the Island. According to parish records, in 1901 John Mojecki donated four lots on John Street in Port Richmond for the church. The church was incorporated as the Polish Roman Catholic Church of Saint Adalbert on February 7, 1901. The incorporators were Michael Augustine Corrigan, Archbishop of New York; Vicar General John Murphy (later Cardinal) Farley; Saint Adalbert rector John A. Strzelcki; and lay trustees John Mojecki (donor of the four lots) and Peter Bolewicz. The church was named in honor of Saint Adalbert, a bishop of Prague, who was martyred in Poland in 997. The cornerstone of a church to replace the John Street one was laid in December 1901, and the church officially opened on May 3, 1903. The parish acquired more property in four transactions between 1907 and 1920. The school, at the current Morningstar Road location, was finished and in use for the term beginning in September 1960. The present church, a strikingly modern brick and glass building topped by an 85-foot cross, was dedicated in December 1968. (*Staten Island*

Advance, June 3, 2000, B1.) One of a number of radically modern Roman Catholic churches on Staten Island, this structure is dramatically sited to be seen by traffic on the Willowbrook Expressway, which it abuts. A more reserved façade greets those entering the church from the local street; and the interior, with its upswept ceiling and modern stained glass is the best feature of all. (Willensky, 820.) The principal of the parochial school in 1999 was Diane Hesterhagen.

Saint Ann's School stands at 125 Cromwell Avenue in Dongan Hills (Block 3318/1). It was incorporated on May 31, 1922 by Patrick Joseph (later Cardinal) Hayes, Archbishop of New York; Vicar General Joseph F. Mooney; Saint Ann rector Joseph A. Farrell; and two male lay trustees. Dongan Hills Realty sold the parish a 151' x 190' parcel for the shchool in 1932. Construction for a new nine-room elementary school began in 1954, with plans for a student population of 320. The school currently offers classes from kindergarten through the eighth grade. Its principal in 1999 was Michael Mazella.

Saint Charles Seminary stands at 209 Flagg Place on Todt Hill (Block 1891/1), which was built as the estate of Ernest Flagg. (Willensky, 842.) Its current owner is the Society of Saint Charles-Scalabrinians, an institute of Roman Catholic priests and brothers founded by Blessed Giovanni Battista Scalabrini (1839–1905) in 1887 to provide pastoral care to immigrants in transit and in their new homes. On April 5, 1941, in Massachusetts, the Scalabrinians incorporated a seminary "Promoting the greater glory of God by cultivating Christian perfection, and to render assistance to the Roman Catholic Bishops in the United States of America." The incorporators were the Rev. Nazareno Properzi, President; the Rev. Louis Toma, Treasurer; the Rev. John Peona, Secretary; and, as trustees, the Rev. Leonardo Quaglia, the Rev. Ugo Cavicchi, the Rev. Arnaldo Vanoli, the Rev. Flaminio Parenti, the Rev. Pietro Maschi and the Rev. Peter Gorret. On August 16, 1948, Betsy Melcher and Boyd E. Wilson, Executors of and Trustees under the Last Will and Testament and Codicil of Ernest Flagg and his widow, Margaret Elizabeth Flagg, sold the Flagg estate to the Scalabrinians for $65,000, and the Scalabrinians decided to put their seminary there. The Scalabrinians have since adopted other methods for training their seminarians. They divided the Flagg Estate between a section used for

424

meetings and special events and the Center for Migration Studies (CMS), incorporated in 1964 to collect and disseminate information on contemporary human international migration. CMS has been headed since 1976 by Executive Director Lydio F. Tomasi, Ph.D. For further information, *see* Silvano M. Tomasi, foreword to Alba I. Zizzamia, *A Vision Unfolding* (Staten Island: Center for Migration Studies, 1989.)

Saint Charles Borromeo Roman Catholic School stands at 200 Penn Avenue in Oakwood (Block 4279/1). Saint Charles was incorporated in 1960 at 214 Peter Avenue with the following officers: Terence Cardinal Cooke, President; James P. Mahoney, vice president; Robert J. Kelly, treasurer; and Raymond Perry and Joseph Nicita, trustees. The approximately 200' x 400' property for the two-story convent and school and one-story church was acquired on October 17, 1960. The school principal in 1999 was Sister Jeanine Conlon.

Saint Christopher's Parochial School stands at 15 Lisbon Place (Block 3576/23) Grant City. The Catholic parish sponsoring the school was incorporated in 1926. On July 17, 1957, it purchased, at public auction, old P.S. 33, which was a one-story wooden frame building on a 261' x 175' lot at 148 Midland Avenue. The church built its school on that lot, orienting it so that its address was on Lisbon Place. Saint Christopher's serves students from prekindergarten through the eighth grade. Its principal in 1999 was Catherine Mizzi-Gilli.

Saint Clare's Religious Education Center stands at 110 Nelson Avenue (Block 5244/lot 36) in Great Kills. The Church of Saint Clare was incorporated on October 9, 1925, by Patrick Joseph Cardinal Hayes, Archbishop of New York; Vicar General John J. Dunn; Saint Clare rector David O'Connor; and lay trustees Daniel J. Buckley and Angelo C. Scavallo. The property on which the parish house was erected was acquired on July 1, 1917. The parish house, a two-story house of twelve rooms, was the administration office of the parish church. On October 16, 1919 and again on August 23, 1923, the pastors of the Church of Saint Patrick took title to the property that was to become St. Clare's. It was intended to "erect a rectory, school and convent in connection with the church." Under the Rev. D. M. Dougherty, Pastor of Saint Clare, a site for the erection of a parochial school was designated in 1935. The principal in 1999 was Sister Rosemary Ward, P.V.B.M.

Saint John's Lutheran School stands at 224 Windsor Road, Castleton Corners 10314 (Block 707/243; the church is at 663 Manor Road.) Saint John's used a 2-1/2-story 24' x 36' frame building on Catherine Court for a parochial school from 1860 to September 1914. Thereafter, the church used the building for church societies and confirmation classes, and allowed the sexton to occupy the top floor rent-free. The church acquired its current school on June 12, 1952. The lot is 273' x 270'. The building is 50' x 116'. The building was constructed in 1952 and had fifteen rooms by early 1960, including four basement classrooms, four more classrooms, a library, teachers' lounge and two offices on the first floor, all for 42 children. In 1999, the principal was Richard Leischeidt.

Saint John's Villa Academy Elementary School stands at 57 Cleveland Place in Arrochar (Block 3089/50). This institution was incorporated on July 22, 1921 by the Sisters of Saint John. On August 22, 1922, the sisters acquired a 450' x 450' lot from Thomas Leopold Imbery. On June 15 and 22, 1956, certificates amending the purposes and powers of the Sisters of Saint John the Baptist were issued. The certificates outlined the sisters' mission

as follows: 1) spiritual and moral improvement, religious and literary purposes and settlement work; 2) imparting knowledge of the history, doctrines, good works and practices of the Roman Catholic Church; 3) establishing and maintaining Saint John's Villa Academy, a boarding school for children of Roman Catholic parentage; and 4) establishing and maintaining in Manhattan Our Lady of Loretto Day Nursery for children. Exemption records circa 1976 show an application for a building permit to erect an elementary school at this address. At that point, ownership of Saint John's was vested in Sister Ann Marie Damiani, Administrator. The principal of Saint John's in 1999 was Sister Rosaria Demaro.

Saint John's Villa Academy High School stands at 26 Landis Avenue in Arrochar (Block 3087/1). The Sisters of Saint John the Baptist, who operate this institution, were incorporated on July 22, 1921. They acquired this property on August 14, 1922. The University of the State of New York admitted Saint John's Villa Academy as a high school on February 11, 1938. On February 1, 1945, the sisters filed an amended certificate with the New York Secretary of State "To establish and maintain an old age home, and a boarding school for children under 12 years of age of Roman Catholic parentage." Records of 1958 show this to be a new Catholic private high school for girls, with headquarters located at Cleveland Place. In 1999, the principal was Sister Anne Dolores.

Saint Joseph Hill Academy stands at 850 Hylan Boulevard, Arrochar 10305 (Block 3095/21). The school has its roots in Saint Mary's Home for Working Girls, incorporated on September 17, 1923 by Olympia Bauer, Francesca Kovacsics, Elizabeth Chabay Agnes Arvay and Helen Ulimeyer, all of 205 Major Avenue, Arrochar Park, Staten Island. On September 29, 1923, the Reverend Charles A. Cassidy, pastor of Saint Peter's Church, conveyed the property to the Saint Mary's Home. The institution functioned as a school prior to its present incorporation, which happened on November 17, 1947, when the Congregation of the Daughters of Divine Charity were incorporated to conduct an elementary and high school known as Saint Joseph Hill Academy. The incorporators were Francis Joseph Cardinal Spellman, Archbishop of New York and Mary Margaret Gergely, Mary Myriam Kovach, Mary Amabilis Eslinger, Helen Philomena Terelmes, and Helen Gregory

Tobias (all of the women resided at Arrochar). The principal in 1999 was Sister M. Mercedes Sterlein, S.D.C.

Saint Joseph-by-the-Sea High School is in Huguenot. The Sisters of Charity built the school in the early 1960s as a private, Catholic, all-girls academy. The school went coeducational in the 1973–1974 school year. The school's statue of Saint Joseph is noteworthy. Robert Cushing sculpted the twelve-ton, eighteen-foot-high statue in 1882. In 1922, it was moved from Manhattan to Mount Loretto, and on February 4, 1999, to Saint Joseph-by-the-Sea.

Saint Joseph and Saint Thomas School stands on Maguire Avenue, Pleasant Plains 10309 (Block 6975/85). Saint Joseph's, then "at Rossville in the Town of Westfield, Richmond County," was incorporated on December 24, 1878. The incorporators filing with the Secretary of State at the City of Albany were John Cardinal McClosky, Archbishop of New York; Vicar General William Quinn; Saint Joseph's pastor Patrick Mahoney; and trustees Patrick McKern and John Mooney. The parish bought a 388' x 417' lot for its school at a City of New York public auction for $7,100. The school serves grades K through eight. The principal in 1999 was Theresa Simmonds.

Saint Mary of the Miraculous Medal School stands on 1124 Bay Street in Rosebank (Block 2847/86). The Roman Catholic Church of Saint Mary, "erected in the Village of Clifton." was incorporated on March 17, 1886, under a New York State law entitled "An Act supplementary to the act entitled 'An Act to provide for the incorporation of religious societies, passed April fifth, eighteen hundred and thirteen,' passed March 25, 1863." The incorporators were Michael Augustine Corrigan, Archbishop of New York; vicar General William Quinn; Saint Mary's pastor John Lewis; and two laymen whom Father Lewis had selected, August Thiery and Daniel T. Cornell. The school currently serves children from the prekindergarten stage to the eighth grade. In 1999, the principal was Virginia Savarese.

Saint Patrick School stands at 3560 Richmond Road, Richmond (Block 4424/1). Saint Patrick's parish was incorporated on November 8, 1878. The incorporators were John Cardinal McCloskey, Archbishop of New York; Vicar General William Quinn; Saint Patrick's pastor Patrick Mahoney; and lay trustees

Lawrence Seaver and John Gonund. On September 18, 1956, the Sisters of Saint Dorothy, Inc. conveyed to the parish an academy at the southeast corner of Saint Patrick's Place and Centre Street (Block 4438/62). The property then consisted of an eighteen-room, three-story frame building with approximate dimensions of 40' x 40'. The academy lot was 100' x 129'. The school currently serves grades K-8. The principal in 1999 was Sister Mary Ferro.

Saint Peter's Boys High School stands at 200 Clinton Avenue, also known as 196 Henderson Avenue in New Brighton (Block 92/1). The owner of Saint Peter's Boys High School is the Church of Saint Peter's "erected in the Village of New Brighton, County of Richmond." The church, though organized many years before, was not incorporated until January 29, 1886. At that time, the incorporators were Michael Augustine Corrigan, Archbishop of New York; Vicar General William Quinn; Saint Peter's pastor John Barry; and lay trustees Peter McQuade and Louis Benziger. (R.D.) In 1948 documents, the Reverend Joseph Farrell, pastor of Saint Peter's, stated that this property was acquired in 1946 from Manhattan College for $152,000.00. It consisted of a parcel of land less than six acres, with two buildings used exclusively for school purposes and for a home for the Christian Brothers who taught in the school. The school building, 117' x 62' was built in 1937. It consisted of a gym, lavatory, showers, cafeteria, 6 classrooms, office, faculty room and library. (R.D.) On July 7, 2000, the Richmond County Savings Foundation awarded Saint Peter's Boys High School a $100,000 grant. The grant was given for Project 2000, Saint Peter's building campaign, for the construction of a 10,000-square foot addition to the 87-year-old school. Plans for the new $3.25-million building call for state-of-the-art laboratories for chemistry, physics/biology and computer technology, library and office space and classrooms to accommodate an additional 100 students. (*Staten Island Advance*, July 7, 2000, A4.) Saint Peter's principal in 2001 was John Fodera.

Saint Rita's School stands at 30 Wellbrooke Avenue in Meiers Corner (Block 770/9). Saint Rita's church was incorporated in Port Richmond on January 10, 1922. The incorporators were Patrick Joseph (later Cardinal) Hayes, Archbishop of New York; Vicar General Joseph F. Mooney; Saint Rita's rector Emanuel Tav-

erna; and lay trustees Vincent Cannateli and Thomas Carnavelle. The groundbreaking for the school took place on June 4, 1956. The principal in 2001 was Ms. Janet McGee.

Saint Roch's School stands on Villa Avenue in Elm Park (Block 1132/46). Saint Roch's church was incorporated October 16, 1922. The incorporators were Patrick Joseph (later Cardinal) Hayes, Archbishop of New York; Vicar General Joseph F. Mooney; Saint Roch's rector Catello Terrone; and lay trustees Giovanni Sforza and Domenico Palladino. The church acquired lots on October 16, 1922, and recorded them on September 23, 1923, October 29, 1923, and March 22, 1957. Together, the lots constitute one big lot 428' along its east-west axis, 143' feet along its south side and 162' along its north side, with extensions. In 1960, the one-story building included eight classrooms, a principal's office, nurses' room, teachers' lounge, and all-purpose room, among others. The principal in 1999 was Mary Patricia.

Saint Sylvester's School stands at 884 Targee Street in Concord (Block 3152/52). The Church of Saint Sylvester was incorporated on June 30, 1921. One lot, acquired in 1929, was converted into a convent. Commencing in 1938, the Sisters of the Presentation used it while they taught in the parochial school connected with the church. The principal in 1999 was Nancy Bushman.

Saint Teresa's School stands at 1632 Victory Boulevard in Castleton Corners (Block 695/28). The Church of St. Teresa of the Infant Jesus, the church's full title, was incorporated in New Brighton on March 19, 1926. The incorporators were Patrick Joseph Cardinal Hayes, Archbishop of New York; Vicar General John J. Dunn; Saint Teresa's rector Philip S. Conran; and lay trustees Edward J. Ross and Francis E. Finnigan (these trustees were required by the Religious Corporation Law of 1895). Saint Teresa's serves grades K through eight. Its principal in 1999 was Sister Mary Joseph Deasaro.

Yeshiva of Staten Island stands at 1870 Drumgoole Road East at Bloomingdale Road (Block 6998/24). This institution was incorporated on May 12, 1933 as an elementary school, high school, college and post-college school, and as a synagogue and a seminary for rabbinical students. Its incoporators were Samuel Nelson, presiding officer; Ephraim Pessin, secretary; Rabbi Joseph Adler and Louis Brisman. The institution was reincorporat-

ed on April 24, 1953. This process changes the name to Mesivtha Tifereth Jerusalem of America. It amended and enlarged the institution's purposes to include: 1) Hebrew orthodox religious training; 2) secular instruction, resident instruction, and a dormitory and home for boys of Hebrew parentage; and 3) a place for Hebrew Orthodox worship for its members and for communicants of the Hebrew faith. The property deed was filed by the corporation on July 17, 1970 and consisted of an irregular lot of approximately 9 acres, with a masonry building of approximately 37,000-square feet consisting of a basement and three stories. The site was obtained from the Sisters Marianites of Holy Cross from Le Mans Sarthe, France, with an office at 1870 Drumgoole Boulevard, Staten Island. In 1999, its principal was Rabbi Stanley Bronfeld.

68, 70, 78, 104, 120, 123, 128, 139–140, 151, 164

Richmond Turnpike Company, 78–79

Richmond Valley, 57, 62, 81, 136, 218

Richmond Valley School, 94, 136, 218

Richmond Restoration, see Restored Village at Richmondtown

roads, 34–35, 77–78, 139–140, 225–226

Robbins Reef, 36, 168, 229

Robbins Lighthouse, 168, 229

Robin Hood Park, 141

Robinson, Henry

Also known as Harry, Robinson was the black engineer on the ill-fated *Westfield* ferry that exploded on Sunday, July 30, 1871. Born on or about January 21, 1831 in either Richmond or Norfolk, Virginia, Robinson began his steamboat career about 1851 out of Pough-keepsie. He moved to Stapleton about 1860. He had held engineer licenses for about fifteen years at the time of the *Westfield* disaster, and was highly regarded by Jacob Hand Vanderbilt, the president of the Staten Island Rail Road Com-pany (SIRRC), which operated four ferries between Manhattan and Staten Island. The *Westfield* was one of those ferries. Robinson was in his sixty-eighth year when he died on January 4, 1899, in Manhattan. He was buried in Staten Island's Woodland Ceme-tery. (R.D.)

Robinson Street, 79

Robinson's Atlas, 133

Rockland Avenue, 99, 134, 148, 216

Roman Catholic Churches, 59–60, 169–170

Rose and Crown Tavern, 40, 45, 64; see also Parkinson House

Rosebank, 25, 33, 58–59, 68, 100–102, 110, 115, 119, 128, 135, 138, 145, 157, 165, 169, 201, 203, 207, 217, 234

Rosebank Storage Warehouse, 122–123

Ross Castle, 55

Ross, (Colonel) William E., 58, 64

Rossville, 3, 20, 33, 43–44, 53, 58–59, 62, 68, 77, 79, 92, 98, 103, 118, 121, 128, 136, 158, 204, 207, 218, 249

This area is also known as Blazing Star. Note sandy soil, proximity to water for food and transportation. Site of old Blazing Star Ferry to New Jersey. Patriots crossed the Arthur Kill at this point during the American Revolution. During stagecoach days several inns were located near the water. Once a thriving farm community. Lovely old homes. Tollhouse was on Arthur Kill Road at foot of Rossville Avenue. Building moved and remodeled, now at 77 Poplar Avenue. The Sleight Family Graveyard on Arthur Kill Road near Rossville Avenue has been designated a City Landmark. Gravestones date back to 1750. (E.H.)

Rossville African Methodist Episco-pal Zion Church Cemetery, 101

This cemetery, opened in 1852, stands on Crabtree Avenue in Charleston (Block 7092/22). It is a major surviving element of Sandy Ground, a nineteenth-century settlement integrated by free black oystermen and their families who moved to Staten Island from Virginia and Maryland. The cemetery contains the burial sites of at least thirty-four African-American families, some of whose descendants still reside in the area. It adjoins the Sandy Ground National Register Archaeological District. Its telephone number is (718) 356–0200. (Dolkart, 294.)

Rossville Avenue, 66, 77, 218

Rossville District School, 75, 136

Rossville Hotel, 66

Rutledge, Edward, 41

Ryerss' Ferry, 53, 66

S

S.S. White Dental Manufacturing Company, 121, 125, 164, 198
This business was formerly at the foot of Seguine Avenue in Prince's Bay. It became a subsidiary of Pennwalk Chemicals Corporation, and most of the operations moved to Holmdel, New Jersey, in 1971. (E.H.)

Sabine Pass (Texas), 89

sailing vessels, 78

Sailors' Snug Harbor, 28, 53, 63, 73, 79, 105–106, 130–131, 142, 174, 186–187, 210–211
This area, now an 83-acre park known as Snug Harbor Cultural Center, stands at 914–1000 Richmond Terrace in New Brighton (Block 76/1). The five buildings and the front fence were designated New York City Landmarks on October 14, 1965. (Dolkart, 271.) It is also a New York City Urban Cultural Park, a national historic landmark, and on the state and national historic registers.

The site includes 28 historic buildings, a collection of nineteenth-century Greek Revival, Beaux Arts, Second Empire, and Italianate architecture that is being preserved and adapted for the visual and performing arts and for use by other cultural groups and institutions. Founded in 1801 by Robert Richard Randall, Sailors' Snug Harbor was the first maritime hospital and home for retired sailors in the United States.

The City of New York purchased the site in the early 1970s, and Snug Harbor Cultural Center opened in 1976. Current programming includes contemporary art, theater, recitals, outdoor sculpture, concerts, various workshops and special events. The complex is being restored and converted in a series of projects based on a comprehensive master plan. The restoration and preservation of the buildings, the infrastructure and of the landscape and various site features, with public as well as private funds, represents the largest endeavor of the kind in the country today. (DGS Report on Public Landmark Buildings, September, 1992.)

Saint Alban's Episcopal Church, 101
This church stands at 76 Saint Alban's Place. R.M. Upjohn designed it in 1865 as the Church of the Holy Comforter (Episcopal) and enlarged it in 1872.

Saint Alban's in Eltingville, a rare example of board-and-batten construction in New York City, is one of the city's finest rural Gothic Revival wood-frame buildings. The church was built in 1865; in 1872 it was moved to its present site and enlarged by the insertion of transepts between the nave and chancel. In 1951 the Holy Comforter parish merged with Saint Ann's Great Kills, to form Saint Alban's. In 1990 the church completed a restoration (Li-Saltzman Architects) that included repainting in historically accurate colors. (Dolkart, 291.)

Saint Andrew's Episcopal Church, 23, 29, 32, 43, 46, 54, 58, 92, 212, 254
This church, attributed to George Mersereau, stands at 50 Old Mill Road at Arthur Kill Road (Block 2294/30).

This stone edifice housing Staten Island's oldest Episcopal congregation is located just outside Historic Richmond Town. Construction of the original church began in 1709. This structure burned in 1867 and again in 1872; surviving sections of the original walls are encased in the present stonework. With its rounded windows and carefully delineated nave, tower, and entrance porch, the church resembles the Norman parish churches erected in twelfth-century England. Its phone number is (718) 351–0900. (Dolkart, 286.)

Within the church are tablets to Queen Anne; to the Reverend Aeneas Mackenzie, the first rector; and to the fourteen rectors who have served the church. Outside is a Daughters of the American Revolution plaque in memory of the American patriots who overcame the enemy there and a plaque dedicated January 1963 in memory of relatives of Mother Elizabeth Seton who are buried in the graveyard. Observe Washington bicentennial plaque on portal of stone gate. (E.H.)

Saint Andrew's Parsonage, 61; *see also* Moore House
This home was built in 1830. In 1959, it was moved from its original spot on Center Street to 40 Old Mill Road in Richmond-

town. Originally called the Bedell House. A wing was added in 1946. Former parsonages were at 3393 Richmond Road (used until 1924) and at 3531 Richmond Road. (E.H.)

Saint Austin's School, 137; see Garner House

Saint Charles Seminary, 238; see also Flagg Estate.

This building, the earliest part of which was erected circa 1898, stands at 209 Flagg Place on Todt Hill. Seminary occupies former Flagg Mansion. Note interesting gatehouse to estate, gambrel roof on mansion and open "captain's walk." Old Water Tower now a private home. (E.H.)

Saint Dorothy's Academy, 172, 222; see also Religious and parochial schools

Saint Francis, 224

This school, erected in 1928, stands on Todt Hill Road near Ocean Terrace in Dongan Hills.

Saint Gaudens, Augustus, 73

Saint George, 1, 19, 35, 42, 55, 65, 90, 100, 109–110, 114–115, 124, 127, 138, 141–144, 147, 152, 157, 160–161, 163, 168, 171, 175, 177, 185, 208–209, 224, 226, 229, 231–232, 236, 248, 251, 253

Saint George Coast Guard Base, 71, 90, 100, 168

Saint George Library, 160, 190

This branch of the New York Public Library stands at 5 Central Avenue in Saint George. The library contains issues of the *Staten Island Advance* on microfilm from 1921 to the present, Works Progress Administration (WPA) tax photographs and a special collection of Staten Island historical materials. (E.H.)

Saint George/New Brighton Historic District, 65; see also Camp Washington.

The genesis of this New York City Landmark extends back to the 1835 creation of New Brighton, one of the earliest planned communities in the New York area. (Dolkart, 274.)

A prominent businessman, Erastus Wiman, on properties owned by George Law and others, began Saint George, in the town of Castleton and Village of New Brighton. Wiman wanted to buy the area for a train and ferry terminal, a power plant and casino, and a stadium. But Law resisted. Wiman, it said, then played on Law's vanity, promising to "canonize" him by naming the Terminal Saint George. A deal was struck. (SIIAS, 1992.)

Saint George Post Office, 160, 209

Saint George Theatre, 160, 184, 187

Erected in 1930, this theater stands at 27 Hyatt Street in Saint George. The architects were Eugene DeRosa and James Whitford. (Lundrigan and Navarra, 1998, 65.) The ornamentation was by John Skiba (1882–1962), an internationally known sculptor. (E.H.)

Saint George's (Bermuda)

When Richard Moore, the first Governor of Bermuda, arrived in July 1612, one of his first actions was to found the town that he named for the patron saint of England. But he probably also bore in mind the name of Admiral Sir George Somers, whose British ship, en route to Jamestown, Virginia, ran aground off what is now Saint George's Island in 1609. The name of the town is either "Saint George's" or "the town of St. George" — not "Saint George," please. (Rushe, 150.)

This is the second English town to be established in the New World and it continues with its own lively; way of life while the first, Jamestown in Virginia, has long since been abandoned, though a replica town and museum keep its name alive. (*East End.*) *See also* Walker family.

Saint John's Avenue, 111

Saint John's Episcopal Church, 58, 102

This church stands on 1331 Bay Street in Rosebank (Block 2832/17). It is a New York City Landmark, and also on the state and national historic registers. The congregation was organized in 1843 and built a wooden church in 1844. The rectory was built in 1862 and the parish house about 1865. Arthur D. Gilman designed this church between 1869 and 1871. Gilman was a well-known architect in Boston before moving to Staten Island and receiving the commission for this church. His design reflects nineteenth-century theories of Episcopal Church architecture, especially in its clear delineation of such building parts as nave, side aisles, transepts, chancel and tower. See the "Landmarks of New York" plaque on the side of the church facing the courtyard. (E.H.) For further information, *see* Dolkart, 280.

Saint John's Methodist Episcopal Church, 104

Saint John's Evangelical Lutheran Church, 61

Saint Joseph's-By-the-Sea, 214, 221

This school stands at 5150 Hylan Boulevard (Block 6475/1) in Huguenot. The site has seen varied use. It overlooks Arbus Lake and was once the site of a short-lived resort, Arbutus Beach. Then steel magnate Charles Michael Schwab (1862–1939) and his wife E. Eurana, had a summer estate on this site.

Then the Sisters of Charity of Saint Vincent de Paul entered the site's history. This community of Catholic sisters filed their incorporation papers on January 26, 1849, with Deputy Secretary of State Archibald Campbell, with the consent of Justice of the New York State Supreme Court, E. P. Hurlbert. The five trustees and directors affixing their signatures were Elizabeth Boyle, Mary Ely, Eleanor Hickey, Eliza Knoll, and Ann Obermeyer. Ellen Timmons, Mary J. Hadden and Marie Wallace, nonoffice holders, completed the list of eight incorporators. The incorporation was for the purpose of "Instruction of youth, the care of the sick, the erection of hospitals for the sick and destitute, the visitation of hospitals, and rendering generally to the poor and destitute spiritual and corporal assistance and relief."

In an indenture of December 11, 1909, Charles M. Schwab and his wife E. Eurana Schwab conveyed to the Sisters of Charity of Saint Vincent de Paul sixty acres of land plus 2,430,00 square feet of underwater land deeded to George Conklin in 1881. Charles Schwab had purchased these parcels from the Richmond Beach and Railway Company in 1902. The sisters used it as a year-round home and annex for children who needed country air, taken from the New York Foundling Hospital, which the Sisters also operated. Eventually, the need for such institutions declined.

The sisters had a tradition of involvement in education; they also operated Mount Saint Vincent College in Riverdale and Elizabeth Seton College in Yonkers. In 1962, they started construction on a high school on their Staten Island site that one leading architect considered "awkward looking." (Willensky, 860.)

In September 1963, with their building still unfinished, the sisters began operating the all girls' high school at temporary quarters at Our Lady Star of the Sea School, 5411 Amboy Road Staten Island. In its first year, Saint Joseph's-By-The-Sea had 105 girls in three classes and a faculty of four sisters and two lay teachers. Exemption documents indicate that the girls' high school building, then under construction, was expected to open in the fall of 1964.

In 1971, the Board of Regents, for and on behalf of the Education Department of the State of New York, granted Saint Joseph's-By-The-Sea an absolute charter. Its incorporators, who were also the first board of trustees, were Evelyn M. Schneider, Emma Reagan, Margaret Downing, Mary E. Gallagher, Louise R. Slattery and Rita King. Saint Joseph's-By-The-Sea purchased about fifteen acres of property in Huguenot in 1978. (R.D.) The school went co-educational during the 1973–1974 academic year. (*Staten Island Advance*, November 23, 1993.)

On Wednesday, February 3, 1999, Saint Joseph's-By-The-Sea received a twelve-ton, eighteen-foot-tall bronze statue of Saint Joseph that had been at Mount Loretto for 75 years. The Reverend John Drumgoole, Mount Loretto's founder, had commissioned the statue in 1882. Prior to being transported to Mount Loretto, the statue had stood on Lafayette Street in Manhattan outside a building that housed the former Saint Vincent's Home for Boys. (*Staten Island Advance*, February 4, 1999, A15.)

The church stands at 347 Davis Avenue, West Brighton, at Castleton Avenue.

The Reverend John A. Gleason, President of Saint Michael's Home in 1918 described a 100' x 125' parcel as used for the raising of corn for cattle, salt meadows for bedding for cattle and potatoes and other vegetables for the support of the children of the institution.

In 1938, Mother M. Alphonsus, Superintendent, filed a report with the Department of Taxes and Exemptions. It stated that of a certain parcel of 100 acres, 52 were used for the raising of hay. The hay was used for feeding the cows and cattle used in the maintenance of the home. Ten acres were used for raising corn, some of which was used to feed the orphans, the remainder for feeding the cattle. Twelve acres were set aside for recreational use, on which a donated football gridiron was constructed for the use of the orphans in the home. Eighteen acres were in salt meadow, and annually the salt hay was collected and used for haybagging.

The Right Reverend Monsignor George H. Guilfoyle was Secretary of the Catholic Charities of the Archdiocese of New York in 1957. In a filed statement, he indicated that Saint Michael's Home conveyed their property to the Catholic Charities on July 5, 1952. The conveyance was carried out pursuant to a proceeding in the Supreme Court of the State of New York on June 25, 1952. Saint Michael's was a home for the care of dependent and neglected children, practically all of whom were public charges of the City of New York.

Saint Nicholas Day, 32

Saint Patrick's Roman Catholic Church, 92–93

This parish was incorporated in 1862. Its church, at 45 Saint Patrick's Place in Richmond (Block 4438/18) dates from that era. Located across the street from the Richmondtown Restoration, Saint Patrick's is an integral part of the old community of Richmondtown. The church is a dignified example of the Early Romanesque Revival style. (Dolkart, 289.)

Saint Paul's Avenue, 58, 103

Saint Paul's Memorial (Protestant Episcopal) Church, 58, 103

This church stands at 225 Saint Paul's Avenue (Block 516/21) in Stapleton. The church and rectory are New York City Landmarks and are on state and national historic registers. Together, they form one of the finest High Victorian Gothic religious complexes in New York City. The noted architect Edward T. Potter created a dynamic work using a dark gray stone with lighter-colored Con-

necticut brownstone banding and polished granite dwarf columns on the entrance porch. Erected between 1866 and 1870, the church was damaged by fire in 1940 and again in 1985; restoration took place following both fires. The 2-1/2 story rectory, resembling a rural English parish house, complements the church. (Dolkart, 276.)

Saint Paul's Methodist Episcopal Church, 57

Saint Paul's Roman Catholic Church

This church stands at 134 Franklin Avenue at the corner of what is now Cassidy Place (73/20). In December 1923, Saint Peter's Roman Catholic Church purchased the site of Saint Paul's. It was intended as a chapel for Saint Peter's parish. The Right Reverend Monsignor Joseph A. Farrell, the first pastor, opened Saint Paul's School in 1924 in the newly built Mission style he favored. Many children from Saint Paul's parish who were attending Saint Peter's school started to attend classes at Saint Paul's. At first there were just five grades; after the fifth grade, students again traveled to Saint Peter's. The Presentation nuns who were assigned to teach at Saint Paul's came to New Brighton every morning from Saint Michael's Home in Greenridge, and returned there every night.

After the Parish bought a three-story rambling old Victorian mansion on the corner of Cassidy Place and Clinton Avenue, it became the first "real" Saint Paul's School. The nuns moved into the third floor and used it as a residence, sparing them the tedious cross-island commute.

Eventually, seventh and eighth grade classes were added. The first class to complete all eight grades graduated in 1934. Among the graduates were Catherine Dee, William Higgins, Irene Sandrowski, James Molloy, Margaret Fosket, William Mulligan and Dolores Kiernan (who eventually became Mrs. Paul Wood and resided in a home at Tysen Street at the corner of Cassidy Place, purchased in 1987 by a future borough historian).

In 1931, the executors of Eugene Alexander arranged with the Reverend Robert Gibson for the acquisition of the 3-story property where St. Paul's is located today, on Clinton Avenue and another corner of Cassidy Place. One portion of the property was converted into Saint Paul's School, serving until the present building opened in 1954. In 1963, with the Franklin Avenue church near collapse from irreparable structural problems, the Reverend Francis Xavier Doyle oversaw the dedication of the chapel, auditorium, and school cafeteria. Later, the Right Reverend Monsignor Michael O'Donnell was responsible for moving the rectory from Franklin Avenue to the Cassidy Place site, and for relocating the convent to the current pastoral center and rectory.

Father Vincent Bartley became Saint Paul's pastor in 1993. In 1999, the Saint Paul's Building and Construction Subcommittee of the Seventy-fifth Anniversary Committee, headed by John Tobin, submitted three options to provide a long-range legacy for the Saint Paul's parish and community. (*Saint Paul's Seventy-fifth Anniversary Journal,* 1999.)

Saint Peter's German Evangelical Reformed Church of Kreischerville, 104

This building stands at 19–25 Winant Place in Charleston (Block 7400/171). It is a New York City Landmark. This small wooden church complex reflects the immigrant history of the Kreischerville area. The church was a gift of Balthasar Kreischer, owner of the Kreischer Brick Works, to the many German workers in his factory. Hugo Kafka designed the church in 1883 and the parish hall in 1898; Royal Daggett designed the rectory in 1926. By the early twenti-

enacted repressive laws to encumber free black entrepreneurs. Targets of this campaign were free blacks who had become successful in the oystering industry focused on Chesapeake Bay. In response to these restrictions, a planned migration of black families occurred in the 1840s and 1850s.

In 1850 the Sandy Ground free blacks founded the African Methodist Episcopal Zion Church. Its first wood frame structure "seating about 150 persons" was completed in 1854. The church became the focus for black social life on Staten Island. (Designation Report, 1982.)

In 1899, Comptroller Bird S. Coler approved a lease request of the Commissioners of the Sinking Fund for the A. M. E. Zion Church, at Rossville. It was to be leased for one year, at an annual rental of $400, with the privilege of renewal, to include janitor's services, heat and light. The premises consist of a one-story and basement frame building, in fair condition. (Board of Education Minutes, February 3, 1899, 71.)

Sandy Hook, 40, 72, 168, 223
Sandy Hook Lighthouse, 168
Sanitation Department, 141, 162
Saturday Morning Advertiser, 71
schepen(s), 13, 27
Schmid, August, 70
Schoharie Street, 63

school, 30–32, 75–77, 93–94, 133–139, 216–225, 252
School Board, 54, 134
school commissioner, 79, 84
school day, 32
School District No. 3, 57
school dress, 32
schout(s), 13, 27
Scott-Edwards House, 27

This house stands at 752 Delafield Avenue in West Brighton (Block 230/33). Erected in 1730, it is a New York City Landmark and is on the state and national historical registers. Captain Nicholas Manning probably erected the original one-story brownstone house on this site in the first part of the eighteenth century. At a later date the second story was added; the Greek Revival portico was most likely placed on the building in the 1840s, perhaps by Ogden Edwards, the first New York state supreme court justice from Staten Island, shortly after he purchased the house. (Dolkart, 282.) The original unwhitewashed fieldstone walls are still visible on the side. It's too bad about the addition of dormer and vents to the graceful roof line. (Willensky, 836.)

Scott's Farm, 210

This farm stood on the south side of Sand Lane between Hylan Boulevard and South Beach, where private homes now stand.

the Richmond County Poor House. It was established to assist and to house poor people, who received shelter and food in exchange for labor. The earliest surviving dormitories, opened in 1904, are in the Dutch Colonial Revival style and use brick and fieldstone, gambrel roofs, and classical porticoes to evoke the Colony's past history as a farming community.

In 1914, Seaview Hospital was constructed on adjacent land belonging to the Colony and became the largest institution in the world dedicated to the cure of tuberculosis. Its red tile roofs, stuccoed walls, and tile and mosaic decoration recall Spanish Mission architecture. In 1915, the New York City Farm Colony was merged with Seaview Hospital. Currently, the Farm Colony is under the jurisdiction of the Department of General Services and Seaview Hospital is under the jurisdiction of New York City Health and Hospitals Corporation. For more information on this site, *see* Dolkart, 284–286 and DGS 1992, 58.

This stone house, erected in 1720, stands at 361 Great Kills Road in Great Kills, overlooking Great Kills Harbor. It is the former home of "Schooner" John Poillon. a member of the Committee of Safety. It is also known as the Poillon House. Some historians believe that George Washington stopped here in May 1776. (E.H.)

Replaced by underground storage tanks. (E.H.)

Baltimore and Ohio Railroad freight yards in Saint George. When the North Shore railroad was planned, the club purchased the Delafield estate in Livingston between Davis Avenue and Bard Avenue, near the Staten Island Athletic Club. The Delafield mansion was used as the clubhouse from 1886 to 1931 when the city bought the property. Annual cricket matches were played between American teams and English, Canadian, and Australian teams. Among the Staten Island players were Eugenius H. Outerbridge, and Randolph St. George Walker. Tennis became a more popular sport than baseball and in 1906 the name of the club was changed to the Staten Island Cricket and Tennis Club, retaining that title until 1931 when it became the Staten Island Cricket Club. Cricket matches are still held at the city-owned Walker Park, as this property is now known, named in memory of St. George Walker, Jr., a casualty of World War I. (E.H.)

Staten Island Diet Kitchen, 132

This philanthropy was incorporated on June 6, 1882 for the "relief of the destitute sick of the County of Richmond, by the preparation and distribution of nourishing food, and otherwise." The names of the managers for the first year were Sarah B. MacFarland, Eliza Mac-Donald, Margaret A. Johnston, Ann Charlotte Meyer, Elizabeth W. Clark, Clara K. Oehme, Mary T. Ripley, and Caroline L. Peniston. These managers, plus Reverend J. C. Eccleston and Louis Henry Meyer witnessed the instrument of incorporation. In 1885, the Staten Island Diet Kitchen acquired a red brick house at 190 Van Duzer Street and Grant Street in Tompkinsville.

In a 1926 letter to the Board of Tax Commissioners, Marie Alice Kennedy, President, stated "last year we served 38 families giving from one to four quarts (of milk to the City's poor). This work is done by a Board of Managers (30 women) who do all the work themselves, having no paid Secretary or Treasurer." She also mentioned an endowment of about $8,000. They had a tenant in their building, whose rent and the interest from the endowment went into purchasing milk for the "sick and needy poor." Calls came for the milk through the Social Service, Visiting Nurse Association, Baby Health Stations and other welfare organizations.

Mrs. Kennedy (then of 314 Westervelt Avenue in Tompkinsville) elaborated further on the organization in the forty-second annual report. In the light of a real estate boom, the board of management decided to alter their headquarters into a private dwelling for one family. It was then rented for $780 per annum and the money used to extend their work. The needy sick, by sending a doctor's requisition could then obtain milk from the Port Richmond Baby Health Station, New Brighton Tuberculosis Clinic, Richmond Borough Dairy and Stapleton Baby Health Station. Diet Kitchen also worked with the Society for the Prevention of Cruelty to Children, the Staten Island Tuberculosis Committee, and Staten Island Hospital; adopted Ward 44 at Sea View Hospital and furnished milk to anemic children at P.S. 14. (Mss. New York City Department of Taxes.)

The Diet Kitchen's building is still standing. (E.H.)

This building stands at Bay Street and Central Avenue in Tompkinsville. Integral to its history is the biography of Michael J. Kane Jr. Born in Rosebank on October 23, 1871, Kane worked first for the *Staten Island Leader*. In 1896 he joined *The News Letter*. He then became a partner in the purchase of the *Staten Islander*. At first the newspaper's headquarters were located on Richmond Terrace in Saint George on the site of the present County Court House. In 1915, prior to the groundbreaking for the new Court House, the newspaper headquarters was transferred to the new Tompkinsville building at the tip of Central Avenue created by Bay Street. This configuration later became Pershing Circle. Shortly thereafter, the newspaper moved to larger quarters at a nearby location, and less than two years later it ceased publication. Mr. Kane died November 12, 1930.

The motto of the paper, inscribed in the now obscured cornerstone of the 1914 building, read: "With malice toward none and good will toward all, the aim of this paper is to present the news in a wholesome and healthy way; to promote the interest of the community; to expose sham in all its forms and to continuously hold up before men sound ideals, the contemplation of which inspires better living and purer thinking." (Leng and Davis, 1930, IV, 520.)

Tompkins looms large on Staten Island's map, but he was born in Fox Meadows (now Scarsdale) in Westchester County, June 21, 1774, to Jonathan Griffin Tompkins (1736–1823) and Sarah Hyatt (1740– 1810). In 1798, he married Hannah Minthorne (1781–1829), daughter of wealthy New York City alderman Mangle Minthorne.

Tompkins was Governor of the State of New York from 1807 to 1817. President James Madison appointed him Comman-der of the Third District Militia, covering southern New York and northern New England. He served during 1814–1815, part of the War of 1812, a war during which the British navy menaced New York City and reduced Washington, D.C. to a smoking ruin.

In Tompkins's last year as governor, his message to the legislature initiated the final abolition law of New York State, a process completed in 1827. That same year, Tompkins became vice president of the United States under President James Monroe, and served in that position until 1824.

Tompkins's connection to Staten Island began in 1816, when he founded the village of Tompkinsville. He named the streets in the area for family members: Hyatt Street commemorated his mother, and Arietta Street, Griffin Street, Minthorne Street, Hannah Street and Sarah Ann Street were named for his children. The same year, Tompkins acquired an interest in the steamboat monopoly of Robert Fulton and Robert R. Livingston, exercising it in 1817 in conjunction with Adam and Noah Brown. He also had an ownership in the steam ferryboat, *Nautilus*, and a related transportation business over the Richmond Turnpike (now Victory Boulevard), which he had constructed.

Tompkins died on Staten Island, June 11, 1825, of alcohol related illnesses brought on by financial difficulties, and is buried in the Mangle Minthorne vault, Saint Marks Episcopal Church, Manhattan. The church grounds also has a bust of Governor Tompkins contributed by the Daughters of the War of 1812. (R.D.)

was used as a tavern during the American Revolution. (E.H.)

This New York City Landmark, erected in 1835, stands at 27 Tyler Avenue near the intersection of Broadway and Clove Road in West New Brighton.

Tysen lived from 1841 to 1928.

This house, known variously as the Tysen-Neville House, Neville-Tysen House and the Old Stone Jug, was erected at 806 Richmond Terrace (Block 70/24) circa 1800. It is a New York City Landmark and on the state and national historic registers. Plans call for relocation in Richmondtown (E.H.)

The builders of this exceptional farmhouse of rough sandstone (now whitewashed) were probably Jacob and Mary Tysen. Rehabilitation work on the façade in 1991 revealed an unusual two-story veranda, which was added at an unknown date, perhaps in the late nineteenth century. The house assumed its present configuration around 1910, and the hexagonal cupola was added at that time. For part of the nineteenth century, the house was used as a tavern, known as the Old Stone Jug, which was frequented by residents of Sailors' Snug Harbor. The building is often referred to as the Neville House, after Captain John Neville, a retired naval officer who purchased the property in the 1870s. (Dolkart, 272.)

In 1991, when the roof and porch had begun to fail, a coalition, made up of the New York City Historic Properties Fund, the Department of Housing and Urban Development of the United States government, the New York City Landmarks Preservation Commission and Neighbor-hood Housing Services of New York saved it with a $91,000 package of loans. Li-Saltzman Architects Manhattan served as project architect and Island Housewrights, a restoration firm run by Conrad Fingado and Russell Powell, rebuilt the two-level porch and replaced the roof in 1992.

After a coalition of public and private groups salvaged the structure, its owner, Beulah Crute, became ill and entered the Silver

U

Island to maintain lighthouses along the East Coast from Maine to Delaware. A remarkable series of buildings were erected here that reflect the architecture, and the building technology of the 1830s through the 1870s. The federal government was dealing with an essential service at the time, aid to navigation, and a high quality of design and construction was attained at the maritime site. With the advances in lighthouse technology, this depot no longer provided all the needs of the Coast Guard. However the Coast Guard remained on the site for many years after the area became technologically obsolete, moving to Governor's Island only in the 1960s.

By 1983, four of the twelve buildings remaining on the five-acre site had been designated historic landmarks by the federal and state governments, and one of the four was also declared a New York City Landmark. The New York City Depart-ment of Transportation built a ferry maintenance building on the waterfront between the structures. (Department of General Services, 1992, 60–61.)

In July 1998, the United States Lighthouse Service site was chosen for the $18 million National Lighthouse Center and Museum. Henry Stephenson,

Chair of the Lighthouse Museum Board of Directors and Chair of the Community Board 1 Waterfront Committee, announced the decision to Borough President Guy V. Molinari. (Giannini, 1–2.)

The Friends of the National Lighthouse Center and Museum were introduced to Lewis Johnson, newly appointed director, who outlined his plans for future developments of the museum during a meeting on January 11, 2001. (*Staten Island Advance*, January 12, 2001, A19.)

United States Gypsum Company, 121, 199

This building stands at 561 Richmond Terrace, New Brighton. J.B. King's Windsor Plaster Mills were established on this site in 1876, and were bought out by U.S. Gypsum in 1924. (R.D.)

United States Medical Corps, 165

United States Navy, 120

United States Public Health Service Hospital, 80, 101, 169, 210

United States Public Health Service

United States War Department, 89

United States War Veterans, 163

University Temple, 111

Upjohn, Richard, 102

Upper Bay, 1, 109, 196, 208, 228

Upper School, 138

V

Vale Snowden, 65

Valley Street, 115

City Landmark and on the state and national historic registers. It is thought to be an eighteenth-century structure onto which a Greek Revival porch, possibly salvaged from another house, was added. It is of indeterminate origin, and came to this address from another site. (Dolkart, 276.) It is privately owned.

Verrazano-Narrows Bridge, 115, 157, 167, 226, 235, 242, 249, 253, 255, 259–260

The bridge was opened in 1964 as a project of the Triborough Bridge and Tunnel Authority; currently it is under the Metropolitan Transit Authority. It spans Fort Wadsworth and Brooklyn. A memorial to Giovanni da Verrazzano stands at the Bridge Plaza. (E.H.) Note that there are two Zs in Verrazzano's name, but only one in the name of the bridge.

Verrazzano, Giovanni da, 11, 40, 227, 242; see also Watering Place

Veterans Park, 182

This park stands between Bennett Street, Vreeland Street, Park Avenue and Heberton Avenue in Port Richmond.

Victoria Home for Aged British Men and Women

This philanthropy stood at 297 Jewett Avenue (Block 238/30). The Imperial Order, Daughters of the British Empire in the United States of America, Inc., purchased a private residence on this site in 1915. The charitable purpose was extended by the parent body when turned over to the Victoria Home in 1919. The large frame building between Jewett and DuBois Avenues had a vegetable garden and fruit trees on the DuBois side. The fruit was canned and preserved and the vegetables used in the summer. By 1929, records indicate that the property was sold to Hollenbec and Bernstein. Apparently the extent of the property had constricted in the 1930s and the address of the house became 82 DuBois Avenue. (Mss. New York City Department of Financing, 1915–37, R.D.)

Victorian-style mansions, 65, 74, 99, 106, 110

Victory Boulevard, 33–34, 55, 57, 60, 62, 69, 70, 77–78, 99, 104, 106, 119, 120, 123, 127, 129, 139–140, 151, 164, 171, 185, 193, 196, 207, 251

Villa Hotel, 111, 112

village halls, 98, 147

Virginia, 67, 111, 118

Volunteer fire companies, 50, 99

A Borough Hall mural shows volunteer firefighters in action. (E.H.)

volunteers, 87, 94, 99

Von Briesen Park, 108; see also Hudson, Verrazano-Narrows Bridge.

The park stands at the end of Bay Street at Fort Wadsworth. The family of Arthur Von Briesen, president of the Legal Aid Society, donated the property to New York City. From this park one can see the Verazzano-Narrows Bridge, the Shore Acres real estate development, Fort Wadsworth, New York Harbor and Brooklyn. (E.H.)

von Straubenzee, Turner, 44

Voorlezer's House, 15, 22–23, 29, 31, 46, 49, 77, 254; see also Historic Richmond Town

This building, erected in 1695, stands on 63 Arthur Kill Road in Richmondtown. It was designated a National History Landmark on November 5, 1961, was placed on the National Historic Register on October 15, 1966, and on the State Historic Register on June 23, 1980. (New York State Office of Parks, Recreation and Historic Preservation to R.D., April 15, 1997.) Erected in 1695, the building has the original clapboard construction; hand-hewn beams, wooden pegs, wide floorboards and fireplaces. Currently, the building bears a plaque on the left of its doorway and a bronze plaque in its interior, the latter a gift of Queen Julianna of the Netherlands. Historic Richmond Town has restored the building to its original use as a schoolteacher's house and school, and one can visit the teacher's living quarters and a schoolroom with a display of historic school equipment.

Vreeland, 36

Vroom, 36

W

W.S. Pendleton House, see Pendleton House

Wach Oaks, 94; see also Watchogue School

Wagner College, 65, 66, 131, 163, 187, 192, 211, 223, 224, 225, 237, 240, 252; see also Cunard Mansion, Ward Mansion.

This institution stands at 631 Howard Avenue on Grymes Hill. Its history goes back to the incorporation of the Lutheran Pro-Seminary of Rochester, New York, on October 1, 1885, by Alexander Richter, John G. Wagner, Frederick Schlegel, David Banteleon, Robert Kuhn, Josh Christ, and Jacob Margrander, all of Rochester. Justice James L. Angle of the New York State Supreme Court in Monroe County (Rochester), New York, ordered the name changed to Wagner Memorial Lutheran College of Rochester, New York, on September 1, 1886. This was done to honor George Wagner, whose father, John G. Wagner, donated money for the Rochester campus. On March 29, 1928, the Regents of the University of the State of New York granted an amended charter to Wagner Memorial Lutheran College for the relocation to Staten Island. (R.D.)

Wagner College's present campus is 370 feet above sea level, affording excellent views of surrounding countryside and of New York Harbor, Brooklyn, Sandy Hook and the Manhattan skyline. It incorporates tracts from several previous landowners; the Cunard family owned land on the hill (and the family home is part of the campus building plant), and the library is on property that had belonged to Jacob Vanderbilt. Note development of extensive landscaping program. (E.H.)

Dr. Norman Smith, who is Wagner's seventeenth president, arrived at the college in 1988. During his tenure, the college achieved ranking in the "top tier" in the 1999 ranking of best colleges by *U.S. News and World Report*, has received donations of over $30 million from college alumni and friends, and expanded its campus with the acquisition of the former Augustinian Academy. (*Staten Island Advance*, September 17, 1999, B3.)

Walker family

The first Walker in the United States was named John. He had been born in Yorkshire, England, but came to the United States from Rothesay, Scotland, in 1824, to engage in tobacco planting. (Walker, 12.) Three generations later, John's grandson David and

his wife, the former Amanda Norvell, had a home in Lynchburg, Virginia, where, on November 16, 1830, Amanda gave birth to her second son, Norman Stewart. On November 17, 1852, Norman Stewart married nineteen-year-old Georgiana Freeman Gholson (born May 22, 1833, Petersburg, Virginia; died 1904, Staten Island.) Their wedding trip was a tour of Europe. In 1855, Norman and Georgiana moved to New York where their second child, Norman Stewart, Jr., was born on March 18, 1856.

Norman Walker received the rank of major during the Civil War. He occupied an important post in the Confederate service, being the agent of his government in Bermuda, where many blockade runners loaded their cargoes for the dash through the federal fleets off Wilmington, North Carolina, and Charleston, South Carolina. Major Walker facilitated the transportation of food and war munitions for the Confederacy, kept the blockade-runners supplied with coal, and smoothed out the difficulties that arose through protests made by the American consul at Bermuda.

In 1866 Major Walker and his father-in-law, Thomas S. Gholson, opened a cotton importing business in Liverpool and the family moved to that city.

461

The business was ultimately a failure. The Walkers' final home in England was the "Hut" near Bracknill, Berkshire. Leased in June 1877, the house was a rambling structure of approximately thirty-five rooms. It proved to be a pleasant residence for only a year, for in 1878 the family returned to the United States, making their home in Richmond, Virginia. In 1883 Major Walker joined a cotton brokerage firm in New York, and the family established a new, and final, residence on Staten Island. (Walker, 136.) The Walker family soon moved in elite Staten Island social circles. On December 11, 1889, Norman Stewart, Jr., married Minnie Affie Morrison Wiman, daughter of Erastus Wiman, Staten Island's most prominent businessman. *The Staten Islander* called the event "the grandest wedding Staten Island has ever seen, one that not even the Greek God Hymen assisted by the nine Muses could have improved upon."

Norman Stewart Walker, Sr. died Monday, September 15, 1913, at 9:00 p.m. at his Dongan Hills residence. After a funeral at Trinity Protestant Episcopal Church in New Dorp on Thursday, September 18, 1913, at 3:00 p.m., Major Walker was buried in Moravian Cemetery. He was sur-

vived by five of his nine children: Norman S. Walker, Jr., of Staten Island; Randolph Saint George Walker; John T. Walker of Orange, New Jersey; Mrs. Bryce Stewart of Winchester, England, whose husband was a colonel in the British Army; and Miss Edith Stewart Walker of Staten Island, with whom he had been living since his wife's death nine years earlier. (*Staten Island Advance*, September 17, 1913; *World*, September 20, 1913.)

About that same time, the daughter of Norman Stewart Walker, Jr., also Edith Stewart Walker (1891–1982), married. Her husband was Maurice Iasley Pitou, the son of Squire Pitou of Clinton Avenue. The wedding took place in Christ Church on a Wednesday afternoon. Anna Minnie Hope Walker, the youngest sister of the bride, was the maid of honor. (*Richmond County Advance*.) Described as a Manhattan stockbroker and president of the Richmond County Country Club, Maurice Iasley Pitou died suddenly, after a brief illness, at Saint John's Hospital, Baltimore, Maryland on January 26, 1931. (*Staten Island Advance*, January 27, 1931.)

Randolph St. George Walker also had a long history on Staten Island. He was born June 15, 1863 at Saint George's, Bermuda.

It is open to conjecture, but it would seem that he was named in part for George Wythe Randolph (1818–1867), a grandson of Thomas Jefferson, Confederate brigadier general and, from March 18, 1862, to November 15, 1862, Confederate Secretary of War. Norman Walker knew General Randolph well. In part, Randolph St. George Walker may have also been named for the town of St. George's, where he was born. Ironically, his brother Norman Jr. married the daughter of Erastus Wiman, the man who gave the name Saint George to a part of Staten Island. (Mss. Dickenson, 1996, no page number.)

Randolph St. George Walker came to Staten Island in 1883. In his work life, he was a Wall Street executive and for 23 years the treasurer of the New York Cotton Exchange Clearing House. In his leisure time, Mr. Walker served as president of the Staten Island Cricket and Tennis Club until it dissolved in 1923, and was a life member of the Saint George Society of New York, which he headed for two years. The fourth of their nine children was Randolph St. George, born June 15, 1863 at Saint George's, Bermuda.

The Walker-Blafield-Yates Post American Legion and Walker Park were named for his son. At the time of death, March 29,

1949, he lived at 33 Central Avenue, Saint George. He was survived by a daughter, Helena Randolph Walker of the same address, and three grandchildren. (*Staten Island Advance*, March 30, 1949, 2, and Walker, 137.)

Walker Park, 114, 183

Once the estate of prominent businessman Henry P. Delafield, his father, Rufus King Delafield, a Wall Street cement manufacturing merchant, and his grandfather, William Bard, Walker Park's five acres were purchased by the Staten Island Cricket and Tennis Club for $40,000 in 1886 (it had 664 active members that year). The club played its inaugural cricket match there on July 5 of that year. Erastus Wiman had encouraged the club to leave its first home courts at the former Camp Washington grounds so that he could unify the ferry service at a terminal and create a sport and amusement center in St. George. But, well prior to that, in 1874, Mary Outerbridge and her sister Laura are believed to have played the first tennis game in the United States on those grounds.

By 1923 the former Delafield estate was purchased by the Staten Island Academy as a recreation area. In 1930, the New York City Parks Department bought the land for $110,000, and commenced work on a recreational area it planned to call Livingston Park. However, the Randolph St. George Walker, Jr., Post of the American Legion requested the park be renamed in honor of their namesake, and in December 1933, the Board of Aldermen approved the change.

The renaming ceremony took place Sunday, May 27, 1934, as part of Memorial Day observances. There was a large parade from Bard and Henderson Avenues to the grounds of the park at Delafield Place and Bard Avenue, with three hundred people witnessing the combined dedication and memorial services. Borough President Joseph A. Palma dedicated the grounds as Walker Park. Allyn Jennings, director of operations for the Parks Department in the five boroughs, formally accepted the new name. Among those present to speak were Miss Helen Walker, sister of the fallen hero, and their father, Randolph St. George Walker, Sr. (*Staten Island Advance*, May 28, 1934, 1.) The ceremony included unveiling a nickel plaque that read in part "Dedicated to Randolph St. George Walker Jr., Private First Class, Company 'K,' 107th Infantry. United States Army. Killed in action, age 20, in the attack on the Hindenburg Line, September 29, 1918."

The plaque is now at the park entrance at 50 Bard Avenue. The park grounds include a French Provincial clubhouse, built in 1934. (E.H.) For further information, *see Staten Island Advance*, September 11, 1989, B2.

French speaking Calvinists from Belgium who escaped religious persecution by going to Holland and coming to America with Dutch settlers. Huguenots, also French-speaking Calvinists, came from France. Walloon Street is near P.S. 44. (E.H.)

Staten Island War Memorial Skating Rink opened in Clove Lakes Park in 1970. Look for other memorials in immediate community, including War Memorial Playgrounds (Nicholas DeMatti, Austin J. McDonald, R. E. Kaltenmeier). (E.H.)

The eighteen-room mansion, known as *Oneata*, built in 1865, stood at 636 Howard Avenue on Grymes hill. General William Greene Ward made it his home in 1864, and General Ulysses Simpson Grant often visited there. The home remained in the Ward family until 1942. It was an example of Victorian architecture, full-length windows, large French doors opening on porches, high ceilings. (E.H.) It has been demolished. (R.D.)

Ward-Nixon House, 62

This house, also known as the Caleb T. Ward House, stands at 141 Nixon Avenue (Block 571/242) on Ward Hill. Designed by Seth Geer circa 1835, it is a New York City Landmark and is on the state and national historic registers.

Located at the crest of Ward's Hill, with a magnificent view of New York Harbor, this monumental mansion is the finest Greek Revival country house surviving in New York City. The house has brick walls stuccoed to simulate stone and an impressive two-story portico. Geer, the builder of Colonnade Row in Manhattan was involved in a number of Staten Island building projects. (Dolkart, 276.)

Ward Schools, 76

Ward's Point, 163, 181

In 1858, while excavating the foundations of the Cole-Decker House, workers came upon

Native American burial ground. This discovery gave the place one of its variant names, Burial Ridge. (NHL Nomination, no date.)

It turned out that Ward's Point contains the largest and best preserved assemblage of archeological resources chronicling historic contact between Munsee people and Europeans along the Atlantic coast during late sixteenth and early seventeenth centuries. Concerned by threats posed by developers and vandals to what most regarded as an important link with Staten Island's past, local historians and politicians unsuccessfully tried to get the New York State Legislature to vote funds to acquire the Conference House in 1888, 1896, 1901, and 1909. In 1925, Staten Island preservationists finally convinced investors purchasing much of the land around Ward's Point to donate the building and eleven adjoining lots to the City of New York. The donation changed hands on April 29, 1926. Gradually expanding the park to its present 68.5 acres, New York City presently maintains Ward's Point and its environs as a conservation area. (National Historic Landmark Designation Study, October 29, 1992.)

The Conference House, near this site, had been a national historic landmark since 1966 and a

New York City Landmark since 1967. On March 16, 1976, an area designated Ward's Point and encompassing 68.5 acres was determined eligible for the National Register in the context of the United States Environmental Protection Agency's Oakwood Beach Water Pollution Project, based on "the information it may provide on prehistoric and historic Indian subsistence and settlement on Staten Island." (National Register Nomination Form, August 6, 1982.) The site was placed on the state register of historical places on August 6, 1982, and on the national register on September 29, 1982. The whole site comprises 33.5 acres; the part relevant to Native American history accounts for twenty of these acres.

Washington, D.C., 72, 238, 259

Washington, George, 40–42, 227

Washington Hotel, 92

Washington Park, 98

Watchogue Road, 111

water pollution, 163

Watering Place, 11–12, 33–34
This site stands in Tompkinsville at Victory Boulevard and Bay Street. *See* Tompkinsville Park.

Watson, Walter Reno, 174

Webb and Knapp, Incorporated, 196

Weed, (Brevet Brigadier General) Stephen, 166–167
General Weed was born November 17, 1831, at Potsdam, New York. He died July 2, 1863, at the Battle of Gettysburg, and is buried in the family plot at Moravian Cemetery in New Dorp. (R.D.) Battery Weed at Fort Wadsworth is named for him.

Weissglass Stadium, 178, 194
This former stadium, at 1971 Richmond Terrace in Port Richmond, was named for Julius Weissglass (1873–1946), founder of Weissglass Dairy. (E.H.)

Weitzman's Photo Shop, 125

West Baptist Church, 59

West Brighton, 79, 101, 142, 176, 178; *see also* Factoryville

West Brighton Ferry Landing, 141

West Division, 28, 52

West New Brighton, 21, 28, 44, 53, 57, 58, 62, 63, 68, 70, 77, 81, 89, 91, 92, 94, 105, 108, 117, 120, 122, 123, 129, 135, 137, 138, 141, 150, 159, 171, 172, 176, 182, 184, 196, 198, 200, 205, 211, 217, 219, 236

West Shore Expressway, 226, 253

Westchester, 19

Westerleigh, 101, 105, 111, 123, 218, 236, 237

Westerleigh Collegiate Institute, 112, 138
This institution is located on College Avenue, West New Brighton, Village of New Brighton, on land known as the Koch property, between Jewett Avenue and Manor Road, immediately south of the grounds on which Read Benedict then lived.

The school's articles of incorporation, published in 1900, describe Westerleigh Collegiate Institute's purposes as: 1) To establish an English and Classical School, in which the best work shall be done, for the young of both sexes, by employing the best teachers and utilizing the most approved methods and . . . meet the requirements of the Board of Regents of the University of the State of New York; 2) and include a Primary Department for pupils 3 to 9 years of age, from kindergarten to grammar school; a Grammar Department of four years for pupils from about 9 to 13; and a High School and College Preparatory Department for pupils from about 13 upwards.

Westerleigh Collegiate Institute's site, worth $5,000, was donated to the school. The school's proposed building was expected to cost $10,000. To meet the costs, the founders offered a prospectus for a subscription at $100 per share. The founders also noted their future intent to open a Westerleigh College for Culture for advanced instruction in science, art, literature, philosophy, etc., and a Westerleigh University Extension Center. As a result of their endeavors, by 1901, William F. Van Clief, then President of the WCI was able to say that "a large

and flourishing school has been built up in a section of the Borough of Richmond in which educational facilities was very much needed; the school now numbers upwards of 200 pupils, and has a corps of 17 instructors. The buildings belonging to the Institute are handsome and commodious and constitute a marked addition to the neighborhood in which they are located." In addition, the institute maintained a free public library in one of its buildings, open from 9:00 a.m. to 5:00 p.m. daily.

The Regents of the University of the State of New York granted Westerleigh Collegiate Institute a provisional charter on December 12, 1894, and appointed twenty-four trustees, in accordance with the recorded application of its Incorporators. The First Board of Trustees appointed by the Board of Regents consisted of Otto Ahlman, Mrs. Amelia D. Alden, Frank Burt, Guy S. Brantingham, Read Benedict, Edward D. Clark, Edward P. Doyle, J. P. Decker, Clarke Dunham, George T. Egbert, Isaac K. Funk, D.D., Benjamin F. Funk, Daniel S. Gregory, D.D., C.A. Hart, Cassius L. Haskell, William T. Holt, Jacob I. Housman, Azel F. Merrell, William H. Perry, John B. Pearson, George M. Purdy, William J. Quinlan,

William S. Van Clief and Calvin D. Van Name.

On January 15, 1895, the stockholders elected twenty-one trustees. Two of these proved to be not eligible, leaving a board of nineteen trustees. Dropped from the original board were Frank Burt, Read Benedict, J. P. Decker, Clarke Dunham, Jacob I. Housman, Azel F. Merrell and John B. Pearson. Added to the elected board were William Bryan, John Snyder and Edward J. Wheeler.

There were two especially interesting provisions of the Articles. One was concerning religion: "While the Westerleigh Collegiate Institute shall be recognized in a general sense as a Christian Educational School, all denominational and all sectarian influences shall be forever excluded from its counsels, and its funds shall forever be kept free from prostitution to merely selfish, secular and political ambitions and ends." The second provision was concerned with Temperance: "The course of Scientific Temperance Instruction shall be taught in the use of the Text-Books prescribed by the laws of the State of New York."

The stockholders adopted the articles of the institute at their first annual meeting, January 15, 1895; the board of trustees elected at that meeting ratified

the decision. On October 6, 1898, the Board of Regents issued Westerleigh Collegiate Institute a full charter and incorporated it as an academy. (Application to the Commissioners of Taxes and Assessments of the City of New York, for remission of tax levied on the Westerleigh Collegiate Institute for the year 1900; R.D.)

Westerleigh Park, 112, 182; *see also* Immanuel Union Church.

The park stands at the junction of Maine Avenue, Willard Avenue, Neal Dow Avenue and Springfield Avenue in Westerleigh.

Western Electric Company, 201

Western Union, 208

Westervelt Avenue, 70, 103, 109, 113, 115

This road goes through the Tompkinsville area.

Westfield, 53, 57, 79, 88, 97, 136–137, 142, 152

Westfield Times, 130

Westfield (ferry) 70, 79, 88, 139, 142

Westfield   Township   District Schools, 76–77, 94

No. 5, now Tottenville P.S. 1 Annex, 58 Summer Street between Yetman Avenue and Academy Avenue (Block 7898/1). The original building dates from 1878. Pierce and Brun designed an enlargement for a two-year high school, erected 1896–1897. This modest neo-Grecian school of brick with stone trim was originally capped

work going on for the "proposed $12,000,000 state institution for mental defectives at Willowbrook." Some six dormitory buildings and a drainage diversion canal were to be initially constructed.

By January 1941, more than forty buildings were under construction, with about thirteen more planned. Completion of construction was forecast for 1943, with a partial opening by fall 1941. Some 3,000 patients were expected to be on the grounds of the hospital. (*Staten Island Advance*, January 7, 1941.) Over the next generation, the resident population became dangerously overcrowded.

The reason for the construction was that Willowbrook's mission was being expanded to include medical care to military personnel. Halloran Hospital, named for Colonel Paul Stacy Halloran, a U.S. Army Medical Corps leader, was activated on October 19, 1942. It closed as a hospital for active-duty personnel in 1947 and reopened immediately as a veterans' hospital. The veterans' hospital closed in 1951–1952, and Willowbrook took over its physical facilities for its own clients' use.

In 1972, Willowbrook faced a class-action suit on behalf of patients held in overcrowded conditions poorly suited to improving their mental health. In 1975, the court ordered Willowbrook to reduce its population to 250 by transferring most of the patients to more modern environments, such as group homes. Willowbrook closed, and in 1989 the City University of New York purchased the land for the College of Staten Island campus. The College of Staten Island opened at the former Willowbrook site in 1993.

Wiman, Erastus, 27, 109, 115, 127, 129, 131, 143–145, 160, 198, 226; *see also* Erastina, Woods of Arden House

The Historical Museum contains the Wiman Room, a replica of a room in Wiman's former home on Saint Mark's Place, Saint George, known as Tantallon. The mansion later became the Elk's Club. It was razed in 1963. (E.H.)

Wiman Place, 145
Winant (Winant Family, p. 16), 56
Winant House, 27

This house was erected in 1780.

Winant Place, 145
Winant's Pond, 69
Windsor Castle, 64
Winter Avenue, 146
Winter, William, 146
Woglom Family, 56
Wolfe's Pond, 101, 182, 249
Women's Auxiliary, 75, 131, 211
Wood, John, 57
Wood House, *see* Abraham J. Wood House

Woodland Cottage

This New York City Landmark stands at 33–37 Belaire Road (Block 2860–68) in Rosebank, and is known as the 33–37 Belair Road House. It was built in 1845 with an addition in 1900.

In the 1830s Staten Island's farms began to undergo suburban development. Woodland Cottage, which was built as a rental unit, is one of the few surviving examples of the picturesque Gothic Revival houses that were quite common in Clifton in the early years of the area's suburbanization. The original cross-gabled section has steep roof slopes outlined by bargeboards; the house features diamond-paned casement windows with drip moldings. Between 1858 and 1869, the cottage served as the rectory of Saint John's Church. (Dolkart, 280.)

Woodrow, 76, 101

Woodrow House, 61

This house was erected in 1810.

Woodrow Methodist Episcopal Church, 55–56, 63

This church stands at 1101–1109 Woodrow Road (6110/14) in Woodrow.

The congregation worshipping here predates the church by some time; the oldest marker in the cemetery, that of Judith Mersereau, dates to 1767. Bishop Francis Asbury, founder of American Methodism, preached at the home of Peter Van Pelt in 1771; a memorial tablet commemorates his visit. The congregation was formally established in 1787. A large marker indicates the grave of the Reverend Henry Boehm (1775–1875). There are also markers of individual Revolutionary War veterans and a Daughters of the American Revolution tablet on the church portico in memory of men of Westfield who served in the American Revolution. (E.H.)

The simple Greek Revival church was erected in 1842 on the site of Staten Island's first Methodist church, which had been destroyed by fire. The parsonage dates from 1850. The tower was added in 1876. (Dolkart, 293.) The complex is now home to Woodrow Methodist Church, and is a New York City Landmark.

Woods of Arden House, 27, 82, 145; *see also* Frederick Law Olmsted House

This New York City Landmark stands at 4515 Hylan Boulevard in Eltingville. Built in 1720, it is also known as the Poillon House. Its early owners were Jacques Poillon and Dr. Samuel Akerly. Note original stone portion of old farmhouse. Observe unusual trees, especially two Cedars of Lebanon planted by Frederick

Law Olmsted. Visualize theatrical performances given on grounds by Erastus Wiman. (E.H.)

WPIX, 105

Wren, Christopher, 23

Wright, Frank Lloyd, 175

Wyeth House, 64, 107

This house, erected 1850, stands on Meisner Avenue in Egbertville. Observe large home with cupola. Located on hillside, it commands an excellent view. (E.H.)

Wyeth, (Judge) Nathaniel Jr., 107, 187

Wynant, 18

Y

Yetman, Hubbard R., 217

Yetman Avenue, 103, 217

York Avenue, 90, 108, 160

Yorkshire, 28

Yorktown, 89

Young Men's Christian Association, 117, 185, 192

The original YMCA building stands at 1590 Richmond Terrace in West New Brighton. The cornerstone of this building indicates the YMCA of the North Shore was organized in 1867. The building was used later as a police station. In 1974, it was Hercules Oil Company. A new building at 651 Broadway, West New Brighton, opened in 1956. The T. Robjohn House, erected about 1845, remains on the property opposite the Staten Island Zoo. (E.H.)

Although the building is not a designated landmark, the Landmarks Preservation Commission judged it historically significant, and asked that it not be destroyed. The roof of the two-story French Second Empire brick and brownstone building collapsed from a suspicious two-alarm fire in November 1989. According to Loring McMillen, then Staten Island's official historian, it is among several 1800s era buildings that have survived along Richmond Terrace, then called Shore Road, which harken back to a time when that strip was the commercial center of West Brighton. In the 1880s the building became the police department's first precinct stationhouse. The building has since served as an auto repair shop and a diesel engine repair shop. (*Staten Island Advance*, July 5, 1990, A13.)

The Works Progress Administration Tax Photo of Block 187, Lot 138 shows a Sinclair gas station on the property, possibly at the same time, after late 1936, that the Hercules Contracting and Hauling were the owners. The current owners, Karen and Mario Canzoneri, were described in a story by Michael J. Paquette in the *Staten Island Advance* of June 23, 1999. In it, Mr. Canzoneri had located the report of the YMCA of the North Shore

Staten Island that included an engraving of the YMCA building shortly after the groundbreaking on March 20, 1871. When the building was dedicated on November 22, 1872, it had dimensions of 48' x 84,' and cost $19,000. The population in 1872 was pegged at 8,000.

This report lists the 1867 incorporators as Matthew S. Taylor, George A. Middlebrook, Mulford D. Simonson, John D. Vermeule, and Eugene DuBois. The 1870–1871 president of the association was Frank Barrett, with vice-presidents Charles F. Cox, John M. Hawkins, S. Judson Raynor and Eugene DuBois. The report's appendix lists the officers filling other posts, *e.g.*, corresponding and recording secretary, treasurer and directors. There was also a listing of the most recent members elected, as well as their 320 extant life, honorary, counseling active associate and lady (associate) members. (R.D.)

Y

Youth Squad, 161
Yserberg, 36
Yvette Yacht Club, 172

Z

Zion Lutheran Church, 104

EDITED/REVISED APPENDIX

This is a revised edition of Evelyn Morris King, "The Black Man on Staten Island," which originally appeared as Chapter XXVIII of *Black Man in American History*, published in 1971. Its footnotes come primarily, but not solely, from Richard B. Dickenson, *Census Occupations of Afro-American Families on Staten Island, 1840–1975* (Staten Island: Staten Island Institute of Arts and Sciences, 1981.)

The history of Staten Island has not been fully presented because of the paucity of records, and the lack of research into the role of blacks in the development of the community. At the present time organizations are working to fill this gap in the history of Staten Island. It will be interesting to follow these developments.

For the purpose of this guide, some facts are given to show the relationship of black people to the entire community from the earliest time until now.

SLAVERY ON STATEN ISLAND
STATISTICS

Records indicate that there were free black people on Staten Island as early as 1690, but no additional information is available.[1] An unofficial 1698 census showed that there were 71 slaves and 654 whites living on Staten Island.[2] Some whites were probably indentured servants brought by the Dutch.[3]

A 1737 census revealed the presence of 349 slaves and 1540 whites.[4] Slave ownership increased concurrently with the white population because the economy of staten island was based on agriculture, and slaves were used to work on the farms and to serve within the household. Records indicate also that there were indentured servants here, both black and white. In 1771, there were 594 slaves and 2253 white people. By 1790 these numbers had increased to 819 slaves and 3123 whites. Available records reveal that slaves were mentioned as bequests in the wills of their owners.[5] At one time Richmond County was recorded as the wealthiest county in New York State, wealth being based on the value of property and slaves were considered as such.

SLAVE LIFE

Few references have been made to slave life on Staten Island during colonial days, but J.J. Clute, in his *Annals of Staten Island* writes the following description:

Every farmer was the owner of one or more slaves, the males being the assistants of the masters in the field, and the females of the mistress in the kitchen. They were invariably treated with kindness by the Dutch, but the French, and especially the English settlers, were disposed to draw the line of social equality more rigidly. Slaves were generally well taken care of, perhaps not always so much from matters of humanity as of interest. They always had their own sleeping apartments and their own separate tables. As the life of a slave was doomed to be one of labor, intellectual cultivation was deemed unnecessary; some few, however, were taught to read the Bible. It was not unusual to see master and slave working together in the fields apparently on terms of perfect equality. In the kitchens, especially in the long winter evenings, the whites and blacks indiscriminately surrounded the same huge fire, ate apples from the same dish, poured cider from the same pitcher, and cracked nuts and jokes with perfect freedom.[6]

GRADUAL DISAPPEARANCE OF SLAVERY

Many Staten Island owners manumitted slaves during the period between 1790 and 1825. County court records attest to this. The following are some of the manumissions recorded:
- Elizabeth Ward, freed by Edmund Seaman in 1806;
- Fortune Perine, age 8 months, claim relinquished by Reverend Peter Van Pelt in 1805;
- Frances S. Henry, age 28, freed by Obadiah Bowne in 1808;
- John Jackson, age 39, freed by Edmund Seaman in 1809;
- Joseph Ryerss, freed according to will of Gozen Ryerss, estate probated in 1811;
- James Thare, freed by same will signed by Judge David Mersereau;
- Harry Ryerss, freed by his father, Joseph, on the same day he gained his freedom.

In 1799 the State Legislature of New York enacted a law stating that no child could be born into slavery after July 4, 1800, but that the owner of the child's parents, if he supported it during infancy, could have its services until age 25 if a female and age 28 if a male.[7] They were in effect "bonded servants." However, many owners on Staten Island freed such children at birth. Town Clerks kept records of such renunciations.

It is reasonable to believe that some Staten Island blacks may have joined Revolutionary forces, but the writer has not had access to such records.[8] If so, they too were freed according to a New York state law of 1781, which freed slaves serving in the state's armed forces. Four years later a law was passed prohibiting the importation of slaves for the purpose of sale within the state. They could be imported for personal use, however.

EMANCIPATION

Governor Daniel D. Tompkins, who lived on Staten Island after the close of the War of 1812, had been a bitter opponent of slavery. During his term of office he wrote to the state legislature urging that complete abolition of slavery within the state be accomplished by July 4, 1827.[9]

It was on July 4, 1827 that all slaves on Staten Island were emancipated. Despite the gradual disappearance of slavery prior to that date there were still 698 slaves liberated on that day. The census according to township revealed the following distribution:

- Westfied, 230;
- Castleton, 132;
- Northfied, 182;
- Southfield, 154.[10]

A great celebration in honor of this momentous event was held at the Swan Hotel, which was located on the Shore Road (now Richmond Terrace west of Broadway, near the present site of P.S. 18 in West New Brighton.) Freedmen came from all over staten island to join in the festivities, many walking great distances.[11] Since no provisions had been made for them, most of the emancipated blacks returned as freedmen to the homes of their previous masters.

SLAVE RECORDS

Detailed records of only a few slaves are available at this time.

Perhaps the earliest story is of a slave family named Richmond. The pastor of Saint Andrew's Church in Richmondtown, Reverend Charles C. Charlton, purchased this family and brought it to Staten Island in the 1700s. A son Bill, born to the family in 1763, was sold to General Earl Percy and taken to England where he became an expert cabinetmaker and professional boxer, known as the "Black Terror."[12]

Benjamin Perine was born December 2, 1796, to a slave in the home of Peter I. Van Pelt. When Benjamin was about 18, he was sold to Mr. Ridgeway who lived on what is now Victory Boulevard between Bulls Head and Travis. There he remained until after 1825, at which time he was emancipated. Perine married Diana DeHart on December 28, 1835. He lived to be 104 years old, and is buried in the Second Asbury (Old Slaves/ Cherry Lane) Cemetery, also known as Old Slaves or Cherry Lane Cemetery, under Anguilli Plaza on Forest Avenue.[13]

Joseph Ryerss who had been manumitted by his master, County Judge Gozen Ryerss in 1811, purchased in that year from James Barton 5$\frac{1}{2}$ acres of land with a house on it for $1,215. This property became part of the Staten Island Cemetery, following Ryerss's death, about 1842.

Nicholas Dehart, affectionately known to many Staten Islanders as "Claus," was born a slave May 7, 1800, two months before the law went into effect decreeing that children born of slaves "shall be deemed born free." "Claus" was in the household of the Merserau family who at that time lived in a house at the corner of the present Richmond Terrace and Delafield Place, West New Brighton. When Mr. and Mrs. Mersereau died, "Claus," with the other Mersereau household slaves, was given to the daughter, Margaret Mersereau, who had married Abraham Crocheron. There he lived until slavery was abolished on Staten Island. He became a gardener for the Parker, the Goodhue and the Willcox families, all well-known on staten island. Nicholas DeHart in his later years engaged in the oyster business. He bought the oysters from the boats in Kill Van Kull and his wife, Mary, prepared them for wealthy people who lived in the Livingston area. He also was a cook on the steamship "Bellona" which made a stop on Staten Island as it plied between New Jersey and Manhattan. Nicholas DeHart maintained his family in comfort in a home on Shore Road, now Richmond Terrace, between Broadway and Van Street in West New Brighton (then called Factoryville). He earned the respect of the community. The *Richmond County Gazette* of December 5, 1885, featured a story about "Claus." It noted: "His funeral was attended by Hon. Erastus Brooks, Mrs. Francis George Shaw contributed an ivy wreath and Mrs. Duffie, and her sisters, the Misses Pelton, erected the gravestone." Nicholas De Hart was buried in the Staten Island Cemetery, adjacent to the original old Ascension Church .

Peggy DeHart, sister of Nicholas, reportedly was the first member of the DeHart family to receive her freedom. She was purchased by the freedman, Joseph Reyerss (previously mentioned), manumitted and then married to his son Harry. Descendants of the DeHart family have lived on Staten Island continuously.

ABOLITIONIST MOVEMENT

Prior to the Civil War there was a very active group of abolitionists on Staten Island. Their leader was Sidney Howard Gay, editor of the *Anti-Slavery Standard*, the New York abolitionist paper. He later was the managing editor of the *New York Tribune* from 1862 to 1866. His wife's family, Quakers, had been prominent in antislavery activities for two generations. The Gay's cottage on what was then called Haley's Lane (later Davis Avenue), West New Brighton, became the meeting place for the neighborhood people who believed in and worked for the emancipation of slaves. The best known of these was the Albert Oliver Willcox family. Others were George Curtis, after whom Curtis High School and P.S. 19 are named, Francis George Shaw and George Cabot Ward. Most of these people were Unitarians who had come to staten island from New England. The Gay home was used as a "station" on the underground railroad. It has been reported to the writer that a tunnel was used for the safe transportation of the slaves from the water's edge to the Gay home. This was an excellent hiding place for fugitive slaves.

Among the well-known New Englanders who visited the Gays were John Greenleaf Whittier, James Russell Lowell, William Lloyd Garrison, Wendell Phillips and Lucretia Mott. It is interesting to note here that P.S. 18 bears the name of John Greenleaf Whittier. Mrs. Mary Otis (Gay) Willcox, daughter of the Gays, relates interesting anecdotes of this period in the *North Shore Legends*.

All Staten Island residents did not agree with the abolitionists or "Black

Republicans" as they were called by the opposing party. On Staten Island, as elsewhere in the State, the freedman did not have equal civil rights. New York State permitted black men to vote only if they paid a tax. Many whites feared competition of the black people in the labor market.

CIVIL WAR PERIOD
DRAFT QUOTAS

In July 1863, serious riots occurred in Manhattan to protest the Federal Conscription Act. This riot action spread to Richmond County as some whites became enraged and vented their anger on black people and upon the Abolitionists. Again we acknowledge *North Shore Legends*, in which Martin Gay has written about incidents of those days. According to his childhood memories, he reports that the citizens of Port Richmond, determined to have no violence in the village, placed "a small cannon at the bridge where the Shore Road crosses Bodine's Creek (presently Richmond Terrace and Jewett Avenue) and let it be known that no rioters would be allowed in that village and no attempt by them to get in was reported." This incident took place a short distance from the present location of P.S. 20.

ESCAPE TO NEW JERSEY

Many blacks escaped from Staten Island across the water to New Jersey. Some left their homes and hid in the woods. Others were beaten. Mr. Gay reports "a confectioner's store in New Brighton kept by a respectable colored man was attacked and gutted."

ABOLITIONISTS BEFRIENDED BLACKS

Some stories are recorded that indicate how the Abolitionists on Staten Island befriended blacks during these critical days. When Mrs. Louis T. Hoyt discovered a group of black refugees hidden in the woods near her home (Bard and Castleton Avenues) she sheltered them in her barn and personally fed and cared for them, fearing that her servants might inform the leaders of the mob.

Mr. Gay recalls another incident:
Mr. Charles G. Thorpe, driving to the boat one morning, met a colored man pursued by a mob. The man was at his last gasp, and begged for help. Mr. Thorpe seized the reins, pitched the coachman, whom he dared not

trust, into the road, pulled the exhausted man into the wagon and drove him to safety.

ABOLITIONISTS IN DANGER

The abolitionists also lived in terror of mob attacks. Many threats of violence were reported. Under the cover of darkness, some families left their homes to seek safety with neighbors who had protected themselves with firearms. Mrs. Gay and her children took refuge in the home of George Cabot Ward. Her husband's safety was threatened in his New York office where he was stranded.

JULY 1863 RIOTS

Rumors of disorder on Staten Island spread as the draft riots in Manhattan became more violent. At this time there were nearly 1,000 blacks on staten island in a total population of about 26,000.[14] Angry mobs of whites seized thirty muskets from the Tompkins Lyceum on Van Duzer Street, Stapleton, and from other drill rooms, set fire to homes and stores, and threatened innocent African Americans who lived on McKeon Street (now Tompkins Street) Stapleton. This is near the present P.S. 14. The rioters then burned the car barns of the railroad at Vanderbilt's landing, Clifton. Damage to property in these July 1863 riots was great. After investigation by the Board of Supervisors, the county was ordered to pay the African Americans damages amounting to $9,314.69 and to the whites in the amount of $1,710.96. The claims of the white people were settled almost immediately but the cases of the black claimants were delayed for two or three years.

SANDY GROUND

A small community of black families exists today on Bloomingdale Road between Drumgoole Boulevard and Arthur Kill Road. The name of this area, Sandy Ground, appears in records dating back to 1779.

The soil there was well suited for the growth of strawberries and asparagus. For years the produce was shipped from the Rossville area to the Manhattan markets by steamboat. At the present time air pollution, caused by nearby New Jersey factories, prevents the growth of profitable crops.

It was in the 1830s and 1840s that a group of free blacks from Snow Hill, Maryland, came to Sandy Ground. There had been black families living in the section prior to this. The newcomers had been oystermen in their home state and migrated to Staten Island because of the excellent oyster beds here. The oyster captains from staten island also brought some of the blacks to staten island to prepare the oyster beds and plant the oysters.

These free blacks owned their own homes and in 1850 founded the Zion African Methodist Church on Bloomingdale Road. The first minister was Reverend William Pitts. The church is presently known as the African Methodist Episcopal Zion Church. Old time residents of the community recall the religious revival meetings or camp meetings that the church held, to which people came from all over staten island. During the summer children looked forward to the strawberry and watermelon festivals that were held on the church grounds. Hayrides, by horsedrawn wagon in early days and by open trucks in later years, made the journey to Sandy Ground a gala event, particularly for the children who lived "on the other side of staten island." Sunday School picnics were also fun for both young and old.

For about seventy years, while oystering flourished, the African Americans in Sandy Ground successfully maintained their families. When the New Jersey factories so polluted the waters that the oyster beds had to be abandoned, the African Americans of the community had to find other employment. Some went to work in the factories in New Jersey, some learned trades and some among those well educated during the years of prosperity engaged in professions. Many moved elsewhere. One African-American woman, Mrs. Esther Purnell, operated a private school. White children of the neighborhood also attended this school. Other children went to the county schools.

New families have moved in throughout the years, but descendants of some of the original families from Snow Hill still live in Sandy Ground or in other parts of Staten Island. The family names of some of the founders of the Zion African Methodist Church are familiar names in the black community: Henry, Williams, Harris, Landin, Henman, Purnell, Robbins, Jackson and Bishop.

Records of the sale of property to the African Americans in Sandy Ground are available to the researcher. The first seems to be the sale of 2 1/2 acres by Isaac Winant to John Jackson, in 1828. Seven years later he and a Thomas Jackson purchased eight acres of land for $600. It has been told by old inhabitants that John Jackson owned and operated a ferry between Rossville and Manhattan. His sister married a Henry and became the mother of John Jackson Henry, grandfather of the present generation of Henrys, several of whom were teachers. Dorsey Landin owned and operated the first ferry that plied between Rossville and Perth Amboy.

Joseph W. Bishop was one of the free African Americans who came from Maryland in the 1840s. He was a skilled woodworker. In 1888 his son, William Arthur Bishop, opened a blacksmith shop at 1448 Woodrow Road. He was a wheelwright and farrier, as well as a blacksmith. The shop is operated now by Joseph W. Bishop, who bears the name of his grandfather. The business is chiefly in ornamental ironwork, welding and automobile work. The original forge is still in use.

Another well-known black family associated with Sandy Ground and members of the church there, although not residents of the community, was the Cooley family. Joel A. Cooley, who lived on his grandfather's property on Sprague Avenue, Tottenville, was well-known for his prize dahlias of enormous size. For five successive years, he won special awards in the Annual Flower Show that was held in the old Madison Square Garden. Mr. Cooley also raised figs, asparagus, yams, strawberries and chickens. In his early years, he had been an oysterman.

Other family histories are noted in Minna Wilkin's articles in the *Staten Island Historian* of October 1943, to December 1943.

WORLD WAR I

Many black men on Staten Island served their country during the first World War. These names have been reported to the writer: Daniel Smock, Augustus Riddick, John Dixon, Clarence Crowley, Carol Jackson, Walter Fox, Walton Jackson, William Spellman, Samuel Bryant, Cornel Jones, Walter Jones, Samuel Landin and Robert Walls. They all returned home with honorable discharges, after serving with New York's 369th Regiment, which was cited for bravery eleven times. Cornel Jones later returned to Paris where he started an orchestra.

The first base hospital established in the United States during World War I was the Hospital at Fox Hills between Grasmere and Rosebank. Wounded soldiers were sent there for observation, then assigned to other hospitals according to their needs. Some were basket cases, some ambulatory. Janet Smith, the second registered black nurse on staten island, was on the medical staff that greeted soldiers at the piers and escorted them to the hospital at Fox Hills.

There was a unit of the Red Cross for black women known as the Blue Cross. It performed services only for black troops.

Before the war, Malcolm Smith, a native Staten Islander, had served aboard a mine layer, the USS *San Francisco*. He received a citation for Naval Service and was honorably discharged in 1914. After his return to staten island he drove the first metered taxi here. He died in 1968.

WORLD WAR II

During World War II, Fox Hills Army Camp, located close to Vanderbilt Avenue and Targee Street, was a unit of the New York Port of Embarkation where approximately 3,000 black soldiers served in a stevedore battalion. Richmond Borough President Palma was among the hundreds of civilians who witnessed a first anniversary observance of the installation. The day started with troop review and demonstrations of various phases of the soldiers' work and ended with a wrestling match. Probably an unforgettable event to most of these soldiers was the assignment of Joe Louis, the world heavyweight champion, to their unit as a member of the Army Special Services.

A branch of the same outfit was the first black contingent of the Women's Army Corps, the WACS, which was stationed nearby on Osgood Avenue. The women possessed varied backgrounds and were on duty at the Army offices, laboratories, post office, post exchange, medical clinics and even drove hi-lows used for loading and unloading the ships. The special talents of these men and women were often displayed at War Bond rallies in the Paramount Theater in Stapleton and at canteen social events.

In 1942 the Booker T. Washington Service Center opened not far from Public School 16. This was considered the most active Island canteen. It was later moved from Bethel Community Church on Van Duzer Street to Montgomery Avenue and finally to Sand Street in Stapleton. Influential in making this center a reality was Dr. C. Asapansa-Johnson who was the church pastor, Mrs. Sarah Sparks Brown, Mrs. Bertha A. Dreyfus, Reverend Carl J. Sutter, Clarence DeHart, Nathan DuJohn and Nettie Carter-Jackson. An average of 1,000 men benefited from the Center, most of whom were stationed at the Fox Hills Base or at the Saint George Coast Guard Station. Approximately 575 hostesses were on duty, having come from all over the Metropolitan area. The center closed September 27, 1946.

Romance was ever present, for some servicemen fell in love with WACS and hostesses, married them, remained on or returned to Staten Island, moved into the Fox, which was a converted barracks, and sent their children to P.S. 12.[15]

EMPLOYMENT OF THE BLACKS

In the early 1800's the economy of Staten Island depended largely upon farming. There were only a few factories, breweries, and shipyards. The oyster industry was the only one open to blacks and competition in it was keen. Elsewhere in industry there was job discrimination. After emancipation black people were employed as gardeners, cooks, maids, coachmen, and in other household positions. Some gladly accepted sleep-in domestic jobs.

Economic opportunities remained limited until after World War II although an occasional shipyard or factory job became available. More janitorial and night watchman jobs were open. There were only a few blacks employed in government services. Two worked in the Sanitation Department. Daniel Butts was the first black mail carrier to the rural areas of Staten Island. Samuel A. Browne was a regular letter carrier, retiring from the Post Office in 1938. Mr. Browne, who celebrated his ninety-sixth birthday in 1969, has the distinction of being the only known black from Richmond County to have served in the Spanish-American War.

Sea View Hospital, on Brielle Avenue, opened as a sanatorium for tubercular patients in 1913. At one time this was the largest tubercular hospital in the world. During the early 1930s many black nurses were employed there, some being recruited from the South. Sadie Poole Bomar, the first known black registered nurse on Staten Island, was one of the first black nurses on the Sea View staff. Her family history dates back to the slave days on Staten Island.

Now Sea View Hospital and Home specializes in geriatric care and the integrated hospital staff works in harmony as it renders fine service.

The first black visiting nurse was Georgia Stone Hayden who is now a nurse at Willowbrook State School. Willowbrook employs a large number of black people in many different capacities. Martha Kirnon was the first black nurse in the public schools. Gertrude Farley was the first of her race to become a supervisor in the Department of Health.

PRIVATE ENTERPRISE

At the turn of the twentieth century there were only a few businesses privately owned by blacks. One of the best known was the William A. Morris Moving and Storage Company. Mr. Morris, who was born in Elizabeth City, North Carolina, in 1876, came to Staten Island in 1895.

Space is given here to a brief biography because Intermediate School 61 bears the name of William A. Morris.

As a young man, Morris worked hard and invested wisely. He hauled freight, delivered coal, and worked for the Richmond Storage and Moving Company. Soon he was able to purchase a team of horses and a van and was in the moving business for himself. As his business prospered, he was able to expand and bought another team of better horses and a new van. Gradually the volume of business increased, moving vans were motorized, and Mr. Morris bought the old Tompkins Department Store building on Richmond Terrace and Van Street. After renovating the building, he permitted the National Auto Show to be staged there before he started to use it as his warehouse.

The business ultimately expanded to nine tractor-trailers and two small rack trucks. A spacious garage was built on Barker Street with private gas tanks on the premises (now the location of Wacker's Express, Inc.). The Morris homestead was adjacent to this property.

One of the first Interstate Commerce Commission licenses was granted to Mr. Morris. His modern vans traveled the highways from coast to coast. He gave steady employment to 35 employees including a mechanic, auctioneer, accountant and full office staff as well as to his drivers and movers. In spite of adversities, he brought his business through the Depression.

Mr. Morris engaged in various community activities. He organized and was first president of the local branch of the NAACP, was founder of the Staten Island Van Owner's Association, builder of the Shiloh Church, an original member of Everyman's Bible Class and was on the Board of Directors of the West New Brighton Bank.

He established a housing corporation for black people to aid them in their efforts to find decent housing. He was also very charitable and donated food, clothing, furniture, and money to less fortunate people. His small trucks were always available for community affairs.

Mr. Morris and his wife, Susie DeHart, had nine children, most of whom reside on Staten Island today. Mr. Morris died in 1951 at the age of 75 and Mrs. Morris died in 1969 in her ninetieth year.

Other moving companies organized by blacks were the Glover Moving Storage Company and the Great Kills Moving and Storage Company.

Another independent businessman was Archie Poole who owned a taxi and tire Company and was authorized to sell license plates. He was also one of the founders of the *Amsterdam News*, one of the first black newspapers in the country. Mr. Poole set up a printing press in the basement of his home but later opened a printing business at 57 Ann Street, Manhattan, from which he retired in 1961.

Some of the older businesses that are still in existence include Palin's Ice, Coal and Wood Company (now Palin Ice Company), Honablue Fuel Company (now Superb Fuel Oil Service), Broadway Cleaners and Dyers, Tucker's Cleaners, C. and L. Cleaners, Dujon's Jewelry Store, Brighton Floor Service, Billups Funeral Home and Chambers Funeral Home (now McClendon Funeral Home). There are also several more recent painting and decorating firms, beauty and barbershops, tailor shops, food stores and a few restaurants.

In 1965, Hazel Claire Brown, a teacher at P. S. 18, established the Hazel Claire School of Charm, Inc. As owner-director, Mrs. Brown states that the school is "a cultural-non-sectarian, Volunteer Service organization." It aims to improve the "total physical self-image of women," to provide college scholarships for minority students, to assist students in realizing their fullest potential, and to assist in community affairs.

Munro's Gardens at 1498 Woodrow Road is a florist business resulting from the experimental gardening efforts of Bromley Munro and his wife, Mabel Lambden Decker, forty years ago. Now they have a flourishing business, growing their own hyacinths, poinsettias and chrysanthemums and buying other flowers from wholesale florists.

THE EMPLOYMENT SITUATION TODAY

It was World War II that opened up the employment field for black women on Staten Island. With men away, women were called to industrial and hospital jobs. Today we find them as x-ray and medical technicians, laboratory assistants, in dietary positions and as nurses and nursing supervisors. This employment is in the private as well as city hospitals, in the United States Public Health Service Hospital, in the Department of Health, at the Staten Island Medical Group offices, and in the privately operated nursing homes. Men have also entered these fields. Known to the writer are two dentists, two physicians, an anesthetist, and three dental technicians.

Many blacks, both men and women, are employed in civil service positions on Staten Island as social workers, policemen, firemen, detectives, parole and correction officers, as postal and transit authority employees and as employees of the Sanitation Department.

Blacks are on the payrolls of nearly all the larger industries on Staten Island. Many are employed in service occupations, such as laundry and dry cleaning operations, as janitors, chauffeurs, elevator operators and longshoremen. Administrative and staff positions are held by blacks in the New York Urban League, in government housing projects, in federal recreational programs, and in antipoverty programs such as the Staten Island Community Corporation, the Stapleton Organized Community Council, the West Brighton Community Action Program, the Staten Island Mothers for Adequate Welfare, the Silver Lake Day Care Center and Regional Manpower Opportunity Center.

Blacks are represented by over fifty members in the educational system on Staten Island. These include college professors, assistant principals, other supervisors and many teachers. Opportunities are open for both men and women to participate in education through school programs involving the services of para-professionals. In the legal profession are three black attorneys and an assistant district attorney. In 1970, Mr. Arthur Lewis was appointed as the first black man to occupy this post on Staten Island.

The presence of black people in diversified occupations has been the result of a long struggle for equal educational opportunities and equal opportunities.[16] The local NAACP, the ministers of the black churches here and black members of the community have been instrumental in upgrading employment through the years on Staten Island. Unskilled labor still faces an unresolved problem of gainful employment. Staten Island, as the rest of the nation, is governed by the Civil Rights Act of

1964, designed to end discrimination in employment by employees, employment agencies and labor unions. The Equal Employment Opportunity Commission was created to investigate and correct violations.

HOUSING

The same housing problems that have faced blacks in other parts of the country have faced them on Staten Island. Some black families have owned their own homes for generations. Others have had to fight for decent housing, The eight public housing projects have provided facilities for hundreds of black families.

The first of these was the Edwin Markham Houses, completed in 1943. This project was designed originally to house defense workers who were arriving in the area for employment in the shipyards. Former site dwellers, both black and white, were guaranteed preference of occupancy. When the dwellings were completed, however, blacks were not admitted. The problem was resolved when the local NAACP's Housing Committee brought pressure to bear against the New York City Housing Authority.

As the black population increases on Staten Island, greater opportunities must be made through community effort for these new families to secure adequate housing. A committee is actively engaged at the present time in fighting housing discrimination on Staten Island.

Black residents have tended to concentrate in certain areas of Staten Island, just as all national groups have done throughout history. It is estimated that there are 30,000 blacks on Staten Island today. Many live in the following sections: Sandy Ground, Mariners Harbor, Port Richmond, West New Brighton, New Brighton, Tompkinsville, Stapleton and Meiers Corners. Some few families are scattered throughout Staten Island.

Among the black families on Staten Island today who can trace their ancestry back to the nineteenth century are those that bear the following names: Agard, Armfield, Boone, Bryant, Carter, Cooke, Crowley, DeGroat, DeHart, Dixon, Dungee, Forting, Fox, Glasco, Hogard, Hughes, Jackson, Johannus, Lawrence, Leary, Mathis, Newcombe, Oliver, Overton, Poole, Prime, Robinson, Seaman, Spicer, Thompson and Washington.

EDUCATION

It is through education that any group is able to improve its status and make worthwhile contributions to the larger community. The earliest reference to teaching black children occurs in the records of Saint Andrew's Church in Richmondtown. Reverend Aeneas Mackenzie was interested in public education and in 1707 requested that teachers be sent over from England. His request resulted in the appointment of Adam Brown and Benjamin Drewitt "to instruct the poor whites, and black children also, if any such are brought to him, gratis." Further research may reveal whether any blacks came for instruction. During slavery, we know that few were given the opportunity to become literate. In Manhattan the New York African Free School started in 1785 as an outgrowth of manumission. In 1787 there were twelve pupils and in 1797, that number had grown to 122. Records also indicate that there were 44 slaves attending evening school in that year. As we trace these records we find that New York City itself and interested white citizens contributed to these efforts of the blacks. By 1820 there were 500 pupils in the African Free School No. 2 and by 1832 (after state emancipation) there were seven African Free Schools with about 1400 students. A year later the Manumission Society sold the schools to the Public School Society.

It is unlikely that any children from Staten Island attended these schools across the Bay. However, it is hopeful that research will reveal similar efforts being taken here to ensure an education for black children. We know that Mrs. Esther Purnell had a school for the children of Sandy Ground after the Civil War. We know that black children went to the county schools before consolidation in 1898 and that public schools were for all the children, regardless of color, after that date. However, instances of discrimination have been reported. A first hand account of Catherine Johannes Brown, written in 1969, gives us a glimpse into the schools at the turn of the century. She writes:

> In 1891 there were laws in Richmond County forbidding discrimination in schools because of race, but Stapleton Village was one of the many that disregarded the law. There was a school on Broad and Brook (now Wright) Streets for whites and a one-room building for Negroes on Tompkins and Center Streets. My mother visited the Negro school on several occasions and found the children running around the room and the teacher sitting down knitting.
>
> My mother [Catherine Wester Johannes] entered me in the school for whites as an East Indian because my father was a native of

that country, but I was dismissed when one of my friends told that my mother was a Negro. We were told about the school in Tompkinsville on the corner of Grant Street and Saint Paul's Avenue. My mother received a note stating no Negro non-resident might attend. My mother was advised to see Mr. Methfessel, a member of the village Board and, fine American that he was, he told her, 'We have no schools for Jews, Italians, Negroes — our schools are for all,' that she was to send her little girls back the next morning. She did. Someone got tired of the agitation and burned down the little one-room building in Stapleton. All the Negro children were then admitted to the new school (old P. S. 14).

Consolidation came in 1898. Then high school departments were established in Stapleton, Port Richmond and Tottenville. I was the only Negro child in that high school department. This department was a wonderful experience for me. What a fine group of dedicated, unprejudiced teachers they were! Now the schools are better equipped, but I don't think my grandson's college education is equal to what I received there in Stapleton.

Mrs. Grace Hunt and I were the first Negro teachers to be appointed on Staten Island after it became a part of New York City. My sister was the first Negro graduate from Curtis High School and even went on to be a teacher in the same school where I had been denied entrance.

I taught at Public School 12 for many years. I cannot say that either my sister or I was badly treated during our careers, so perhaps things are changing for the better. I retired twelve years ago and am now 85 years of age. I live with my husband, Samuel A. Browne, Sr., who was the first Negro mailman on Staten Island. He is 95 years of age.

CHURCHES

All the black churches on Staten Island have had similar beginnings as mission churches. It has been difficult to find any recorded churches before the 1800's, nor were there any ordained ministers until that time. The churches evolved when the efforts of hardworking people were brought to fruition after years of informal worship in private homes and small buildings and in segregated sections of white churches.

The oldest church in Stapleton, Union African Methodist Episcopal Church on Tompkins Avenue, organized in 1839. Its first minister was Reverend Isaac Barney. Its present minister is Reverend Charles C. Davis. The church was rebuilt in 1923. There was a graveyard in the rear of the church at one time prior to the expansion of the United States Public Health Service Hospital.

The Rossville African Methodist Episcopal Zion Church on Blooming-dale Road, Sandy Ground, was founded in 1850, mainly by freed slaves and free people who had migrated to the area from Maryland. In 1875 a second church was organized — Mount Zion Methodist Episcopal — and an edifice erected in 1879. The present minister is Reverend Wallace Lee.

Saint Philip's Baptist Church, organized as the North Shore Colored Mission in 1879, was dedicated ten years later under its present name. Its first minister was Reverend Granville Hunt. The present minister is Reverend William A. Epps, Jr. In 1966 the congregation moved from Faber Street in Port Richmond to the building on Bennett Street that had been the Zion Lutheran Church.

Shiloh African Methodist Episcopal Zion Church was a mission in 1906. The cornerstone was laid in 1914. Its first minister was Reverend J. T. Tilghman. The present minister is Reverend Lemuel L. Turner. This church is located on Henderson Avenue in West New Brighton on property deeded to the church by Mr. and Mrs. William Willcox, members of the abolitionist family active on Staten Island in the 1860's. (P. S. 48 is named in memory of William G. Willcox.)

Bethel Community Church on Van Duzer Street, Tompkinsville was first established in 1896 under the ministry of Reverend Henry Hall. Its present minister is Bishop C. Asapansa-Johnson.

The Church of God in Christ, on Clove Road, West New Brighton was organized in 1929. Its first minister was Elder Drake. Its present minister is Elder St. Clair Burnett.

In addition, there are a few smaller church organizations in the community. Also, many black people on Staten Island belong to the congregations of largely white-member churches.

BURIAL GROUNDS

Before the creation of public cemeteries, burials took place in church graveyards and in private family cemeteries known as homestead graves. Slaves were often buried behind the master's burial grounds. Records, indicate however, that the Reverend Peter I. Van Pelt had one of his slaves buried in the cemetery of the Reformed Dutch Church in Port Richmond.

Many blacks were interred in the Staten Island Cemetery, dating from 1851, adjacent to the site of the Old Ascension Church on Richmond

Terrace. This is where Nicholas DeHart was buried in 1885 and his granddaughter, Ellen DeHart Day, as late as 1958. Unfortunately, this cemetery and the Fountain cemetery adjacent to it have been vandalized and the inscriptions on most of the tombstones are not discernible.

The Frederick Douglass Memorial Cemetery was organized on Amboy Road in Oakwood in 1935. It was the result of the efforts of a funeral director, Rodney Dale, to find a place where black people could be buried with dignity. Most cemeteries either did not allow interments of blacks or permitted them to be buried only in neglected sections. From his Harlem office, the director stated that there have been more than 25,000 interments of all nationalities in this Staten Island cemetery since its opening. Including such well-known figures as Reverend John Robinson of the million-dollar Saint Mark's Church, Mamie and Bessie Smith, singers, the father of James Baldwin and Rodney Dale himself. A memorial plaque near the entrance to the cemetery bears a likeness of Frederick Douglass.

SOCIAL, FRATERNAL AND CIVIC ORGANIZATIONS

The black residents of Staten Island enjoy the same kinds of social activities as the rest of the population. They have dances, picnics, barbecues, house parties, fashion shows and club and church-sponsored bus and boat excursions and ocean cruises. They also have their fraternal and civic organizations.

The Lambda Chapter of the Lambda Kappa Mu Sorority was formed on Staten Island in 1948, by Sarah Tennessee Baker, R.N. It conducts a program for the elderly, provides a scholarship for a needy high school student, gives financial help to the less fortunate, enters a debutante in the NAACP's cotillion and encourages a group of Koppelles, "little sisters" of high school age, to attain their maximum potential.

The Saint Martin's Association consists of a group who banded together to give financial help to churches, hospitals and other institutions on the Caribbean island of Saint Martin.

The Brown Bombers Social and Athletic Club dates back to 1937. It was disbanded during World War II, but reorganized in 1946. The original aim of the members was to compete as gentlemen in sports activities, as did their idol, Joe Louis, who was known at that time as the Brown Bomber. The club gives financial support to athletic and charity organizations, sponsors a women's bowling team and a debutante in the NAACP cotillion.

The Bradley Bombers Athletic Club was organized in 1965 to provide activities and adult supervision for teenagers. It has had measurable success in keeping young people in school. Two other organizations (Afrasia, and the Bachelors Social Club) with the same purpose, joined with this group in 1970, renaming themselves the Unity Club.

The Armfield-Kittrell American Legion Post was chartered in 1945 under the leadership of Charles West. This group sponsors free tutoring service for young high school students who are on the verge of dropping out. It is active in the antidrug program. One of the highlights of the year is the annual Christmas party for children.

The Women's Civic and Political Union was organized in 1919, largely through the efforts of Drusilla W. Poole. Its main purpose has been to encourage suffrage among black women and a realization of the effect of politics on their daily living.

The Staten Island Branch of the National Association for the Advancement of Colored People was organized in 1925 to protect a black family that was being harassed because it had moved into an all-white neighborhood. Its first members included William and Susie Morris, Samuel and Catherine Browne, Daniel Butts, Augusta Riddick, F. Everett Henry, Dan Smock, Archie and Drusilla Poole, Alfred Spellman and Isaiah Andrews. This branch of the NAACP has supported the efforts of the national organization for justice and equality and has led the fight for improvement in employment, housing and education on Staten Island. For years it held an annual charity ball that has been replaced by the cotillion.

The League for Better Government was founded in 1945 as a nonpartisan organization to seek better government through increased participation of black people in the political arena. Charter members were: Samuel Browne, Herman Butts, Clarence DeHart, Rudolph West and James Sumner. The league holds conferences with politicians and takes stands on current issues.

A Staten Island Chapter of CORE was organized in 1960 by Richard Prideaux, and Clarence and Edith Overton. The group concentrated it efforts on housing, voter registration, employment and education. It negotiated with merchants to hire blacks and Puerto Ricans. These businessmen contacted the Junior Chamber of Commerce and as a result, funds were provided to pay for skills training. It conducted Operation Open City whereby it attempted to improve living conditions for minorities.

The Staten Island Chapter of the New York Urban League was founded in 1960 as the Urban League Guild, largely through the efforts of Mamie Asapansa-Jackson, Mrs. D. Pierce, Ernest Dow and certain members of the white community. The league encourages involvement of the black people in programs that will aid in solving health, housing, economic and educational problems. It also helps new residents adjust to the Staten Island community.

The Staten Island Council for Civil Rights was organized in April 1962 by Dr. Norma Owens. The following groups became members to combine their efforts in the cause of civil rights: The Women's Civic and Political Union, the Staten Island Branch of the NAACP, the League for Better Government, the Urban League Guild of Staten Island, the Staten Island Chapter of CORE, the Nettie Carter Jackson Democratic Club and the Staten Island Civil Liberties Union. Later the Lincoln Republican Club and the Catholic Interracial Council became members. The Staten Island Council for Civil Rights was active until July, 1966.

The Catholic Interracial Council of Staten Island, branch of the citywide organization, was founded in 1963. It has been influential in the areas of education, housing, employment, and welfare. The Fipocos Society was organized in 1965 by Benjamin Washington and Al West, deriving its name from the first two letters of the job titles held by its members: firemen, policemen, correction officers. It seeks individual, community and organizational betterment. Its members have appeared in schools, in uniform, to explain their jobs to the youth.

In 1967, a group of women organized a local chapter of the National Council of Negro Women, calling it the North Shore Division. Charter members were Willie May Taylor, Louise Brown and Muriel Carrington. Its main purpose is to render community service as the need arises. Currently the group is active in a drug prevention campaign.

The Dr. Martin Luther King Heritage House was established a few days after Dr. King's assassination April 4, 1968. It has a dual purpose: to memorialize Dr. King's name and to seek solutions to local problems. The founders were Mamie Asapansa-Johnson, Reverend St. Clair Burnett, Hazel Brown, Daniel M. Davis, Jr., Dorothy and Ernest Dow, William Givens, Ben

Harris, Rabbi Marcus Kramer, and Lemuel Turner. The group has arranged exhibits by black artists, conducted public forums on relevant topics, and held special programs during Negro History Week.

In April 1970 many organizations decided to combine their efforts to achieve common goals and formed the Federation of Black Community Organizations of Staten Island.

The above are some of the organizations in which the Blacks of Staten Island are active. Membership is held also in other groups, some of which have been organized by the white community.

VISITORS TO STATEN ISLAND

Prominent blacks who visited Staten Island were Blind Tom, the slave who became famous before Emancipation as an entertainer. He was managed by Colonel Bethune, his master, Booker T. Washington, educator and spokesman for his people, "Black Patti" (Sissieretta Jones), who sang with her troubadours in the Staten Island Opera House, which was located on the corner of Henderson Avenue and Broadway, (present site of P. S. 18).

In more recent times, the following well-known people have visited here: Robert Russa Moton, Arthur Schomberg, Roy Wilkins, Adam Clayton Powell, Jr., James Farmer, Whitney Young Jr., Shirley Chisholm, Cab Calloway, Duke Ellington, Dick Gregory, Daisy Bates, Althea Gibson and Floyd Patterson.

LOOK INTO THE FUTURE

As elsewhere in the nation, black people on Staten Island are seeking identification and are playing import roles in community life. The young people are concerned about their heritage and eagerly attend after-school classes in Afro-American history. They participate in the federally sponsored education programs. Some of the schools have already implemented "Black Studies" as part of the curriculum and others are preparing to do so. School libraries, as well as public libraries have a wealth of material awaiting the reader.

Our hope for a well-integrated community can be realized if all Staten Islanders, by becoming more knowledgeable of others' basic ideas, ideals and needs, gain greater understanding, and together work toward solution of mutual problems.